# THE METAMORPHOSES OF TINTIN

# THE METAMORPHOSES OF

# TINTIN

## OR TINTIN FOR ADULTS

Jean-Marie Apostolidès

Translated by Jocelyn Hoy

Stanford University Press
Stanford, California

Stanford University Press
Stanford, California

The Metamorphoses of Tintin was originally published in French in 1984 under the title Les Métamorphoses de Tintin © Seghers. This translation is based on the third edition of Les Métamorphoses de Tintin © 2006, Flammarion.

This book has been published with the assistance of the French Ministry of Culture—National Center for the Book.

Printed in the United States of America on acid-free, archival-quality paper

Library of Congress Cataloging-in-Publication Data
Apostolidès, Jean-Marie.
    [Métamorphoses de Tintin. English]
    The metamorphoses of Tintin, or, Tintin for adults / Jean-Marie Apostolidès ; translated by Jocelyn Hoy.
        p. cm.
    "Originally published in French in 1984 under the title Les métamorphoses de Tintin, Seghers. This translation is based on the third edition of Les métamorphoses de Tintin, 2006, Flammarion."
    Includes bibliographical references.
    ISBN 978-0-8047-6030-0 (cloth : alk. paper) — ISBN 978-0-8047-6031-7 (pbk. : alk. paper)
    1. Tintin (Fictitious character) 2. Hergé, 1907–1983. Aventures de Tintin. I. Title. II. Title: Metamorphoses of Tintin. III. Title: Tintin for adults.
    PN6790.B44T592313 2009
    741.5'9493—dc22

                    2009015732

Designed by Bruce Lundquist
Typeset at Stanford University Press in 10.5/14 Bembo

TO "L'OISEAU"

# CONTENTS

## PART TWO: HADDOCK

# CONTENTS

# PREFACE

While Steven Spielberg is moving forward on the production of the first of a series of films featuring the adventures of Tintin, to be followed soon after by a second film directed by Peter Jackson, it is important to say a few words to the American audience about Hergé's cartoon character.

Tintin appeared for the first time in 1929, but by the eve of World War II he had already become a notable cultural figure. In the 1930s, his adventures first appeared in a newspaper for children, *Le Petit Vingtième* (*The Little Twentieth*), and were collected each year in an album. During the war years, rather than cut back on his work, Hergé continued to produce a daily version of the exploits of his little hero in a collaborationist newspaper called *Le Soir* (*The Evening*). His drawings appeared side by side with the anti-Semitic caricatures of Jam as well as the brilliant but conformist articles by a young Belgian critic, Paul de Man.[1] From 1942 on, despite the scarcity of paper, *The Adventures of Tintin* also appeared as albums in color. It was during the war years that Hergé realized the full scope of his work, and in that time period he produced the most gripping adventures. Between 1940 and 1945, he published *The Crab with the Golden Claws*, *The Shooting Star*, *The Secret of the Unicorn*, *Red Rackham's Treasure*, and *The Seven Crystal Balls*, in that order. In these adventures Tintin was no longer a journalist commenting on world politics from the standpoint of the Right, as he was between 1930 and 1939. Now he was transformed into a kind of literary hero acting in a purely fictitious world. Next to Tintin appeared Captain Haddock and then Professor Calculus—a trio of friends whose exploits took place all over the world.

After the war, Hergé was put out of commission and had to remain silent until 1947. When Hergé's years of penance were up, Tintin's adventures re-appeared in a new magazine devoted to children, *Le Journal de Tintin*. Hergé resumed work on *The Seven Crystal Balls*, completing the adventure with the famous episode *The Temple of the Sun*.

In France and Belgium, children born after the war—the so-called baby boomers—grew up with Tintin. Children eagerly followed the new adventures as they appeared in *Le Journal de Tintin*. They also had access to the earlier episodes that Hergé Studios had reworked and Casterman Press reissued in album form. In a few years, Tintin had become more than just a commercial success. He had been transformed into a mythical figure whose task was to cope with the perils and challenges of modernity. His fame and influence spread well beyond the Catholic youth whom Hergé was addressing at the outset. Tintin was not merely a passing fad but a formidable social phenomenon. It is no exaggeration to claim that Tintin was part of the education of most of the young Francophone boys and girls growing up after the Second World War. With Tintin, they discovered the world; with Tintin, they developed the taste for adventure. Taking Tintin as their role model, they learned generosity, daring, tolerance, openness, self-control, and the need to understand and explain everything. Moreover, children learned to speak just like the characters in the adventures. On this point it is important to note that Hergé was as great a writer as he was an extraordinary artist.[2] Many of the children learned by heart the numerous dialogues and rejoinders in Hergé's albums as if they were verses in a sacred text.

I was one of those thousands of boys whose youth was marked by Hergé's hero. Approaching my forties, and having become a father myself, I wanted to undertake a positive reassessment of the many values I had learned through Tintin's adventures. Thus, between 1980 and 1983, I began a systematic rereading of the adventures, which were published in this book in 1984. Although my book has been republished in its original form by three different presses, at its initial publication in 1984 the field of "Tintinology," or "Tintin studies," was at its infancy.[3] At that time the most important piece was the 1959 pioneer study by Pol Vandromme.[4] But Vandromme was both suspicious of and frankly hostile to academic jargon, and he refused to engage in any in-depth analysis of Hergé's world. Even though many of Vandromme's insights were subsequently confirmed, his ideas were not presented in any systematic way in his book, and most readers of his day thus overlooked them. Fifty years later, studies of Tintin include more than one hundred scholarly books and surely many more hundreds of scholarly articles. In addition, there are four or five biographies of Hergé that allow us to learn more about the personal context of his creative work. Also, regular conferences and subsequent publications are dedicated to Tintin.[5] Moreover, a museum dedicated entirely to Hergé is soon to open in Louvain, Belgium, to spread public knowledge and appreciation of his work. One is surely justified now, if not before, of speaking of Hergé's work as a classic.

In order to orient the American reader, let me clarify two points. First, this book initially was addressed to those readers perfectly familiar with the Tintin albums. Thus, I did not always clearly explain the circumstances of one or another particular adventure, for I supposed they were already known to my readers. Second, the systematic use of scholarly language—among others, that of psychoanalysis—to interpret the adventures of Tintin was intended to highlight the fundamental oppositions that seemed to me to be the underlying framework of this saga. In particular, I focused on the opposition between Tintin the "foundling" and Haddock "the bastard." Although today a majority of readers may have assimilated these psychoanalytic notions, the vocabulary might seem heavy or outdated. If that is the case, I ask your pardon. However, in a study I intended to be entertaining, I was still very much concerned with showing that a domain typically consigned to children is indeed amenable to legitimate scholarly interests.

# ABBREVIATIONS

| | |
|---|---|
| TC | Tintin in the Congo |
| TA | Tintin in America |
| CP | The Cigars of the Pharaoh |
| BL | The Blue Lotus |
| BE | The Broken Ear |
| BI | The Black Island |
| KOS | King Ottokar's Scepter |
| CGC | The Crab with the Golden Claws |
| SS | The Shooting Star |
| SU | The Secret of the Unicorn |
| RRT | Red Rackham's Treasure |
| 7CB | The Seven Crystal Balls |
| PS | Prisoners of the Sun |
| LBG | Land of Black Gold |
| DM | Destination Moon |
| EM | Explorers of the Moon |
| CA | The Calculus Affair |
| RSS | The Red Sea Sharks |

# INTRODUCTION

*The Adventures of Tintin* has been translated into some sixty languages, with more than 200 million copies sold to date. There is no doubt that Hergé's work is of compelling interest. Philosopher Michel Serres, for example, sees it as a twentieth-century classic, an enduring masterpiece. On the occasion of Hergé's death, Serres confided to a journalist that "no other French author can be compared to him in influence and reputation."[1] To be sure, Hergé also has vehement detractors. Several years ago a critic of Tintin wrote, "This hypocrite, this boy feigning innocence, this ugly little monkey cannot fool us any longer. It's time we exposed him for what he really is. Tintin is a forty-year-old dwarf, a colonialist, and a zoophile, with homosexual tendencies to boot. This is the despicable character we set up as a hero for our dear little children."[2]

The accusations leveled at Hergé are many but almost always play on the same themes. His hero is accused of misogyny: indeed, women are almost totally absent from his work—along with workers and Catholics. Moreover, he is suspected of promoting a right-wing ideology, of being a colonialist, racist, and anti-Semite. In most of his interviews, Hergé had to respond to these accusations, and his defense varied little from one interview to the next. Thus, one can summarize it as follows. Tintin was born at the end of the 1920s, when his author, who had grown up in a right-wing, Catholic environment, was only twenty-two years old. The first two albums are witness to "the sins of his youth," subsequently disavowed. The first, which smacks of an elementary anticommunism, was republished only much later and only as an archival document. The other represents a colonialist ideology of the 1930s. If the hero bears a certain paternalistic attitude toward the blacks, he is not really racist because we see that he actually defends them against the wicked whites. Later on, Tintin consistently takes the side of the underdog, and we see him coming to the rescue of Native Americans as well as oppressed Chinese. As for the accusation of anti-Semitism, even if Hergé admits to having presented "a disagreeable businessman with Jewish features and a Jewish name," still he pleads innocent: "Who could have foreseen that Jewish stories would end in the way we know they did, that is, in the death camps of Treblinka and Auschwitz?"[3]

That one can appreciate Hergé's work and the ideology it promotes is due at least in part to the author's managing to cloud the issue by getting us to forget his hero's origin. Tintin is a character without a past. Hergé was constantly touching up his work for more than fifty years, not only to improve the graphics but also to eliminate whatever aspects appeared anachronistic, poorly executed, or too caught up in an ideology he no longer espoused. Just as in George Orwell's *1984*, where old newspapers are rewritten so that the present seems to flow seamlessly from the past, so too Hergé recast his work to form a whole, to escape history and thus be able to transform itself into myth.

The first albums consisted of three versions. From 1930 on, the first series, often inaccessible, was produced from day to day and appeared in daily or weekly newspapers. The second already differed from the first, even though it was published in the same year as an album in black and white. In 1941 the albums were published in color with a format of sixty-two pages. The third version consists of albums reappearing after 1949, when the success of Tintin reached such unprecedented levels that Hergé was able to capitalize on it by recirculating the first adventures. One's critical appreciation of Hergé's work varies according to which version one has in mind. Hergé himself does not make it any easier for his critics. On the one hand, he does not endorse any particular interpretation of his work;[4] on the other, he never clarifies to which version he is referring. Thus, the Tintin from before the war gets credited with a liberalism acquired only later.

There are two ways of studying the adventures of Hergé's hero. The first is diachronic: It consists in following the stories in their order of appearance and situating them in the concrete context in which they appeared. From this point of view, the first versions, partially reedited in the collection *The*

*Archives of Hergé*, are of particular interest.[5] The second method is synchronistic: It consists in taking the adventures as a whole in order to examine the internal development of this fictional universe, as coherent and self-enclosed as the world of Honoré de Balzac. In this case, it is better to analyze the most recent versions since they more readily exhibit Hergé's overall vision for his work, which he continued refining until the end. Depending on which point of view one chooses, one ends up with a different evaluation of Tintin.

What interests me here is to bring these two methods together to study both the genesis of the work and the metamorphoses of its hero. These metamorphoses are of various kinds. As external to the text, they depend on the ideological changes and disavowals of the author. As internal to the text, they have to do with the development of the stories as a whole, the aging of the characters, and the establishment of their interpersonal relationships. On another more immediate level, the metamorphoses of Tintin are equally about their author's knack for dissimulation to dodge his enemies. Bringing these two approaches together may allow for a more adequate appreciation of the role of Tintin in contemporary culture.

# BOOK ONE
# TINTIN IN HISTORY

In the end, you know, my only international rival is Tintin! We are the little guys who don't let the big guys bully us. No one has ever noticed that, because of my size.

—Charles de Gaulle, cited by André Malraux in
*Felled Oaks: Conversations with de Gaulle*

Thomson: "Can you perhaps think of some famous last words?"
Thompson: "U-uh . . . 'San Theodorians, I have understood you!'
Will that do?"

—*Tintin and the Picaros*

## CHAPTER ONE

# THE CHILDHOOD OF A LEADER

## THE ORIGIN OF TINTIN

Hergé has often recounted the circumstances of Tintin's creation in 1929. When Hergé had been employed for two years at a Belgian newspaper, *The Twentieth Century*, a Catholic daily running some twelve thousand copies, his new director, Father Norbert Wallez, decided to spark some interest in his own ideas among young people. He launched a weekly illustrated supplement, *The Little Twentieth*, and handed it over to Georges Remi, already working under the pen name Hergé. Hergé had previously published a comic strip in *The Belgian Boy Scout* called *The Adventures of Totor*, and he adapted his former hero to the new circumstances. Whereas Totor was a scout, Tintin would be a journalist, but like his Boy Scout ancestor he would remain accessible to his readers, whom he hoped to win over. Just like real journalists, Tintin would conduct investigations on the state of the contemporary world. His model, Albert Londres, was at the height of his career. The first *Adventures of Tintin* constituted in effect an overall assessment of the situation in Europe in the 1930s, particularly the place of Belgium in that world. Instead of analyzing his country from within, however, Tintin would look elsewhere for a satisfactory reflection of his world. "Are we still the best?" This was the implicit question he would pose on his trips to the four corners of the globe.

Two circumstances determined the birth of Tintin: first, he was involved in dramatic historical times, and second, his exploits were addressed to children and adolescents. Having to appeal to the psychology of children in the

1930s gives the series a certain didactic character. Tintin becomes the model teenager, a virtuous and heroic young man caught in a world of corruption that he tries to redress. He harbors no doubts whatsoever, especially about his own values. He has the soul of a soldier, ready to take up arms to defend the moral and political order in which he believes.

Tintin's initial stance is undoubtedly the result of Hergé's own memories of World War I. Born in 1907, too early to have actively participated in the war, Hergé nevertheless retained some fairly clear memories of that time. As he recounts in interviews, his career as cartoonist is probably tied to these images of the world war.[1] He managed to combine political demands with those of adolescent psychology, but the initial results were fairly mediocre. The first albums seem both flawed and unsatisfying. Hergé was still far from matching his ideal, Alain Saint-Ogan, whom he visited in May 1931.

Initially, Tintin adopts the mannerisms of Joseph Rouletabille, the young reporter in Gaston Leroux's famous detective series, but Tintin is even more naïve and humorless. Snowy, in contrast, emerges full blown from the world of Benjamin Rabier, illustrator of La Fontaine's *Fables*. In the guise of a dog, he represents Tintin's younger brother, who imitates the elder and to whom Tintin reveals the secrets of the universe. Snowy laughs and cries like a child. He behaves less like a typical animal and more like a somewhat uneducated and awkward human being. In *Tintin in the Land of the Soviets*, we see him elegantly grooming himself before his return to Brussels (*AH*, I, p. 179). In *Tintin in the Congo*, he sports a colonial helmet and holds the barrel of a rifle in his paws (*AH*, I, p. 185). In *Tintin in America*, he sips his friend's drink through a straw (*AH*, I, p. 313). Snowy is Tintin's Émile, with Tintin himself his sole educator. To protect the dog's youthful innocence from corruption by the evil world, Hergé has Snowy speak only to Tintin. Occasionally Snowy addresses other "inferior" animals as he would domestic servants, but other humans do not understand his language. Nevertheless, Snowy chatters away, multiplying the puns and flattering commentaries on each of his master's exploits.

Splitting the hero into two characters, Hergé makes it easier for his readers to identify with them depending on their age. The younger ones identify more readily with Snowy, whose canine appearance is no obstacle to his being their friend. Beneath his furry coat, he is quite similar to Tintin. The older children, twelve to fifteen, identify more readily with Tintin himself, endowed as he is with an imaginary superhuman strength. Confronting a hostile universe, Tintin emerges victorious, no matter what the conditions.

In 1930 the European nations realized that World War I had marked an end to their supremacy. Among capitalist nations, the United States had surpassed them and was promulgating its own values. In *Scenes from Future Life*—a source of inspiration for Hergé's *Tintin in America*—Georges Duhamel predicted that this technological, materialistic society was in the process of "conquering the Old World."[2] To the east, Russia constituted a danger that was poorly assessed, either because the Soviet achievements were overestimated or because they were judged as catastrophic. Contrary to the expectations of most Western governments, the Bolshevik regime remained in power. Other countries could no longer treat it as some kind of puppet government about to disappear in the near future. Despite their relative weakness, the European countries—whether Belgium or France—maintained their power by controlling large colonial territories. But what sorts of relations should exist between the ruling governments and their colonies? What sort of model of life should they pursue?

The fascism that was developing simultaneously in Italy and Germany and finding many adherents in other countries as well was at least one response to these questions. In promoting a strong youth movement, "virile" and "pure," this brand of fascism was not only dealing with the problems arising from the economic crisis but also promoting a solution to the "moral decadence" of the West. In opposition to the materialistic values flaunted by America, fascism looked to the past. The glory of the past was to become the antidote to the current decadence and offered an alternative to the United States and the Soviet Union, both of which were rejected unconditionally. Unregulated capitalism was abhorred even more than communism to the extent that capitalism represented the loss of qualitative values—the end of "moral civilization"—in favor of the reign of the quantitative.

In Belgium, from 1930 on, one saw the rise of the Rexist movement, whose basic ideas of nationalism, Catholicism, and anti-capitalism were very close to those of fascism. The main figure of this movement, Léon Degrelle, published articles on South America in *The Twentieth Century* before he founded his own weekly, *Vlan*.[3] The Rexist movement spread rapidly. During the elections of March 24, 1936, it carried seventy-eight seats in the provincial elections.

Although Hergé was not officially a member of the Rexist movement, he was close to the traditional right wing. Similarities between the ideology of the Rexist movement and *The Adventures of Tintin* have already been pointed out.[4] The first three adventures take their hero to Soviet Russia, the Belgian Congo, and the United States, respectively. In theory, Tintin is a reporter, but one sees him draft an article for his newspaper only in the first adventure (*AH*, I, p. 76). In reality, he is the symbol of this "new youth" promoted by the right-wing movements as the emblem of a rejuvenated West.

Tintin barely seems like a creature of flesh and blood: he has few needs, no personal problems, and no financial difficulties, even though he doesn't handle money. He is much more an abstract and imaginary figure. His face is round, expressionless, with two black dots for eyes. He wears his hair in a kind of tuft, or "quiff," at the top of his head. Everyone can readily identify with his "full-moon" face and project onto it all their desires. Tintin invites his readers to identify with him all the more because he himself embodies a certain ideal: he incarnates Western Christian values at a precise moment of history.

Although Tintin's first exploits are as dated as the newspapers in which they first appeared, they also seem to take place in the present. In *Tintin in the Land of the Soviets*, he departs from the train station in Brussels and returns there at the end of his trip. He has some problems with the German police, as one might expect, and reveals to his readers the sorry state of the Soviet economy. In the Congo, he teaches the native children about the wonders of the Belgian state (*AH*, I, p. 247).

His nationalism is sometimes less pronounced. Although he is proud of his country, he presents it as the ideal model only implicitly. He himself comes to embody Western technology and constitutes a modern variant on the "trick-

"My dear friends, today I'm going to talk to you about your country: Belgium!"
*AH*, I, p. 247. © Hergé/Moulinsart 2007.

ster" in traditional tales.[5] Wherever he goes, he instinctively knows how to use the latest means of transportation: car, airplane, boat, and locomotive. In the Soviet Union, he is able to build an automobile from scraps of iron without using a single tool (*AH*, I, pp. 60–61). Later on, he repairs a racing car without reassembling all its parts. "Wow! That works so much better without all the pieces!" (p. 104). When an airplane propeller breaks, he cuts another from a tree with a simple penknife (pp. 155–157). He repairs the gas tank of his airplane while it continues to fly without a pilot (pp. 157–158). In the Congo he is just as inventive. For example, he uses a powerful electromagnet to deflect his enemies' arrows. No situation leaves him at a loss; he always finds a solution. Following Tintin's example, Snowy comes up with a number of little "inventions" himself that save the day just when his master gets stuck in difficult straits. For example, when a member of the GPU, the repressive Soviet police, threatens Tintin with a gun, Snowy picks up a long stick with his mouth and literally mows down the agent by running through his legs (p. 75).

Although Tintin doesn't really understand how the technology works and never formally learns how to use it, he nevertheless masters it. Thus, he seems to have magical powers. For example, in the Congo, he films some villains (p. 226) and records their conversations on a tape recorder. Without going to a lab to develop the film—after all, he's in the bush—the next day he projects his film for the Africans, who are as astonished as his readers by these unprecedented feats. One easily understands why the natives hail him as their "great white witch doctor" and kneel before him whenever they meet him.

Far from aiding development in the colony, however, the hero's behavior creates an unbridgeable gap between himself and the blacks. They never learn how to master this mysterious technology. Even what access they have to it is always in some inferior or ridiculous form. Consider the case of the natives' railroad. The engine is made of scraps glued together, and the cars, from wooden boxes. When Tintin's car collides with it, the train is derailed, and the hero tows it back to the station with his own vehicle (p. 217).

When Tintin's tricks do not work in a particularly desperate situation, he has one more solution, as effective as the appeal to technology: he calls on God. For example, a leopard enters the classroom where he is teaching. Defenseless before the wild animal, like the Christian martyr delivered over to the beasts, the hero begins to pray: "My God, give me the strength to endure this mighty battle" (p. 247). God hears his prayer. The leopard turns out to be as gentle as the lion of Tartarin. Later on, tied to a dinghy and facing certain death, Tintin cries out: "My God! Protect me! A waterfall! I'm going to be crushed on the rocks!" (p. 257). God does not turn a deaf ear to his plea. A branch miraculously grows out of a rock, saving the hero. A few hours later, fighting with the bandit Tom, Tintin falls over a steep cliff: "My God! I'll be smashed to bits on these rocks!" God once again hears his prayer. The rock turns into a hippopotamus, and Tintin safely bounces off the hippo's back. Tom the villain has less luck; he falls into a river where he is devoured by crocodiles. Witnessing his enemy's death, Tintin—not one to hold a grudge— begins praying for him: "God save his soul!" (p. 265). On his adventure in America, Tintin has a similar experience. As he is about to be killed by one of Al Capone's thugs, Tintin offers up his final prayer: "My God! Receive my soul! And now, let me die bravely, like a true Belgian!" (p. 308). God promptly intervenes, this time inspiring Snowy with a trick that saves his friend's life.

If the hero's existence is punctuated by miracles, this only emphasizes the sacred character of his mission. Like Joan of Arc, whom the Church had canonized only a few years before, Tintin not only has to free Europe from Evil but also to impose Western nationalist values on the rest of the world. Divine intervention clearly shows that Tintin is an instrument of Providence. In not listening to others but only to his own conscience, he also shares with the heroine of Domrémy the virtues of courage, youth, and virginity.

To bolster his character's credibility, the chief editor of *The Twentieth Century* staged the following scenario. The newspaper recruited a young man resembling Tintin. Tintin's look-alike went to the train station in Louvain, took the local train from Cologne that was supposedly returning from Russia via Berlin, and then got off in Brussels, where he made a grand entrance like the sacred kings or bishops of old. His triumphal welcome signaled the deep accord between the fictional hero and his readers. Tintin embodied the ideas of his day. The pseudoevent of his triumphal return to Brussels, reproduced three times, emphasized the close relation between the character and the immediate historical present.

## NEW IMPRESSIONS OF AFRICA

Although Tintin symbolizes a certain ideal of Belgium, at the beginning of his adventures he paradoxically has little contact with his fellow Belgians. He *is* the Belgians; he embodies the nation. The foreigners he comes into contact with are of two sorts: the Good whom he can convert to his values, and the incorrigibles whom he has to punish. The majority of the blacks are among the Good. Embarking on his trip to the Congo, Tintin carries with him all the stereotypes of Africa that his experience will confirm. Far from being affected by his contact with reality, he imposes on the natives his own point of view, which they reflect in a somewhat caricatured fashion. Thus, he never really sees this continent for what it is. On the contrary, Africa gets to know him better. Tintin possesses a kind of innate knowledge that has no need of justification. Being a white man is enough; his whiteness is an essence bearing its own conviction. Except on safari, when he agrees to follow the bush beaters, he always gives the orders. His "boy" Coco teaches him nothing about the country. Faced with his master's raised finger, Coco always responds: "Yes, Master." The little African is assigned only menial tasks: watching the car, preparing the meals, and carrying their equipment. Only once does Coco take any initiative: to free Tintin from being held captive in a hut. Even in this case Coco is merely imitating his young master. In each of his encounters, Tintin interjects the prejudicial platitudes he shares with his readers: the crocodile is a "frightful beast," the rhinoceros is a "monster" like the buffalo, the Aniotas' tribal dress is "ridiculous," the Pygmies he meets are "unbelievably fearful, just like all of their race." Elsewhere he compares the natives to the Huns, a term we find later in the mouth of Captain Haddock.

The hero is a model the natives are supposed to imitate. Their task, of course, is hopeless; Tintin is too perfect for them. But encouraging them in the right direction, Tintin preaches and sets a good example, as in the following incident. Snowy falls into the water, and a "brave" African sailor throws him a life buoy, calling out politely, "Master Dog!" (*AH*, I, p. 193). Since the sailor has bad aim, the buoy conks Snowy in the head, at which point Snowy sinks to the bottom of the sea. The black sailor, in his "weakness" of wanting to preserve his own life, hesitates to jump in to save him, especially since the waters are full of sharks. Tintin doesn't hesitate to make the sailor feel ashamed of his cowardice: "And you've done nothing to save him? Well, now you'll see how a real man acts!" (p. 194). Without fear of the formidable sharks, Tintin jumps in. Similarly, when the leopard bursts into his classroom, Tintin's conscience calls out to him: "Careful, Tintin! You must protect the children, whatever the cost to yourself!" (p. 247). When the Pygmies attack the hero, his first reaction is to run away. But he soon gets hold of himself: "Whoa there, Tintin! Running away? That wouldn't be like you! Face up to these little Moors and fight valiantly to your death!" (p. 268). The "little Moors" aren't very threatening after all, and they soon embrace Tintin as their king.

In the Congo adventure, the blacks are represented as children: friendly, naïve, cowardly, and lazy. One has constantly to prod them to work, even when their own interests are at stake. Thus, when their train derails, they let Snowy take up the job by himself. "Me too tired! Me get dirty!" But in the face of Tintin's threats, they finally give in, and the dog backs up his master: "Come on, you lazy bunch! Get to work!" (p. 216).

Tintin's main task is to educate. He follows the missionaries who wanted to Christianize Africa. Without questioning his own competence, he takes on their various duties and sets out for the Congo with an amazing amount of supplies: camping gear, colonial-style clothing, hunting weapons, preserved foods, scientific equipment, and medicines (p. 185). One can see why the natives impatiently await Tintin and Snowy and give them a huge welcome: "Our reputation precedes us," he says to Snowy with false modesty. As soon as they land, a cheering crowd carries the two friends triumphantly in a procession: "These blacks are certainly nice to carry us to our hotel!" (p. 198). To reciprocate, Tintin will share with them the benefits of Western progress. We see him in various roles: doctor, teacher, railroad engineer, foreman organizing workers, peacemaker settling quarrels, and commanding general leading the war against the enemy M'Hatuvu. In the eyes of the natives, Tintin embodies the modern State that takes good care of its citizens.

Although the Africans take the Europeans as their model, they are nevertheless not their equals. On the boat, the menial tasks fall to the blacks, whereas anything requiring more ability or education has to be done by the whites. Hergé's Africa is strangely underpopulated. While the natives act like children, the Europeans represent the more mature stage of development and so "naturally" impose their values on the immature, as parents do on children. The socioeconomic changes in Africa are conceived in psychological terms. Just as Tintin represents all of Belgium, each black person is potentially all of Africa. The natives are not differentiated from one another. They have the same stereotypical faces, the same character, and even the same sorts of indistinctive names. When they are named at all, they typically have nicknames such as "Coco" or "Snowball," suggesting their desire to become white. Left to themselves, children enjoy imitating adults. Similarly, the Congolese copy the whites, but their imitations turn into parodies. Their railroad is more like a merry-go-round, and their clothing is made of the faded finery of the Europeans. More frequently they sport the remnants of military uniforms—hats, helmets, leggings, and epaulettes—instead of their native dress. The local kings wear crowns, sit on thrones made of wood, and smoke pipes or cigars. The king of Ba Baoro'm has a rolling pin for a scepter—an appropriate sign, given the name of his tribe. The king of the M'Hatuvu has a pet turtle. When the M'Hatuvu king declares war on his rivals, he reviews his army "trained and equipped in the European style" and thus feels guaranteed of victory. His main piece of artillery is a homemade artillery rifle that looks like a blunderbuss mounted on wheels, like a child's toy. The weapon explodes the first time it is used (p. 234). Whenever Tintin addresses these bogus chieftains, it is always ironically: "Hail, king of Ba Baoro'm." He knows full well that he himself is the only genuine master of Africa.

For the natives, he is a sacred, all-powerful individual, a *boula matari*. They speak to him with respect, call on him with their slightest problems, and kneel before each of his miracles to show their adoration. He is not only the "good white" but also the god of the blacks, a model beyond reach who nevertheless serves as their guide. Each tribe recognizes his superiority and abandons its traditional chieftain in favor of him. "You are a chief of Ba Baoro'm. You are their Great Chief" (p. 230). He dispenses justice like King Solomon. He soon puts an end to all tribal warfare by conquering the enemy tribes one by one and uniting them under the same law—his own. Thus, he repeats in Africa the history of Europe and becomes the "true" founder of the Congo.

He would have completely pacified the entire region had he not encountered three kinds of resistant forces. First, the alleged laziness of the Africans themselves prevents them from working as hard as the whites. Second, the local leaders dispossessed of their power and prestige vent their hatred on him. Finally, the wicked whites, profiting from the ignorance of the natives, exploit them to gain control of the riches of Africa for themselves. Tintin leads the struggle against the native secret societies combating European influence, especially the so-called leopard-men, the Aniotas, whose numbers include the former witch doctor of Ba Baoro'm, Muganga.[6]

Since Muganga is not sufficiently powerful to defend himself against Tintin, he joins up with Tom, Al Capone's "lieutenant." Muganga and Tom conclude a deadly pact, toast each other with whiskey, and set out to eliminate the hero. While Tom reveals to his new accomplice the projects of Al Capone, the witch doctor declares the origin of his hatred: the arrival of the whites has compromised his power. He wants to keep his tribe ignorant in order to profit from their gullibility. As for himself, he obviously doesn't believe in spirits, fetishes, and magic spells, but he makes use of them to control the people of Ba Baoro'm. Just in time Tintin shows up to film the confessions of the villains and thus opens the eyes of the natives, who then revolt against their witch doctor. Our hero cunningly tricks the American gangsters and has them arrested by the local police. If Tintin's stay in Africa does not completely transform the continent, at least he puts it on the road to progress.

Upon his departure, our hero realizes that his task has not been accomplished: "Good-bye, Congo. There's so much more for me to see here" (p. 291). The very last image of this album nevertheless ends on an optimistic note. One of the natives lies prostrate before a statue of Tintin, who has his arms opened wide like a Christ figure, while next to him an African dog worships a fetish representing Snowy. At a nearby café table, two customers fantasize about the world of the whites: "They say, in Belgium all little whites are like Tintin." Below, a mother scolds her little brat: "If you not good, you never be like Tintin!" In front of a straw hut (*la case à palabre*), an old man reminisces: "I've never seen such a *boula matari*, all-powerful, like Tintin." Another native, who finds Tintin's camera, learns that it will belong to him in a year and a day. Although Tintin is gone, ascending into the heavens in an airplane sent to pick him up, he nevertheless remains alive among his disciples. This last image, with its evangelical overtones, recalls the situation of the apostles after Jesus ascends into heaven. The apostles talk about him and prepare to spread his word. Thus, Hergé presents a kind of "animistic" Pentecost, parodying the Christian one. The Africans receive the gift of tongues, recite the acts of their god, and set off to imitate his example.

One might be astonished by the deification of the hero of a comic strip in an overtly Catholic newspaper. But rather than Tintin being transformed into a pagan idol, the reader is led to believe Tintin himself is combating paganism and actually preventing any sacrilege against the Christian mysteries. I think there are at least two reasons for this. On the one hand, the local beliefs of the natives are considered merely "childhood mythology." Scarcely more dangerous than tall tales invented by children, these apparently idolatrous beliefs would disappear once Africa reaches maturity. On the other hand, Tintin is suitable for adulation not only because he brings technology to Africa, as Prometheus brings fire to humankind, but especially because he embodies the modern State. Just as the European monarchical State had sought a kind of transcendence vis-à-vis the Church, and thus invoked Greek and Roman mythology to lend support to heroic images of the king—comparing him to a god in the classical tradition, when such deification would have been heretical in a strictly Christian context—so too Tintin takes advantage of the local beliefs and customs to demonstrate his superiority. Using technology that the natives cannot comprehend, he passes for a kind of magician and proves that his gods are more powerful than the Great Spirit invoked by Muganga, his rival.

To the extent that he *is* the State, Tintin has to situate himself outside the civil society that he organizes. He has access to a mysterious, all-powerful "beyond" that he manifests in wondrous feats incomprehensible to the people. As the abstract representation of European order, the hero does not have any ordinary human faults. Because of the modern separation of the religious from the political, however, his deification does not challenge the Christian understanding of the world. Just as the State in previous times supported its authority with an appeal to a transcendence that makes State power seem incontestable, so too does Tintin profit from the animistic belief system. He does so before the traditional, "primitive" religion is transformed into folklore, just as the absolute monarchs of the Renaissance and seventeenth century made use of the remnants of Greek and Latin paganism to bolster their claims to legitimacy.

## TINTIN AND HIS ENEMIES

Tintin's enemies come from many places. Among them one finds all those groups in France and Belgium who at the time were denounced by the rightist polemicists as subversives. First of all, there were the Communists. If they weren't the largest group, they were the ones against whom Tintin was initially fighting. During January 1928 in Brussels, a Soviet exhibition was the scene of hostile demonstrations by the National Youth Movement. Degrelle, the future leader of the Rexist movement, took part in a rowdy student demonstration during which the students, armed with cudgels, smashed a bust of Lenin.[7] This same year, Joseph Douillet, a former Belgian ambassador who had served thirty-five years in Russia, ten of which were spent under the Soviet regime, published in France a pamphlet hostile to the new Soviet government. In the pamphlet he denounced the crimes of socialism, contrasting its meager accomplishments to those of the czarist regime.[8] Douillet's *Moscou sans voiles* (*Moscow Unveiled*) vehemently attacked socialism per se more than Stalinism. The author, familiar with several Soviet prisons, recalled the general misery of the population, the massacres of the peasants, the internment camps, the ubiquitous propaganda, and the cynicism of the new leaders, whom he linked with murderers and convicts. Since Douillet's hostile attack was one-sided and simply idealized the previous regime, his book lacked the power of conviction and political finesse of Boris Souvarine's *Staline* written some years later. Douillet's book nevertheless appealed to the expectations of rightist circles less eager to spread word of the crimes of the Soviet monster than to denounce enemies who would justify their own ideological choices. On the eve of the worldwide economic crisis, the effects of the bloodbath of World War I were still being felt in Germany and France. Socialism with its pamphlets attempting to revive the morale of the working class constituted a decided threat to the bourgeois regimes. Without being able to impress the working class with the benefits of economic liberalism, one could at least expose the less worthy results of a regime allegedly founded on the dictatorship of the proletariat.

*Tintin in the Land of the Soviets* is clearly inspired by *Moscow Unveiled*. For the hero, communism represents absolute Evil. However, in his Soviet adventure he tries neither to transform communism by persuasion nor to conquer it by force, but merely distances himself from it. He succeeds only in more specific actions, like rescuing some unfortunate person or preventing the GPU from seizing a peasant's wheat. Tintin records the extent of the evil, but because he does not understand its origin, he does not directly engage with but merely observes this world of misery.

Tintin constantly gives the slip to representatives of the police or the party. Like Tintin himself, however, they are merely blind servants of ideology. Their opposing belief systems vehemently clash without really undermining each other. Tintin does not have any effect on Soviet Russia, a country that rejects him as a hopelessly foreign body. The hero's final words sum up his Soviet experience: "Good-bye, inhospitable land!" (*AH*, I, p. 151). What brings a smile in this first adventure is not its systematic anti-Soviet message but the imaginary omnipotence of its main character. Neither the ravages of winter nor the bullets of enemy fire are able to touch him. By himself he is stronger than an army. He doesn't incite a revolution against the "Reds," as Joseph Douillet constantly predicted, perhaps because in spite of everything he remains at this time an agent of order.

In Russia, as in the other countries he visits later on, Tintin discovers a fundamental law of its society: what the people glimpse of government is but a deceptive appearance. For example, he meets a group of British Communists "who have been shown the wonders of Bolshevism" (p. 69). The guide shows them a factory, while affirming: "Contrary to our detractors, our factories are running at full productivity." Tintin wants to verify this claim and discovers that the factory is a fake: "This is actually a stage set. Behind the facade they're burning straw to make it look like smoke coming from the factory" (p. 68).

The adventure among the Soviets does not follow a preset plan. Rather, it probes deeper and deeper beneath the appearances until the hero hits the kernel of reality never before glimpsed by ordinary eyes. In the course of a trip outside Moscow, he comes across a toppled *isba*, or hut, apparently uninhabited. Inside he takes refuge from a raging blizzard but is soon over-whelmed by nightmares: a clock strikes thirteen, skeletons begin to move, and a ghostly voice threatens him (pp. 137–142). Tintin soon discovers what this macabre scenario conceals, namely, the hiding place "where Lenin, Trotsky and Stalin have amassed the treasures stolen from the people" (p. 143). To avoid having the people catch on to their actual practices, the Communist leaders, according to Hergé, have constructed a scenario in miniature that they intend to impose on all of Russia and even beyond, on the free world. Their "program" is really an apocalypse leaving behind nothing but cadavers and ghosts. The same movement disguises the ghastly results while revealing the true intentions of the leaders. Those who hold the reins of power con-stitute a secret society whose goal is to amass their own power and wealth rather than to benefit the people.

In this first adventure the theme of conspiracy, very popular among the extreme Right before the war, is not very specific, but this theme shows up in various guises in later episodes. In the Congo the hero battles the Aniotas, and in America, the mob that runs Chicago. Beneath a surface legality, these groups carry on all kinds of illicit activities: bootlegging, kidnapping, extortion, and murder. Despite the rivalry of the clans, the mob maintains an underground society of mutual aid, and the mob sets out to eliminate Tintin (p. 406).

In the United States, according to Hergé, there is little difference be-tween the gangsters and the industrial giants. They use the same methods to set up a culture of appearances. "Here, everything is phony," remarked Georges Duhamel. Hergé keeps that in mind when he presents a false knight advertising cans (p. 391), an imitation castle (p. 392), some factories produc-ing tainted food (p. 400), and a mock weight-lifting contest (p. 412). What-ever the industrial leaders do not obtain with money, they get by resorting to violence, legal or illegal. Unregulated capitalism is shown to be just as disastrous as socialism, perhaps even worse to the extent that the more successful it becomes, the more Europe follows its dangerous example.

After Tintin's stay in Chicago, Hergé depicts several capitalists that confirm his point of view. For example, in 1935, we have Basil Bazarov in *The Broken Ear*, modeled on the real Basil Zaharoff. Bazarov is an arms merchant with refined manners who sows the seeds of death wherever he goes, maintaining constant tensions between rival countries that inevitably result in war (*AH*, III, pp. 339–341). Next to him we have an American industrialist with the head of Groucho Marx: the villainous R. W. Trickler, executive of General American Oil. In this same adventure, Trickler tries to corrupt General Alcazar and push him into war to assure his society of exclusive rights to the oil fields of Gran Chapo. When Tintin tries to prevent the war, Trickler hires a gunman to "disappear" this worrisome idealist. Some years later, we find this same shady businessman quietly dealing with countries in the East: money recognizes no borders and disregards ideologies (*CA*, 47, IV, 2).

During the period 1931–1935, when Hergé was denouncing capitalist ideology, he propagated an idea of government he held on to for a long time: the idea of secret societies that make all the important decisions. Between 1880 and 1930 people often talked about secret societies, and the public had a greater tendency to exaggerate their powers than to examine their organization and actual roles. In *The Cigars of the Pharaoh*, Tintin runs into one of these secret organizations. Although never explicitly so designated, it is easy to read this group of initiates assembling in the interior of the Egyptian pyramid as the image of the Freemasons represented in right-wing circles before the Second World War.[9] They were thought to be a "State within a State" with various religious aspects. According to the right wing, this international organization was aiming at worldwide domination by fomenting revolutions everywhere that would eventually serve their cause. In the French Revolution of 1789 as well as the Bolshevik Revolution of 1917, the right wing saw the same almighty hand of the Masonic lodge.

Hergé took up the anti-Masonic theme by showing how a group of Egyptologists, through their arms and drug trafficking, aim to control both mind and body. When Tintin eventually exposes them, he discovers in their membership a political adviser, a military officer of high rank, some international dealers, and some bankers, Mr. and Mrs. Snowball of the Indian and India Bank Ltd. Only in the next episode, *The Blue Lotus*, does Tintin learn the name of their leader, Roberto Rastapopoulos.

Although Rastapopoulos has a Greek surname, this corrupt millionaire represents the Jewish stereotype, exactly as caricatured in the right-wing newspapers of that time. He has bushy eyebrows, a pronounced nose, a cowardly and obsequious character, and dreams of nothing but getting rich and doing evil. To Tintin, Rastapopoulos admits his governmental connections: "The higher-ups have asked me to take advantage of my stay here by observing everything very carefully. So, if you don't mind my asking . . ." (*AH*, III, p. 43). Later on Hergé represents one or two other Jews as villainous and as well established as Rastapopoulos: the director of the English Company of South American Petroleum (*AH*, III, p. 358) and, especially, Mr. Blumenstein, of the Blumenstein Bank of New York. Blumenstein is the villain in *The Shooting Star*, an adventure appearing in *Le Soir* in 1942, just when the collaborationist governments were handing over the Jews in exchange for improving their own situations.

Whether they are Communists, Freemasons, Jews, capitalists, or perhaps some combination of these, the enemies of Tintin are portrayed as representing absolute Evil. They are portrayed as engaging in a death struggle against the national governments, particularly against those with a long tradition of working closely with their people, such as the liberal monarchies of Belgium and England. The hero and the expatriate crooks are locked in a constant battle to find out which of the two camps will be able to impose its values on the people. For the right wing, moreover, "the people" are thought to be passive, weak willed, and ready to follow any government, no matter what its political stripe.

## HERGÉ AND "THE MORTAR"

Although it is undeniable that the first episodes of *The Adventures of Tintin* took up the themes of the right wing before World War II, many other influences on the author allow us to nuance this claim. Hergé was both a young nationalistic cartoonist and a careful reader of *The Mortar* (*Le Crapouillot*). Edited by Jean Galtier-Boissière, this magazine focused on art and literature and, in addition, specialized in denouncing the "lies" of the First World War. Between the world wars, *The Mortar* published a number of special editions that tried to expose the real role of governments and the influence of special money interests on world politics. Under the same banner of anticonformism, one found in these publications journalists of the Right and the Left, pamphleteers, nationalists, and anarchists, among them the extreme rightist Pierre Dominique and his leftist cohorts Victor Serge and René Lefèbvre.

In Tintin's first two episodes, Hergé wholeheartedly endorsed the traditional right-wing agenda, but the third adventure, *Tintin in America* (1931), reveals a more ambivalent stance. Although Hergé admits that this episode was influenced by Georges Duhamel, it was perhaps equally influenced by Josef von Sternberg's 1927 film *Underworld*, which featured for the first time the gangster type as hero. Hergé had specially researched the October 1930 issue of *The Mortar* dedicated to Americans, particularly the article "America and the Americans." Returning from the United States, Claude Blanchard described Chicago as "the capital of crime, where murder is accepted, savored like a stew, and served every morning with the newspapers."[10] In the adventure in America, Hergé sticks to this line so strictly that he does not show anything of the United States except gangsters, police, Native Americans, and some businessmen. In the character Bobby Smiles one recognizes the gangster George "Bugs" Moran, whom Blanchard described as having "a face of a Methodist preacher." He was the leader of the principal gang rivaling Alphonse "Scarface" Capone's. Hergé shows him in the act of offering Tintin this strange contract: "I'm hiring you at ten thousand dollars a month to help me bring down Al Capone. If you rub out Capone himself there's a bonus of twenty thousand dollars. Agreed?" (*TA*, 14, I, 2; see *AH*, I, p. 319). From Blanchard's article, Hergé borrows the scenario of the shoot-out from one building to the next (*AH*, pp. 323–324). Like Duhamel, Blanchard also described Chicago's slaughterhouses, which Tintin eventually visits. Blanchard cited the exact name of the restaurant where Tintin eats, "Swift and Company," though Hergé changed the name slightly to "Slift" (p. 398).

Tintin's episode with the Native Americans is inspired in part by the article "Among the Red Skins of New Mexico." Numerous details that lend this album its local color belong to this report. The fact that the police themselves consume confiscated alcohol is made public on the radio: "Some 150 gallons of Javel champagne have been seized by the police. The district attorney and twenty-nine policemen have been hospitalized" (p. 364).[11] Especially because Hergé had not yet visited America in this time period, he depended on the photographs from *The Mortar* when he set the scene or drew real characters. This is true for his portrait of Al Capone, the armored car used by the gangsters (copied from a photo of such a vehicle belonging to gangster Spike O'Donnell), or even advertising labels. For example, a report from *The Mortar* provides the model for the "The Knight's Preserves" (p. 391) as well as the drawing of Tintin's attempted lynching (p. 366). Similarly, Hergé used a photo of a building in San Francisco and transposed it, almost exactly, to Chicago (p. 316).

The implicit conclusion Tintin draws from his stay in the United States echoes the pessimistic vision of Georges Duhamel and, especially, of Claude Blanchard. Disembarking from the Port of New York, the hero remarks: "Pity! I was almost beginning to get used to it!" (p. 417)—exactly the words of the reporter from *The Mortar*. Nevertheless, the reporters from *The Mortar* recognized how much their own values had been strongly affected by this new world, how much this frenetic life had seemed inhuman to them, a conclusion Tintin could equally subscribe to: "All the wonders the United States offered me seemed like a travesty of the Old World that gave human beings a life worth living."[12]

Between 1931 (*Tintin in America*) and 1935 (*The Broken Ear*), Hergé often used information gleaned from *The Mortar*. For *The Cigars of the Pharaoh*, he may have taken advantage of a 1932 article by Lucien Farnoux-Reynaud, "The Secret Societies," illustrated with a photo of a Masonic lodge. For *The Blue Lotus*, he probably used a February 1934 article by André Viollis, "L'impérialisme japonais est une menace pour le monde" (Japanese Imperialism Is a Threat to the World). Indeed, if the daily press presented the Sino-Japanese War from the point of view often favorable to the Japanese, the "defenders of civilization," Hergé favored the Chinese camp, as did the author of the 1934 article. In this adventure, Hergé introduced a new American businessman, W. R. Gibbons, director of a steel company and pompous defender of Western values: "Where are we going to end up if we can't even educate these dirty Yellows with some sense of etiquette? It's hopeless to try to instill the spirit of civilization into these barbarians!" (*AH*, III, p. 155).

For *The Broken Ear*, Hergé was inspired by several special issues of *The Mortar*. On the one hand, the March 1932 issue featured an article by Xavier de Hautecloque, "Sir Basil Zaharoff, the Magnate of Sudden Death." Although Hergé changed the name of the arms dealership from Vickers to the "Vicking Arms Company, Ltd." (*AH*, III, p. 339), he kept for Bazarov's character the same features and dress as in the original magazine photo. On the other hand, he undoubtedly used an article by the German economist Antoine Zischka, "One Drop of Oil Is Worth One Drop of Blood," when he alluded to the Gran Chaco war between Bolivia and Paraguay. The character of W. R. Trickler was styled after J. D. Rockefeller, the powerful director of Standard Oil, while his rival, the Jewish banker who pushes Nuevo Rico into the war, was a copy of Henri Deterding, the boss of the Royal Dutch–Shell Company. For all the episodes that revealed the tight connections between political interests and high finance and industry, Hergé found material in many special editions: "Maîtres du monde" (World Leaders) from March 1932; "Marchands de canons contre la nation" (Arms Dealers Against the Nation) from October 1933; and "Menaces sur le monde" (Threats to the World) from February 1934. It is also possible that Hergé's attacks on the press were partially lifted from two issues dedicated to "L'histoire de la presse" (The History of the Press) by Jean Galtier-Boissière and René Lefèbvre (June and November 1934).

Reading *The Mortar* noticeably altered Hergé's point of view, or at least allowed him to integrate into *The Adventures of Tintin* anticapitalist elements, even anti-Western ones, which later on provided him an excuse. After the war, the mood in Francophone intellectual circles was generally anti-American. On this point at least, Hergé's work had to undergo little revision.

## CHAPTER TWO

# DISCOVERING THE OTHER

## THE VOYAGE TO CHINA

In 1933 Hergé's vision of the world began to change. In that year he became acquainted with Chang Chong-jen, a young Chinese student at the
Academy of Fine Arts in Brussels. Before *The Blue Lotus*, there were two
instances of Chinese people in *The Adventures of Tintin*, one in Moscow and
the other in America (*AH*, I, pp. 108, 411). In both cases they were sadists
specializing in sophisticated methods of torture and putting their "talents"
to work for Evil, whether the GPU or the underworld. Although in these
early episodes the hero manages to escape their wiles, his opinion of the
Chinese remained particularly negative. Tintin envisions the Chinese eating
young dogs, and Snowy imagines himself served up on their plates.[1]

Hergé sent "Mr. Tintin" in 1933 to Chiang Kai-shek's China, threatened
at the time by Japanese imperialism. Through Hergé's reading of *The Mortar*
and his discussions with his Chinese friend, he came to discover a different
China, culturally mature, full of traditions, very different from the way he
had caricatured it thus far. From then on, he saw China through the eyes of
Chang, who had a hand in creating the new adventure. He agreed with the
point of view of the Chinese government and inscribed his faith in it on the
walls of Shanghai. Even today, in the new version, the political slogans have
not been deleted, allowing the reader to follow the adventure in its original context. Since the majority of readers do not understand the Chinese
writing, however, this historical aspect of the adventure is lost on them. The
Chinese script is merely part of the decoration with no political content.

**25**

Scrolled along the pages are both inducements to boycott Japanese goods (*BL*, 9, I, 3; 45, III; 55, IV, 1) and anti-imperialist slogans (7, I, 1; 26, I, 1), also recalling "the three principles of government" of Sun Yat-sen.[2]

What amazes us today in this album is not so much the allusions to particular historical facts, such as Japan's departure from the League of Nations or Tokyo's annexation of China, but all that is not even mentioned. In 1934 Chiang Kai-shek's power was already declining. He had to face the military factions of Fong Yu-siang and, especially, the Communists contesting his government. Mao Tse-tung organized the peasant resistance. Despite the slogan "unification first, then resistance" that marked the beginning of the grand campaign to wipe out the Reds, the official government did not prevail. The year Hergé drafted *The Blue Lotus* was also the year of the "Long March."

Despite this album's flaws, it marked a turning point in Hergé's career. It was the first time the author spent time on the details of the scenario and developed a general narrative. The preceding adventures had been drafted from day to day. In the first four episodes, the story was narrated in the form of a newspaper report, more like a series of successive impressions than an adventure with a distinctive story line. With *The Blue Lotus*, Tintin achieves the status of a hero in a novel. Rather than control all the action, he now takes part in a more encompassing plot. This is also the first adventure to be concerned with the realistic details of the setting, the uniforms, and the landscape—a concern that becomes markedly more and more essential in the following years. Equally important, this is the first time Tintin really opens up to a non-Western world, the first time he lets himself listen to the Others rather than simply impose his own values on them.

In fictional form Hergé tells the story of his meeting with Chang. Tintin meets a young Chinese boy, appropriately named Chang, who—unlike the little African Coco—does not let himself be dominated by his friend. On the contrary, Chang teaches the hero details of his native country and familiarizes him with its values. To be sure, their friendship grows because each of them is willing to get beyond his own ethnic shortsightedness. Tintin teaches Chang that not all foreigners are like the "wicked who massacred his grandfather and grandmother" during the Boxer Rebellion. In exchange Chang disabuses Tintin of the common prejudices he had circulated about China. When Tintin admits that "many Europeans think that all the Chinese are cunning and cruel, wear a braid, and spend their time inventing tortures" (*AH*, III, p. 227), he is on the way toward becoming self-critical.

The "discovery" of cultural relativity will have many consequences in Hergé's work. It marks the beginning of the author's personal evolution. Gradually he abandons the right-wing ideology to adopt a different world-view. Tintin's world will be transformed, but this evolution will not have any abrupt breaks. It will continue over a number of years, with each adventure revealing some marked differences from the preceding ones. Beginning with *The Blue Lotus*, Tintin is no longer the symbolic representative of the Christian West. Although his values still harbor an implicit Boy Scout fervor, he no longer constantly invokes God. The miracles disappear. The hero is a layman who has to get out of tough situations on his own. Instead of the story of a heaven-sent saint, Hergé relates the adventures of a kind of "superchild" who through sheer willpower manages to accomplish seemingly impossible tasks. Tintin's character also becomes less caricatured, his omnipotence more limited. When Tintin finds a way to get out of trouble, the author takes care to explain it logically. Tintin the journalist becomes Tintin the detective. He thinks he is Sherlock Holmes, Snowy tells us! While remaining an extraordinary individual, he is less the embodiment of an ideal than an actual person who represents only himself. Despite all that, of course, there is not a complete break with the character from the earlier adventures. Hergé retains the main qualities that make his hero exceptional but tones them down, even to the point of Tintin's occasionally doubting himself. Nevertheless, Tintin remains a model of strength, loyalty, and purity.

As Tintin becomes more human, Snowy becomes more animal. Granted, he does not lose the gift of speech provided by his creator, but he uses it less frequently. Snowy stops commenting on each of his master's exploits as he had done in the first four adventures. He loses his sarcasm; his sense of humor becomes more discriminating. He sees the human world differently. Far from sharing human values, he feels they are strange, barbaric, even incomprehensible. Little by little, he comes to reclaim his animal consciousness, not only different from but often even opposed to human consciousness. Most important, the role Snowy had formerly played beside his hero will henceforth be occupied by humans. Chang is the first of these privileged interlocutors, awaiting the arrival of Captain Haddock. The transformation of the two main characters in the adventures leads to a decentering of the story. The interest is now focused less on Tintin himself and more on the world in which he operates. Beginning in 1934 Hergé concentrates much more on the actual external circumstances. Without completely rejecting his former values, he reintroduces his character into a world of ambiguity and relativity.

## ATTEMPTS AT ACCOMMODATION

The discovery of the Other makes Tintin more vulnerable. In 1935, in *The Broken Ear*, he no longer controls the events but is determined by them. He manages to secure only one positive result: explaining the mystery of the Arumbayan fetish. To distance this episode from the real world, Hergé situates it in a fictitious universe. The propelling idea is to report the atrocities in the Gran Chaco war, but rather than set the stage in Bolivia or Paraguay, Hergé invents two imaginary countries, San Theodoros and Nuevo Rico, to give himself more scope for creativity. Before this album, Tintin plunged into an imaginary world by not facing reality. In *The Blue Lotus*, Hergé partially documents the world he claims to be describing, but the correspondence between his fictional character and the real world is rather tenuous, and he subsequently abandons this way of working. *The Broken Ear* marks a greater distance from the influence of ideology. At the same time, Hergé more thoroughly explores the creative potential of his character. He wants to see how far he can push Tintin's personality without totally losing the coherence that gave him his initial appeal.

In 1937 Tintin takes up the role of detective. *The Black Island* unfolds on the northern coast of Scotland, a real country, where Hergé had visited before beginning work on this adventure. A band of counterfeiters takes Tintin prisoner. After the First World War, counterfeiters were using such sophisticated techniques that a special international convention was held in Geneva in 1929 to try to put a stop to their practices.[3] Tintin himself also takes advantage of contemporary technology to stop the gangsters. He takes an airplane, talks on the radio, and watches a television show at a time when these technologies were not available to the general public. He becomes a hero along the lines of Charles Lindbergh, Wiley Post, or Francesco Agello, whose feats appeared in the newspapers the preceding years.[4] What is more striking, this album presents an extraordinarily powerful gorilla that terrorizes the population of Kiltoch. The original film version of *King Kong* dates from 1933, and the Loch Ness monster made headlines in the newspapers several times in 1936. Hergé takes advantage of these two sources to create his own suspense thriller.

In 1938 he drafts *King Ottokar's Scepter*, combining detective-style intrigue with contemporary political elements but, as in earlier adventures, taking place in two imaginary countries, Borduria and Syldavia. Hergé begins the story immediately after the *Anschluss*, Germany's annexation of Austria, just at the time when Hitler's troops were marching into Czechoslovakia. While in Belgium Léon Degrelle was calling for appeasement with Germany, Hergé was illustrating here in fictional form what separated him from National Socialism.

Borduria represents Nazi Germany. The Bordurian military uniforms are exact replicas of Nazi uniforms, and their squadrons are equipped with German Heinkel aircraft. The Bordurians dream of annexing their neighbor Syldavia. They even have a plan of invasion resembling Hitler's. In Syldavia, a fifth column, the Iron Guard, stirs up constant unrest. (If their name recalls the German steel helmets worn by the SS in 1933, their actions evoke Colonel Robert de La Roque's "Cross of Fire.") The head of their party is named Müsstler, a name combining the first letters from *Mussolini* and the last from *Hitler*. Tintin defends the traditional monarchy and manages to prevent the annexation of Syldavia. In this album, the description of social phenomena as significant as mass revolution remains schematic. Nothing in *King Ottokar's Scepter* allows us to understand Müsstler's power. Internal conflicts in the country, even economic problems, seem nonexistent. Syldavia is presented as an ideal little kingdom ruled by a good king, beloved by his people. One cannot understand why, in such circumstances, Müsstler finds so much support and collaboration among the people. He is apparently endowed with magical powers, and his actions lack real historical causes. (Hergé never depicts him explicitly; he is the Evil One without a face.)

Following this episode, Hergé begins working on *Land of Black Gold*, which also takes place in an imaginary country, Khemed, on the eve of World War II. In this album he alludes to the struggle of Jewish organizations (the Stern, Irgoun, and Haganah groups) against British occupation before the independence of Israel. This adventure appears in 1939 in *The Little Twentieth* and in *Coeurs Vaillants*, but in May 1940 it is interrupted on page 25, following Hergé's military induction.[5] It reappears in a different format in 1948, after the *Prisoners of the Sun*, and is revised again in 1971. In the latter version the episodes recounting the struggle between the British and the Jewish organizations are deleted. One might be surprised to see that here Hergé presents the Jews in a different guise, given that he generally takes up again his anti-Semitic caricatures. Tintin is mistaken for an Israeli leader, Goldstein, and finds himself freed by a Zionist organization. One explanation is that in 1939 Hergé shared the right-wing opinion that Jews are fine, provided they stay where they belong! Whatever the explanation, the album was never finished according to its original plan. When the author was liberated, he launched his hero into adventures where politics plays no apparent role.

*The Crab with the Golden Claws*, which unfolds in Bagghar, an imaginary city in Morocco, begins in 1940. Before coming out as an album, this story was published weekly in *Le Soir-Jeunesse* from October 17, 1940, to September 3, 1941, then daily as a comic strip in *Le Soir* from September 23 to October 17, 1941. *The Adventures of Tintin* now targeted the general public, not simply young people. After the defeat of Belgium, *Le Soir* became a collaborationist newspaper. During the years Hergé was publishing his work there, he was torn between two positions: the first, to distance himself from everything political; the second, to give his opinion of contemporary events but only in a disguised fashion. *The Crab with the Golden Claws*, as well as *The Secret of the Unicorn* and *The Seven Crystal Balls*, represents the first position. The first of these albums is a banal detective story, where Tintin is taken prisoner by a gang of international drug traffickers. The double album dealing with *The Unicorn* affair runs in *Le Soir* from June 11, 1942, until September 23, 1943. Here Hergé involves his characters in a treasure hunt that turns out to be at the same time a search for their roots. Does the reunion of Tintin's cohort in the course of this adventure signify that in 1942 one has to turn toward tradition to remain united? Apart from this implicit appeal to national unity in a country deeply divided by the occupation, it is difficult to see any direct allusion to the contemporary drama. Tintin distances himself from everything political, even when the next album, *The Seven Crystal Balls*, published in *Le Soir*, is interrupted by the Liberation. In contrast, in *The Shooting Star*, preceding the *Unicorn* episode, Hergé offers his opinions on the war, if only obliquely. Appearing in *Le Soir* from January to May 1942, this story is an allegory of contemporary events. The character Philippulus, a mad scientist who predicts the end of the world, can be read as a critic of some political "prophets" who were heralding the imminent destruction of the West and appealing to the people to repent. At this time in France, the Vichy government under the leadership of Marshal Pétain exploited the French sense of guilt. The war was said to be punishment from on high for the errors of the nation, namely, its lack of foresight before the war and the Popular Front movement itself. This album especially is characterized by an anti-Americanism that the journalists of *Le Soir* were promoting in the regular columns of their paper. The villain in this adventure is the Jew Blumenstein, a New York banker. He embodies the brand of capitalism that tries to procure the scientific discoveries made in Europe to promote nefarious ends. In 1942, for a collaborationist newspaper like *Le Soir*, the real enemies are the British and Americans. At the same time that Hergé was publishing his adventures, the cartoonist Jam was constantly caricaturing Franklin D. Roosevelt and Winston Churchill. In the January 31/February 1 issue, for example, one sees the American president addressing Congress. Among the many businessmen in attendance, several have the same stereotypical Jewish facial features Hergé gives to his Blumenstein. Moreover, on several occasions *Le Soir* published extracts from a recent book by the economist Anton Zischka, whose articles Hergé had read in *The Mortar*. Zischka's book was titled *La Science brise les monopoles* (*Science Breaks Monopolies*). It appeared in Germany in 1937 and was published in French as an edition of the *Toison d'or*. The book analyzes in detail the crimes of American capitalism, its role in the colonial wars, and its belligerent imperialism. Hergé tacitly endorses this point of view, even if the crew of the *Peary*, the ship chartered by Blumenstein to compete with the *Aurora* for the "Funds for European Scientific Research," are less unscrupulous than their backer. Thus, when Tintin is about to land for the first time on the meteorite island, one of the crew from the *Peary* prevents a fellow crew member from shooting the hero.

During the war Hergé seems torn between two paths: either to continue to make Tintin a reporter and have him take part in the big questions of the time; or to transform him into a purely fictional hero involved in a totally imaginary world. In the first four adventures, he opted for the first solution, openly speaking to the political conflicts of his day. *The Blue Lotus* marks the turning point in the sense that the author steps back from the right-wing ideology that he had until then espoused. He looks for a way to adapt to the situation by putting his hero's actions into perspective and especially by involving him in adventures where politics does not play a major role. When Tintin does act politically, it is in imaginary countries, thus at least partially disengaging the author's responsibility. During the German occupation Hergé distances himself from the collaborationist propaganda of *Le Soir*, except in *The Shooting Star* episode, where he registers his hostility toward the Allies.

## THE CONVERSION

The liberation of Brussels on September 1, 1944, put a temporary stop to *The Adventures of Tintin. Le Soir* completely overhauled its staff. The journalists who had worked on the paper during the war were arrested and tried as collaborationists. Although Hergé was spared,[6] he was called as a witness during the trial and was more or less blacklisted for two years. His cartoon character would not reappear until September 1946 in a new weekly magazine, *Le Journal de Tintin*, dedicated exclusively to children. There Hergé published the double album of the adventure *Prisoners of the Sun*, slightly modifying the graphics as they had appeared earlier in *Le Soir*. Although Tintin had been the shining model of the Good, with the Liberation he finds himself if not exactly in the camp of the wicked, at least suspected of having consorted with Evil. Tintin had shown his other side.

To clear his hero's name, Hergé does two things: the new adventures consistently take place in imaginary places, and he cleans up the albums published before the war. This new approach is so successful that by 1949, the author feels free to go back to his earlier stories. Hergé recognizes that the adventures have a kind of unity or wholeness that allows Tintin the possibility of becoming a mythical figure, but only on the condition that he distance himself from actual historical contexts. The journalist who once investigated stories for a Catholic publication is now transformed into a new kind of hero: he no longer investigates; he acts. He turns away from politics to participate in scientific explorations. For example, he is the first voyager to the moon. Thus, Hergé takes up a path he had already explored during the war.

The adventures, which had unfolded until then according to the rhythm of contemporary history, shift to another temporality. Earlier, each episode was separate from the others; from now on, they would be connected. Before the war, Tintin was presented as a "true Belgian." Now he becomes an international figure. It is not clear where he lives—it could be Brussels or any other European capital, at least until he takes up residence in Marlinspike Hall, "somewhere in Western Europe" (*TP*, 6, I, 3). On his adventure in the Congo, where he had formerly taught the African children the wonders of "their country, Belgium," he now teaches them calculus. Although Hergé continues to use an imaginary dialect based on one found in an area of the city of Brussels, he eliminates from the albums any obvious "Belgianisms." From now on his characters speak standard French. Thus, in *The Secret of the Unicorn*, the dealer at the flea market who sells the scale model to Tintin says in the original version, "That might have worked, Sir! But I just sold it to this young man." In the later version he says more simply, "I'm sorry, Sir. I just sold that to this young man" (*SU*, 3, III, 3).

When Brussels becomes the capital of the European Union, Tintin acquires an international reputation. He adapts to the postwar ideology and represents the technologically advanced West in contrast to the Eastern bloc. When he comes into contact with any government officials, either he does so as a private individual or the governments in question are purely imaginary. If he visits the East or even South America, he travels there only to get his friends out of a tight spot. If in *Tintin and the Picaros* he works to hand over power to General Alcazar, he does so rather unwillingly, and he harbors no illusions about the consequences of this coup d'état. The choices are Alcazar or Tapioca, two variations on the theme of tyranny. Between the two, the only difference is the color of their uniforms!

The same situation occurs with the Communist bloc country, although the country is never named. Hergé merely alludes to "a great foreign power" without further details. Of all the adventures after the war, *The Calculus Affair* is the most political. Professor Calculus is kidnapped by spies who try to steal his scientific discoveries. Tintin and Haddock meet up in Borduria to rescue him. The party in power is the "Moustache Party," and its leader, Marshal Kûrvi-Tasch, is reminiscent of Stalin more than any other totalitarian leader.[7] Although in the first adventures, especially *Tintin in the Land of the Soviets*, Tintin handles a gun with ease, he later embraces a more holistic pacifism. In *The Picaros* he wears on his motorcycle helmet the acronym of the International Peace Movement. Having moved away from the extreme Right, Hergé's hero fifty years later finds himself on the side of the Liberal Left. But there is still room for many ambiguities. For example, in putting together his final album, the author admits to having been influenced by the Régis Debray affair.[8] Yet Tintin displays such political skepticism that it is impossible to situate him comfortably with the Left. He is politically engaged only when his personal interests are directly threatened—for example, when his own clan risks dissolution.

The evolution of Hergé's work is striking only if one examines the early versions published in the newspapers before the war or in Hergé's *Archives* (*Archives Hergé*). If one is limited only to the albums accessible commercially, this evolution is less noticeable because each adventure has been touched up so many times to adapt to contemporary liberal ideology. The first album,

*Tintin in the Land of the Soviets,* for example, would be considered irredeemable from the postwar standpoint. This adventure was simply eliminated from the "complete works" and for a long time was out of print.[9] However, as pirated editions began to multiply, Casterman Press republished it in 1973 as an archival document. Despite the poor quality of the graphics, this volume is very interesting because one can see clearly Tintin's initial ideological stance, one that some claim Hergé never completely renounced. All of Hergé's ideas are "recycled"—reappropriated, refined, and reappearing in different episodes where they take on different meanings. For example, the episode of the train in *Tintin in the Land of the Soviets* (*AH*, I, pp. 51–52) reappears in *Tintin in America* (*TA*, pp. 30–32). When Tintin disguises himself as a ghost to frighten the Bolsheviks (pp. 81–84), this skit reappears in *Destination Moon* when Haddock tries to cure Professor Calculus of his amnesia (*DM*, p. 49). The boat race (p. 93) reappears in the episode of the capture of Allan (*CGC*, pp. 59–60). The gag with the snowball (p. 127) shows up in the Incan episode (*PS*, p. 33). This "recycling" even includes Tintin's use of the Thom(p)sons' famous "to be precise." Another anomalous expression (*plaît-il?*) that he uses to address the member of the GPU also shows up much later in the mouth of Professor Calculus (*F714*, 7, III, 2).

In light of the problems with the adventure among the Soviets, *Tintin in the Congo* is considered the first album of the adventures. Since it is heavily laden with the colonialist ideology of the 1930s, it was difficult for Hergé to republish it without making a number of changes. First, the relationship between Tintin and Snowy is revised. In the initial version, they were two brothers—one in human form, the other dog—but in the new version they are simply man and dog. Snowy speaks much less and acts more like an animal. Moreover, between the two friends there is less self-congratulation. Snowy is less arrogant and stops continually flattering his master. With regard to the Africans, who are no longer "Negroes" and become "blacks," Hergé changes the adventure in two ways. First, without really changing the story, he expunges from the text and from the pictures anything that bears a directly negative appraisal of the natives. Thus, on the boat *Thysville*, Tintin avoids reprimanding the black sailor who does not jump in to save Snowy and merely says, "We must save him at all costs" (*TC*, 7, I, 2). When he meets Coco for the first time, Snowy doesn't find him "very resourceful." In the later version, Snowy dispenses with all commentary, and even Tintin no longer emphasizes how "nice" the blacks are to carry them triumphantly to their hotel. The natives' locomotive, initially described as a "dirty little machine," is now merely an "old choo choo." Tintin becomes more tolerant regarding disputes. He no longer considers the African villages "his" and even refuses the crown offered him. From now on Africa is for the Africans. The M'Hatuvu tribe, who were called "Huns," are now the "famous warriors." The Pygmies are no longer "gullible," and the pejorative term "little Moors" (moricauds) previously applied to them simply disappears. The Pygmies are now simply referred to as "those folk." Toning down the vocabulary and displaying greater tolerance also apply to the animal kingdom: the crocodile ceases to be "a frightful beast"; giraffes, the "satanic animals"; the rhinoceros, "a monster"; and the buffalo, "ferocious." In the new version, the white fathers continue their missionary activities, but Tintin no longer shares their beliefs. If he remains a religious hero, it is in quite a different sense of the word. To the extent that he no longer represents Belgium, he stops speaking of it in the third person, acquires a sense of humor, and no longer claims to teach anything to the Africans.

In the new version the superiority of the whites is deemphasized. To lessen it even further and thus extract this album from its historical context, Hergé resorts to a second technique. Instead of erasing certain paternalistic characteristics, he accentuates them to give them a different meaning. For example, where the blacks had previously appeared in full dress, he redraws them totally naked except for loincloths. Now the blacks are no longer realistic characters but conventional figures drawn from folklore. They come to represent the "good savage" invented by Western culture, a notion we would only smirk at today. But with a blink of an eye, Hergé claims to distance himself from his previous point of view. In the early version, the natives do not all speak at the same level of proficiency. The "common folk" speak "pidgin"; the local chiefs and witch doctor speak more like the whites with whom they fight. In the new version, they all follow the same linguistic stereotype so that the historical context of their struggle disappears.

As in the previous example, this technique creates a kind of complicity between the author and the reader. Rather than being presented with a story of colonization, the reader sees the newer version of *Tintin in the Congo* as an imaginary adventure to a land of good savages. No doubt, that is how one is supposed to have read the first version of *The Red Sea Sharks* in 1958, in which the Africans all speak "pidgin." But at the time of decolonization, Hergé chooses to give them a language closer to standard French.

In the following albums, all references to the blacks susceptible to any kind of racist interpretation are eliminated. In *Tintin in America*, the little black child whose cries moved Tintin to action is now white (*TA*, 47, IV, 4). In *The Crab*, Haddock is taken prisoner by some bandits and was originally beaten up by an enormous black man (*AH*, IV, p. 336), who is later replaced by a white giant. In the early version, Haddock later on chases his tormenter and yells out various insults at him: "Little Moor! Piece of coal! Coconut! Fuzzy-wuzzy! Cannibal! Anthropithecus! Blackbird!" (*AH*, IV, p. 341). In the new version, the first two insults are replaced by "Piece of plaster" and "Black beetle," and the last one by "Iconoclast" (*CGC*, 56, II, pp. 2–3). The insults the author retains are now addressed to a white man, so they lose their former racist overtones. Hergé can therefore assert in his interview with Numa Sadoul that just tone of voice determines Haddock's vocabulary.[10] In the same album the black sailor whom Allan beats after the sailor had been tricked by Tintin is now white (18, II, 3).

In regard to Jews, one sees that after the war Blumenstein from *The Shooting Star* becomes Bohlwinkel, a name that in Brussels means "candy shop."[11] This unscrupulous banker no longer runs his business in New York but now in the imaginary Sao Rico. As in the preceding example, Hergé no longer associates violence and evil with a distinctive Other, such as blacks or Jews, but with his own ethnic group, whites and Belgians. Although sparing Tintin by having him lose his Belgian identity and become a person without roots, in the new versions the author implicitly engages in self-incrimination. Only the Western male has the innate capacity for evil; other people are simply the victims of the white man.[12] Since the stereotypical Jewish villains rarely appeared in the prewar volumes, Hergé does not have to redraw them. Rastapopoulos, who originally was a Jew and a Freemason, is modified in a different way. *The Cigars of the Pharaoh* is reworked after the war. The two policemen known as X33 and X33A when Tintin meets them for the first time are later renamed Thomson and Thom(p)son. Señor Oliveira da Figueira is no longer presented as an arms dealer and is not murdered by the Masonic sect, as he was formerly. Now he moves into the "good" camp and remains a loyal friend of Tintin. The misadventures of the hero no longer take place in Mecca but in a city without a name. His exploits are both simplified and less implicated in the context of the founding of Saudi Arabia in 1932. If in the new version Rastapopoulos is still always called "Grand Master" by his followers, his group is no longer seen as a Masonic gathering of the rich and powerful. Mr. Snowball is no longer a banker. In the albums where Rastapopoulos shows up, he loses his former "religious" traits. Now he is simply an international crook, half worldly, half gangster.

To clear himself of all accusations of anti-Semitism, Hergé represents all the "bad guys" after the war as having a Nazi past. This is already the case with the Bordurian military. In *King Ottokar's Scepter*, the Bordurians try annexing Syldavia with the aid of Müsstler. They subsequently go from being Nazis to being Communists without changing their methods or mentality. Hergé combines them into one to show us two sides of totalitarianism. In *The Red Sea Sharks*, we meet Kurt, who is specifically designated as a former officer in the German army (*RSS*, p. 60). In *Flight 714* we find the shady Dr. Krollspell, whom the author openly accuses of working in the concentration camps, and the sinister Officer Hans Boehm, whose face is covered with scars. By associating these two former German officers with Rastapopoulos, Hergé manages to put into question Rastapopoulos's Jewish image. The proof that he cannot be taken for a Jew is that he surrounds himself with Nazi thugs to perpetrate his crimes.

By eliminating the traces of an ideology he ostensibly renounces, Hergé unwittingly reproduces it in the newer works he drafts after the war. The lunar adventure, *The Calculus Affair*, or *The Red Sea Sharks* can be read as a "plea to the house." Although he never officially was brought to trial for collaboration and anti-Semitism (charges against him were dropped), he continues in effect to prosecute his case in order to establish his innocence.

Professor Cuthbert Calculus is the main character of the two lunar adventures. Cuthbert is inventor, scientist, and artist. In *Destination Moon*, Tintin returns to Syldavia, the land of the Good, summoned by Calculus to participate in an important scientific experiment. This adventure is allegedly exempt from overtly political or military objectives. As the professor claims: "It goes without saying that all the research is for humanitarian purposes. No question here of making atomic bombs. In fact, we are seeking a way to protect humankind from the dangers of these weapons" (*DM*, 9, II, 3). Contrary to the professor's intentions, politics is inevitably implicated. Some spies try to steal the scientist's discoveries to use them for evil ends. Calculus himself may be unaware of the political implications of his research—he thinks he is doing something for the good of humanity—but Tintin sees right away that this kind of project, in itself neutral or even positive, can be diverted from its initial objective. He helps Calculus stay with the forces of Good,

but he cannot prevent the forces of Evil from participating in the conquest
of the moon. In their spaceship, Tintin discovers Boris Jorgen, former military adviser to Muskar XII, the traitor from *King Ottokar's Scepter*, who now
works for a totalitarian superpower. *The Calculus Affair* develops the same
theme and treats the potential culpability of the inventor in the same way.
Professor Calculus is again presented as the solitary genius who does not pay
attention to the consequences of his actions. Like Hergé himself during the
war, Calculus carries out his project without looking beyond it.[13] His final
invention—a device generating sound waves capable of destroying windows
at a distance—radically disturbs daily life at Marlinspike Hall, but its creator
doesn't even notice. What Calculus considers merely a "modest" discovery
could become a formidable weapon in the hands of politicians or the military. Meanwhile, poor Calculus's own invention turns against him. With its
help, he is traced, kidnapped, and led to Borduria, where he is imprisoned
in a fortress. While he continues to believe in his own innocence, the public
comes to see him as a traitor, a collaborator with the totalitarian regime.
Colonel Sponsz arranges that he will be released only on the condition that
he hand over his blueprints, allowing the Bordurian engineers to put them
to use in creating a terrible weapon. But Colonel Sponsz also arranges that
no one will believe in the scientist's innocence when he is released: "If we
set the professor free, it will be in the presence of two representatives of the
International Red Cross. He'll have to declare in front of them that he came
to Borduria of his own free will, to offer us his plans" (*CA*, 55, III, 1).

Thus, the inventor, the scientist, and the artist inevitably collaborate with
Evil, because they are surrounded by people who can distort the meaning
and hijack the purpose of their work. Tintin and the captain manage to free
the professor and save his reputation. In the course of this adventure, Calculus
learns that inventing is never innocent. Between the forces of Good and Evil,
between Syldavia and Borduria, the border is "open," allowing the opposing
sides to come to resemble each other. To avoid causing misery in the future,
Calculus burns the blueprints to his invention. Like Hergé himself, the professor eliminates what he had created so that it will not be put to wicked ends.
From then on, he spends his time cultivating roses and inventing household
appliances. *The Calculus Affair* is the last time Calculus appears in public, the
last time he concocts an invention that could be used politically or militarily.

*The Red Sea Sharks* is a kind of retrospective of Hergé's work. A number of characters reappear—Castafiore, Alcazar, Allan Thompson, Dawson,

Dr. Müller, Sheik Ben Kalish Ezab—either as defendants or witnesses in a trial Hergé does not acknowledge. The author brings them together in a story where the wicked share the same cynicism and thirst for power. Rastapopoulos collaborates with Dr. Müller and the former Nazi Kurt. Even Castafiore, the symbolic embodiment of art, compromises herself in accepting the invitation of the dubious Marquis di Gorgonzola, alias Rastapopoulos. Tintin has the whole world against him. Along with Haddock he finds himself lost at sea on a life raft, at the mercy of the sharks that appear less dangerous than the humans. Despite his limitations, Tintin manages to reinstall the forces of Good, or at least temporarily to limit the powers of Evil. This adventure is presented not only as a review of the usual characters but especially as a kind of reclamation of the hero's own past. He meets his former acquaintances to change his standing in their eyes—in effect, to delete the past.

In this story Tintin is not the one fascinated by the luxuries and manners of Rastapopoulos, as he was in *The Cigars of the Pharaoh*. Now it is Bianca Castafiore's turn. Tintin is wiser and more ordinary at the same time. In the first frame, we see him, just like ordinary folks, anonymously enjoying a film. If this adventure does not really extract him from the cozy comforts of Marlinspike Hall, no doubt he will remain like the ordinary viewer, an individual without a history who has no memories other than those of the films he enjoys on Saturday nights with Haddock. Here the drama extracts the character from his past, as Hergé had done in previous adventures. Rastapopoulos is now closer to the Nazis than the Jews; the blacks are now industrious rather than lazy, as they were in *The Congo*. Not only does Haddock no longer appear racist but he also participates in liberating the blacks from slavery. Relying on unconscious projection, he accuses the blacks of unjustified violence: "I let you out of that dungeon, and what thanks do I get? You knock me flat!" (*RSS*, 47, II, 1). Suddenly the blacks understand the captain is innocent. Haddock is on the side of their liberators, so he cannot be confused with the "wicked white" slave traders.

Hergé also takes advantage of this story to revisit his anti–Americanism. At the end of the adventure, as at the end of the Second World War, it is the American army that saves the hero's life. In a sense Tintin and Haddock embody the Resistance that could not have triumphed without the help of the Allies. Meanwhile, to avoid the pitfalls of a predetermined Manicheanism, the author saves one of his characters from taking a wrong turn toward the forces of Evil: Piotr Skut, an airplane pilot who takes orders from Müller.

Having shot down his plane, Tintin saves Skut's life. Tintin refuses to judge him, and his withholding of judgment allows Skut, the once "trigger-happy thug," to join the forces of Good.

Finally, in the last album one still recognizes the same persistent themes. *Tintin and the Picaros* is also a "retrospective album" in which many of the usual characters reappear. Tintin's past pursues him. Recall that he was a partisan of General Alcazar. Even if the hero refuses to compromise himself with Tapioca, knowing that Tapioca is "a real tyrant, vain and cruel," Tintin finds himself the victim of numerous lies that frame him among the accused, like the others. Coerced to show up in San Theodoros, he is taken prisoner, although only in an unofficial capacity, and escapes the police dragnet thanks to the intervention of a monkey. Having reluctantly become a member of the Resistance, on television he watches the trial of his friends—in effect, his own trial. In addition to Castafiore—the artist compromised by her attraction to fascist power—the two Thom(p)sons are also condemned. In a sense, the detectives represent the hero's superego, the superego that the author seems to hold responsible for his own political errors. Of course, the detectives too will have to be found innocent, since they belong to Tintin's close-knit "family." Even if the trial is a mockery, it risks ending tragically. With the help of Haddock, who in this instance is more idealistic than Tintin, Tintin manages to save the world. Nevertheless, despite his own misgivings, he re-installs Alcazar as the country's leader. The moral of the story is that neither Tintin nor anyone else in his clan is a collaborator. The only person from the group who could be accused of supporting whatever political regime surfaces is Jolyon Wagg, who, on the very last page, echoes Tintin's former salute: "Good old Alcazar! Give him a big hurrah!" (*TP*, 62, III, 1).

The transformations of the first albums aim at extricating *The Adventures of Tintin* from their historical context. Hergé reworks them in connection with the adventures drafted after the war. He not only changes the characters, the sets, and the intrigue but also reintroduces into the first adventures characters invented much later. For example, the Thom(p)sons now appear in the first frame of the first album, *Tintin in the Congo*. Their appearance there is fraught with significance. From *The Cigars of the Pharaoh* on, Allan Thompson (not to be confused with one of the twin detectives) becomes the accomplice of Rastapopoulos. This changes not only the meaning of this adventure but also many others, such as *The Crab*, where he works for Omar Ben Salaad, *The Red Sea Sharks*, and *Flight 714*. When Allan Thompson is not working for his usual boss, one suspects the latter to be in prison. Hergé gets his readers to imagine the existence of his characters outside their actual appearances in the albums.[14] Moreover, to make each adventure self-contained, the author introduces at the opening the silhouettes of those who will show up later in the episode. For example, in the new version of *The Secret of the Unicorn*, one catches a glimpse of Aristides Silk on the first page (*SU*, I, II, 2).

Instead of having Tintin embroiled in history, from now on we have the history of Tintin, where each album recounts a different exploit. The overall story is not strictly linear or static, where the reader would have to follow the order set out by the author. The main character and his friends do change from time to time, but their evolution seems less a matter of historical circumstances than of the "laws" of Hergé's own universe. The author does not want his readers to find in *Tintin* the story of the development of the extreme Right into an acceptable liberalism. Rather, he presents the adventures of a hero who starts out alone in the world and ends up building an entire "family on paper," as Numa Sadoul puts it. The world in which Tintin develops from now on is a world without a history, or at least a world whose history is cut off from concrete reality. Hergé does not talk about this change. He simply represents it, and this re-presentation is itself the sign of this historical distancing. From the first to the last adventure, the hero apparently lives by his own devices. He does not deny himself anything, but he simply matures. Hergé's reworking of his material consists in extracting Tintin from history to change him into a myth. Nevertheless, this myth, although it appears unified, tells another story, as telling for the understanding of Tintin as the archaeological, historical reconstitution through which we have just worked.

# BOOK TWO
# THE HISTORY OF TINTIN

# PART ONE
# TINTIN

He came into the world with a tuft of hair on his head.
That's why we named him "Tufty Ricky."

—Charles Perrault


And here's his pal "Tufty-Ricky!"

—*Flight 714*

# CHAPTER THREE

# THE PRIMORDIAL UNIVERSE

## TINTIN AND SNOWY

The first two frames of the new adventure series capture the relationship be-tween Tintin and Snowy. In the first frame, on the platform of some unnamed train station, the hero is surrounded by friends who have come to say good-bye: some scouts in uniform, some journalists, and Quick and Flupke, two young men from the Marollian district of Brussels, heroes from Hergé's former series. Although he is leaving, Tintin takes with him their knowledge and values. In spite of his new international reputation, he remains Belgian. He retains his Boy Scout fervor, even when he becomes a so-called reporter. In the back-ground, the Thom(p)sons remark: "It seems that a young reporter is leaving for Africa." In reintroducing the Thom(p)sons at the beginning, Hergé em-phasizes their dual role of surveillance and protection. The two detectives do not seem to recognize Tintin, but they still keep on eye on him. Less involved than actual parents, they are more like uncles watching their nephew set off on a long trip. In the next frame, Snowy mingles with his fellow creatures—dogs. He tells them about his future adventures in the manner of Tartarin of Tarascon: "Yes, I've had enough of this boring life, so I decided to go on a lion hunt."[1] One never knows to what life Snowy is alluding. Tintin's life begins here, with the adventure. What one gleans about his former life is merely a hypothetical construction. In reintroducing his inseparable pair, Hergé situates them within a long tradition of famous masters and servants. As they travel the world, one thinks of Don Juan and Sganarelle in Sicily, and especially of Don Quixote and Sancho Panza, whom they resemble even more.

Tintin and Snowy are opposite and complementary at the same time. Within the narrative structure, Tintin represents the male and Snowy the female. The boy wears his hair in a tuft, or quiff, on top of his head, and the dog always has his tail pricked up in the air. Snowy is very proud of his tail, but it is constantly threatened. In the first adventure it is operated on, and in America, pierced by a sword. Snowy gets his tail stuck in doors; Haddock steps on it, crushing it with his heel; a parrot pecks at it, and so on. Tintin plays with the most secret anxieties of his friend, as if he unconsciously wanted to be the sole possessor of the virile attribute:

> "So, if you had to have your tail cut off, that wouldn't really be so terrible, would it?"
> "Uh! you think so? That would be unbearable. I would lose all my beauty!" (TA, 56, IV, 1)

Throughout his long career, Tintin always defends the values of Boy Scout leadership, sincerity, loyalty, and purity. He is literally obsessed with doing Good, to the point of identifying himself with it in the first episodes. For the master, goodness is a moral concern, whereas the dog tries hard to attain it physically. Although Snowy may occasionally rummage through garbage cans, he is really horrified by dirtiness. After all, he is an elegant dog, narcissistic and vain. Decked out in his fur coat, he is very aware of the impression he makes on others: "I believe I'm going to be a sensation" (*EM*, 27, III, 1). What makes him really unhappy during a visit to an atomic factory in Sprodj is not so much that he has to put on a protective spacesuit but that it does not fit him well (*DM*, 12, IV, 2). Snowy is afraid of all kinds of "creepy-crawlies" associated with dirt, especially spiders. To keep his coat as white as a baptismal dress, he is on the constant lookout for water. From the very first album, we see him taking a bath: "Ah! It's lovely in the water! It's marvelous!" (*TC*, 12, II, 1). During another adventure he waxes eloquent on the purifying virtues of water: "A quick bath and I'll soon be rid of all this mud!" (*SU*, 39, IV, 2). As a Christian is purified by baptism, Snowy is rejuvenated by the bath: "Ah! It's good to be nice and clean again!" (*SU*, 39, IV, 4). The Tibetan monks come to appreciate the metaphorical equivalence of his white coat and pure soul in baptizing him "Snowy" and his master "Pure of Heart" (*TT*, 44, III, 1).[2]

The strong relationship between these two depends as much on their complementarity as on their shared values. The master remains a model for the dog without ceasing to be his opposite. Tintin is brave, while Snowy is fearful; the former is a pacifist, but the latter is always looking to pick a fight with the animals he doesn't like, such as cats and parrots. Tintin is prudence itself, while Snowy acts without thinking about the consequences. Tintin is sober and moderate; Snowy is a gourmand and shows an excessive love for alcoholic beverages. In the new version, the master, who is fairly reticent in any case, can never be heard bragging about his exploits. The dog, meanwhile, remains an incurable braggart and boasts about imaginary feats: "Let me tell you about the time I killed an elephant!" (TC, 42, I, 2). He is affected and self-indulgent, a real show-off. Tintin gets annoyed by his faults and never ceases to scold him, especially in the first episode. He tries teaching him about the human world, as if he wanted to humanize him. But mocking the hero's self-righteous attitude, Snowy resists his training and even turns against him. He doesn't miss an opportunity to turn the tables and patronize the master: "My poor Tintin, you are just not up to speed," he says, after the young man misses his shot. "Take care; you'll do better next time." On several occasions, he cautions Tintin to be more careful, and, as things turn out, Snowy is right (TC, 42, III, 2). Snowy sometimes even imitates his master's humility. After a particularly courageous feat, he says with false modesty: "Oh, you know, it's just a lion. That isn't nearly as bad as it seems" (TC, 23, II, 2). Snowy's parodies inject into his master's situations a dry wit resembling Mark Twain's or Jerome K. Jerome's. With his humorous refrains, he thus introduces a certain levity into Tintin's adventures that might otherwise proceed too ponderously and predictably. When they are going to have a fight, Snowy announces: "Attention: there's going to be a row!" (TC, 18, II, 1). In the face of the witch doctor Muganga's powerless rage, he comments: "Wow! He's really angry!" When Tintin hits one of his enemies, Snowy exclaims: "Bull's eye!" When Tintin is meting out justice, Snowy pipes up: "Look at Tintin playing little Solomon." Snowy's commentary on each episode prevents the reader from too easily identifying with the hero. Thus, while the hero stands apart in the circle of great men, ordinary folks can share the point of view of his dog. From the outset, then, Tintin and Snowy represent an opposition between the world as it ought to be and the world as it really is—the opposition between the ideal and the real. For Hergé, the ideal is more important: essence precedes existence. The ideal can be manifested, however, only in a degraded, "fallen" form. The characters in Tintin are constantly searching for paradise lost. Their taste for adventure is primarily an escape from "a boring little life"—ironically, from an ambiguous, fluctuating world where Good and Evil coexist.

Despite the distance separating them, Snowy doesn't hesitate to appropriate his master's victories, or at least to claim his part of the glory. To suggest that they both share in the action, the dog usually speaks in the first-person plural: "What hunters we are, right?" (*TC*, 16, III, 3). "We're some pair of aces!" (28, II, 2). Tintin willingly shares his adventures with his companion, but since he is the boss, he most often uses an imperative form, as he does later on with Haddock: "Keep going," "Try harder," "Let's go," "Hurry up," and "Let's get back to our hut." Each one speaks for the pair, but in a different mode. Tintin organizes and commands; Snowy carries out the orders, obeys more or less willingly, and always turns up in time to celebrate the victory. If he acts like Tintin, Snowy will be saved from the forces of Evil.

In the face of the enemy, or simply strangers, the two comrades act as one with two bodies—one human, one animal. In the first episodes, Tintin's life is so closely tied to doing Good that he comes to embody it. At this period, Snowy tries to recover a kind of primal unity, a fusion with his master. For him, that is the only way to escape the world of Evil. He and Tintin live together in a mutual harmony that overcomes their differences. They help each other out as the need arises. The first crisis comes when Tintin saves Snowy from drowning and being eaten by sharks (*TC*, pp. 7–8). Later, Tintin tries to save him from the jaws of the crocodile. A third time, he retrieves his friend from the clutches of a monkey. Snowy thus finds himself indebted to his master. He owes his master at least as much in return, if he doesn't want to fall back into a world of corruption. Even when Snowy is not feeling particularly courageous, he nevertheless throws himself at the lion carrying off Tintin in his jaws. The debt is paid, and this time Tintin feels himself indebted: "My brave Snowy! Without you I'd have been eaten alive!" (*TC*, 23, II, 2).

The bond between Tintin and Snowy also serves as the prototype for Tintin's connections with his future cohort. In the original world, the connection is really just with Snowy. Coco, for example, plays no more than a minor role and can be easily forgotten. With Snowy, the relationship is an open camaraderie, an unconditional friendship of a kind one develops in adolescence, a feeling that replicates with a person at once like and unlike oneself the primordial existential fusion of the first months of life. Tintin and Snowy are the original couple; in becoming separate, in accepting ambiguity and difference, they engender the complex world of *The Adventures of Tintin*.

## HUMAN WORLD, ANIMAL WORLD

The similarities and differences that unite Tintin and Snowy likewise generate between the human and animal species a relationship not, strictly speaking, biological but much more poetic. In the first part of his work Hergé is
heavily influenced by Benjamin Rabier, illustrator of La Fontaine's *Fables*.
Hergé creates an imaginary middle world between humans and animals. In
the new version of *Tintin in the Congo*, the laws of this universe are still per-
ceptible. Without completely disappearing in the later albums, they become
increasingly less important, giving way to a world governed by different laws.
Nevertheless, one can glimpse traces of the original ones even in the final albums. Hergé never gets rid of anything. The many layers of his work are able
to accommodate and recycle in different form certain "fossils" from preceding adventures. Even if Snowy's canine nature never completely loses its early
privileges, one sees him gradually becoming more human. In the train Snowy
takes to the port, he presses against the windowpane as a child would (*TC*, 1,
II, 1). After a doctor on board cures Snowy's bite wound, Snowy stands up on
his hind legs and begins to dance for joy, the "noble sentiment" connecting
him with humans (*TC*, 4, II, 3). Snowy laughs and cries like a baby who cannot control his emotions. When the Pygmies make him their leader, Snowy
wears the crown with a royal dignity: "Approach, devoted subject," he says to
Tintin, whom he allegedly just surpassed in reputation and prestige (*TC*, 50,
II, 3). Even if he brags less, he still uses human language with a lively wit and
an excellent sense of repartee. He uses human language with his fellow creatures, too, the dogs and other animals. Although he is not on intimate terms
with just anybody and snubs the Red Skin dogs (*TA*, 16, IV, 2), he defers to
beasts of impressive size: "Good day, Madame Cow!"[3]

Snowy's move toward humanization does not mean a complete surren-
der to the human model. In fact, he often resists his human training so as not
to lose his canine identity. One sees Snowy becoming more and more conscious of his animal nature, especially once Tintin loses the imaginary omnipotence that had characterized him from the beginning. Snowy remains a
dog and is proud of it. When Sheik Patrash Pasha insults Tintin by treating
him like "a piece of dog," Snowy retorts, with wounded pride: "And you,
mind your language, you piece of man!" (*CP*, 15, III, 2). When Snowy swears,
he doesn't hesitate to say "in the name of man!" Gradually he acquires an
autonomous conscience that Hergé illustrates with a canine form of "good
angel–bad angel." The same irreducible duality that exists for humans is also

found in the animal world. The bad angel pushes Snowy toward drink, while the good angel prods him to keep his dignity. "It's whiskey, you miserable fool! Alcohol! Dragging an animal down to the level of man!" (*TT*, 19, I, 2).

For Snowy, consciousness of his uniqueness emerges slowly and does not really mature until the break between the primordial duo and the separation of the human world from the animal. Just as colonized peoples turned against the Europeans by invoking the very same intellectual arguments that had formerly been used against them, and their independence is at first secured by the most "educated" of their population, so too, without engaging in an overt revolt, Snowy wins his animal independence and spurns the humans' lessons of how to live.

In the primordial world, anthropocentrism tends to prevail throughout all the levels of living creatures and puts an indelible stamp on the animal kingdom. Following Snowy's example, all the animals express themselves like humans. Seeing Snowy, a monkey cries out astonished: "What a funny little animal!" (*TC*, 16, IV, 2). A boa constrictor swallows him and says: "I feel awful! I need a dose of bicarbonate of soda!" (*TC*, 34, III, 2). Just like Jonah in the belly of the whale, Snowy stays in the belly of the boa until he can make a hole to get out. His paws come out first, transforming the snake into a fabulous new creature. The boa is the first one to be amazed at this transformation: "How weird! It's the first time I noticed I have paws!" (34, IV, 3). The push toward humanization, however, has its limits. Certain animals never speak, or they just stupidly repeat, like the parrot. What's more, only Tintin among all the humans can understand the animals when they do speak. For ordinary adults, Snowy is simply barking.

This tendency toward humanization is counterbalanced by the inverse leaning toward animality. Tintin is the first to sense his attraction toward animal forms, at least while he is close to his companion. When Snowy is kidnapped by the monkey, Tintin disguises himself in the skin of another monkey that he has just killed. He swings from a tree and chats with the poacher in monkey language (*TC*, pp. 17–18). In his human life, Tintin is able to walk with the supple, undulating movement of a cat. He jumps, pounces, and swings into the most unlikely places, displaying his close affinities for the feline species. His close connection to the animal world at times attains a mythic level. In *Prisoners of the Sun* he is attacked by a condor (*PS*, p. 20), but he uses this fantastic bird as a parachute. Becoming one with the condor, he falls from the sky before the very eyes of his flabbergasted companions. Half man, half bird, in this scenario he incarnates the Bird-God (*Démon-Oiseau*), one of the divinities of the pre-Incan pantheon.

Tintin's capacity for metamorphosis allows him to display the privileged connection he shares with Snowy. They transform themselves sometimes into a single creature, man or animal, and thus escape their pursuers by re-configuring the primordial couple. In one case, in *The Congo*, we see both of them put on the skin of a giraffe. In *The Blue Lotus*, they disguise themselves as a Japanese general, Snowy hiding himself as the fake belly of his master.

The primordial world of Tintin, however, has several incomplete aspects. Its laws are unstable and unpredictable, based not on science but on po-etry. The hero dwells in an undifferentiated world where anything can hap-pen. His capacity for metamorphosis, meanwhile, allows him to explore the world in various directions. He travels on land and sea, beneath the earth and into the heavens. Just as in fairy tales, there is no time lapse between a project's conception and its realization. The external world does not present any huge obstacles to Tintin's will, and thus he is able to achieve his goals. Hergé's world has not quite discovered its own modus vivendi. However, the hero's unflappability and omnipotence are presented to young readers as a compensatory myth in the face of the world of adults who ignore them or appear outright hostile. Although the author's creation preserves the feelings of the world's hostility and strangeness, he inverts reality: the adolescent does not have to conform to the external world; rather, the external world magi-cally submits to the wishes of the almighty Tintin.

In Hergé's world, the human-animal distinction is less significant than that between Good and Evil. In the first albums, the demands of the Good provide the overall structure. Hergé situates his "Genesis"—*Tintin in the Congo*—within a long tradition that runs from *Le Roman de Renart*, the medieval bestiaries, the *Fables* of La Fontaine, and continues today in *Les Contes du chat perché* (*The Wonderful Farm*) by Marcel Aymé. Its classification of living creatures is based on a theology lost to us today but that flourished in the twelfth century. According to pre-Scholastic Christian doctrine, man is created in the image and likeness of God. This means that human beings are higher in the spiritual hierarchy the closer they come to their creator. Even when he disguises himself as a beast, Tintin maintains his angelic de-meanor. In contrast, the wicked tend toward animality, even more so when they believe themselves distanced from it. The day Rastapopoulos comes face-to-face with a nose-ape, he finally becomes aware of his own apelike appearance. Snowy, who is always trying to imitate his master, has the most valued human features: the ability to laugh, a sense of good and evil, and the capacity to repent and seek forgiveness. According to church fathers in the twelfth century, virtue keeps human beings in the region of harmony (*resemblance*), whereas sin throws them into that of discord (*dissemblance*).[4] By listening to the devil that reigns over the lower regions and urges giving into carnal appetites, one becomes akin to the beast.

In his first works, Hergé illustrates this theology that the church has promulgated in popular form until recently. Distinguishing human from animal, the author establishes a complex hierarchy based on their merits. In the class of human beings, Tintin at the beginning of the adventures holds the highest place by embodying the Good. Others who follow closely behind by imitating his example include Coco and, especially, Chang. Young boys of a right-wing bent generally come before adults whose likeness to animals is more noticeable. Hergé indicates the stamp of the lower world, the world of sin, on his characters by giving them either animal faces or surnames suggesting animals. One thinks immediately of Captain Haddock, but in the course of the work one meets two people named Gibbons, the Bird brothers, a traitor named Wolff, a journalist named Jules Rouget, a Professor Boléro from Calamari, the concierge Mrs. Pinson, the nice pastor Mr. Peacock, and so on.[5]

That a name evokes some animal does not necessarily mean that the bearer of the name is either treacherous or wicked, but only that there is something impure about him for which he ought to atone. Moreover, there is an implicit hierarchy in the names and creatures. For example, there is quite a difference between Haddock, a rather pacific seafaring man, and the Bird brothers, who definitely act like birds of prey. The presence of the engineer Wolff in the Sprodj factory presents the theme of the wolf in the sheep pen; whereas Mrs. Pinson, Tintin's concierge, is a talkative bird but perfectly harmless. Without having to look for an absolute coherence or system when the author is simply giving free rein to his imagination, one can nevertheless note that an animal name does situate a person on a certain rung of the hierarchy of being. The more vicious the person, the more likely the resemblance to allegedly fiendish animals will be accentuated.

In the adventure in *The Congo*, Hergé creates a kind of poetic bestiary that classifies the animals according to their virtue or vice. Snowy, of course, is at the top of this animal hierarchy, parallel to the human one. His merits reflect on the whole canine species, but not all dogs are like Snowy. Those trained by humans to attack other humans do not receive strong marks on the virtue scale; their unsympathetic treatment is not unlike that of puppies pushed away by a dried-up bitch. Despite Snowy's lukewarm feelings for cats, they also get a plus for virtue, which is not at all the case for the frequently appearing parrots. Although cows are situated on the scale at "degree zero," monkeys who think of themselves as very close to the human species fall into the negative category. Among the large animals, some change from one value to another. At first the elephant is considered dangerous but then, in *The Cigars of the Pharaoh*, shows itself to be a human's true friend. The same goes for Ranko, the gorilla in *The Black Island*, but in this case wicked humans put his colossal strength at the service of Evil. Among other animals that always get a negative score are the serpent, the crocodile, and especially, the shark. The shark occupies the same rung in the animal kingdom as the notorious criminals do in the human world.

In his work Hergé creates an entire mythology about sharks similar to the one about the giant octopus in the novels of Victor Hugo and Jules Verne.[6] The shark is the rapacious animal par excellence. With his beady little eyes, turned-up nose, chinless face, and razor-sharp teeth, he is predisposed to blind violence and hatred. He appears on several occasions: in *The Congo, The Cigars, The Crab, Red Rackham's Treasure*, and *The Red Sea Sharks*.[7] On each occasion the sharks attack the innocent as well as the guilty. At the end of *The Red Sea Sharks*, we hear that Rastapopoulos has been devoured by the Red Sea sharks, but that is really not true: sharks do not eat each other! In Hergé's work the shark plays the role of the wicked witch in children's fairy tales. It incarnates the all-powerful, wicked stepmother. Tintin encounters the shark on several occasions. A shark tries to eat Snowy, and then Tintin himself. A shark makes off with the chest said to hold the treasure of Red Rackham. When Tintin is lost at sea, floating in a sarcophagus, he catches a shark with the help of a lucky hook. When Professor Calculus first appears and immediately acquires an eminent place in Tintin's universe, he does so partly because he invents an apparatus designed to protect against sharks. It possesses a "secret ingredient" that overcomes the most basic fears from Tintin's childhood. Calculus makes an agreement with Tintin's cohort because he wants to share his secret with them. His solution to the problem of sharks consists in confronting them with the same appearance they have; in other words, by outfitting oneself in a steel shell that gives humans the same power as the devouring animal.

After a moment of hesitation, Tintin willingly tries out the professor's steel submarine (*Red Rackham's Treasure*).

In Hergé's primordial universe, the animal and human worlds are open to each other and change their contours when they come into contact. These encounters do not destroy them but incite transformations. In the Congo, while Tintin is teaching the little Africans 2 + 2, a leopard barges into the classroom. Tintin throws a sponge at him; the leopard swallows it and then drinks a bucket of water to help his digestion. The sponge swells up and the leopard inflates, becoming an obese, deformed creature that Tintin chases out of the classroom with a few kicks (*TC*, p. 37). As in paradise, the human, or at least the child, is the measure of nature. Ferocious animals are subdued, with the exception of the shark, and—like the lion that Tintin dreams of taming—even wild animals come to serve the hero (*TC*, 24, II, 1). In the new version Africa takes on the aspect of a child's world, joyous and undisciplined, perfectible with the help of education. Goodness triumphs without difficulty, despite the presence of sharks and crocodiles. When this circuslike world evolves, the original rapport between humans and animals will be modified, but it will still preserve traces of the primordial condition. When Tintin gathers his little group around himself, each of its members finds himself under the influence of an animal totem whose qualities and defects he will share. Humans and beasts go their separate ways, but governed by a mysterious kinship. Tintin follows the sign of the pelican, whereas the Thom(p)sons remain close to the monkey. At Marlinspike Hall, Haddock and Calculus come to understand each other just as the estate's dog and the cat understand each other. Meanwhile, Castafiore tries her best to disguise her deep affinities with the parrot, her emblematic animal.

## ORDER AND SYMMETRY

Once freed from its political dimension, *Tintin in the Congo* plays up its religious aspect, even though the hero stops acting like a martyr. The story does not claim to be realistic. Like the first book of the Bible, it tells a myth about the origin of Tintin's world. Tintin is greeted in Africa as the redeemer: "You see that big ship, Snowball? Well, Tintin and Snowy are on that boat" (*TC*, 9, II, 2). The welcome the natives give their hero is not less enthusiastic than in the original version, but it has a different meaning. Now it is not the white man who is carried in triumph, but the Good itself. Tintin incarnates the messiah awaited by the blacks and promised them by the missionaries. To erase any doubts, the Great White Father recognizes him as the messiah by twice saving him from death. Tintin brings peace, progress, education— abstract and universal values that now seem detached from their historical origin. The album does not present a highly structured adventure but, rather, consists in a string of miracles performed by the hero. Once the local chieftains are pacified, they offer him the crown, as they did formerly. They propose that he stay and live with them, but Tintin declines all their offers. His kingdom is not of this world; the ideal he represents is more spiritual than material. Also, he does not want any earthly attachment other than to Snowy. Coco cannot sustain his friendship. When the foreign correspondents suggest holding a news conference, he refuses so as not to get involved in any commercial activity (p. 11). As the Christ figure, he lives from day to day, feeding himself on the gifts of the people or the fruits of the land. His mission consists in spreading the "good news" that now is less political than spiritual: he preaches order and harmony.

Hergé's Africa is in limbo, awaiting salvation. It has not yet achieved social stability because it is pulled in opposite directions by Good and Evil. If the behavior of the blacks is presented as somewhat ridiculous, the reason is that they have not firmly chosen one and rejected the other. In contrast to the natives, Tintin himself never laughs. In this first adventure, comedy is a symptom of the Fall. What is funny is the attempt of all those creatures trying to recover paradise lost without recognizing Tintin as the redeemer. Africa is close to heaven, and its fall is recent. It is almost a virgin continent, sparsely populated, still in a primordial state close to the original paradise. The black man is rooted in the state of nature; he dwells in an amorphous universe. The hero arrives like Robinson Crusoe to his island and imposes a law that no one can escape. These childlike people would achieve complete happiness if they were not constantly tempted by the devil, which ironically shows up here with the face of Al Capone. While Tintin raises the country up, the gangsters drag it down, arousing among the weakest a thirst for possession, the first step toward damnation. As the Christ figure, Tintin is betrayed by his own, by the whites, and handed over to Al Capone's thugs, who condemn him to death. He is on the verge of being executed when he falls from the cliff with Tom, thus symbolizing the Fall into Evil, into discord. But Tintin is a divine being that cannot die. He escapes unscathed and returns to the natives to carry his mission to its conclusion. Once the gangsters are behind bars, he ascends into heaven—in a flying machine sent in his honor. We can read the final pages of this album as a Pentecost: his disciples will spread his word. The epic of Tintin in this idyllic, imaginary Africa will be handed down from generation to generation.

The work of the missionaries aims at making the Africans like Europeans, and so establishing a symmetry between blacks and whites. But the nature of the land, as well as the weight of tradition, opposes that: imitation turns into parody. One sees the shapes of natural creatures shifting and interpenetrating, creating a circuslike universe where humans and animals exchange their attributes. Although the perpetual alteration of creatures and things is a source of comic effect, it risks leading to the chaos fought by the white fathers. Thus, Tintin takes up their task. To raise the blacks to the level of the whites, he emphasizes their existing similarities so that a world of order may gradually be established. Symmetry will bring harmony to counter the multiple forces of Evil that hold the country in check.

What destroys the symmetry is the "mimetic desire,"[8] the desire to imitate others, to seize what the others possess, but only in order to surpass them. This desire turns up in various forms and degrees in all creatures, from animals to humans, and from primitive tribes to complex contemporary societies. In *Tintin in the Congo*, Hergé exposes this basic instinct by focusing on the monkey, the imitative animal par excellence. A monkey meets a cute white dog (Snowy), snatches him up, and makes off with him to distinguish himself from his "pals"—in effect, disrupting the balance and order of his group. Later, the same monkey sees a fellow monkey sporting a colonial helmet, as the humans do. It is really Tintin in disguise, but our monkey is too foolish to recognize him. He proposes exchanging the dog for the helmet, and then the latter for a rifle he thinks would give him absolute superiority. The desire to possess and dominate is interminable. Tintin puts an end to it by scolding the monkey: "Down on your paws, my boy! Don't you know what is going to happen now?" (*TC*, 18, II, 1). The same mimetic desire exists among the humans. An African finds a sailor hat and makes off with it, thus making his friend jealous. Since there is only one hat, the dispute degenerates into a fistfight. Tintin reestablishes their original symmetry by satisfying each of them: he cuts the hat in two. "The white master very fair! Him give half hat to each one!" (*TC*, 27, IV, 3). The same process also works at the tribal level. The Ba Baoro'm try to destroy the equilibrium with the M'Hatuvu by securing the exclusive services of the hero. But the hero puts an end to their rivalry by becoming *boula matari* in each of their tribes.

After his stay in Africa, Tintin heads for America to pit himself directly against the incarnation of Evil, Al Capone. In America he discovers the rivalries between the whites and the Native Americans. Weakened by internal divisions, the Native Americans do not have the wherewithal to confront the new claimants of the West. What Tintin discovers most of all is that the world of Evil has a structure very similar to that of the Good. In Chicago, the rival gangs all deal in various villainous practices: selling contraband goods such as alcohol, racketeering, kidnapping, and blackmailing. Al Capone introduces himself as "the king of the Chicago mob" (*TA*, 5, IV, 1), but his status as "king" is far from absolute. His success creates enemies, and he has to deal with those seeking to overthrow him. Among them is Bobby Smiles, who tries to distinguish himself by enlisting the services of Tintin. Tintin turns him down with virtuous indignation. "You know, I've come to Chicago to defeat the gangsters, not to become one myself," he replies to Smiles in an uncharacteristic surge of passion (*TA*, 12, I, 3).

The principle of symmetry is enough to create order.[9] Tintin tries to reestablish order, at least in the world of the Good, without necessarily being in symmetrical relation with someone else. Of course, he is not alone; Snowy is always his companion. But the man and dog have a dual relationship of both opposition and complementarity. Tintin actually finds his strength in disharmony, and it is disharmony that propels the course of his adventures and their dynamic evolution. Although he is not alone, he is unique: he is the One, incorruptible, indefatigable, and self-sufficient. His round face makes it easy to project one's fantasies onto him. Hergé recognizes this himself: "The circle is the perfect form. One can write on it whatever one wants."[10] The hero's name also contributes to marking him out as extraordinary, single-minded, and autonomous. His name, after all, is composed of twin syllables, *Tin-tin*, that do not associate him with anything external. To say he is unique is to claim he is in harmony with himself and that he becomes unbalanced only in his relation with the external world. It is not surprising, then, that the forces of both Good and Evil try to enlist his services. From the beginning, he is the incarnation of the Good, the goal of human beings of goodwill. Gradually he becomes a force capable of disrupting equilibrium or of reestablishing it. Although he has been endowed by his creator with the power of metamorphosis, he does not apply it only to himself. Just as "Riquet à la Houppe," or "Tufty Ricky," has the gift of making himself identical to the one he loves and transforming the silliest of beauties into ones of wit and intelligence, so too Tintin possesses the capacity to transform the world around him. Nevertheless, in the first two adventures, he does not yet realize the marvelous gift that the good fairies left in his cradle. He is content with exploring the world and establishing order and justice.

# CHAPTER FOUR

# GOOD AND EVIL

## THE SENSATIONAL APPEARANCE OF
## THE THOM(P)SON BROTHERS

At the circus, the children excitedly await the entrance of the clowns. Similarly, in the *Tintin* albums, they love the two Thom(p)sons. The creation of the twin detectives belongs to the original period of the adventures, and they make their stunning entrance in *The Cigars of the Pharaoh*. Hergé typically takes a long time before launching new characters, but he creates the Thom(p)sons almost in one fell swoop. In *Tintin in America*, there are a few characters prefiguring the "Siamese twins": the two Yankee policemen who crash into each other while chasing Tintin (*TA*, 8, III, 2); and Mike Mac-Adam, the private detective who turns out to be a braggart, a coward, and an incompetent (*TA*, pp. 45, 46, 58). The Thom(p)sons are idiosyncratic in not being biological brothers (as one can see from the different spellings of their surnames) but otherwise being perfectly identical. Only one detail distinguishes them: the shape of their moustaches. Thomson's is wavy at the bottom, whereas Thompson's curls under, thus appearing straight. In every other respect they are identical, including their comments and their characters.

The Thom(p)sons embody a kind of unintelligent and inflexible order. We have discussed in the previous chapter that order comes from symmetry. No doubt that explains why the Thom(p)sons duplicate one another. They internalize the principle of order to such an extent that they become its incarnation. They lay down the law not only in their speech but in their very being. Their appearance alone reminds us that we ought to be like

others and not stand out. When Thomson tacks on his famous "to be precise," most of the time he doesn't add anything but simply repeats what the
other just said. Their parroting of each other indicates a lack of individuality.
Although their common name does not distinguish them from masses of
people named "Thom(p)son," their repetitive comments reduce them even
more to a single figure reflected in a mirror. Not twins by blood, they have
become twins by their submission and conformity to social conventions.
Their "twinness" surpasses appearance: they have identical spirits. They are
completely normal, in the sense that they follow the norms, but they do so
to the extent that they become exceptional. The drive to be in such perfect
harmony is so deeply ingrained in their skulls that any situation involving
a third party seems monstrous to them and ought to be eliminated. For example, when they are following Tintin's tracks with Haddock, they hesitate
about which of two directions to take. Thomson proposes that they split up:
half of them go one way, the other half the other. When Haddock remarks
that half of three equals one and a half, we can see by their expressions that
they would like to cut him in two (*PS*, 11, III, 2).

Once they show up on the scene, the two characters are established full
blown. Hergé may refine them, nuance their characters a bit, polish their style,
but they do not really change. Until the early 1980s, they wear the same detective's uniform from the 1930s, with a bowler hat, stiff collar, and hard-soled
shoes—all the trappings that mark them more convincingly as police than
simply the uniform itself. Throughout the adventures, their character does
not change, only their role in the intrigues. Born under the sign of Gemini,
or the Twins, they remain the same from beginning to end. Neither history
nor experience holds any surprises for them; they never learn anything, as do
other characters in the albums. Even more, they are ignorant of their origins.
They forget the time when they were not identical as they are today. At their
trial on San Theodoros, when the chief prosecutor accuses them of wearing fake moustaches to imitate the followers of Marshal Kûrvi-Tasch, they
exclaim together in one voice: "That's a lie! We've been wearing moustaches
since we were born!" (*TP*, 47, III, 1). The Thom(p)sons do not have any history; they constitute an essence. They embody Obedience and Normalcy, just
as Tintin embodies Good.

In Hergé's albums, the two detectives achieve perfect symmetry. As the
superego in Freudian theory, they are old-fashioned, punitive, and irrationally
inflexible. If one were to get rid of them, one would not know how things

might turn out. They represent the primal prohibitions learned in infancy that remain through later life. The Thom(p)sons roll their eyes, threaten others with their canes or revolvers, and are constantly ready to blow up. When you hear them, you realize they have a particularly loud voice.[1] According to the Law, they punish the guilty indiscriminately, no matter who they are. Their blindness to particularities and differences does not suit a complex world where appearances do not match reality. Since they only believe what they see, they constantly pursue Tintin, at least in the beginning, because they take him for a villain. To vanquish Evil, Tintin the hero does sometimes borrow its trappings. For example, he disguises himself as a gangster to infiltrate the mob and wipe it out (*TC*, p. 51). Similarly, the villains sometimes disguise their nefarious deeds under the appearance of Good. In the Congo, Tom dons the cassock of the white priest to fool Tintin (p. 42). At the level of appearances, there is a perpetual tug-of-war between Good and Evil, where one turns into the other, and vice versa. But the Thom(p)sons stick only to the surface. For them it is sufficient if someone tips them off that Tintin is a cocaine trafficker and they find the drugs in his dresser drawers. They arrest him without further investigation.[2]

The Thom(p)sons' constant fixation on appearances and their resulting blunders are part of the dynamic between Good and Evil underlying the primordial universe. From *The Cigars of the Pharaoh* through *The Black Island*, in the three albums where they directly participate in the action, they are constantly pursuing Tintin. The primordial universe is a kind of illustration of the psychic world of the adolescent, the age group to which these albums were initially addressed. On the one hand, the ego-ideal is set extremely high. Tintin as its embodiment is, after all, a kind of superman. Moreover, adolescents generally ignore the constraints of the real world and, instead, occupy themselves with a projected ideal that serves as a compensatory fantasy in a world that otherwise ignores them. Dreams of future success, quite apart from the question of their attainability, serve as a kind of revenge by anticipation. In identifying with the figure of the hero, adolescents manifest their aggression toward their own families whose modest ambitions they thereby spurn. On the other hand, the superego is punitive, even sadistic, and its demands are incompatible with those of the ego-ideal and the narcissistic satisfactions of personality.

Hergé's universe is thus in tension between the Law, defended by the Thom(p)sons, and Adventure, personified by Tintin—a tension between the

demand for symmetry and order, and the need for difference and noncon-
formity, factors in evolution and progress. The Thom(p)sons pursue Tintin,
but they do not understand that they are all working to achieve the same
goal. In other words, the two detectives aim at maintaining a superficial
order, while Tintin aspires toward a transcendent order that cannot be fully
incarnated in one being or one political regime. Only at the end of a story,
when justice is once again reestablished, do the Thom(p)sons recognize their
mistake. They then make honorable amends, more or less willingly, but set
off again on their pursuit of Tintin in the following episode. Sometimes they
note a certain discomfort at arresting someone they call their friend (*BL*,
46, I, 3), but they do not let their personal feelings stand in the way of their
obsessive obedience to their orders.

To vary the narratives and also to lessen the unconscious guilt he may be
attributing to his hero, Hergé eventually casts the Thom(p)sons in a different
light. He drops the Thom(p)sons in *The Broken Ear* only to pick them up
again, virtually unchanged, in *The Black Island*. He presents the same pattern:
pursuit of the hero, followed by a final reconciliation once the villains are
behind bars. In *King Ottokar's Scepter*, they start off as usual suspecting Tintin
who, once more, has appearances against him. But this time the detectives and
Tintin meet up again when a bomb explodes in the Thom(p)sons' hands, leaving them half undressed. There they are, without their starched collars (*KOS*,
12, I, 2)! At the same time, the twins also shake off some of their weighty psychological hang-ups, for the constraints of habit rule the body as much as the
soul. At the moment of this literal explosion, the Thom(p)sons finally realize
that Tintin is innocent, and they never go back on this conviction.

With *The Scepter*, the superego and the ego-ideal learn to live together,
if not in complete harmony, at least side by side without perpetual conflict. This transformation is due as much to the lowering of the ego-ideal—
Tintin becomes a more human hero—as to a more realistic, less oppressive
paternal image. In this adventure Tintin takes hold of the scepter, symbol of
royal power. Although he is not yet an adult (and in fifty years he ages only
about three or four years), the hero learns that the Father can be replaced,
that the scepter can pass into other hands.

That two figures as noteworthy as the Thom(p)sons, who represent "the
Normal," reappear in Hergé's revised world does not mean that the author
totally accepts the point of view of contemporary social morals. Doctors are
as badly treated by Hergé as they are by Molière or Marcel Proust, but the

cops get the worst treatment. Their inflexibility constantly trips them up, and they bring about exactly the opposite of what they plan. They supposedly embody order but are constant sources of disorder, arresting the innocent and allowing the villains to escape. One day Thomson bitterly complains: "The one time we manage to catch the culprits, they turn out to be innocent!" (CE, 60, III, 2). Their clumsiness is legendary. They can't walk down a flight of stairs without tripping or get close to a rope without getting tied up in it. Even though their mission is to "announce" the law, by a malicious quirk of fate they have a speech impediment. Their "sonorous voice" (*grosse voix*) becomes an unintelligible cacophony. They "belch" nonsensical verbiage and create all sorts of linguistic nonsense, mindless repetitions, equivocations, slips of the tongue, verbal gaffes, and spoonerisms. They literally fart from their mouths, turning that noble orifice into its inferior opposite. Their incongruous noises always come at an inopportune moment. Moreover, although having a clean uniform is the rule for the police force, somehow the Thom(p)sons always manage to get dirty, as if they were secretly attracted to filth.[3] If it's not pigeon droppings on them, they manage to fall into the gutter. They end each day by wetting their clothes, like babies who still cannot control their natural functions. Their hats—their pride and joy—are forever getting "beat up." The hats blow off, get dirty, are crushed by trucks, or are used by Abdallah as a wastebasket for old newspapers.

To integrate themselves into the local populations, the Thom(p)sons, like Tintin, often resort to disguise. But for Tintin the capacity for metamorphosis is something spiritual, whereas for the Thom(p)sons it only further reinforces their own defects. With them, the mask takes on its original function: to identify rather than disguise. On each expedition they deck themselves out in the traditional local costumes, only to make themselves the laughingstock of the community. Only one time do they receive the gift of metamorphosis, but at their own expense.

In the desert of *Land of Black Gold*, they amass a substance they swallow like aspirin but that was designed for the combustion of gasoline. Since they act so much like a machine, the substance naturally acts on them as well and blows them up. The two human robots morph into two robotic clowns. Along with their internal rumblings, they suddenly sprout red and green hair. They cannot stop the process: masses of curly hair keep growing out of their heads, like an unstoppable, multicolored diarrhea. Later, on the lunar spaceship, they have a relapse. Haddock wipes them off and cuts their long locks, where Snowy has made a cozy bed—but the hair keeps growing back. It is as if suddenly everything escapes through their skin—everything they had kept locked up inside them their whole lives, all their filth and internal disorder they had repressed within themselves to try to contain the disorder of the external world. Since they don't know how to use their brains, their exploding heads assume the anal function. On the adventure to the moon, the Thom(p)sons' character seems similar to that of a type of clown (*auguste*). They become whiners, indecent, with a bunch of multicolored hair sticking out of their heads, their ridiculous spacesuits evoking the baggy costumes of clowns.[4]

Thus, the Thom(p)sons' disguises do not really integrate them with the community but merely ape the strangers around them, manifesting their deep affinity with the world of monkeys. Their style of imitation is mechanical and superficial, unlike Tintin's ability to blend with the spirit of a land. When two monkeys later come face-to-face with the Thom(p)sons, they create a mirror effect that can even become dangerous. On the island of his ancestors, Haddock risks being killed because the monkeys imitate the detectives (*RRT*, pp. 30, 31).

Despite all the Thom(p)sons' faults, one can understand why children love them. The Thom(p)sons parody the principles of parental education. Just as there are different kinds of clowns at the circus, the detectives' roles are different from Tintin's. Tintin is the self-possessed white clown who succeeds in all his projects. The Thom(p)sons, the unlucky clowns, are charged with laying down the law that they themselves inevitably transgress. In effect, their behavior ridicules "law and order," showing both its demanding character and the many ways one can break it. According to Freudian typology, the superego they embody develops mainly during the anal stage, the stage during which one learns language and rules of cleanliness. But the Thom(p)sons breach the very law they expound. They remain fixated at the pre-Oedipal stage, never achieving emotional autonomy.

The way the Thom(p)sons use language is "magical," as it is for small children learning to speak. They think that merely saying something is real is enough to bring it into existence (*7CB*, 23, III, 3). If the detectives are not afraid of anything, not even death, it is simply because they have not reached the developmental level of symbolic relations and cannot put themselves in the place of the other. Facing the firing squad, their only concern is to affirm in a final and involuntary wordplay that they accept the law whatever it may bring: "San Theodorians, I have understood you!" (*TP*, 60, IV, 1). Through them, law and order are constantly caricatured. Not only are the twins stupid, unfair, and egoistic, but they also show that absolute symmetry equals death. Repeating the same tics and the same gestures, one retraces one's steps and goes in circles. For these detectives, everything happens twice. Each time, only Tintin's presence, or an order from Haddock in the spirit of their leader, permits them to escape a vicious circle.

Despite their absence in several adventures, the Thom(p)sons are the first to enter Tintin's world and pretty much stick around until the end. Whereas Tintin becomes less heroic, the detectives become less cruel. After their adolescent period, the time when the ego-ideal and the superego are at war, they manage to be on good terms with the hero, living more maturely with a unified and reconciled ego.

## THE TRICKS OF THE DEVIL

*The Cigars of the Pharaoh* opens with a disappearing manuscript. Professor Sarcophagus has in his possession a papyrus indicating the exact location of the tomb of Kih-Oskh. The many Egyptologists who have tried to discover this tomb have mysteriously disappeared, but Sophocles Sarcophagus tries hard to succeed where others have failed. He invites Tintin to accompany him, and the hero accepts. Hergé uses the discovery of the tomb of Tutankhamen for the point of departure for this story.[5] When Tintin manages to get inside the tomb, he does not find the king's mummy but instead the mummified bodies of the numerous missing Egyptologists. Three empty sarcophagi await their future cadavers: Sophocles Sarcophagus, Tintin, and Snowy! The message from the past, the pharaoh's will, is shown in hieroglyphics. In reality, the tomb is guarded by a band of foreign gangsters who want to keep away any curiosity seekers. Tintin tries to decipher their omens, particularly the mysterious cigars with the label bearing the insignia of King Kih-Oskh. The bandits use the ancient heritage to assuage the local peoples and escape the researchers. We've seen this pattern before. In the Congo, Muganga utilized the people's animistic beliefs to control them. In America, the mob takes advantage of America's legal system to perpetrate their crimes. They organize many underground societies, as if murder and kidnapping were industries like any other. During Tintin's religious period, Evil takes shape in secret societies. They constitute a kind of inverse world, lodged underground, in caves, tombs, and ruins: the Kingdom of Death.

Like Good, Evil also has its rites and hierarchies. At the head of the mob stands a villainous figure, the inverted image of the good leader, generally a king. In the different albums, this villainous leader is named in turn Al Capone, Wronzoff, Müsstler, or Rastapopoulos. The latter, Tintin's most dreaded enemy, first appears in *The Cigars*. His first name, Roberto, suggests an Italian parentage, persisting in his pseudonym later on, the "Marquis di Gorgonzola." Although he is French speaking, his surname suggests his Greek heritage. One can detect in his name the conjunction of two words: *Rasta-something-or-other*, on the one hand, and *populo*, on the other. These two words, normally mutually exclusive, come together in the character of someone Hergé wants us to understand after the war. Rastapopoulos is both a "rasta," a mixture of a high liver and adventurer, and at the same time has the tastes of "the people." Hergé always accentuates his vulgarity. With a cigar always hanging from his mouth, Rastapopoulos wears loud suits, fashionable caps, flashy shoes, and a monocle. In *Flight 714*, he is rigged out in a cowboy outfit, music-hall style: blue jeans, pink shirt, workers' boots, and a dark monocle. At the same time, the overtones of the name Rastapopoulos also evoke Mephistopheles. The two names have five syllables and end with *l* followed by a final sibilant consonant. Whereas Mephistopheles has a dominant *e*, Rastapopoulos has a dominant *a*. The first name repeats and prolongs the *phis* in the *phe*; the latter, the *po* in the *pou*. In each one, there is a sibilant before an occlusive (*ista* and *asta*); the conjunction of these syllables strikes the ear in a way that makes the two names more resonant. Indeed, Rastapopoulos's name expresses his very being as an indelible mark. Although he is no longer either Jewish or Freemason, he retains the highest place among the forces of Evil and has many dealings with the devil.

The members of the sect that he directs meet secretly. They have contacts with other similar groups in India, China, and, no doubt, all over Europe: they are an international crime organization. They recognize each other with secret passwords and tattoos. Parodying the emblem of the Good, the sign of the pharaoh Kih-Oskh is a circle. Outside their meetings, the followers of Rastapopoulos wear a hood reminiscent of that of the Ku Klux Klan. They hide their faces and are known only by their actions. They do anything to further Evil. Moreover, they have superhuman powers: some resort to hypnotism, others to magic, yet others to drugs. Importantly, they use the terrible *radjaidjah*, the poison causing madness. The followers of this sect infiltrate the ordinary world up to the highest echelons. One is counselor to the Maharaja of Gaipajama, another a colonel in the army. Their wealth procures drugs—opium and cocaine—that they push everywhere, making people totally dependent on them. Their organization blends scientific techniques with religious folklore. Although they all call each other brothers, they are ranked. The structure of their sect is reminiscent of the Catholic Church, with Rastapopoulos as the black pope of this satanic cult. His governing seat is not in Rome but in Cairo; his throne is not in Saint Peter's but in the tomb of Kih-Oskh. Here, the dead take the place of the living, just as Evil takes the place of Good. Instead of spreading the truth, Rastapopoulos pushes drugs that numb the spirit and the soul. Instead of following the example of the founders of the church, he subverts the connection of the present to the past and renders the royal message of the pharaoh incomprehensible. Each territory occupied by the sect has a "bishop" at its head, whose job is to increase the number of followers. Mitsuhirato in Shanghai is counselor to the Maharajah of Gaipajama, who transmits the orders from the supreme leader. So that these orders are scrupulously followed, each bishop has at his disposal a hierarchy of clerks. From among these international crooks, some stand out: the fakir ("the shame of our corporation") in India, and Yamato in Shanghai. They command a chain of hired hands responsible for various menial chores. The organization is structured both vertically and horizontally. Allan Thompson provides the liaisons between one point and another. He also smuggles opium concealed in the cigars from Egypt to India and China. Each member of the sect is personally connected to the leader by a pledge of allegiance. Members address Rastapopoulos as "Grand Master" and show him unconditional loyalty. As those who have sold their souls to the devil, the members of this counterchurch enjoy all kinds of honors and wealth in the ordinary world. They are joined by the same secret, the despicable origin of their power. Whoever betrays their cause is irreparably punished, for the devil knows all! The punishment consists in another inversion along the social hierarchy: once an admired person, the traitor finds himself deprived of his standing and falls to the lowest level on the human scale. Even a traitorous intention suffices to call for this punishment, which transforms the existence of a false "brother" into hell. For example, the writer Zloty receives the poisoned arrow even before handing over to Tintin the name of the leader of the infernal sect (*CP*, 43, I, 4).

What most strengthens the power of the counterchurch is its infiltration into the ordinary world that it corrupts. In Shanghai, Mitsuhirato has powerful contacts in politics as well as in industry, the army, and police. For example, he makes Dawson, the chief of police of the international concession, inform on his colleagues. His power in Shanghai is as great as Al Capone's in Chicago. He organizes international opium trafficking for Rastapopoulos and acts at the same time as a Japanese secret agent in China. In this capacity he has direct influence on local affairs. With the villainous powers so entrenched in civil society, the forces of Good find themselves sidetracked from their goals and embroiled in the world of Evil. Everything leads to Rastapopoulos, endowed with superhuman, satanic power.

As we see, then, the first part of *The Adventures of Tintin* is still theological, as if the Absolute that Hergé does not find in politics could be detected elsewhere. Nevertheless, this theology is not at all connected to any revealed religion, even if it is strongly infused with Catholicism. On the contrary, it is open to a kind of religious syncretism even while its author's personal beliefs become more agnostic. This theological bent also serves especially to connect Tintin's obsession with Good to a social movement. Earthly life is interpreted as an immense Manichean drama: the issue is nothing short of the salvation of the universe. God and the devil carry out their struggle on earth through the work of their principal lieutenants. Although God has endowed his champion Tintin with the virtues of courage and strength indispensable for leading the forces of Good, this tremendous duel nevertheless renews the combat between a David and a Goliath. The current forces are unequal. Therefore, Tintin has to take advantage of his capacity for metamorphosis to win out. In the face of that challenge, the devil has to reinforce Rastapopoulos, his strong supporter. Rastapopoulos is thus endowed with supreme cunning, the great capacity to deceive. To bolster that power, he has tremendous knowledge gleaned from his agents, who transmit to him all the secrets of the powerful on earth, and he also possesses a superhuman mobility. Surrounded by the police in Cairo, for example, he magically escapes and pops up in India. The devil always catches him when he falls. Experiencing a fall that would kill anyone else, Rastapopoulos walks away unscathed. Sure signs of his diabolical nature are his numerous seductions. Those who serve him have already succumbed, but there are countless innocents who let themselves be taken in by his false promises. He offers to fulfill their dreams, but only in an illusory manner. Like his master, Satan, he always deceives because he panders illusions. He sells drugs that numb the spirit. Those who buy into his deceptions no longer know how to distinguish Good from Evil, reality

from fiction. Rastapopoulos sells the dream of a better world to those in a
hopelessly imperfect one. Although certain chiefs of state manage to establish relative peace in their countries, the sole solution for escaping worldly
corruption is to retreat into oneself and cultivate one's garden.

Rastapopoulos seduces even Tintin and keeps him fooled for a long time.
The hero should have stuck to his first impression and recognized the mark
of the devil. At their first encounter, the villain beats up on a weaker person,
and Tintin intervenes to stop the unfair fight. Nevertheless, the hero who
adores the movies is soon seduced by Rastapopoulos's popular image as millionaire and director of the cinema company Cosmos Pictures.[6]

Their second meeting is important for understanding the role of the
unconscious in Hergé's work. Tintin is walking in the desert and glimpses a
town that he does not immediately recognize as only a film set. Our young
hero suddenly hears the cries of a woman coming from behind the rocks.
Like a child outside the closed door of his parents' bedroom, he tries to
find out what is happening, what they are hiding from him, and he rushes
in. What he discovers horrifies him. A young blonde woman, her clothes
disheveled, is lying on the ground and being sadistically whipped by two
Arabs. We can interpret this as the equivalent of the "primal scene" Freud
discusses several times in his writings. Whether the primal scene is pure
fantasy or has something to do with a real fact reconstructed from memory,

*CP*, 16, III, 2. © Hergé/Moulinsart 2007.

it is common to most neurotics and "probably to all human children." The scene of sexual intercourse between the parents is interpreted by the child as an act of violence on the part of the father. The father figure becomes split in two, as is often the case in Hergé's work. It is interesting to note that Tintin does not remain passive in confronting this scene. He brandishes his gun like a club, beats up the attempted rapists, and introduces himself as the hero to the lovely young woman: "Don't be afraid, Miss. You've seen the last of those ruffians" (CP, 16, IV, 2). In the film Rastapopoulos is producing, Tintin takes the place of the male star waiting in the wings ready to accomplish the brave deed that Tintin just acts out. Only after being thoroughly insulted by the film crew does Tintin—now exposed as a mere pseudohero, even a mythomaniac—finally realize his blunder. At that moment Rastapopoulos arrives on the scene and tells him about a film in the making called *Arabian Knights.*

The scene of sexual violence that Tintin just interfered in appears so fascinating that Hergé uses it a second time in *The Blue Lotus.* The second time, Tintin relives it only as an image, without participating in it. At the cinema in Shanghai, he is astonished to see the action that he had interrupted the first time (BL, 33, II, 1). Rastapopoulos's power of seduction rests not only on his social status as film producer but also on his capacity to unveil this scene in Tintin's unconscious. Tintin can accept the seduction scene only to the extent that he denies its reality, for these sexually laden desires run contrary to the ideal he allegedly incarnates. He can accept his desires only because they supposedly do not spring from him but from projections of an ambivalent father figure. His interior psychic life is illusory, confused with cinematic images. Having interrupted the film's shooting, he feels sufficiently guilty to reconcile himself with Rastapopoulos, and at this point he shakes hands with the devil.[7]

Tintin does not realize the consequences of this act of trust. Intoxicated by his effusive charm, Tintin is taken in by his enemy. *The Cigars* and the album following are in this respect modeled on *The School for Wives* by Molière. In Molière's comedy, Horace constantly confides in Arnolphe without recognizing him as his chief rival. Hergé uses the same theme, but in this case the adult is powerful enough to read the soul of the adolescent who is his enemy. Sure of his triumph, Rastapopoulos goes so far as to tell Tintin the truth in the form of friendly advice: "My dear chap, it's exactly like a film. Anyone would think there was a plot to get rid of you!" (CP, 22, III, 3).

By their third meeting, Tintin is completely blinded: he submits to Rastapopoulos, confides in him, accepts his presents, and once again shakes his hand. At this point, the hero is in debt to the devil. Things look grim! Rastapopoulos reveals who he really is only at the end, when he thinks Tintin is completely overcome. Tintin can't believe it: "You? Leader of the gang? Impossible!" (*BL*, 57, II, 2). Tintin spends the greatest part of his first voyage to the East harboring illusions, a prisoner of appearances. It is only at the end, because one of his assailants remains masked, that he understands that the fight was fixed.

## THE UNIVERSE OF THE GOOD

In *The Cigars*, the principal father figure is the pharaoh referred to in the title, but he remains absent. He withdraws to the realm of the dead and abandons the earth to the greed of the wicked. The insignia of the king and the sacred places such as the royal tomb are appropriated by Rastapopoulos for establishing Satan's kingdom on earth. It goes without saying that this is no positive royal figure but only one on the defensive. The Maharajah of Gaipajama is a good king, close to his people. The crowd applaud him when he defends them against the weakest attacks of the bandits. But the bandits terrorize the population, force them to give up cultivating rice, and, instead, substitute poppies, whose harvest the bandits purchase at a low price. In exchange, the gangsters sell the peasants' wheat and rice at a high price. Since the peasants depend on these products for their daily diet, they fall into debt and are at the mercy of the villains (*CP*, 52, II, 3, 4). Without compromise, the monarchy runs serious risks. The two preceding sovereigns, the father and brother of the current one, paid dearly for fighting against the drug traffickers. Rastapopoulos had presented them with a gift: the poison that drives one mad. The current ruler is the last member of the royal family who can govern, for he has only one son too young for the throne. If the maharajah falls to the bandits, the social order will collapse. The power of the prince is also sapped from within. Unbeknownst to the maharajah, the palace basement serves as a hideout for the traffickers. Many good members of Gaipajama have been duped by the forces of Evil, and the kingdom is on the brink of disaster. Having met Tintin in a most unconventional manner, the maharajah receives a warning: like his predecessors, he too will soon be the victim of a terrible poisoning. In this context of the imminent collapse of society, Tintin has to take action, and he (barely) manages to restore the shaky monarchy.

With these few political examples Hergé preserves in his later work, one can see how Tintin remains a "classical hero." He acts only in the kind of space depicted in Pierre Corneille's classical tragedies: a small kingdom or federation where the government is closely tied to the people. The traitor is often an adviser to the king or someone in his inner circle. This kind of political world, about to disappear in 1940, paradoxically allows Tintin to escape from history insofar as he seems to belong to a different temporal order. From the reworking of the first adventures, one now sees them less as a matter of good government and more as a story of the initiation of a young man into the adult world.

Good has to set limits to its own power; otherwise it runs the risk of turning into Evil. This intrinsic vulnerability often obliges its defenders to use the cunning of the devil. The Chinese in Shanghai choose this strategy. To counter the threats to them, the entire population becomes a secret society. The resistance to the Japanese invasion strengthens traditional customs and solidarity. The ruling caste regroups around the sage Mr. Wang Jen-ghie. Its members establish a committee of resistance charged with coordinating their actions. They take the name "Sons of the Dragon" and function in a way similar to that of Rastapopoulos's sect. They act secretly and try to convince Tintin to work with them. They delegate Didi, the son of Wang, to protect the hero, but on each occasion Tintin misinterprets the actions of his bodyguard. Hergé portrays his protective measures as acts of aggression (*BL*, 8, IV, 3) or attempted murders (9, IV, 4). Only when thinking about the incidents later on does Tintin realize their meaning: "If I've got it right, the man who assaulted me was saving my life!" (*BL*, 9, III, 1). The author prolongs the misunderstanding up to the moment when the hero meets the central committee of the Sons of the Dragon. He is then "initiated," that is, learns how to decipher the complex signs in Chinese society, and thus how to distinguish Good from Evil. Only the true face of Rastapopoulos remains unknown to him. Learning that Rastapopoulos is in Shanghai, Tintin goes to visit him, renewing their pledge of trust and prolonging the suspense. When he manages to figure out the meaning of the omens, it is too late. Didi has been shot with the poisoned arrow and pays dearly for his generosity. Little by little his madness undermines the Wang family, just as the treason of the adviser destroys the maharajah's power.

*The Cigars* and *The Blue Lotus* form a single adventure. On the one hand, we see the contamination of Good by Evil as a breakdown of the strict

Manicheanism of the primordial universe. Tintin must now face a more complex world. Evil is like a poison that lodges at the heart of Good and strikes it with impotence. On the other hand, we see the symmetry of the two poles of absolute morality. Good and Evil resort to the same tricks, and both form secret and hierarchical societies. Rastapopoulos is called "Grand Master"; Mr. Wang is named "The Venerable." Good and Evil are no longer confused in an undifferentiated world, but they do share similar appearances that at times make their distinction problematic. Because of their constant and numerous interconnections, Tintin's actions are no longer spontaneous. He learns to reflect before "pulling the trigger." He investigates beforehand, taking on the role of Sherlock Holmes, as Snowy reminds him.

Good and Evil are like two magnetic poles of society that attract both positively and negatively. Each person is pulled by one side or the other. If the attraction of one of the poles is too strong, or if the capacity to resist is annihilated, the individual is no longer free. To counteract the attraction of Evil, people form support networks. They help each other out, even cling to each other, to try to maintain a neutral equilibrium. The traditional social hierarchy is one of the support networks they forge. When it collapses, as we see in the albums drafted after the war, family and personal emotional ties constitute another chain of support. When some of the support structures break down—and not all of the links have the same strength to resist—one has to tighten the connections or re-form the network, so that the pull of the planetary underground cannot obliterate the fundamental desire of most human beings to seek perfection. At first, the absolute opposition between Good and Evil creates the dynamic of Hergé's universe. But then the two poles become the inverted image of each other: they form two worlds both opposite and complementary.

## SO SAYS THE MADMAN OF SHANGHAI

In the primordial world of the first two albums, when Tintin embodied the values of the Christian West, the villains attacked him personally. After that, the villains aim more broadly at the support network that structures the world of the Good. Tintin is no longer at the center of that universe. He participates in adventures external to and larger than his individual character. He throws himself into the fray and rushes to aid a good cause, but he ceases to be the sole incarnation of Good. The heroic personality of his character no longer is the focus of the entire story.

Beginning with *The Cigars*, his character shrinks quite a bit, or splits off into several other characters. Hergé creates new characters that establish their right to exist beside his hero. Thus, one finds the appearance of the Thom(p)sons and several paternal figures: Rastapopoulos, the ambivalent father figure, or Sophocles Sarcophagus, a preliminary draft for Professor Calculus. Professor Sarcophagus is a scientist with few social skills, and the poisoned arrow that pierces him only accentuates his penchant for the ridiculous. Other father figures at the juncture of politics and family—Mr. Wang and the Maharajah of Gaipajama—have more solidity. But ultimately Tintin and Snowy are the ones to engender the objective world, even if the hero reproduces only by parthenogenesis.

What can be said about the paternal figures equally applies to fraternal figures appearing at this same time period. At the level of the family, Tintin acts as if he is driven by destiny. He repairs the support network wherever it breaks down, starting with the weakest link. At the end of *The Cigars*, Rastapopoulos and the fakir kidnap the maharajah's son. The hero is immediately in hot pursuit and brings the young prince home. At the insistence of the prince, he accepts the hospitality of the sovereign. He supports the character of the son in the maladjusted network by occupying the same role in the family. But turning the son into "twins" does not sit well for someone whose place has always been considered unique. Tintin soon cuts the ties that seem too binding to pursue his adventures in China. Having reestablished the power of the maharajah and bolstered his family, Tintin could not live in the house of the Father. Living with the father figure renews the risk of suffering further restriction of his personality—or at least, he worries about that. Tintin does not accept any law other than the one he promulgates, even if that leads to endorsing the dominant values. This explains why he prefers the company of boys younger than himself, such as Coco, the maharajah's son, Chang, or Zorrino: he can be their role model.

Mr. Wang's family is also dysfunctional. The family network is broken because of the madness of the son, the weak link in the chain. Although Didi's illness does not immediately lead to a total breakdown of the family, it does prevent the boy's development. He regresses since he cannot openly rebel. Didi's actions have a negative value in a positive universe. After being Tintin's protector, he becomes his executioner. Didi inverts the model of justice ruling the world of the Good. Instead of giving life, he threatens death.

Before his madness, Mr. Wang's son had many affinities with Tintin. First, his name is also formed from "twin" syllables, *Di-di*.[8] He certainly seems older than the hero, but we know that Tintin is more mature than his years. Even if Hergé does not endow his hero with eternal youth, after several years he does come to resemble Didi more and more, even with respect to his Asian facial features. The two young men share a kind of feline suppleness, a devotion to good causes, and the patience of a wild animal stalking its prey. Didi tails Tintin when he arrives in Shanghai and is so discreet that the hero doesn't even notice him. Didi is efficient, inscrutable, silent, crafty— qualities he shares with Tintin. Before his madness, Didi's actions are heroic, but they are interpreted the wrong way. The author lets us see them the way the Thom(p)sons see Tintin's exploits. But then the secret poison carries Didi off into another world, and for several moments Tintin follows his brother to the threshold of madness. We do not know if the hero is pretending madness to trick Mitsuhirato or whether some poison in the bottle is affecting his mind. In any case, Tintin seems to be the victim of some sort of delirium (*BL*, pp. 23–24). We see him regressing first to the animal world by squawking like a chicken, and then to infancy by obsessively reciting nursery rhymes, jumping rope, imitating a plane, and acting mad in every way. He thus replicates the mad symptoms of Sophocles Sarcophagus, the writer Zloty, and even the inmates in the asylum in Gaipajama.

If Tintin's madness, real or simulated, is a "mild case," Didi's is both much stronger and richer in significance. Mr. Wang's son is obsessed with the idea of cutting off people's heads. He thinks of this beheading as a necessary step toward enlightenment: "Lao-tzu said: 'You must find the way!' I've found it. You must find it too. So I'm going to cut off your head. Then you'll know the truth!" (*BL*, 13, IV, 3, 4). The madman of Shanghai, as Tintin calls him before recognizing his identity, expresses his fantasies with the logical rigor of a syllogism. He believes that decapitation does not lead to death but opens the door to another, richer life of the spirit. Decapitation is not the end of earthly existence but, rather, a rebirth by way of the separation of a bodily member that the "sane" consider vital: the head. For Didi this is an appendage one should lose, and this loss allows one to attain the highest degree of wisdom preached by Lao-tzu.

Along with the anxiety present in the child in his Oedipal rivalry with the Father, we can interpret this decapitation as a substitute for castration. Perhaps this is Tintin's situation, but Hergé maintains Tintin's innocence by separating him from all affective life and displacing the anxiety onto his

double. For Didi, the poison acts like an omen of truth, and the unconscious freely expresses what is denied in Tintin. The poison eliminates the
conscious level and frees the libidinal drives repressed by education and
channeled into socially valorized activities. Didi's regression to the more
primitive stage of development is aided, no doubt, by the fact that he is
the only child and thus more attached to the family. One can translate all
this in these terms: (1) Lao-tzu, the religious father whom I revere, has said,
"You must be castrated." (2) I have been castrated. (3) You must imitate me.
(4) It's my turn to castrate you. (5) Thus, you will be like me. To whom is
this message addressed? First, to Tintin, Didi's "twin"; and then, to Snowy,
who again finds himself the object of sadistic violence perpetrated by the
older brothers. But it is chiefly Mr. Wang whom Didi addresses in making
him witness the decapitation. At the moment when he is going to cut off
Snowy's head, he invites his father to watch: "Come in, Father, and see an
interesting experiment" (BL, 19, I, 3).

The villains know how to take advantage of the son's unconscious desire
by inviting Didi to realize his fantasy and decapitate his father. When Yamato
puts the saber into his hand, Didi jumps with joy. The faces of Rastapopoulos and Mitsuhirato also flush with pleasure. Although he prevents the
execution, Tintin lets the sadistic scenario play out almost to the end, as if he
wants to see the spectacle without being responsible for it. The two Fathers
are face to face: Mr. Wang, who embodies Good; and Rastapopoulos, Evil.
Everything seems lost: in one split second, Tintin holds the fate of the world
in his hands. At the very last minute, Tintin gives the orders to Chang, who
is hidden in a barrel, to shoot and break the blade of the sword hanging
over Mr. Wang's head. The paternal castration would have led the father to
the same situation as the son, thus suppressing the all-important difference
between them.

# CHAPTER FIVE

# THE DEFLATION OF VALUES

## THE INFERNAL MACHINE

*The Blue Lotus* lays the ground for Tintin's psychological world, and *The Broken Ear* establishes the basis for a "tintinian" anthropology. This basic structure remains virtually unchanged in the adventures to come, up to the concluding episode, *Tintin and the Picaros*. The design of *The Broken Ear* contrasts with that of the preceding albums insofar as the author distances himself from Western values. He accomplishes what Roger Caillois calls a "sociological revolution" in trying to look at his own culture from the point of view of the outsider.[1] This album compares so-called primitive and civilized societies, although the "primitive societies" are not presented directly, for the cultural shock to the "civilized" might be too overwhelming. Rather, they are presented from the viewpoint of a misanthropic explorer who chooses to live out his existence in the Amazon jungle. The "civilized" are observed with the same sort of detachment and the same style except without the personified intermediary.

Although this adventure is more contrived than the previous ones, it is also more superficial, even in the most dramatic scenes. The adult world is seen from the point of view of a mischievous or skeptical child, whereas previously the external world had been viewed through the eyes of the "wise" child indoctrinated by the moral precepts of his elders. Tintin himself does not escape this shift in viewpoint. Although he remains a hero, he loses some of his credibility. He is no longer the sole point of identification for his readers but becomes more like one character among others.

The story of *The Broken Ear* is rather confused and at times incoherent. It opens in the previous century when an ethnographer, Charles J. Walker, goes to South America to stay with the Arumbayas. As a sign of their friendship, the Arumbayas give the ethnographer a fetish, a wooden statue with a broken ear. Among the members of Walker's expedition is a mulatto named Lopez, who steals from the Indians a precious diamond warding off the serpent's bite. Unbeknownst to Walker, Lopez hides the diamond inside the statue. When the Arumbayas discover the theft, they round up the expedition and kill nearly everyone, with the exception of Walker, who escapes and returns to Europe with the fetish. Lopez is wounded and flees from his hiding place but is not able to recover the diamond. Before he dies, he writes down his secret on a piece of paper that years later ends up in the hands of a South American named Rodrigo Tortilla. Tortilla manages to locate the fetish, exhibited in an ethnographic museum in Brussels, and sets out for Europe. In the course of his travels, he loses Lopez's scrap of paper, and now it falls into the hands of his fellow countrymen Ramon Bada and Alonzo Perez, who also meet in Europe. To obtain the diamond, Tortilla resorts to a trick: one night he hides in the museum, snatches the fetish, and brings it to a sculptor named Balthazar. Tortilla orders Balthazar to make a copy that he intends to substitute the next day for the original. But Balthazar does not follow orders. First, he sculpts the two ears of the statue just alike, although on the original, one of the ears is broken. Second, he makes not one but two copies, giving them to Tortilla and keeping the original for himself. Tortilla, believing he is now in possession of the diamond, kills the sculptor who, after all, could still "talk," and then turns on the gas in the sculptor's studio to make it look like suicide. Meanwhile, the theft of the fetish is announced on the radio, and Balthazar's death puts three people on Tortilla's tail: Perez and Bada, who are after the diamond, and Tintin, who has already figured out part of the story. The chase begins! Right away, Tortilla is murdered by Perez and Bada, and Tintin is made an unlikely colonel in the San Theodorian army. To escape death, he flees to Nuevo Rico, where he becomes embroiled in several wild and extravagant adventures. He goes to see the Arumbayas to find out about the mystery of the fetish and ends up literally getting hold of the original at the same time as Perez and Bada. The latter two drop the statue, the diamond falls into the ocean, the bandits drown while trying to fish it out, and Tintin brings the pieces of the statue back to the museum. Thus, the fetish originally given as a sign of friendship is transformed into an object of hatred. Because of human greed, the diamond curing the deadly bites of the serpent becomes itself a source of death. Lopez, Balthazar, Perez, and Bada each die in their attempt to possess the diamond. They all commit the same error: transforming a "sacred" object into a marketable piece of goods.

On another level, *The Broken Ear* is pure vaudeville. The album begins with a melody from Bizet's *Carmen*, sung by the caretaker of the museum, and proceeds with the pace of Offenbach. A theatrical mood prevails, including the names of the generals, Alcazar and Mogador. This world is as flimsy as a cardboard box; it lacks depth and is malleable at will. The psychology of the characters, the good as well as the bad, is totally superficial. Hergé draws us some marionettes lacking any human feelings and thus seeming to dance lightly across his stage. The people are more like the fetish, hollowed out inside. It is not surprising, then, that a parrot and a statue—symbols of this circuslike humanity—lead the conga line at the finale. None of this flamboyance detracts from the episode's drama. No other has as many deaths. But in this context nothing seems very serious, and the actions lack significance, as if they have no consequences. Every action is equivalent to every other, for none bears the imprint of an absolute. Motivated by "the holy lust for gold," the actions are merely interchangeable signs within a general process of exchange. Tintin abandons his typical heroic role and joins up with the other players on the world stage. Although he still engages in many feats, the most heroic of them—facing a firing squad—is only the product of his own drunkenness. He is mistaken for "the most loyal follower of General Alcazar," even though he has never heard of the man. Soldiers carry him aloft in triumph, and he accepts this unseemly honor, borrowing from Snowy his love for puns and wordplay: "Long live Alcazar! Give him a big hurrah!" (*BE*, 21, IV, 2), a salute one finds later almost word for word coming from Jolyon Wagg in the final episode (*TP*, 62, III, 1). Tintin is rewarded with the title of colonel, becomes the aide-de-camp to the general, and as his most important duty plays chess with his superior. Later, he is again condemned to death—by Alcazar this time, and for reasons just as ill founded. The general himself, like a character straight out of the farcical theater of Henri Meilhac and Lucovic Halévy, is violent, weak willed, and corrupt. But on the side opposing his regime, reasons for revolting against him are not very serious. Diaz joins a secret society out of spite for being demoted. He attempts to assassinate his former leader several times, but this career officer doesn't even know how to handle explosives and is killed by his own bomb just at the moment when Alcazar reappoints him to his former position.

In this album no character stands out from the others. Even the hero of the adventure is just one of the competing puppets. The author stages a world of actions and interactions operating like a giant machine. The humans are simply cogs, large and small, while the machine itself alters its course when an important piece of the machinery gets jammed or changes direction. Alcazar wins one round in the race for power: all his soldiers cheer for him, allegedly ensuring the "triumph of the revolution," and jeer his opponent Tapioca, "the infamous tyrant." But when Tapioca prevails, Alcazar takes over the role of infamous tyrant and calls Tapioca's revolution merely a rebellion. From top to bottom on the social scale, people change their views as quickly as actors change their costumes. The pleasure in reading this album comes from watching the play of shapes and their constant change.

Metamorphosis is not Tintin's exclusive privilege but belongs to the entire world. Although Tintin still shows his positive orientation toward Good, the overall motivating structure of *The Broken Ear* works like an infernal machine, run by the deceptive and almighty devil—money. In this world cut off from salvation, the characters no longer act but are simply buffeted about to the point of madness. The machine may get thrown off course, for it constantly breaks down because of the competition between its various parts and risks exploding at any moment. Although the war between San Theodoros and Nuevo Rico quickly comes to an end, it is likely that their hostilities will resume under the slightest pretext. Human folly might lead to a general conflagration if Tintin did not lead the battle against the forces of Evil.

## THE DOUBLES AND THE UNIQUE

*The Broken Ear* is to some extent an adaptation of the world of Feydeau in comic-book form.[2] But among the many marionettes playing on its stage one also finds the author's usual suspects: the distracted museum curator, the professor on the moon, the unscrupulous gangsters, the crooked politicians, and the businessmen ready and eager to go to war to fill their own coffers. One also notably finds a more systematic analysis of the structure of "doubling," or duality. Once Tintin admits the existence of an objective world, its structure is like that of the "realist" superego: "twinness," or duplication. Hergé explores all sorts of possible symmetries, both individual and collective, and the conflicts they engender. On countless occasions, "twins" are after the same unique object. Here are some examples. The gangsters form two rival clans to secure the single fetish and end up destroying themselves. One of the groups is itself made up of two symmetrical individuals in conflict. Ramon Bada and Alonzo Perez, the "tall skinny one" and the "short fat one," never cease squabbling with each other, like an old married couple. The newspaper publishes two similar ads for one parrot. Balthazar makes two copies of the one original fetish. In San Theodoros, two generals want to hold the unique position of chief of state. The country is itself a twin with Nuevo Rico, ruled by General Mogador, the double of Alcazar. Two companies, General American Oil and the British Company of South American Petroleum, fight over the rights to the oil fields of Gran Chapo. Although Tintin is fooled by the substitution of his bag with another identical to it, he is attacked by two rival assassins. When he escapes into the Amazon jungle, he discovers the two similar tribes, the Arumbayas and the Bibaros, engaged in a relentless war.

Faced with these twin structures or parallel situations, some unique individuals get out when the getting is good. Among the "bad guys," Basil Bazarov the gun trafficker goes from Nuevo Rico to San Theodoros to peddle his "products," and he assures each ruler that his guns will help conquer their rivals. Thus, he maintains the two states in perfectly balanced terror. Among the "good guys," two unique individuals, Tintin and Ridgewell, meet and square off. When they first meet, Tintin and Ridgewell seem antagonistic toward one another, but after a while they recognize they are similar, like "brothers," for they have many things in common. One is a reporter; the other, an explorer—two similar professions. They both have a tendency to be withdrawn and self-sufficient. They both are leaders and help others without worrying what people will say. Ridgewell is an Englishman soured on the allegedly "civilized" world, who goes to live among the Arumbayas and teach them golf. He learns the indigenous language and thus gains a certain power in the tribe. His situation is similar to Tintin's among the Ba Baoro'm. There also the Arumbayan witch doctor tried to recover his lost power by eliminating "the white guy" (BE, 51, II, 2). Ridgewell is a kind of Tintin, grown old among the natives, solitary and ill humored. Mistaken for a young man, skillful, courageous, and generous, he also has a touch of the gift for metamorphosis, at least with respect to his voice. His talents as a ventriloquist save their lives when they are taken prisoner by the Bibaros, the tribe known for headshrinking.

Finally, in this album there is one unique object, the object of all desire—
the fetish. Michel Serres rightly sees *The Broken Ear* as "a treatise on fetishism."[3] For the Arumbayas, the small statue is a special object endowed with
a soul, a *mana*, making it sacred, although blessed with both beneficial and
harmful powers. After Lopez's crime, the fetish continues to circulate among
the whites in a mysterious way: it brings death. The Arumbayan fetish avenges
itself, in a sense, by becoming the instrument of the natives' revenge on the
"civilized." Despite all their science, the latter find themselves impotent to
stop the circulation of the fetish originally given as a sign of friendship.[4] For
the Westerners, the power of the fetish relies on two factors: the diamond that
it contains and its broken ear. The sculptor Balthazar does not notice this detail and makes two copies with the ears intact, thus making them doubly symmetrical with respect to themselves and to the other. The original, by contrast,
does not have a double (for there is only one diamond) and is not symmetrical
with the others (for its ear is broken). The bandits also practice fetishism, but
in Marx's sense of the term: commodity fetishism. For them, the object does
not have any religious or use value, but only monetary exchange value. Their
greed blinds them to the uniqueness of the object, and they dash around the
world in search of copies without any value. Ordinary people who wait for
riches to fall down from the skies are susceptible to the same sort of blindness. Balthazar's brother keeps the original he finds among Balthazar's rags,
but he does not realize that he possesses a treasure. The only use he makes
of the fetish is to duplicate its form—this time, exactly—without probing
its significance. He is also in the grip of reification, for he does not see in an
object anything other than the abstract monetary value one can get from it.
To save face, he hands over the original—no doubt at a modest price—to an
American millionaire ignorant of what he has bought. Mr. Goldwood, with
his suggestive name, also practices fetishism in the sense that he collects objects and prices them, regardless of their utility or sacred origin.

The unique object, of course, does not have a higher price than that of
a unique human being, for the value of a human being is unquantifiable.
The unique object is originally acquired as a gift, bearing certain sentiments
between individuals or peoples that cannot be bought or sold. Reconciler of
destinies, Tintin is able to bring harmony among the individuals, stop their
false rivalries, and restore health to their societies. Here indeed is a unique
individual who cannot be bought or sold. Even the sight of banknotes is
enough to make him angry, as Mitsuhirato knows full well. But the diamond

in the fetish does have the power to reopen mortal wounds. When one tries to buy it, Good turns into Evil. Lured by its commercial value, Ramon Bada and Alonzo Perez die in one another's grip. When they are not able to keep the fetish, their shared greed unites them in death.

Tintin is similar in the human world to the fetish in the world of objects. What characterizes the uniqueness of the hero is his soul, as pure as the diamond. His purity assures his membership in a spiritual universe, a membership that will become manifest to human beings. His soul is enveloped in a human body that also possesses a distinctive mark: his tuft of hair like Ricky's marks him as exceptional, like a creature from fairy tales. What constitutes the uniqueness of the fetish is the diamond, as clear and hard as the soul of a saint, imprisoned in a body of wood. The broken ear points to the statue's dissymmetry. Similar to Tintin's tuft of hair, the broken ear is a sign of uniqueness. The relation of the original to the copy is like quality to quantity. But between Tintin and others like him, there still exists an unconditional difference. The hero points toward a transcendence above and beyond the ordinary world where everything is merely relative and quantitative. In the quantitative world, "soulless" human beings are mere cogs in the supermachine. When one cog malfunctions, it is replaced by another exactly like it.

The risk facing Tintin in this adventure is that he will become like these hollow puppets. He discovers the paradox of symmetry: one's qualities may change into their opposites by mindlessly imitating others but not attending to any sort of deeper connection between them. This problem of "twinness," of mimicking the other, first affects individuals, then groups, and finally nations. The mimetic desire motivates countries to compete with each other, in the end escalating to war. Moreover, copies of the fetish circulate around the globe at ever-increasing speed. This incessant process of duplication reproduces the monetary inflation overwhelming the West just a little before Hergé drafted this album. The fetish robbed of its monetary worth—that is, without the diamond—is now reduced to the level of a worthless banknote not backed by any precious metal, whether gold or silver. Since the whites deny the fetish's religious value, it becomes an empty sign without any roots in the concrete, social world. It depreciates rapidly, and the speed of its circulation increases in proportion to the depreciation of its exchange value. Balthazar sculpts two copies, and his brother makes hundreds of them that he disseminates in the market like counterfeit dollars. The first copy Tintin comes across costs about forty dollars; shortly after, he discovers two others for sale at four dollars a pair. When he finds the workshop where the copies are made, he realizes they are worth no more than the wood from which they are made. Even stripped of its diamond and smashed to pieces, the original fetish is still worth more than the copies. Tintin convinces Mr. Goldwood to return the small statue to the museum. After all, isn't that the place to exhibit objects that have lost both their use value and their exchange value, and that have thereby acquired merely an "imitation" value? Once returned to the museum, the fetish recovers a degraded value as an art object, the only kind of value the modern West is able to assign it.

## THE AMBIVALENCE OF THE SACRED

This frenetic society, cut off from its religious roots, paradoxically recovers a sense of the sacred precisely in its agitated activity itself. In societies caught in a crisis of regeneration, the sacred is no longer to be respected but only to be transgressed.[5] In *The Broken Ear*, the feeling of living intensely shows up most strongly during political turmoil. The regime change from Tapioca to Alcazar signifies not so much a desire for better living conditions but a desire simply to replace one "used-up" leader by another. In such a context the "utility" of a leader is calculated in terms of commercial interests and is therefore precarious. That explains why the changeover of the elite in power happens so quickly. The elites circulate at the rate of the devalued currency at a time of inflation. To gain in stature and acquire the appearance of greater stability, Tapioca and Alcazar try to pass off their coups d'état as genuine revolutions. So that their revolutionary rhetoric does not appear totally hollow, they act violently, letting the blood flow among their own partisans as well as their enemies. Only with blood can the image of the new leader not confirmed by tradition attain a "sacred" dimension. The revolution is thus less a political act and more a religious ceremony uniting the masses and its head into one body. Up to a point Alcazar succeeds in becoming a genuine king, thanks in part to the strength of his troops but also in part to the errors of his enemies. When his enemies attempt to assassinate him, they make him a martyr, a holy king. The people rush to the palace to hear the news (*BE*, 30, III, 1, 2). Having escaped the assassination attempt, yesterday's traitor becomes God's elect—at least for a while. Alcazar tries to maintain this image by resorting to war. While in power, he enlists the San Theodorians to conquer Gran Chapo, to the great benefit of General American Oil. If in the eyes of his partisans he can thus remain a holy leader who sacrifices instead of being sacrificed, this adventure nevertheless risks an about-face, turning him into a buffoon. One can appreciate this by seeing the Nuevo Ricans filing behind his effigy as if it were the King of the Carnival. From their point of view, Alcazar is only a transitional leader who reigns during the several "holy days" of upheaval. This is a hero made of cardboard that gets burned at the end of the jubilation when one sees him finishing his act on the music-hall stage. During the interregnum, there is complete license: even the sacred laws are transgressed and the people fall into debauchery—and all that happens as if the general himself were merely a stage director. But after the celebration, it is necessary to return to a more serious government, that of Tapioca or Mogador, if the latter manages to annex San Theodoros.

Hergé clearly shares the point of view of Alcazar's enemies, but he does not have a higher opinion of either Tapioca or Mogador, who seem like interchangeable puppets. For him, the revolution does not know how to produce a genuinely sacred leader. Even if the new leader's power originates in blood, such a prince can accede to the throne only according to ancient, venerable rituals that compensate for the impurity of his origin. Baptismal waters redeem the blood. This is the theme the author develops in *King Ottokar's Scepter*. In *The Broken Ear*, neither of the generals truly attains the dignity of a king. They proceed in theatrical disguises, and their revolutions turn into pitiful farce. Blood runs in vain because no one condones the sacrifice.

Tintin not only prevents crimes but also refuses to become a substitute victim. As a unique individual in the political world, he is surely set up for sacrifice. Still, in the economic world it is the diamond that gets sacrificed. The first who obtains the diamond immediately sells it, thereby destroying its sacred value by getting rid of it. The sum obtained will certainly be spent foolishly and extravagantly. In this adventure Tintin is as much the object of pursuit as the diamond. First Perez and Bada try to kill him; then Tapioca's government condemns him to death. At the very moment when he is about to be shot by the firing squad, Alcazar's partisans save him and make him a hero for the day. He is carried in triumph, like a king, except that his heroism is due only to strange circumstances. When Alcazar sees right away that he can take advantage of Tintin's popularity, Tintin is reduced to a mere player in the carnival. Alcazar immediately makes him a colonel and close adviser, implicating him in his own regime to augment its sacred character. But after being protected by this government as its most valuable citizen, Tintin is sacrificed by Alcazar on the basis of a simple, anonymous denunciation.

His death sentence speeds up the action, while Mogador takes advantage of illegally entering Nuevo Rico to declare war. Alcazar's inability to give his power a transcendent dimension comes down partially to this: Tintin treats a sacred object with respect, thus aiming to replace the bloody drama with an equivalent ceremony. In the course of his adventures, the hero is sacrificed but only in appearance; he manages to escape a real act of sacrifice by his capacity for metamorphosis. The general, in contrast, opts for a transgression of the sacred that rests not on the repetition of a past act but on the inaugural event. This sacred is no longer founded on an abstract ritual but on a concrete act, no longer on merely symbolic signs but on the blood evoked as its symbol. Paradoxically, it is this second ritual that Hergé mocks: he sees it as a tragic farce. Although Hergé senses the ambivalence of the sacred, he recognizes it only in the forms approved by the West, that is, only as a representation substituted for a real sacrifice. The hero refuses to acknowledge the other aspect of the sacred that is tied to blood, death, war, and transgression, insofar as it belongs to an irrational universe he dares not confront directly.

Fleeing to the Amazon, Tintin discovers there as well that power can have its origins in a highly valued thing or creature whose uniqueness is sacrificed to establish symmetry. He meets his older double, Ridgewell, and the two men are soon taken prisoner by the Bibaros. The Bibaros decide to punish the two white men who crossed the boundaries of their territory and angered their gods: "Spirits of the forest, we will sacrifice to you these two foreigners" (*BE*, 51, II, 3). This ceremony serves a dual function. On the one hand, it eliminates foreign elements from their native group; on the other, it integrates the strength of the victims into the Bibaroan community. Ridgewell, however, prevents the sacrifice by substituting an equivalent. As in the later incident with Captain Haddock's ancestors, the English explorer is endowed with a special kind of voice that sounds to the natives like the voice of their gods. By ventriloquism, he makes the fetish say it refuses the white men's blood: "The spirits of the forest do not accept this sacrifice. The two foreigners are their friends" (51, III, 1, 2). Thus, Ridgewell and Tintin seem to be elevated to the level of the Bibaroan pantheon. The heroes will take advantage of this same sort of trick again at the end of *Prisoners of the Sun*. The two men forbid an act and replace it with a secular and no longer religious sign that has an ambiguous meaning. For the natives, it is a miracle that affirms their beliefs; for the two whites, it is a conjuring trick that can be rationally explained and thus confirms the superiority of their values.

The same kind of scene takes place among the Arumbayas. Taking advantage of the absence of "the old white man," the witch doctor decides to sacrifice Snowy, whom he recognizes as unique. By doing so, he hopes to regain some of the status and power he lost upon the arrival of the English ethnographer. All of the ethnographer's actions, however, try to adapt the Arumbayan mentality to new living conditions. Although Ridgewell claims to be turning his back on civilization, he is still the vehicle for its principal values. Thanks to his knowledge, he becomes a witch doctor in his own right, both a priest and a healer. In place of the religious ceremonies and celebrations, he teaches a kind of game that is a degraded form of celebration where the playful element—the real risk—is eliminated. He follows this plan by forbidding Snowy's sacrifice. For the natives, he plays a role equivalent to Tintin's, but, given his greater knowledge of how to get things done, he has even more real power than the hero. Being unique like Tintin, Ridgewell forbids blood sacrifices and substitutes more abstract signs. He transforms the religious ritual into a theatrical production: he introduces what had been a self-enclosed society to the carnivalesque dimension of the West. The next installment of *The Adventures of Tintin* takes up this theme and develops it more fully.

## THE MYSTERIOUS ISLAND

*The Black Island* expands on the themes of the preceding adventures. When the Thom(p)sons once again set out after Tintin, he turns around by handcuffing them, making them literally inseparable. Like circus clowns they give an incredible aerial performance without even knowing it! Snowy displays an inordinate attraction to Loch Lomond, and Tintin plays hide-and-seek with a band of counterfeiters. They no longer deal in fake copies of the fetish circulating the globe but with counterfeit banknotes. With a light touch Hergé returns to the problem of inflation compounded by counterfeiting, the process of exchange of empty signs lacking any real worth. Despite their respectable appearance, the gangsters do not have any soul, just as their fake money has no backing in precious metals. Behind the good manners of a provincial officer, Dr. Müller hides his unscrupulous practices. Instead of curing his patients, he makes them mad, using techniques worthy of Rastapopoulos himself. Like the human-animal pairing of Tintin and Snowy, Wronzoff—the leader of the gangsters—pairs up with Ranko, the giant gorilla. Just as Tintin's blond hair matches Snowy's white fur, Wronzoff's long black beard corresponds with Ranko's black coat. Like Snowy, the gorilla is attracted to humans and tries to imitate them. Even when the beast is enraged by the whipping he gets from Wronzoff, Tintin takes him on. The hero throws a stone at him, but the gorilla responds with a rock ten times as heavy. Sporting Tintin's beret, Ranko chases Tintin and grabs Snowy but does not eat him. All of a sudden Ranko becomes fascinated by this tiny, fragile creature at his mercy.

This is the first time Hergé develops the island theme. Like a new Robinson Crusoe, Wronzoff establishes himself on the island as the despot over a band of devoted followers who work for him. His headquarters is the ruined castle of Ben More (read "Ben Mort"), as Rastapopoulos used the tomb of Kih-Oskh. From there he spreads terror, death, and fake bills, the death of the economy. He sets up an international ring of traffickers and uses modern means of communication to extend his power, like concentric waves flowing outward from the island. Despite many obstacles, Tintin manages to reach the bandit's hideout and has to fight Ranko, just as Snowy earlier has to fight Müller's Danish dog. The hero realizes that the relationship of Wronzoff and Ranko is the opposite of his relationship with Snowy. Tintin's own indomitable will and his desire to instill his values are at the service of Good; Wronzoff's will to power is turned toward Evil. Tintin surmises that to defeat the villain, he has to break up the relationship between human and animal, for the man gets all his strength from the beast. He manages to separate Wronzoff from the gorilla, and—just as the soul leaves the body inert at the moment of death—this rupture puts an end to the gangster's superpower. Wronzoff atones for his crimes in prison, while Ranko, despite his tears, is rejected by the other animals and spends his time alone in a London zoo.

To understand the meaning of this encounter, Tintin has to go through many trials. Only when he travels to Tibet does he finally confront his own psychological fantasies. For the moment he still believes that the solution to the problem of the inflation of values is to be found in the public realm of society and politics. Without questioning his own personal beliefs and values, he has a hard time recognizing his inner world as anything but an objective reality, even though it hides its personal origins. At this point, in the monstrous pair Wronzoff-Ranko the hero does not suspect the traits that would make them resemble the pair Tintin-Snowy.

## CHAPTER SIX

# THE GOLDEN PELICAN

## THE REPORTER AND THE SIGILLOGRAPHER

In *King Ottokar's Scepter*, a small, fictitious country in Eastern Europe named Syldavia is the focus of constant agitation by an extremist party, the Iron Guard. Under political cover, the sympathizers with this movement form a revolutionary organization: the ZZRK, the Zyldav Zentral Revolutzionär Komitzät (Syldavian Central Revolutionary Committee). Their leader, Müsstler, is preparing for a general uprising against the Syldavian monarchy. His immediate project is to reunite the two neighboring but longtime rivals, Syldavia and Borduria. As with San Theodoros and Nuevo Rico, "twinness," or duplication in this case, concerns countries. Once again Hergé wants to point out the dangers of a too perfect symmetry. The two similar countries risk becoming merged into one, thus losing their autonomy. Although the legitimate monarchy tries to maintain the symmetry, the totalitarian regime exacerbates the mimetic desire in order to homogenize Syldavia and Borduria. The monarchy is on the brink of collapse, and Tintin intervenes at the last moment to save what can be saved.

*King Ottokar's Scepter* opens with a very banal scene. Professor Nestor Alembick leaves his briefcase on a park bench, and the hero picks it up and returns it to him. Professor Alembick, an ardent "sigillographer," or interpreter of ancient seals, is about to leave for Syldavia on a mission to work in the archives of Ottokar IV, the king in the second half of the fourteenth century. Tintin discovers by accident that a Syldavian group of émigrés to Brussels is strangely interested in the professor and, indirectly, in him. To solve the puzzle of why this is so, he accepts the role of the professor's secretary, and the two set off for the Syldavian capital, Klow. He quickly learns of a plot to overthrow Muskar XII and decides to intervene.

In this album Tintin encounters two principal father figures, one in the public realm of politics, King Muskar XII, the other in the private sector of science, Nestor Alembick. The professor has everything going for him to attract the young man. He is tall, thin, accomplished, hardworking—and even has a white beard that inspires confidence. He is passionately interested in seals, the imprints left by the past, although Tintin is more interested in the signs of the present. Working with the professor, the hero learns that past and present are inevitably connected. At first, Alembick seems distracted, chain smokes, and is so consumed by some inner turmoil that he seems not to recognize even his immediate environment, including the step of Madame Pirotte, his concierge. He is totally oblivious to the fact that his apartment is bugged with tiny microphones. Along with Sophocles Sarcophagus, Alembick is one of those characters that prefigure Professor Calculus. Each of the three has a characteristic surname and a Greek first name. Alembick's is Nestor, the old sage from Homer's epic. For Hergé this Greek heritage seems an essential property of the professor, as confirmed later by the characters Hippolyte Calys and Hippolyte Tarragon. All Hergé's professors and scientists have a fine head of hair to signify their venerability. Their prime motivation is to discover the mysteries of life, of nature, or of the past. But thanks to his exceptional and distinctive creativity, one of them—Calculus— is elevated above the others.

At first totally charmed by the professor, Tintin becomes puzzled over his increasingly strange behavior. Either the professor's attitude has changed unexpectedly, or he is some kind of impostor. Alembick suddenly stops smoking and only pretends to be nearsighted by wearing glasses. When Tintin is the victim of an attempted murder that the professor seems to know about, the positive father figure changes into a monster. His archival studies are only a cover for his participation in the plot to overthrow Muskar XII. Tintin does not unravel the mystery until the end, when the Syldavian minister of the interior reveals that Alembick has a twin brother.

But there is a good and a bad Father, similar on the outside but very different within. The good Father allows Tintin to acquire knowledge and to participate in the intellectual life. The bad Father acts secretively, fomenting plots and trying to kill the young man who gets in his way. The good Father is a true intellectual, whereas the other merely takes advantage of the positive image of his twin. Hergé does not develop the feelings of the twins for each other, but one can infer from this adventure that Alfred is jealous of Nestor and takes advantage of the opportunity to defeat a rival who is both very similar but more gifted. At the end, we find the real Alembick held prisoner in the cellar of a house rented by the Syldavian revolutionaries. Although this professor belongs with the forces of Good, Hergé does not continue to use this character in later adventures. Being a twin makes it difficult to integrate him into Tintin's small "family." The only twins allowed in are the Thom(p)sons, who are absolutely identical. But the passion to know and to create is a mark of uniqueness. Thus, it is Professor Calculus and not Alembick who is allowed into the inner cohort.

## THE KINGDOM OF SYLDAVIA

When in 1938 Hergé drafts *King Ottokar's Scepter*, he does not yet turn his back on political activism. The father figure has two sides, public and private. If the father figure is ambivalent within the private sphere (Alembick), he is wholly positive in the public sphere (Muskar XII). At this point Hergé opts for politics to compensate for disillusionment within the family. After the experience of the war, however, he will reverse this pattern.

Although Tintin is not one of Muskar's subjects, he takes up Muskar's cause. On several occasions, the hero tries to approach the king, but the same thing happens each time. The members of the prince's inner circle, who are secretly backing Müsstler, prevent the meeting. "If the king only knew," he would take measures to arrest the villains, but Muskar is even more in the dark than Tintin. In this episode Hergé develops a theme begun in *The Cigars* of the villainous adviser who stands between the people and the king. In *The Scepter*, Colonel Boris, the king's chief adviser, betrays his king, who has trusted him completely. Boris is a member of a worldwide organization, similar to Rastapopoulos's demonic sect, except Boris's is more openly political.

Muskar XII is a ruler very close to his people. He drives his own car, walks through town, meets with groups of his citizens, and maintains a court open to everyone. Without being bogged down by administration and, especially, by worrying about traitors in his midst, he listens to the lowliest person, like the kings of old—if one can believe in the lofty images of the kings of the ancien régime. Tintin encounters the king by chance. When the young man rushes to the palace to try to talk with him confidentially, the king's car accidentally hits him. The king gets out and gallantly helps Tintin to his feet. This gesture wins the hero's trust, a feeling that quickly becomes mutual. Immediately, the scoundrel Boris denounces Tintin as a committed anarchist out to seduce the king, but Muskar sympathetically listens to the hero's version of the story.

Syldavia is like a medieval enclave within modern times. It is a protected land, primarily geographically, for it is surrounded by the Zmyhlpathian Mountains. Sparsely populated, with 642,000 inhabitants, of whom 122,000 live in the capital, Klow, it has managed to avoid industrialization. Villages such as Zlip do not have paved roads or electricity. The peasants wear traditional costumes without becoming merely folksy. They live peacefully, in harmony with their cows. Even in the city, signs of modernity are integrated with the traditional ways. The modern conveniences do not break with the past but are merely added to what is already there. The medieval castle in Kropow is the heart of the capital, like an organ that pumps life throughout the whole body. Even though no one actually lives there, it stands for the image of the king that the flesh-and-blood monarch is supposed to live up to. It houses the crown jewels and Ottokar's scepter, essential to the preservation of the kingdom. The prince himself lives in a neo-Gothic palace less laden by history but more functional, and whose gates are always open to the public. Although Klow is a modern capital, tradition still prevails. Tintin asks directions from a water carrier whose costume and implements are found today in a museum of ethnography (*KOS*, 33, IV, 1). Syldavia does not break with the past; it is a country rooted in history. The stories of its illustrious monarchs are alive in people's memories, and that living history gives the current king his authority.[1] Muskar XII is an honorable king who replicates the highest deeds of his ancestors.

This glorious history is evoked in the travel brochure Tintin consults before arriving in the country. There one finds the tale of the origin of the rivalry between Borduria and Syldavia, and the stages that Syldavia went through in order to win its independence. In 1127 Hveghi, the chief of the Slavic tribe, came down from the mountains and chased out the Turkish inhabitants from the neighboring villages. He was elected king under the name Muskar, which means the "Worthy King" (from *muskh*, "worthy," and *kar*, "king"). The former capital, Zileheroum, became Klow, the "reconquered city." Although Muskar I can be considered the first king of Syldavia, two other monarchs deserve to be mentioned: Ottokar I, who liberated the country from the Bordurian invasion in 1275; and Ottokar IV, considered "the true founder of the Syldavian fatherland" (p. 21). Ottokar IV ascended to the throne in 1360 and found himself confronted on two sides: from the outside by the Bordurians, and from the inside by the feudal lords, who refused to acknowledge the king's law. Ottokar IV used the tactic of the French sovereigns to overcome the lords. He enticed them to make war outside his borders and thus defeated all his enemies. He unified the country with a modern ideology founded on "arts, letters, commerce, and agriculture." He supported the rising middle class and surrounded himself with lawyers and artists. Despite the absolutist nature of his regime, Ottokar IV remained a medieval monarch in two senses: he consulted his lords on all important matters, and his power could be tested by a stronger rival. The medieval aristocracy and royalty were founded not on heredity but much more on superior force. One constantly had to prove oneself to justify one's lofty social status.

Among the famous exploits of Ottokar IV, one became legendary because it established hereditary succession in Syldavia. It is a story of a divinely sanctioned ordeal, a combat between a baron and the king to prove which one had God on his side. The Syldavian brochure tells the story in these terms:

It was he [Ottokar IV] who pronounced those famous words: "Eih bennek, eih blavek," which have become the motto of Syldavia. The origin of the story is as follows: One day Baron Staszrvich, son of one of the dispossessed nobles whose lands had been forfeited to the crown, came before the sovereign and recklessly claimed the throne of Syldavia. The King listened in silence, but when the presumptuous baron's speech ended with a demand that he deliver up the scepter, the King rose and cried fiercely: "Come and get it!" Mad with rage, the young baron drew his sword, and before the retainers could intervene, fell upon the King. The King stepped swiftly aside, and as his adversary passed him, carried forward by the impetus of his charge, Ottokar struck him with a blow to his head with the scepter, laying him low and at the same time crying in Syldavian: "Eih bennek, eih blavek!" which means roughly: "If you gather thistles, expect prickles." Turning to his astonished court, he said: "Evil be to him who thinks evil!" (*KOS*, p. 21)

This scene serves as an archetype of the Tintin albums. Of the two individuals in the story, the young baron could be the son of the older king. He is defined as the perfect son, for the ending on his name, *vich*, means "son of" in the Slavic language. He shares many qualities with our hero, among them youth and bravery, even to the point of recklessness. Like Tintin he looks for a kingdom where he could be the king. The fourteenth-century manuscript depicting the scene shows the young baron on the ground, rubbing his head, his sword lying beside him. Whereas Tintin wears his sign of virility on top of his head, Baron Staszrvich wears his on his chin. This episode clearly replays the fantasy of killing the father, or of castration, that Didi Wang staged in front of his father. But this time the revenge of the son did not use a scapegoat. He relied on his own physical force to demand the scepter. He laid claim to the symbolic object that defined the king as Father. He provoked the older one to engage in single combat in order to be able to take his place on the throne. The Father accepted the challenge, resorting to cunning rather than brute strength—a trick Hergé attributes to the good as well as the wicked. One does not learn whether the king actually killed the young lord or only wounded him, but in any case he restored him to his place as son. The king laid the young lord on the ground at his feet, in an attitude of complete submission. The king's words signaling his victory— "eih benneck, eih blavek"—became the royal motto, inscribed on his armor as a warning. It reminded future generations of the primal taboo: one may never kill the Father or steal the symbolic object, the Phallus, that defines him as the sole representative of the Law. The Father is the unique, irreplaceable individual. This "Law" is likewise one of Hergé's obsessive metaphors throughout *The Adventures of Tintin*.

From the political point of view, the scene pitted two adversaries against one another, each of whom claimed a different sort of legitimacy and utilized different weapons. The young baron relied on brute strength, and his actions fell within the tradition of knightly chivalry. He was the son of a feudal lord, formerly an independent ruler over his own lands. He challenged another lord, the king, to regain his lost power. From his point of view, his rightful duty was not to respect the king, whom he did not recognize as having any divine right, but to restore his own heritage that he considered despoiled. In addition, he wanted to display the same *virtu*—manly courage—as his ancestors in attacking someone politically stronger than himself. In more ways than one, then, this young baron seemed a worthy ancestor of Tintin.

In contrast, the legitimacy of the monarch could no longer rely on such a long tradition. It had to demonstrate its superiority in other, more concrete ways, or otherwise see the annexation of its feudal lands by another who would usurp the throne as a mere outlaw. Ottokar IV was divided between two forms of legitimacy: the traditional and the new. On the one hand, he could not refuse the ordeal, on pain of being cast out of the feudal hierarchy still in effect. On the other hand, he could not submit to a challenge from one of his own lords whom he ruled. Furthermore, to resort to bloodshed, whoever might win, was a transgression of the Peace of God that the king had sworn to respect. Ottokar IV admirably extracted himself from this conundrum by manifesting his sovereign qualities and allowing the might of his words to prevail over that of his arms. Although the young baron acted out of anger, the king remained calm. When necessary, the king responded with cunning and struck his adversary with the scepter. In doing so, he used an object that was in the most literal sense like "the hand of justice," an abstract symbol of power. His action contributed to sustaining the undisputable value of the scepter. He transformed an object that was verging on becoming merely an empty sign into a living symbol. He proclaimed: "O Scepter! Thou hast saved my life. Be henceforth the true symbol of Syldavian kingship. Woe to the king who loses thee, for I declare that such a man shall be unworthy to rule thereafter" (*KOS*, p. 21).

The ordeal was supposed to put an end, once and for all, to any challenge to monarchical authority. It proved the legitimacy of the prince, and it was the bloody act that consecrated the right of the king. The punishment of Baron Staszrvich recalled the episode of the vase of Soissons when Clovis, founder of the Frankish monarchy, punished his own soldier who had broken his law. This trial in which cunning and secrecy, the "arms" of the monarchy, played the determinant role rather than brute force, equalized the inner world of politics with the external one of battle.

In this album, Hergé depicts such a battle, the Battle of Zileheroum, in the course of which Hveghi, the future Muskar I, routed the Turkish invaders. In the miniature parody of the fifteenth-century drawing on page 20, one sees the battle as a series of duels among many soldiers. Hveghi is in the center on his black horse. A black plume on his helmet designates him as the leader. In single-handed combat he defeats the leader of the adversaries' army, whom we see fall from his horse. On the rest of the field, Hveghi's men pursue the Turkish soldiers. Thirteen years after Bouvines, the fictitious Battle of Zileheroum reproduces that slaughter. It is again a matter of the Judgment of God.[2] The king is dragged down into a subhuman world of violence. He transgresses the law that forbids bloodshed, but then he restores that very law under the sign of divine right. Whether sacrificing or sacrificed, the king puts himself outside the human community. He sacrifices his own person to attain a transcendent dimension. The battle or duel is a kind of sacrament, not of holy water or consecrated oil but of blood. As in the times of the legendary monarchies, this bloody act transforms the leader of a tribe into a king. The royal sanction from the bishop can come only from above. By this bloody trial the prince first has to prove his legitimacy before his former peers, the men who had sworn allegiance to their leader. One finds a confirmation of the sacred character of the Syldavian monarchy on the walls of the castle in Kropow. Frescoes depicting angels of God intervening on the king's behalf emphasize his divine right (*KOS*, 30, IV, 1).

The king accepted the risk and the sacrifice, but it was the young baron who was sacrificed. The son was symbolically "castrated" by the Father. After the monarch accomplished this act, however, he made clear his position as merely the provisional representative of the law. The king is king only by delegation. The king himself must obey the law he lays down and that limits his absolute power. Having established the kingly right against the feudal customs, Ottokar IV set limits to his own power in order to emphasize the difference between a king and a tyrant. In making the scepter the source of legitimacy, he thereby weakened the power of the man who wields it. The person is nothing; the royal exercise of power is everything. Authority does not reside in the royal person, as it does in France, but rather in the sign of royalty, the crown or the scepter, as in England. The king remains king only because each year on Saint Vladimir's Day he exhibits the symbolic object that justifies his position of command. Neither the lords nor the people swear loyalty directly to the prince. They recognize their sovereign in the person who has access to the royal symbols and who agrees to honor them more than being honored by his personal use of them. This explains the relative weakness of the actual person of the king. While he is the most important person because he lives at the source of all symbolism, at the same time he is the most vulnerable link in the social and political universe. If the king loses the scepter or if it is stolen, by that same token he loses the right to rule. His power would no longer have the Right of Authority but only the Might of the Tyrant.

## THE ROYAL ECLIPSE

In the twentieth century, Muskar XII faces a problem similar to that of his ancestors Muskar I and Ottokar IV. He has to take a risk and emerge victorious to prove to his people that he is not called the "Worthy King" in vain. As of old, an individual claiming a different sort of legitimacy is seeking power. Müsstler is applying pressure on the discontented citizens to justify his demands. He reproaches the sovereign for being weak—at least if one judges from the name he gives his own movement: the Iron Guard. Confronting "the men of steel," the prince has to prove his legitimacy by showing that God has not abandoned him. Whereas Ottokar had challenged the young baron by crying out, "Come take it," Muskar XII is challenged by the revolutionaries who demand that he recover the scepter stolen on the eve of the national holiday. The king clarifies the issue to the detectives sent to Syldavia: "Alas, gentlemen, there are only three days! If I am without my scepter on Saint Vladimir's Day, I have no choice but to abdicate" (*KOS*, 44, II, 1). The moment the castle at Kropow loses the royal insignia, the state becomes a body without a soul. Muskar XII is no longer king but simply a man holding an unjustified position. All that remains to him is the strength of his police. Since that is hardly power enough, he calls on the Thom(p)sons to help him recover the scepter. Muskar XII thus relives the drama of Ottokar IV. Risking everything, he descends into the subhuman world of violence and death, to reemerge victorious. He agrees to the sacrifice that will restore his image—or destroy him.

For Ottokar IV the plunge into the world of risk and danger lasted only three days before his successor would take over. During those three days Syldavia's existence was bleak. The monarchy's light was extinguished; shadows covered the land. The forces of Evil emerged from the subterranean world where they had been hiding. But now, for the current king Muskar, the same things are happening: the revolution is at hand! The people complain. "Things are grave, sire! The people are suspicious: there are rumors that the scepter is missing" (*KOS*, 57, III, 3). It is the beginning of the upheaval. The agitators loot the Bordurian shops in Klow to justify the upcoming invasion of Bordurian troops in cahoots with Müsstler. Because of the loss of the scepter's symbolic meanings, the people can no longer distinguish Good from Evil. They are ready to follow the first one to brandish the scepter. This situation spells a veritable eclipse of the monarchy. The lone figure of the prince no longer illuminates reality. Panic spreads everywhere.

This episode reinforces the parallel between Christ and the king, further emphasizing the king's divine nature. After the Crucifixion, the newly emerging Christian world was deprived of its light for three days. Despair was widespread, and the disciples themselves were devastated, doubting the resurrection of their master. Strange phenomena accompanied this spiritual eclipse. According to Mark, darkness enveloped the earth for three hours in the afternoon. The curtain of the Temple was severed in two. Matthew claims that the earth trembled, rocks cracked into pieces, tombs opened up, and numerous bodies of the dead came to life. One has to situate the Syldavian adventure against this apocalyptic background. Muskar XII relives the Passion of his ancestor, as if history were beginning anew, remaining true to its past without ceasing to become new.[3] During those three days, the Father is dead, the castle is empty, and the king has been sacrificed.

The Syldavian emblem, the black pelican, is surely as rare as a white blackbird. Like the phoenix, it exists only as a unique symbol. The two birds, phoenix and pelican, have long been used to characterize the uniqueness of sacred beings: Christ, the king, or the father of a family.[4] The pelican's instinct is to love its offspring to such an extent that it will tear open its belly to feed them on its own entrails. In these scenes from *The Scepter*, Hergé presents a Passion, in the Christian sense of the word: a king is prepared to sacrifice himself for his people as their father. "Rest assured, Prime Minister, there will be no bloodshed. I will abdicate" (*KOS*, 57, III, 4). We witness the symbolic death of the king, and then at dawn on the third day he retrieves his scepter: he is resurrected! Saint Vladimir's Day becomes Easter. Muskar XII enters Klow in a grand, triumphal procession. As he passes by, the people hail him and chant the traditional hymn:

Syldavians unite!
Praise our King's might:
The Scepter his right! (*KOS*, p. 21)

When he can again participate in the symbolic meanings, Muskar XII regains all of his strength. He no longer has to rely upon the Thom(p)sons but on his own army whose effectiveness is now more certain. Giving the revolutionaries no time to regroup, he arrests Müsstler and his henchmen. The king's soldiers quickly capture the strategic points of the capital, and the monarchy is restored.

If Muskar XII repeats (*refait*) his predecessor's accomplishments, Tintin revokes (*défait*) the young Baron Staszrvich's misdeeds. Even after five hundred years, Tintin refuses to be the young baron's double. Although Tintin gains possession of the scepter, the very thing the young baron had coveted for himself, our hero returns the symbolic object and restores the Father's

power. He replays the role of the medieval hero but only to interpret it differently. He has no name, no title to defend. He is called "Tintin," neither a
surname nor a first name but only a kind of nickname.[5] Without a father's
name, he has no heritage to preserve and no ancestor to imitate. For his
model of chivalry he follows the person most like him, Joan of Arc. Like
"the Virgin," he has courage, innocence, youth, purity, and the ability to
conquer. To prove to the king's advisers and to the prince himself that his
own skills are superior to those of the two detectives, he solves the mystery of the scepter's theft. His solution stems from his familiarity with the
world of children. Passing in front of a show window full of toys, he figures
out the secret mechanism of the camera. He takes it upon himself to rout
the Bordurians from the kingdom in order to restore the legitimate sovereign. Just as Charles VII was kept hidden from Joan of Arc, so too the king's
many advisers prevent Tintin from revealing to the king the secret that he
knows. When the hero accidentally meets the king for the first time, Tintin
recognizes him immediately, for the prince has a mysterious aura about him.
But equally astonishing is the fact that just as Charles VII trusted Joan, the
king immediately trusts Tintin. He invites him into his car, drives him to the
treasury, and tacitly confers on him the responsibility for handling operations
during the period of upheaval.

After the scepter disappears, the hero becomes distraught, as does everyone in the realm. His passion is parallel to the king's. He sacrifices himself in
the name of the king, as if he were only the substitute for the sovereign. He
suffers from hunger, cold, and lack of sleep, and he risks his life many times.
The villains beat him and drag him on the ground. The Syldavian soldiers
target him as an enemy, for they are as blind as the rest of the population to
the fact that Tintin is working for them. The hero is betrayed, just as Joan of
Arc was, and is nearly destroyed, as is the pelican in the legend. In the end
Tintin escapes everything in order to be "resurrected" with the king.

By receiving the stolen scepter, Muskar XII owes the hero a debt. He
does not repay him by having him join in his triumph, as the maharajah
had done, but decorates him before the whole court: "My Lords, Ladies, and
Gentlemen. Never in our long history has the Order of the Golden Pelican
been conferred upon a foreigner. But today with the full agreement of our
ministers, we bestow this high distinction upon Mr. Tintin, to express our
gratitude for the great service he has rendered to our country" (KOS, 60,
I, 1). The king thus frees Tintin from his childhood. He knights him, giving

him the opportunity to be recognized by the adults as holding the exceptional place he always desired: to be the One. By solemnly pronouncing
him the Golden Pelican, Muskar XII forever associates him with loyalty and
sacrifice. Tintin accepts this honor along with the king's hospitality. He stays
in a royal apartment where the black pelican decorates the medallion above
his bed. Nevertheless, the hero leaves Syldavia without lingering very long.
Perhaps he remembers that the kingdom of old was founded on the castration of the son? Even if he does not sense any present danger, he does not
want to take up permanent residence in this castle.

The album *King Ottokar's Scepter* is important because in it Tintin discovers his definitive character. Although this adventure was republished, it
received the least amount of touching up after the war. Here Hergé reveals most clearly his own political views and perhaps their hopeless naïveté.
The preceding adventures took place against a background of real historical
events. In this adventure, on the contrary, the events take place in the contemporary period, but they try to correct history. Hergé magically "effaces"
the *Anschluss*. He lays out a fictitious historical course conforming more to
his wishes than to reality, but this choice allows him not to have to modify
this album in any essential way later on.

Syldavia's past is inspired by several European dynasties. In the name
Hveghi one can read Hugues, the founder of the Capetian dynasty. Whereas
the Battle of Zileheroum recalls Bouvines, the role of the scepter makes the
Syldavian monarchy constitutional rather than absolute. And the pomp and
circumstance at the finale openly recall the British king George's jubilee
celebrated in 1935. In this adventure Tintin is most directly involved in
political affairs. While the private father figure (Alembick) is ambivalent,
the public one (Muskar XII) is totally positive. After *The Scepter*, whenever
Tintin comes in contact with political power, he does so only from a private
point of view. When he returns to Syldavia, his return has nothing to do
with Muskar XII or his former role in reestablishing Muskar's monarchy.

Hergé never goes back on his convictions, which are rather close to those
of *L'Action française*, the French Monarchist movement. He claims only that
his ideas in this album did not conform to actual historical events and that he
opted temporarily for a utopian view. The last album, where Tintin becomes
a public figure *The Scepter* is also the adventure (after *The Blue Lotus*) where
the public realm is depicted most unrealistically. The Syldavian monarchy
that miraculously escapes the twentieth century recalls fairy tales or the val-

ues of the ancien régime. Nevertheless, its "non-place" (*u-topos*) allows Tintin to engage in politics one last time. The representation of the Good can unequivocally reestablish order in Syldavia, for this country itself is defined as the location of the Good. When Hergé adopts a more realistic vision of history, no other person will embody the Good. The hero is demoted to the level of ordinary private citizen, and his ambitions no longer include restoring a monarchy but, more modestly, finding roots within a family.

## THE FOUNDLING

In the first seven adventures, Tintin is presented as the incarnation of the myth of childhood—more specifically, what Freud called the *Familienroman der Neurotiker*, "the family romance of the neurotic." According to this theory, during the first years of life the infant tends to idealize his parents, to find security among those whom he divinizes and whose orders and values seem to him absolute. Growing up, the child begins to compare his parents with others, alive or imaginary, and comes to discover that they are merely human, fallible, not always sure of themselves, and far from being the almighty lords that his narcissistic daydreaming had imagined. To overcome his disappointment, the child makes up a story about his family origins and invents a fictitious genealogy that better conforms to his need for security and unconditional values. It is not so surprising to him to be deceived by those who have nurtured him if they are not his real parents. He might be adopted, or a foundling, or the offspring of some prestigious people whom he will trace and who will provide him a better example. These invented parents, close to the ideal beings he previously imagined, seem more like the almighty sovereigns who allow the child to idealize himself. Thus, the weak ego of the child assaulted by the external world finds coherence within a paranoid space that conceals and distorts reality. The narcissistic dream does not encounter any obstacle because it has in advance annihilated the social world that would allow the little dreamer to have an accurate sense of himself and his place in reality. Marthe Robert has argued that much of Western literature, including fairy tales and romantic literature and pioneer adventures such as *Don Quixote* and *Robinson Crusoe*, directly reflect this theme of the "family romance" common to numerous individuals, not just neurotics.[6] What results from this fantasy is a common attitude in the face of reality: the foundling in literature turns his back on real life. Dominated by an overly demanding ideal, he refuses women and sexuality, for he aims directly at the infinite. He can content himself with daydreaming, but if he does act, it is to impose his values on the world, even though his actions may be totally imaginary.

This theory offers the key to understanding many traits of Tintin's personality. Indeed, we do not know the hero's parents, and in all the adventures it is impossible to find a single reference to his family. When Hergé is asked if Tintin is an orphan, he responds with a joke or by a rationalization aimed at deflecting his own personal aggression toward parental figures.[7] Nevertheless, if Tintin's family does not exist anywhere, it ends up existing everywhere, especially in the numerous father figures, monarchical or not, that Tintin meets along the way and comes to help.

The characters closest to Tintin, the Thom(p)sons, who are the only ones to appear in all seven of the first albums, are constantly being ridiculed. First he makes fun of them, then he foils their plans, and finally he helps them out. The attitude of the two detectives reveals the hero's unconscious guilt and his need for punishment. In the first episodes up through *King Ottokar's Scepter*, which marks the reconciliation between the foundling and the father figures, the Thom(p)sons pursue the hero and consider him eminently guilty, even though their judgments are always based on false appearances. On three or four occasions they arrest him as a gangster, and Tintin submits to their verdict with a docility astonishing for a hero otherwise so impetuous. Beneath his apparent anticonformism he hides a deeper conformism evidenced by his actions, which constitute police work and result in restoring order. But Tintin never takes on the Father. On the contrary, he refuses the fight that would make him an "Oedipal" rival. He cannot stand any ambivalence in the father figure; so to escape from it, he resorts to a typical pre-Oedipal strategy.

In the first part of Hergé's work, the mother figure is virtually absent. The hero's ideas of women and sexuality seem to stem from an infantile fantasy. Apart from the scene from the film he interrupts in *The Cigars*, the only maternal figure he comes close to is Castafiore. He meets her in Syldavia, and she intends to charm the young man by displaying her operatic talents. Instead of making herself desirable to him, however, the contralto makes him run away because he cannot stand her feminine voice invading his space: "I would have given any excuse to escape," he says (*KOS*, 28, IV, 2). With regard to women, Tintin's only choice seems to be between the primal scene and flight, a choice that amounts to the negation of sexual difference and of sexuality. The hero resolves the problem of the ambivalence of the father figures by a mechanism of isolation. He rarely confronts a single figure that might be both positive and negative; he always separates them into two. The substitute fathers he meets on his path exist in pairs or, when they are not doubles, Tintin has trouble interpreting their behavior, thus allowing him to deny their hostility (Mr. Wang). The obligation to make the Father innocent is all the stronger when the Father has no wish to kill the son or no interest in subjecting the other to any sort of sadistic violence. In the Congo, Tintin meets a father figure split into two: the good Father who saves him from death several times, and the wicked Tom, dressed up in a priest's cassock, who tries to kill him. In America, Bobby Smiles first seems to have the traits of a police detective but then turns out to be a henchman of Al Capone. The United States is the land of Evil, as is the Soviet Union, and thus Tintin does not encounter any positive father figures in those places.

In *The Cigars of the Pharaoh*, he confronts four father figures. First is Professor Sophocles Sarcophagus, who is initially suspected of being in cahoots with Rastapopoulos (in the first version),[8] but then he is found innocent and considered simply irresponsible. Because he is injected with the poison *radjaidjah*, he ignores the consequences of his actions when he tries to stab Tintin or shoots at him point-blank. The second, Señor Oliveira da Figueira, suffers the same sort of transformation from one version to the next. Initially he is a criminal, then he recovers his innocence, and later he saves the hero's life. With regard to Rastapopoulos as a Father, Tintin is of two minds. Although he is strongly attracted by this energetic man, the hero discovers his true character only at the end. Finally, with regard to the maharajah, Tintin acts as he does later with Muskar XII: Tintin himself bolsters the weakened Father. Thus, he reverses the normal process of creation. It is no longer the Father who engenders the son but the son who allows the Father to exist and to lay down the Law. By this imaginary reversal, the hero hopes to escape conflict, or in other words, to be able to lead a life outside the law and yet to maintain the structure of order intact.

Tintin's anxiety about the father figure is particularly noticeable in the dream sequence in *The Cigars*. Tintin has just entered the pyramid of Kih-Oskh, the most forbidden place, where the Father his hidden his arsenal (the cigars). The hero comes close to acquiring the Oedipal knowledge when he holds in his hand a "cigar of the pharaoh" that he learns much later may not be touched (*CP*, 61, IV, 2). At the moment, he does not have the time to break open the object to discover its secret, which he learns at the end of the adventure in the presence of the maharajah. At the moment when he could resolve the enigma of the Father, Tintin falls prey to the influence of a drug. Before he slips into unconsciousness, his fantasies reveal to him part of the truth, the secret of his relation to the Father (*CP*, 9, II, 2, 3; III, 1, 2).

The first panel shows Tintin imagining himself and Snowy being mummified. He realizes the threat that the Father imposes on him because of his transgression, namely, that he knows what the child is not supposed to know, the scene that he is not supposed to witness without being punished. In panel 2, the green fumes from the drug (green for the color of rejuvenation in the Egyptian religion) are spreading. Tintin is on all fours like a dog, suggesting the regression to the anal stage, and he sees two figures. The larger is no doubt the pharaoh who is coming to get him. Farther in the background is Anubis, the god-jackal, who presides at funerals and embalm-

Panel 1: "No! Not that!!" *CP*, 9, II, 2, 3; III, 1, 2. © Hergé/Moulinsart 2007.

ings. He holds an umbrella, an ambiguous object that has both cultural and individual meanings. The umbrella evokes both the hook that Osiris carries on Judgment Day and the phallic instrument of Professor Sarcophagus. In panel 3, Tintin discovers the forbidden scene. The Thom(p)sons, as archaic parental figures, are slightly differentiated as male and female. The figure on the left is smoking a cigar. He is wearing a "phallic" serpent on his hat and a masculine toga. The figure on the right is feminized.[9] "He" lights his partner's cigar in a gesture of submission. He does not have any masculine attributes and wears a queen's toga that identifies "his" femininity. In the background, Sophocles Sarcophagus reiterates the father figure by carrying a box of cigars, symbols of power and sexuality. We can interpret this scene as a substitute, allowable by the censor, of the primal scene. The Thom(p)sons roll their big eyes, like the strict parents in children's fantasies. Their threatening looks are directed at Tintin, the voyeur of the scene. In panel 4, the hero's voyeurism immediately leads to punishment. The judgment is rendered; one executes the sentence. A box of cigars floats above the scene as a reminder of the Law. We can distinguish in this image two scenes condensed into one: the left part of the panel precedes the right. On the left, Tintin is carried by two creatures down to his tomb. One of the porters is Rastapopoulos dressed as an Egyptian. The other is a kind of "Tintinian" interpretation of the god Anubis: the head of the jackal is replaced by that of Snowy. Here the hero's companion becomes his judge, for he rolls his eyes as the other figures do. The balance of power is reversed: the animal dominates the man, while preserving his human characteristics. The first version of this album clearly indicates that Tintin is being taken down to the sea, whose color green resembles that of the narcotic fumes. The second half of the image reiterates the first but makes it more explicit. The Father condemns the hero for returning to the origin, the Mother. One sees Tintin become tiny, a mere baby, crying anxiously in his sarcophagus-crib. The mummy's wrappings become the infant's swaddling clothes. Above his crib, a menacing Sarcophagus simply looks on rather than comforts him, and the father-professor does not hide his satisfaction at having the son at his mercy.

After *The Cigars*, Tintin always meets up with father figures split into two—the one good and the other bad. The exception to this rule is General Alcazar, an ambivalent Father who honors the hero and then condemns him to death. He represents Hergé's first attempt to present a more realistic, unified father figure. But in contact with such a Father, Tintin sees his own imaginary, superhuman power melt: the ambivalent Father corresponds to the son deprived of his magical powers and having to confront the world with more realistic forces. Hergé chooses to go back to the principle of twinness, of splitting, that allows him to deal with the issue of guilt. In effect, if the "bad" double makes the Father innocent of the murderous desires the son attributes to him, the process is equally applicable to the son. Tintin is constantly encountering brothers filled with desires he does not recognize or understand, thus allowing him to preserve his assumed innocence. The young boys he meets have in common that they are all foundlings, but in order not to see himself in them, Tintin has to deny their "twinness" so that he can remain the One, the Unique. Thus, he constantly tries to reintegrate them with their families, either their own (as the case of the son of the maharajah) or an adoptive family (Chang and, later, Zorrino). The most complex case is Didi's, who is most like Tintin's twin. He is the character closest to the Oedipal situation and threatens to castrate the Father in retaliation for his own castration. Nevertheless, Tintin manages to silence the twin whose madness makes him talk too much. He "cures" him by invoking a traditional father figure common in Hergé's work: the professor. Professor Fang-Se-yeng, friend of Mr. Wang, finds the remedy for the terrible poison.

The refusal to engage in open rivalry and the constant retreat to the more reassuring pre-Oedipal phase explain the hero's characteristics. Resembling characters from fairy tales, Tintin has no personal life or even a real name. More like a nickname, his name is a play on words derived perhaps from the French word for "childish," *enfantin*, or perhaps from the famous illustrator of fables, Benjamin Rabier. Tintin's exploits strongly resemble the Titans' feats from mythology. The hero's capacity for metamorphosis allows him to escape the constraints of the real world. Pursued by the Thom(p)sons, who themselves have the ability to show up everywhere without justifying their appearance, Tintin can morph into an aging woman or an old villager. He also changes into a monkey, a giraffe, a black, a Japanese general, a kid from Chicago, and so on. His mighty powers are, of course, as totally fictitious as those of the forces of Evil that he combats. He simply projects onto the external world the ambivalent, "double" structure of the father figure as his sole "effective" means of escaping ambivalence and relativism, that is, avoiding an adult conception of the social and familial world. Tintin is the little boy who can never grow up, and he understands the world as one big family. That explains why in the first episodes he ignores the differences between individuals and cultures. Jumping constantly from the sublime to the ridiculous, he pushes his adventures to epic proportions rather than simply remain the central character.

With romantic heroes Tintin shares a pessimistic view of the world and projects onto that world a narrowness of spirit as well as the lack of love and unity that comes only from his own immaturity. As Marthe Robert writes, "The romantic desire is always divided between a genuinely Promethean ambition and a mystical communion with 'the world soul' that is the other side of megalomania."[10] Tintin's Herculean feats, which aim at nothing less than imposing on the world his own obsession with the Good and his misunderstanding of sexuality, are as striking as they are imaginary. The hero can do everything because he embodies the dreams of a powerless child who never has an adult relationship. Tintin never marries and, as far as we can tell, never accepts money. Lost in a symbolic universe of the circulation of individuals and material goods, he tries magically to restore paradise on earth, the state of innocence of the little boy before he comes to understand reality. Lacking the power to regain paradise lost (except in those rare moments when he meets up with someone like Chang, who shares his worldview), the hero flees from the corrupt world to find Mother Nature. There, as in the later case of the Yeti, he finds himself on the level of the animals, understands their language, takes care of them, becomes their master, and uses their brute strength for his own work. In short, he takes Snowy's place and regresses to a prior state of indeterminacy. Nature does not seem hostile because his soul lives in unison with the world soul. Other times, Tintin escapes into Robinson Crusoe adventures: he searches for a deserted island where he can restore paradise lost. But the Father, whom he can never definitively eliminate, gets there first and establishes his kingdom of exchange and death. For Tintin each island he lands on becomes a "black" island. He has to start all over again, forever carrying out the same feats. The villains he combats are not flesh-and-blood creatures but midnight phantoms incarnating Evil, evaporating in the light of day.

In the first seven adventures, the hero has no personal history because he refuses situations of real conflict. He accumulates nothing, learns nothing, and has no traits that make him an ordinary human being. His first adventures are like an epic cycle; Tintin always returns to the same starting point because experience makes no mark on him. Everything he could learn about the world he projects onto the "doubles" that Hergé lets disappear as soon as he creates them. This explains why Tintin never ages. In the beginning he lives in an apartment on Labrador Street. "Labrador," of course, is the name of both a kind of rescue dog and a desertlike region. This name is revealing. Despite his wanderings around the world, nothing from those trips ever enters his home, for he keeps no personal souvenirs. There are no indications that he has any kind of personal life, let alone personal feelings. His original home is totally conventional, but also a bit cold and sterile, compared with the warmth of Marlinspike Hall, where he lives later on. His apartment reproduces the bareness of a monk's cell or a jail cell.[11]

The absence of any kind of personal life plus his inexplicable "birth" makes the hero a "soteriological character," one focused totally on salvation.[12] As the Christ, he is the savior of the world corrupted by sin. Miracles are his daily bread. He neither loves nor hates; he is obsessed with the Good, which he believes he incarnates. The spiritual salvation he tries to impose on the world works in the first instance on Snowy. His companion is the constant victim of his master's sadistic demands. When Snowy wants a little break or simply looks for some enjoyment (to have a drink or chew on something tasty), Tintin shows up to prevent him from satisfying his desires. Pleasure counts for nothing in the eyes of the superman whose sole task is to restore the world's lost innocence.

At the beginning of his work, Hergé probably projected much of himself onto Tintin, who physically resembles him and who associates the Good with the absolutist right-wing ideology. Nevertheless, actual historical experience gradually separated the author from his character. Although Tintin manages to prevent the *Anschluss*, Hergé knew perfectly well that Hitler was preparing for war and that fascism was only a caricature of the ideas Hergé defended. After *King Ottokar's Scepter*—the high point of both Tintin's representation as savior of the world and of the adventures' antirealism—the author took a new look at his hero. From then on, the character of Captain Haddock was going to confront Tintin's imaginary powers.

# PART TWO
# HADDOCK

Why bastard? Wherefore base?
When my dimensions are as well compact,
My mind as generous, and my shape as true,
As honest madam's issue?

—*King Lear*, I, 2

## CHAPTER SEVEN

# THE CAPTAIN WITH THE GOLDEN CLAWS

### "DO A TINTIN"

If Tintin is his famous tuft of hair, and the Thom(p)sons their frowning eyebrows, Haddock is above all a mouth—an enormous, eager, greedy mouth, almost always open, tongue out, or teeth sometimes bared. The captain's relation to the external world is lived in the oral mode, passionately and voluptuously. His mouth can just as well kiss or bite, swallow or spit. He rumbles, cries, yells, howls, and threatens. He smokes a pipe, drinks from the bottle, and devours anything he can get hold of when hungry. He sings, dribbles, drools, spits, blows into things he likes, kisses the ones he loves, and has jaws as wide as those of Rabelais's Panurge. He laughs or weeps at high volume and wildly yells for help or chases someone away with equal vehemence. He bursts with affection and with loathing. He doesn't just insult people—he barks at them. But the richness of his vocabulary transcends the level of the dog: his "barkings" are legendary. The wise Tibetan monks recognize the truth and call him "Rumbling Thunder." Like Snowy, Haddock wants to enjoy the good things of life, the taste of comfort and repose, spiced with some intermittent flirting. But also like Snowy, he is rather grumpy, sometimes has a bad conscience, and of course, always has that strong propensity toward alcoholism. Snowy and Haddock understand each other in a flash! If Haddock whines at his fate, however, Snowy—hardly moved at all by any signs of remorse—takes advantage of the situation to sip from the captain's glass. As a realist, the dog finds it a shame to let good whiskey go to waste (*CGC*, 16, I, 1).

Snowy and Haddock almost never speak to each other. They sniff each other out so well and are so much alike that they have no need for explanations. One never knows if they ever fight. Their friendship is unassuming, happy, and without misgivings. The captain comes to take Snowy's place, or, rather, he shares that place in Tintin's life, suggesting that for the first time Tintin actually has a personal life. Having lived so long harmoniously, even symbiotically, with the world of animals and nature, the hero finally enters the complex adult world and shares feelings with his peers. Although none of the young boys encountered on the preceding adventures has left any lasting mark on the hero, Haddock attaches himself to Tintin with the ferocious loyalty of a dog. Thus, Snowy's role becomes less important. Since *The Blue Lotus*, Snowy has lost his "gift of gab." He is no longer the privileged interlocutor. The master relegates him to the animal world from which he had initially managed to extract him. With the arrival of Haddock, the human realm and the animal realm are definitively separated. The animals are no longer described in terms of their affinities with humans but simply according to biological criteria.

*The Crab with the Golden Claws* begins with the episode of Snowy's getting his snout stuck in a can of crab. Similarly, Tintin not only sticks his nose into garbage cans but also follows the trail of one kind of "filth" to another, all the way to a carton of crabs constituting the cargo of the ship *Karaboudjan*. Once again the hero is unknowingly diverted to an opium-trafficking ring organized by a notable Moroccan from Bagghar, a certain Omar Ben Salaad. The ringleader's principal henchman is Allan Thompson, the foil for Rastapopoulos in the episodes where he last appeared. Like Dr. Müller, Allan is happy only in supporting roles, as a shadow to the great scoundrels whom he so much admires. He kidnaps Tintin and keeps him prisoner in the hold of his ship leaving for the coast of Morocco. The *Karaboudjan* is in a worse situation than Syldavia on the eve of Müsstler's occupation. The "king" of the ship, Captain Haddock—theoretically the only master aboard after God—has been dethroned by the forces of Evil. He is prisoner not only of his second mate but especially of himself, his vice—alcohol. Little does he know that his cargo consists of opium, hidden in tin cans of "crabmeat." The captain, always just two steps from a crisis of delirium tremens, cannot distinguish Good from Evil. Like the Thom(p)sons, who cannot tell the difference between real and counterfeit coins, Haddock lives at the level of appearances. When Allan betrays him, Haddock does not stop calling him "brother" because he is too drunk to tell the difference (*CGC*, 16, III, 2). Despite his inebriated condition, Haddock continues to hold the position of authority, so his second mate has to make the others obey by sheer force. Luckily, Tintin's presence aboard ship shatters the world of appearances. Just as Macbeth reacts upon losing his ill-gained powers, the insecure second mate allows the violence to escalate. Allan continually beats up his subordinates, the only ones who could prevent salvation by the exterminating angel, Tintin. The *Karaboudjan* is the foulest place the hero has encountered. Even the corrupt city of Chicago, where the police give the high sign to the gangsters, is less damned than the cargo ship. On the ship there is only one just person, the deposed captain, who sinks into dementia.

Although the previous adventure of *The Scepter* marked a success for Tintin, the fact that Hergé reverted to fiction rather than "live" reporting about contemporary events was much more an indication of defeat. This state of affairs led to a diminution of the hero's paranoia and of his merely imaginary power. *The Crab* marks his real entrance into the community of human beings. For the first time, he takes up his adventure with an "older brother." But Haddock is more miserable, more down and out, than any of Tintin's former young companions. Now the hero has to save not a whole country but, more realistically, only one person. Because Haddock is so bogged down in his chaotic world of drink, for the hero to salvage this wreck from the bottom will require as much energy as saving an entire nation. If Tintin does not have a life of his own, at least for the first time he comes up against a real person worthy of his aid, even if that person seems at first a total neurotic. The young hero does not wish to be a psychoanalyst but a redeemer: he has to lead the lost sheep back to the path of redemption. Tintin plays the role of the good angel in Haddock's life, and thus Haddock no more questions Tintin's bursting into his cabin than a pious child doubts the appearances of the Virgin Mary. The captain follows Tintin with the same naïve faith.

True, their first encounter is a shock: Haddock receives a blow on the head, and then Tintin crashes on top of him. To reach the porthole where he wants to board the ship, Tintin uses a rope that will take on symbolic value in the following albums: the rope signifies their indestructible friendship. Less heavy to carry than a chain and allowing for more flexibility between the partners, the rope proves to be very strong. If one of them tries to cut it so as not to drag the other to death, he cannot do it. Tintin treats the captain the way he has treated Snowy: at first he threatens him, then he reasons with

. him, and finally he lets him act the way the captain wants to confirm the good results of his lessons. Since Haddock's madness is more curable than Didi Wang's, Tintin tries to bring him to reason without the aid of substitute parents. He challenges him by invoking his capacity for judgment. He reminds him of his "old mother," at which point the captain bursts into tears. Tintin especially appeals to his moral conscience: "You must promise to stop drinking. Think of your reputation, Captain!" (*CGC*, 18, I, 1). The hero encourages his companion "to do a Tintin," or in other words, not only to lay off the whiskey but, even more, to imitate him as his model.[1] Haddock promises and remains committed to this young man forever. Of course, he will drink again, but he never falls as low as he had before.

For the first time, Tintin enters the complex adult world without resorting to a process of dissociation. Now there are not twin Haddocks, as in the case of the Alembicks, but only one Haddock, who is ambivalent, both positive and negative, affectionate and violent, courageous and cowardly. What the foundling still does not know is that in the fraternal struggle with the captain, the victor is not the one you expect.

## THE ROAD TO DAMASCUS

From now on the mimetic rivalry is no longer projected onto the external world but is part of the dynamics between the pair Tintin-Haddock that replaces Tintin-Snowy. In the first round of their struggle, the hero tries to draw the captain toward the theological heights that constitute his own universe: "do a Tintin"; follow the absolute Good. After his solemn promise, Haddock surely slips up two or three times, but the young hero is not discouraged. He refuses to abandon his miserable new friend, even when he continually undoes what the other tries so hard to make him do.

Haddock's conversion can easily be read in psychoanalytic terms, and indeed, from now on, Hergé's own work operates at the juncture of religion and psychology. Through Tintin, Haddock lives out his destructive drives, either turned on himself or toward others. Then when he hits bottom, he can rise back up to where his life begins anew. At first, Tintin tries a moralistic approach, one he knows well: "*We* aren't gangsters!" (*CGC*, 26, II, 1). After each relapse, he makes his companion loudly confess his errors, like a medieval penitent: "I'm sorry! I'm sorry! I'm a miserable wretch! I drank the rum I found in the locker! I'm sorry!" (*CGC*, 20, III, 3). Tintin absolves the sinner, who will survive his trial and find his road to Damascus in order to get rid of his former self entirely. He who sins by thirst will be punished by thirst. Haddock lands in the Sahara with his friend. Walking under the burning sun in the desert, without a drop to drink, he hits bottom. When he realizes the kind of death awaiting him, he wanders around in a daze, repeating over and over: "The land of thirst! The land of thirst!" He lets himself be guided by his good angel, without any desire other than to live. One of the most memorable images shows the two of them walking side by side in the immense desert (*CGC*, 30, 30, IV). Snowy is running ahead, carrying a camel's bone in his mouth, while the two men are seen from behind. Tintin is carrying their coats and holding the captain by the hand like a child. They walk a very long time, lose consciousness, and pass out next to each other. Only the help of some camel drivers saves them at the last moment. In the course of this symbolic death, Haddock gets rid of his former self, while Tintin abandons the foundling's daydreaming to confront his own psychic reality.

One detail at the end of the album regarding the implicit twinness uniting Tintin with the captain is especially noteworthy. In one episode Haddock experiences a mishap that his friend has experienced repeatedly in former adventures. Although the captain is full of good intentions to help the Moroccan police and thus to demonstrate his willingness to obey the law, two policemen fiercely pursue him, beat him up, and arrest him. Nevertheless, this incident does not exactly replicate the relationship between Tintin and the Thom(p)sons because the misunderstanding is quickly resolved and the policemen are not twins, even though they do bear a striking resemblance to the Thom(p)sons (*CGC*, 63, I, 2).

The discovery of the captain's unconscious provides the opportunity to look more deeply into the psyche of the hero as well. This exploration of the foundling's unconscious is all the more violent because at that time Hergé was still ignorant of psychoanalytic theory. He later admits to being passionately interested in psychoanalysis.[2]

The hold of the *Karaboudjan* contains two different contraband goods: opium and champagne. The first is sold by the kind of gangsters like Rastapopoulos, who uses it both to numb the weaker individuals and to offer the general public fictitious pleasures, the realization of their most secret fantasies. The second kind of contraband seems less offensive, but it is still morally forbidden. After all, alcohol makes one drunk, and if Tintin believes he can drink it freely, the unfolding of events proves otherwise. Of course, Haddock is totally oblivious to what is going on within the hold of his ship

("Me? I'm an honest man!"), just as innocent as a person whose overly strict superego prevents the libidinal drives from becoming conscious. Tintin intends to bring to light the captain's hidden drives and to confirm his plea of innocence. In making him leave the *Karaboudjan*, Tintin hopes to separate the captain once and for all from the source of Evil where for too long he has been "drinking like a sailor."

Champagne is a drink that frequently shows up in Hergé's work. The first time the hero drinks some,[3] he quickly becomes drunk and finds himself in bed next to Snowy, who is as sloshed as he is. At that period, the hero's companion is more of a young man than an animal. In those albums, sexuality is completed denied, as much for obvious social reasons (Hergé has to submit to the laws for publishing materials for young people) as for the deeper meaning of the story (Tintin is a pre-Oedipal hero who does not know about sexual difference). Sexuality is denied and repressed. One cannot really say that the sexuality is disguised to make it acceptable because it is not even recognized to exist.

One can make the case that drinking champagne—the festive drink for celebrating special social occasions such as weddings—is an unconscious equivalent of having sex. The oblong shape of the bottle's neck and the foamy froth that suddenly spills out are rather obvious phallic symbols. If this hypothesis is justified, then the latent homosexual desire that occurs in Germany (the land of Evil after the war of 1914) between Tintin and Snowy (*Milou* in French can be read as a nickname for a boy named *Émile*) reappears in *The Crab*. In the hold of the ship—the place of the unconscious, of Sin—Tintin proposes to his young friend: "My dear Snowy, let me offer you a drink" (*CGC*, 15, III, 1). This offer is astonishing because Tintin himself usually doesn't drink but especially because it goes against his usual strict prohibition against serving alcohol to minors. However, not only does Tintin not get to enact his proposal but his very desire gets him into trouble. Popping the cork from the bottle alerts his pursuers to his whereabouts. The hero is punished without even consummating the act. This same desire reappears later between Haddock and his new friend. Crossing the desert offers them the occasion for plunging most deeply into their inner selves. The captain feels an irresistible, irrepressible need for champagne. Even if only a few hours earlier he denies knowing anything about what is stored in the hold of his ship, he now "fantasizes" about this particular beverage, even though he normally drinks whiskey (*CGC*, 32, II, 2, 3, 4; III, 2, 3; IV, 1).

Panel 4: "A bottle of champagne! I'll open it!"
Panel 6: "This confounded cork; it won't come out!" "You brute, take that!"
*CGC*, 32, II, 2, 3, 4; III, 2 (Panel 1), 3; IV, 1 (Panel 6). © Hergé/Moulinsart 2007.

Before this scene, Haddock has just met Tintin and is impressed by his many talents and perhaps even a little jealous of his continual success. He already likes this young man enormously and wants to keep him close by. It is Haddock, after all, who burns the oars of the lifeboat so that Tintin can get warm again. Now, in the desert, he has just passed out; his unconscious, freed from the daily censor, can express itself more openly. Haddock identifies Tintin with the drink itself and attempts to rape his young companion, a rape prevented by Snowy. Again, if homosexual desire emerges here with an uncommon virulence, its urge cannot be satisfied.

In *The Adventures of Tintin*, there is another "forbidden" drink that appears more rarely: red wine, the drink more common than champagne, associated for better or worse with the working class, and even with working-class sexuality as more open and uninhibited than that of the middle class.[4] Red, the color of blood, is opposed to white, the color of purity, particularly prevalent in the adventure in Tibet. Although Hergé claims he avoids showing any blood, which he loathes, it nevertheless appears on several occasions. The first time is in the original version of the Congo adventure, when Snowy bites off the tail of the lion, the king of animals. Tintin's young companion thus accomplishes the secret act that later on Didi Wang and the young Baron Staszrvich dream of: the castration of the Father (*AH*, I, p. 221). The deed's violence is softened a bit in the later versions, where no blood is shown flowing from the cut-off tail (*TC*, 23, I, 3).

Blood appears a second time in *The Blue Lotus*. Tintin has just met Chang, and the two friends decide to be photographed to have a souvenir of their meeting. The photographer, however, is a bandit from Mitsuhirato's gang, and his camera conceals a submachine gun. He aims at the pair of friends and wounds Tintin in his left arm. If from one version to another Hergé wipes out the traces of blood, in the most recent versions he keeps in the scene of Chang's wiping the blood flowing from his friend's wounded arm (*BL*, 49, III, 5). Blood is mentioned one other time in a context equally suggestive of sexuality. In the opening of *The Castafiore Emerald*, Haddock is bitten by a little Gypsy girl who lives in the wild, who lives "in Evil"—filth (the sewers). He remarks: "Look at that! She's drawn blood, that little wildcat!" (*CE*, 2, III, 3).

*The Crab* is an album filled not with blood but with red wine. In contrast to champagne, this drink symbolizes a more primitive, undifferentiated sexuality of uncontrolled violence, a pleasure that finds its source in the most basic drives and in which blood always has its part.

Panel 1: "Aha! There's a bottle of wine!" "Where can he see a bottle?"
Panel 2: "I'll uncork it." *CGC*, 34, IV, 1–3. © Hergé/Moulinsart 2007.

The first time red wine appears is in Tintin's dream that seems to be a response to the phantasmic appeal of Captain Haddock (*CGC*, 34, IV, 1, 3). The scene reproduces the previous situation: Tintin and the captain have just passed out, their consciences asleep.[5] The hero recognizes his companion's sexual desire, but he gives it a more violent and anxiety-ridden interpretation. He imagines himself stuck in a bottle of red wine—a prisoner as he was in his previous dream with the sarcophagus-crib. The figure of the captain is ambiguous: it may represent homosexual desire or the ogre devouring a child, an image generally interpreted as "the Bad Mother."[6] On the one hand, the captain's smile suggests an act of engulfing: he wants "to drink" Tintin. On the other hand, the corkscrew suggests a threat of bodily penetration. In panel 3 one can literally see the desire for "red wine" in the captain's look: his eyes have changed into bottles. Here there is a veritable, visual "erection," his eyes glittering with lust. After passing out, Tintin completely represses the nightmare he had foreseen. Several hours later, Lieutenant Delcourt offers him and Haddock a drink. Although it is untrue (we've seen him order a "szprädj" in the Syldavian restaurant in *The Scepter*), Tintin tells the officer that he "never touches spirits" (*CGC*, 35, IV, 1). Following his example, and to expiate the wicked thoughts that had previously overwhelmed him, Haddock also virtuously refuses a drink. But a minute later, his "newfound virtue" doesn't prevent him from stealing the lieutenant's bottles and carrying them off. Just when Haddock is about to take a gulp from the bottle of red wine, a bullet smashes it, and once more Haddock finds his desire frustrated. This scene of the "denial" of "sexual" consumption is particularly important, one that Hergé uses to illustrate the cover of the album.

A bit later in the adventure one returns to the issue of red wine. Tintin and the captain are trapped by the bandits in a wine cellar in Bagghar. The wine cellar is like the hold of the ship: the traffickers use it to store both opium and alcohol. When the bullets from the revolver hit the barrels, the wine spills onto the ground. Tintin tries to take control of the situation—"Now then, no nonsense! This isn't the time for drinking" (*CGC*, 57, I, 3)—but in vain. The fumes from the alcohol affect their brains, including Snowy's. Moments later we see the three of them very happy, presumably having committed "the forbidden act." As Snowy dances on his hind legs and Haddock yodels, Tintin sings at the top of his lungs the aria from Boieldieu's opera *The Lady in White*.[7] This drunkenness on the part of all three of them liberates the captain's brute strength and, ironically, contributes to saving the group. Armed with a liter of red wine, Haddock chases his aggressors, incited by Tintin to go after them—like a dog: "Go on! Ssk! SSk! Bite 'em!" The drinking session—liberating in every sense of the word—constitutes the baptism of an indestructible friendship.

The road to Damascus is only one aspect of the captain's redemption. On the one hand, he learns to control his drives, and at the end of the album he is not only a member of the Sailors' Anti-Alcoholism Society but even its president. On the other, by meeting up with Haddock, Tintin learns to recognize his own desires. At the beginning, Haddock is more or less everything Tintin doesn't want to be. What Tintin shares with the captain goes beyond an unconscious and constantly repressed homosexual desire. Haddock allows the hero to open up to an inner world of fantasies and desires, while Tintin in exchange allows the sailor to display his own desire, no longer belonging to the universe of Evil but to a kind of shared innocence. Although the acts of aggression or sexuality are presented as fantasies incited by something external, such as drugs or alcohol, the two friends can satisfy their desires while not transgressing the law that forbids them.

## THE BASTARD

The transition from the religious to the psychological point of view entails another shift in emphasis. From now on, top billing goes more or less to Captain Haddock. Like Tintin, Haddock can be connected to the "family romance," which he also represents in a certain way.

When a little boy acquires some knowledge of human sexuality, he comes to modify the myth of his family origin. He discovers that the identity of the actual father is never certain, and this discovery allows him to invent his own family history. His mother has had sexual relations with other men—more prestigious ones, of course—but that makes him a bastard rather than just the foundling, as he had previously imagined. The "demotion" from foundling to bastard resulting from these imaginings about the Mother comes at the moment of the Oedipal crisis and is the reverse of the tendency to idealize the mother figure. Thinking of the Mother as a woman "desirable" to other men, not just to the Father, allows the child to satisfy in good conscience the Oedipal drives that push him toward her at the same time.

According to Marthe Robert, the image of the bastard dominates nineteenth-century literature, and she analyzes its main characteristics in authors ranging from Stendhal to Honoré de Balzac. As opposed to the introverted foundling, the bastard takes advantage of knowing that those who conquer society and build their own empires follow Napoleon as the model of all bastards, from Vautrin to Julien Sorel. The bastard wants all the signs of success: women, money, power, and distinction. He treats the world as a battlefield. He doesn't try to transform the world by imposing his own values on it, as does his twin; rather, he wants to avenge himself and take advantage of everything the world has to offer to satisfy his desire to dominate. In another work, Marthe Robert shows that Gustave Flaubert—as much in his life as in his work—is conflicted between the attitude of the foundling and that of the bastard.[8] Their explicit conflict lies at the heart of the author's existence as well as at the source of his stories and literary career. The foundling embraces literature as he had embraced religion. The author as the foundling imposes on himself a rigorous rule for style that he pursues his entire life, just as the penitent puts on a hair shirt forever. The ideal style that Flaubert strives to achieve, if perfected, would escape the ordinary contingencies of writing and become a kind of absolute in its own right, that is, a substitute for religious language.

The same duality exists in Hergé's work and perhaps also in his life. Besides the celebrated Hergé enjoying his success, the brilliant and worldly lover of life's pleasures shown him by his friends,[9] there is also Hergé the rigorous artist, working for more than fifty years at the same task. Hergé complains of being tied to Tintin like a convict to his ball and chain, yet he constantly wants to improve his style. His fanatical perfectionism is legendary. He spends sometimes five or six years completing one adventure. Contrary to Flaubert's, Hergé's clarity of style aimed not to transcend the contingencies of history but to become the most precise witness of an era. This was Hergé's way of escaping temporality. His albums constitute a first-rate compendium of contemporary life, almost a catalogue of twentieth-century material civilization. The author surrounded himself with specialists charged with reproducing actual objects, places, or individuals with the greatest possible accuracy.

The fundamental duality between rigor and success is already noticeable in the first two albums, where Hergé attributes to Snowy or Tintin characteristics of the foundling and the bastard. Beginning with *Tintin in America*, Hergé more carefully inserts each of these tendencies into a different character. Beginning with *The Crab*, then, it is only natural that Haddock takes the place of the fox terrier in the role of the unrepentant pleasure seeker. But to be more precise, one has to see that the captain possesses traits even Tintin had formerly exhibited. Indeed, in *The Land of the Soviets*, it is Tintin the hero who has a penchant for alcohol and hurls insults at people—the same traits found later in the mouth of his companion Haddock. It is Tintin whom we see in the first version of *The Congo* dressed like a dandy from the 1930s going into the Grand Hotel. Finally, it is Tintin, or his ancestor Totor, whom we see reaching the Oedipal stage and pitting himself against the Father to win the woman (*AH*, I, p. 37). Pursuing worldly values is incompatible with the rigorous ideal Tintin otherwise embodies. Thus, Hergé chooses to limit the personality of his character by attributing to him the main traits of the foundling, without totally stripping him of the opposite tendencies. In *The Broken Ear*, for example, Tintin discovers his resemblance to the bastard, but this is the only album written before 1940 in the "lighter" style that cuts through the unremitting seriousness of the others. This is also the adventure where the hero loses his imaginary powers. He is carried in triumph by Alcazar's partisans, but he has not accomplished anything. All he has done is to profit from a play on words under the influence of alcohol at the moment he is about to be shot. This episode really belongs to the character of the bastard that Hergé does not hesitate to revive in *The Crab with the Golden Claws*.

Although his last bottle of spirits has just been shattered, the captain, half sloshed, leaves his place behind the sand dune and rushes to assault the Berber bandits while hurling insults at them. He believes that his howling alone is sufficient to make the enemies flee, but he learns later that his heroism was merely bogus. The men sent by Lieutenant Delcourt managed by themselves, with their rifles, to rout the enemy (*CGC*, pp. 39–40).

In *The Broken Ear*, Tintin cannot resist the prestige of the uniform. He accepts Alcazar's offer of the rank of colonel and title of chief of staff to the new head of state. In this album, for the first time, he also pits himself against the ambivalent father figures. We see him fighting Alcazar, at first only playing a game (he beats him at chess), then in the real game of politics, in making some decisions that the general refuses to ratify (breaking with General American Oil). He also has a rivalry with Ridgewell, who at first tries to chase Tintin out of the forest so that he can remain sole master among the Arumbayas. But Hergé tries to correct this image in the following episodes, particularly in *The Scepter*. He does so because if Tintin too readily gives in to his penchant for the vanities of the world, he loses not only his soul but also the omnipotence that makes him a special sort of hero.

The arrival of Haddock into the series allows for the opposition between the two tendencies without risking the heroic character of Tintin. As the inverse of the hero, defined now as an orphan, the captain immediately calls to mind his origins. Tintin reminds him of that when he says: "What would your old mother say finding you in this state?" (*CGC*, 18, I, 1). At that point the captain bursts into tears, dramatized even more in the original version, which uses capital letters for the sobs of the drunkard: "MAMA! MAMA!" (*AH*, IV, p. 279). Whereas the mother figure is evoked in such a distinctively Oedipal way, Haddock's (biological) father, in contrast, is never mentioned. Thus, the captain feels freer to invent for himself a more prestigious lineage. He discovers a famous ancestor, rich and titled, Lord François de Hadoque, who compensates for the modesty of his actual origins.[10] Of course, Haddock only gradually reveals the defining traits of the bastard. In *The Crab*, the revenge of infantile love is too pronounced for him to know how to take advantage of it in the real world. Moreover, except during their first encounter, the moral demands that the foundling imposes on the captain are too strong for him to freely express the bastard's tendency toward sexual enjoyment. Although this tendency does not cease to exist, it manifests itself most crudely in the captain's immoderate love of drink, with all the ambiguities that one can read into such a desire.

# CHAPTER EIGHT

# THE END OF A WORLD

## PRELUDE TO THE APOCALYPSE

After Tintin meets the captain, he senses that his life has changed even though he still does not understand the sailor's role in his existence. *The Shooting Star* marks the final attempt of the foundling to rid himself of the bastard and to preserve the integrity of his former values. The rivalry between Tintin and Haddock, however, is not just a question of the one being introverted and the other extroverted, or of absolute, religious values opposing secular, worldly ones. In 1942, when Hergé drafted the first version of *The Star*, the time was one of political engagement. Tintin tries one last time to return to his origins and to ignore the presence of Archibald Haddock. Even the Thom(p)sons are absent from this adventure, as they were from the first two.

The end of an epoch is also a new beginning. The album's first thirteen pages are devoted exclusively to the hero. He is taking a walk in a fictitious city, similar to the Moscow of his first exploits, populated with shadows without substance. The people he meets seem unreal; they are simply the witnesses of events they passively record. If the passersby are mute, Snowy in contrast significantly recovers his former talkativeness, at least for several pages. Attracted by a mysterious star that constantly gets bigger and bigger in the sky, Tintin telephones the observatory, but his report is received without interest. Not discouraged by this reaction, he goes to visit the observatory to find out more. The foundling does not like it when the adults keep secrets. Again, they slam the door in his face. Here, the place where one discovers and sets forth the laws of the universe and of life—the observatory, with its telescope towering toward the heavens like a giant phallus—is once again forbidden to Tintin. He is not at all worried, however. He tricks the curator—who looks a lot like Thompson—and sneaks into the place of mystery. Everything there is "strangely quiet and empty" (SS, 3, I, 1). The hero meets another ambivalent father figure, split into the characters of Professors Phostle and Philippulus. The first one, who prefigures Calculus more than any other previous character, is driven by the passion to know. He is distracted, introverted, and proud of his creative powers: "I, Decimus Phostle, have discovered a new metal! I shall give my name to it: phostlite" (SS, 11, IV, 1). He is saddled with a Greek first name, wears his "hairy appendage" at the back of his head rather than on his chin, and has the old-world appearance of all the professors preceding him. At this time, Hergé continued to represent scientists with the image he had of them as a child: old, impractical, unpredictable, living in another time—that is, far from the preoccupations of a child. To fittingly celebrate his discovery, Phostle does not suggest champagne but, more modestly, some soft caramels called "bull's eyes." Tintin, who almost reaches the stage of Oedipal conflict when he meets the captain, regresses with Phostle to the level of oral satisfaction. Although he has no scientific education, the hero is captivated by this old eccentric, and he takes up the role of secretary he played earlier for Nestor Alembick.

The star is more a religious mystery than a scientific one. Tintin seems the perfect one to figure it out in some religious way—that is, unrealistically. If the star of Bethlehem announced the beginning of the Christian era, this star may herald its end. It is a prelude to the apocalypse.

Tintin first meets Phostle's double, Philippulus, in the corridor of the observatory. Philippulus mutters in passing: "A judgment! Yea! A judgment, and don't you forget it!" (SS, 3, II, 1). The scientific discovery he makes with Phostle feeds his derangement, as much political as religious: he awaits the end of the world. Philippulus literally sheds his old self: he takes off his ordinary clothes, puts on the white robe of the prophet, and armed with a gong, accosts the passersby. The prophet urges them to repent, for a great judgment is about to befall the earth: "I proclaim the day of terror! The end of the world is nigh! And the survivors will die of hunger and cold! There will be pestilence, and famine, and measles!" (SS, 7, IV, 3). Numerous signs appear to confirm his mystical ravings. The star shines a "weird light" on the earth, melting the asphalt on the streets and causing the tires on cars to blow out. As in the Middle Ages, the frightened rats leave the cellars in packs and run through the streets. Listening to the dark prophecies, the people on the streets are stunned, terrified. Only Tintin seems above all this, even if he knows the precise hour, minute, and second the star is supposed to collide with the earth. Despite everything, he continues to water his plants, as if life goes on forever. To ease the people's anxiety, he orders Philippulus to go home to bed. This lack of respect unleashes the prophet's rage: "He dares to set himself up against Philippulus the prophet? An advocate of the devil! A son of Satan! A tool of Beelzebub!" (SS, 8, I, 2). Denounced as a public menace, Tintin runs away, pursued by the enraged Philippulus. To calm the prophet's fury, Tintin pours a pitcher of water on his head. He thereby shows the father figure that he "pisses on him," and then he goes to sleep, exhausted. Philippulus reappears in a nightmare (SS, 9, I, 3; II, 2, 3).

In Tintin's dream Philippulus takes over the primordial powers of the Thom(p)sons, the original father figures. He enters Tintin's home as if by magic: "Prophets come and go as they please!" Nevertheless, the hero turns against the Father and gives him an order: "Get out! Leave me alone!" At this point, the Father-prophet resorts to physical violence. Panel 2 shows Philippulus beating up on the young man with his phallic instrument, but on exactly the same place that the hero previously pissed on him—his head, the place where he wears his distinctive tuft of hair. This scene represents the same structure as the encounter between Ottokar IV and the young Baron

Panel 1: "I don't know how you got in, but I know jolly well how you're going out! And get a move on!" "Using threats now, eh?"
Panel 2: "You sit down! And take a look at what I've brought you."
Panel 3: "Yea! Behold the judgment! An enormous spider!"
SS, 9, II, 1–3. © Hergé/Moulinsart 2007.

Staszrvich. In panel 3, the hero contemplates his punishment in the image of the spider, while the triumphant Philippulus keeps striking his gong.

Tintin has already seen this enormous crowned spider on the magnifying lens of the telescope (4, II, 3). For the hero, the spider's name evokes royalty and allows him to free-associate it with the parental figures. He sees it as a devouring monster sent him by the Father as punishment for disobeying his law. Here Tintin shares one of Snowy's fantasies (*BI*, 53, IV, 2), the fear of hairy animals. The hero has a primal fear of being devoured by monstrous animals, such as the gorilla Ranko or the giant spider. But in addition, he projects this irrational fear onto humans whom on first meeting he considers to be monsters, such as the Thom(p)sons or Haddock. All of these have in common thick, black hair around their mouths. Their hairy appearance contrasts with the whiteness of Snowy's fur or the smoothness of Tintin's chin. Here the opposition is in black and white. If for the young man hair is the sign of the fatherly attribute par excellence, its excess belongs to another figure different from the Father, one whose primal, indomitable power wants to dismember and devour the child. Psychoanalysts generally call this figure "the Bad Mother," even though in the infantile phantasmal universe she is sexually undifferentiated.[1]

A little later the young man again encounters Philippulus. After escaping from an insane asylum, the professor takes refuge on the ship *Aurora*. For a while he plays the role of Phantom of the Opera; he steals a stick of dynamite, climbs up the mast, and threatens to blow up everything. Tintin climbs after him to prevent him from doing so, but the madman recognizes him and repeats his curses: "You are the servant of Satan! Keep your distance!" (19, I, 2). The more the young man advances, the higher the madman climbs, staking his pride on not being surpassed. Tintin realizes that he is going to accomplish nothing this way; the only way to vanquish the Father is to elevate himself above the Father—which he proceeds to do quite literally! Armed with a megaphone, he addresses the madman: "Hello, hello, Philippulus the prophet! This is God the Father speaking from heaven. I order you to return to earth. And be careful: don't break your neck!" (*SS*, 20, I, 4).[2]

The first part of this adventure develops some themes that Hergé was working on from the beginning of the Tintin series. The Father is at first seen as all powerful. This is Phostle, the director of the observatory, whose speech is unconditional, rigorous, and scientific; in fact, he self-righteously announces the exact hour to the precise second that the star will collide with the earth. The son does not usually have to contend with such a Father, especially when the Father conceals the origin of his own knowledge. But in this case the Father's "sacred" speech is full of errors. Because of the miscalculations of his assistant (the adviser to the "king," once more, is the one to bring about Evil), Phostle makes an erroneous prediction and is thus demoted to the level of his wicked twin, Philippulus. To be sure, the star does produce a catastrophe, but a relatively mild one compared to the predicted conflagration.

The consequences of the defeat of the Father are twofold. On the one hand, Tintin recognizes that his being judged is only a fantasy growing out of his own guilt for having crossed the forbidden entryway into the laboratory and having tried to steal from the Father the secret of his power. The threat of castration that the bad Father imposes on him is only a nightmare. Philippulus is a dangerous madman but one who can be tamed. Thus, Tintin begins to distinguish his imaginary life from objective reality. However, to the extent that the Father is recognized as fallible, the rivalry with him becomes manageable, and the Father and son could compete with one another. But Tintin does not take advantage of that move. On the contrary, when he sees that Phostle is desperate, incapable of recovering even a small piece of his newly discovered metal phostlite, he comes to his aid to solve the problem. Here Tintin reacts like the typical pre-Oedipal child. He fears that when the Father is reduced to the level of an ordinary human being, that demotion will in turn bring about the son's decline, and the son will lose whatever remains of his power. The son's perennial temptation is therefore to try to restore the paternal power. Thus, not only does he avoid struggling directly with the Father—that is, engaging with him in a real world—but he also suppresses all future desire for vengeance by transforming the meaning of the debt. The Father from now on owes everything to the son, and not the other way around.

## THE RIVALRY

Tintin thinks he is able to treat Haddock the way he has treated all the other ambivalent figures—with the exception of Snowy, whom he believes to have been completely mastered. In other words, he summons the ambivalent Fathers or distances them from himself as he wishes, as if they were nothing but shadows in contrast with the solidity of his own existence. But the captain is dangerously different because he turns Tintin's epic adventures into a novel, thus demoting the hero to merely another character in the story. The epic feeds on heroism and shuns psychology, whereas the novel has room for any sort of hero, provided his personal psychic world interests the reader. *The Crab* already suggests this transformation from epic to novel. Most of the adventure takes place in some exotic land, the Sahara or Morocco. As Hergé himself recalls in the introduction to the fourth volume of the *Archives Hergé,* "A complete mythology belongs to these regions, propagated by song, cinema, and the novel" (*AH,* IV, p. 11). In 1930 Joseph Peyré published *L'Escadron blanc* (*The White Battalion*), which Hergé read and which became a popular film. At this time many such popular films—*Un de la légion, La Bandera,* and *Pépé le Moko*—bolstered the mythology of North Africa. Tintin could no longer be the lone superman who saves the nation. As in *The Broken Ear,* he becomes more an individual adventurer seeking his fortune.

In *The Shooting Star,* he tries to recuperate his soteriological personality—his character as the redeemer—but in vain. Haddock again shows up in his life and takes up the kind of role the Thom(p)sons formerly played. Meeting him again, the hero learns some concrete facts. Water is the captain's element, so he teaches Tintin how to use a compass, read navigational charts, locate the principal shipping lanes, and follow the rules of the sea. At the helm of his ship, Archibald Haddock is like the god of the sea. He reassures the young man by showing him the difference between " a mere draft" and a "raging tempest." Soon Tintin knows enough so that Haddock lets him steer the captain's own trawler (*RRT,* 15, II, 3). Now the hero's successes can rest less on his imaginary omnipotence and more on the knowledge he learns from his more experienced brother.

But the "older brother" is also transformed. Although Haddock does not totally give up alcohol, he drinks more temperately, soothing the rhythms of his manic depression. He revives his taste for life and desire for recognition. The departure of the *Aurora* is an occasion for great ceremony and is broadcast on the radio throughout Europe. In his dress uniform, Haddock receives the bouquet of flowers sent by the Society for Sober Sailors, the society over which he presides. On his new ship, he conducts himself like a true leader: giving orders, overseeing the operations, encouraging his subordinates, and attending to every detail. When Haddock meets with his old friend Captain Chester, Tintin is relegated to second place. The hero is now merely a witness to a world having its own rituals to which he is admitted only upon initiation.

Since meeting Haddock, Tintin has changed his attitude. So has Snowy, who almost gives up speaking. When Snowy has to make himself understood, he starts barking like any mutt (*SS*, 15, IV, 1–3). Moreover, the hero is no longer a solitary victor; he learns to think about the group. He integrates himself into the human community as an equal. Instead of trying to do everything himself, he delegates. Scientific endeavors belong to Phostle and the five other scientists who accompany him on the expedition. Navigation is the business of the crew of the *Aurora*. The hydroplane is piloted by a professional as brave in his domain as Tintin is in his. In short, the hero has to learn to share with others who are just as important as he. It is the group that collectively is on the trail of the wicked, not just Tintin himself, even though he alone is still the hated target of the gangsters.

With this constriction of his personality, the young man looks for new territory to conquer wherever he can shine. He finds it both in daily life and at the intersections created by the specializations of the other protagonists. Until then, Tintin had no private life but totally identified with the public Good. Now he becomes more a hero of the everyday. He discovers needs to eat and sleep; he finds himself indecisive, sometimes angry, or even having to trick the captain to get him to admit his point of view. From now on his heroism entails constant efforts to discipline this human nature emerging from within. For example, he goes without sleep for two days to make sure the scientific mission succeeds. Moreover, whereas he once was merely the eternal spectator of other people's difficulties, he now learns how to relate both to his companion and to all members of the crew. Tintin goes from one to the other to lend a hand. Having no designated place on board apart from representing "the press," he shows up everywhere—next to the captain, in the cabin of the radio transmitter, or behind the pilot of the hydroplane. He becomes the liaison officer for the group, the embodiment of "team spirit," the spiritual glue for the community. Integrated into the group in this way, Tintin can afford to shed some of the foundling's characteristics—introversion, the feeling of omnipotence, the refusal to engage with the Father—in order to acquire some of the bastard's. Thus, the central part of this album is devoted to the apprenticeship in rivalries. There is a rivalry within the camp of the Good, between Tintin and the other members of the expedition who resist his heroism in favor of their own competence. Moreover, there is a collective rivalry between the forces of Good and Evil, represented in the *Aurora*'s attempt to prevent the *Peary* from capturing the phostlite and using it in commerce. Even if Haddock sometimes gets discouraged, he carries the hero in his wake, not yet knowing how his own personality will be transformed.

## THE SINKING ISLAND

The rivalry between the *Aurora* and the *Peary* can be read on one level as a political allegory. Whereas Tintin's expedition is funded by the European Foundation for Scientific Research, the rival expedition is backed by the banker Bohlwinkel, an unscrupulous character who always sniffs out a good deal. Here Hergé pits the incarnation of unregulated capitalism against the spirit of European values. He represents the latter as a union of many European countries, for the scientists come from Belgium, Sweden, Spain, Switzerland, Germany, and Portugal. These European nations are equally represented and animated by a common goal: the disinterested pursuit of knowledge. The discovery of the properties of phostlite is an unmistakable reference to the atomic research carried on by the major superpowers at that time. With phostlite, the mushrooms transform into giant explosions! In the first version, Hergé explicitly takes sides against the Americans who finance the *Peary*, named for the first explorer to reach the North Pole. Opposed to the Anglo-American coalition, Hergé presents a utopian vision that in 1942 smacks of pro-German propaganda. For example, the scientist Otto Schulze from the University of Jena is shown as a "good guy," innocuous and discreet, working in common with the others under the Belgian Professor Phostle. In reality, with a German victory, one knows what outcome was planned by the German chancellor for this "united, equal Europe" opposed by the Anglo-American Allies and Russia.

Hergé's second version of this album is depoliticized. It reads more like a psychological allegory. Supported by his group, especially by Captain Haddock, Tintin can now turn toward his recent past, confront his fantasies, and face up to the magical world of the foundling that he has such trouble leaving behind. It is to this subject that the latter part of the adventure is dedicated. In the name of the entire group, Tintin parachutes onto the meteorite that contains the phostlite. The meteorite is a "divine" place since it falls from the heavens. Tintin plants the flag of the European Society for Scientific Research on the meteorite island and waits for twenty-four hours to be picked up. Here he adopts the image of "the new Adam."

Whereas the first part of the album deals with apocalypse, the latter part concerns rebirth—but it takes on an infernal character. Landing on the meteorite, Tintin leaves the domain of history for that of myth, trying to regain a mythic dimension to his adventure. The island he lands on is uninhabitable, so he cannot impose on it his own laws but must submit to the ones he finds there. The hero has to admit to himself that he has lost his imaginary omnipotence as well as his capacity for metamorphosis. Instead, a weird metamorphosis has transformed the entire island into a monstrous living being. Mushrooms grow into giants in only minutes before exploding, making the island into a veritable war zone. Insects become gigantic monsters dwarfing the humans. Each apple that falls off a tree has the potential to become a lethal weapon, and a butterfly becomes as dangerous as a fighter plane. The trees grow enormous instantly, as if several centuries of vital energy were concentrated into a few seconds. Time and space shrink to almost nothing. Sinking into the sea, the meteorite-island becomes smaller and smaller, but the giant spider, glimpsed earlier on the lens of the telescope, returns from out of the nightmare, ready and waiting to pounce on Tintin and devour him.

In this part of the adventure, Hergé presents the dark side of the foundling's fantasies, the reverse of his omnipotence. Reduced to the level of an ordinary hero, Tintin returns to a primordial world, but without the defense mechanisms that would allow him to deal with it. He finds himself faced with a nature whose "laws" are unpredictable, unstable, and uncontrollable. Deprived of the help of the Father, he risks at each moment being engulfed by the sea, crushed by falling apples as enormous as a giant's chest, run through by a butterfly, and, scariest of all, devoured by the giant spider. These are, of course, childish fears projected onto the external world. Formerly Tintin had enjoyed an almost symbiotic relationship with nature, living happily among the animals and feeding on the fruits of the land. But now he sees nature as hostile and threatening. The island of childhood is uninhabitable, for Tintin cannot control it. All that remains for him to do is retrieve a sample from the meteorite to submit to the scientist, the kind of father figure privileged since the adventure of *The Cigars*. Along with the island itself, the hero's childhood is itself now engulfed. He abandons his myth of childhood after confronting it one last time to try to unravel its secret. But without the Father, it has no predictable law but only the caprice of all-powerful Mother Nature, sometimes good, sometimes wicked, but whose embrace smothers the child and makes him disappear into her breast. Although the Father poses the threat of castration, one has to struggle with the father figure. Besides, one can always try tricking him and perhaps get him to listen to reason. The Mother, however, never listens: she has a voice that calls out and sings, but she has no ears. To escape the world of primitive childhood, one can no longer rely on the character of the foundling but, rather, that of the bastard, who is better equipped to deal with the objective world and the adult world of symbolic relations. The future of Tintin is named Haddock.

## CHAPTER NINE

# FOUNDING THE FAMILY

## THE LEGACY

Although Tintin never clarifies the mystery of his birth, Haddock tries to shed light on his own origins, even to the point of inventing an ancestor who would better suit the aspirations of the archetypal bastard than any actual father could do. The double albums of *The Secret of the Unicorn* and *Red Rackham's Treasure* revolve around issues of this fictitious ancestry. Whereas the preceding album marked the end of the period of infantile fantasy and politics, the new adventure deals with the meanings of symbolic relations within personal life. Tintin, who has implanted in his companion a taste for solving mysteries, helps him search for an ancestor who in the end will resemble them both, the foundling and the bastard. Finding such an ancestor as their family's progenitor, moreover, will make Tintin and Haddock not only good friends but brothers.

The adventure of *The Broken Ear* opened in a museum, but this one starts at a flea market, where Tintin finds a scale model of a sailing ship that he wants to give to the captain. Several people, however, are after this miniature vessel, as they were after the Arumbayan fetish, because it too contains a treasure—not just one diamond but a chest full of jewels whose hiding place is marked on an elusive piece of parchment. Tintin's "clan" sets out on a treasure hunt, but the treasure ends up being very close to home. Their voyage in space is coupled with a parallel voyage in time. Haddock uses this adventure to invent a family genealogy that supports his own imagined destiny, for the treasure once belonged to an aristocrat whom Haddock recognizes as just the Father that he desires.

The story begins at the end of the seventeenth century during the reign of Louis XIV. In 1684, the king rewards the good deeds of his lord and officer of the Royal Navy, François de Hadoque, by giving him a castle dating from the time of Louis XIII. The castle is located in Moulinsart, a territory recently acquired by the French Crown but today belonging to Belgium.[1] Hergé gives Lord Hadoque many of the captain's traits to emphasize the fictional connection between the modern sailor and the ancestral lord. Generous, intelligent, and reckless, Lord Hadoque is a born leader. He has a very loud voice and loves his rum the way his heir loves whiskey. About his personal life we learn one thing: the lord has three sons. In 1698, fourteen years after giving him the castle, the king sends this favored lieutenant to deliver a cargo ("surely of rum," thinks the future Haddock) to the island of San Domingo, which the Treaty of Ryswick had declared a French possession one year earlier. The lord has an adventure in the seventeenth century that will be duplicated by his successor in the twentieth century, but the aristocratic ancestor's success is more illustrious and succeeds without the help of Tintin.

Two days after leaving Haiti, Hadoque's ship, the *Unicorn*—the imaginary animal symbolizing royalty—is chased down by pirates. Lord François de Hadoque has to show that he has all the social skills he needs for success and that he is an able swordsman as well as a good courtier. Like a feudal lord, he kills the pirate Diego of Navarre in a duel. Despite his bravery, Hadoque is taken prisoner on his own ship. His crew is slaughtered, and he is promised certain death after prolonged torture. His situation is all the more perilous because the villain who holds him is none other than the wicked Red Rackham, whose very name invokes the forbidden color of blood and wine. The association with bloody death is displayed by the skull and crossbones the pirate wears on his crimson cape. Even his name sounds evil. "Rackham" evokes both *raca*, the false brother (*faux frère*), *racaille* in Aramaic, and the French word for "scum." "Rackha" is also similar to *Rasta*, and *Rascar*, associated with Rascar Capac, as we shall soon see.

The extreme danger of the situation does nothing to undermine the lord's self-assurance. Tied to the ship's mast, he continues to defy Red Rackham, who has just shown him his latest booty: a chest full of diamonds seized from a Spanish vessel. Wiping off all traces of recent bloodshed from their prize, the pirates sail the *Unicorn* to a nearby island, where they drop anchor. To celebrate their victory in grand style, they break open the barrels of rum and get "abominably drunk." François de Hadoque takes advantage of their drunkenness to free himself, but since he can do nothing against the whole crew of bandits, he decides to jump ship. First, however, he goes down to the ship's magazine, where the munitions are stored. Unfortunately, Red Rackham catches him in the act. Hadoque and the pirate engage in a fearsome duel, but Hadoque defeats the ignoble Rackham and then lights a new fuse beneath a keg of gunpowder. Before leaving the ship in a dinghy, he has time to grab the coffer of diamonds and then rows off in the direction of the island without being noticed. At the moment he lands on the island, the *Unicorn* explodes: "Hurrah! Justice is done!" (*SU*, 26, III, 1).

The first part of the adventure deals with the lord, the captain's ideal ancestor, who represents everything the captain would like to become. The lord is the model bastard: the man who succeeds in everything by cunning and strength and who ends up with a huge fortune whose origin remains secret because it is soaked in blood. Nevertheless, in vanquishing Evil in the person of Red Rackham, François de Hadoque comes to embody the Good, and thus takes on the character of the foundling as well. For two years he lives on the nameless island, reinventing the exploits of Robinson Crusoe, leading the kind of life that Tintin himself would like to have enjoyed. The lord is adopted by the natives, who are immediately fascinated by his voice: "I can just imagine their faces the first time they heard him shout 'Ration my rum!'" (*RRT*, 28, I, 2). Hergé does not dwell on the ancestor's likeness to Robinson Crusoe, Defoe's hero from the novel of 1719, but one can infer that he parallels his contemporary of the famous English shipwreck.[2] Hadoque imposes his own law on the natives, enjoys the riches of the island, lives like an absolute monarch, dispenses justice as he sees fit, and is served by those ready to sacrifice their own lives to satisfy their master. Two years later, a passing ship takes him back to Europe. Upon his departure, the abandoned natives make an enormous fetish in his likeness. They deify the French lord just as the Africans had deified Tintin in the adventure in *The Congo*, a sign of the similarity between the two situations. The statue that will one day stand in the great hall of Marlinspike shows François de Hadoque with a fearsome look and an enormous mouth, proclaiming the Law. As in the adventures of Robinson Crusoe, after the master's departure, the island sinks into anarchy. When Tintin and his companions show up, they can only attest to the irreversible decadence. The natives undoubtedly had returned to their cannibalistic practices and ended up devouring each other. The island is deserted, awaiting a new history. On an ironic note, only the parrots remain faithful to the word of the ancestor; from generation to generation they still repeat his repertoire of insults.

The episode on the island connects the lord to Tintin's own interests. Upon the lord's return to Europe, his ordeal seems to redeem the ignoble origin of his fortune. He can once again assume the character of the bastard, but now with the kind of innocence and lack of shame associated with the foundling. He is thus a winner on two counts and gets busy recording his successes in his memoirs. In addition, to maximize his choices, he constructs three scale models of the *Unicorn*, one for each son, and conceals in the mast of each ship a scrap of parchment inscribed with the secret of the treasure. The "secret" does not just give the hiding place for the actual treasure but is also a kind of trick. On the one hand, the lord tells about the significance of the model only at the end of his memoirs, thus making it necessary to read the whole account and to steep oneself in it. The life of the progenitor of the family becomes the model for his heirs, just as in Syldavia the feats of Ottokar I were exemplary for his heirs from Muskar I to Ottokar IV. The progenitor's existence has to be venerated and reproduced by his heirs, in order to maintain the patrimony. On the other hand, the Father reduces the sons to mere children, to live "castrated," insofar as he orders them to remain one and the same. This message is given by the nature of the parchment itself: one can discover the whereabouts of the treasure only by superimposing the three similar scraps of parchment. The text suggests an analogy between the three unicorns, the three brothers, and the three parchments. As in the fable "The Laborer and His Children," which the lord assuredly knows, the Father transmits his name and his knowledge simultaneously. He lives as the sole founding hero, whereas his children can attain only a lesser fame. (He gives them a "scale" model of the ship, only a toy.) By remaining "twins" with each other, they can preserve the enormous strength of the Father. The message can be clearly interpreted only when the three identical parchments are superimposed on each other and are placed in a direct source of light, such as the sun. The text's play on words ("for 'tis from light that light will dawn") implicitly invites the reader to be faithful to a political order defined by nature, such as the royal house of the ancien régime. The lord received the castle for being a loyal courtier, and he persuades his heirs to serve the prince in a similar fashion. The diamonds are the sign of spiritual as well as material wealth and therefore cannot be exchanged like ordinary material goods. The diamonds are the visible sign of the secret knowledge grasped by the initiated and transmitted from one generation to the next. The sons of the lord can achieve this level of superior wisdom and fortune only if they fully understand and follow the example of the Father. As in the case of the Arumbayan fetish, the precious object is only the outer shell of a spiritual heritage that one has to work to achieve.

## THE HEIRS

For some unknown reason, the lord's sons did not receive their father's inheritance. Perhaps they were not worthy, because they did not carefully read their father's memoirs or because they were crushed by his example and were incapable of following him. After the departure of François de Hadoque, the natives on the island reverted to cannibalism. Similarly, after their father's death, the sons were debased in some way or other and were not able to put together the secret message. For the lord required them to act out a ritual that seemed unimportant: to tilt back the great mast of each of the ships they inherited. Thus, he said, the truth would be revealed. Because they ignored this minor ritual, they did not get their inheritance, and the treasure of Red Rackham lives today, encased in a globe at the foot of the statue of Saint John the Evangelist in the former chapel of the castle of Marlinspike. The three ships were scattered. One lay in the attic of the castle, another belonged to a collector, and the third Tintin purchased at a flea market.

Two hundred fifty years after François's testimony, the two brothers George and Max Bird, unscrupulous antique dealers, buy Marlinspike Hall. Cleaning out the attic, they come upon one of the scale models, now in poor condition, and accidentally discover the first scrap of parchment. They immediately realize that it concerns a buried treasure and set out to hunt for the other two ships. Rather than rely on the castle's butler, Nestor, who is a good man and whom they suspect for no good reason, the Bird brothers hook up with Barnaby, another of their employees. Barnaby gets his hands on the other two models and thus gives the Bird brothers the chance to claim the inheritance.

Meanwhile, just as the fetish brings about the death of all those who try to sell it as a commodity, the three models of the ship lead the antique dealers to ruin. First, the three are unworthy of the inheritance. George,

Max, and Barnaby are not even real brothers. A money dispute erupts between Max and Barnaby. The latter decides to betray the partnership, but to prevent this, the other two accost him just at the moment when he is selling Tintin the clue to the mystery. The police arrest the Bird brothers, but the three crooks do not realize that there is a double message. They know only the bastard's side of the story—the desire for wealth and fame. They forget the other side that exonerates the first—the moral demands and the integrity of the foundling.

Two other characters gain possession of the precious parchments. The first is the collector Ivan Ivanovitch Sakharine, a Russian émigré with the head of Rasputin. Sakharine tries to "sweet-talk" Tintin into selling him the ship, but the Russian does not merit the inheritance. The past serves only his obsession with collecting and not as a lesson for avoiding previous mistakes. For ten years, Sakharine jealously guards the model of the *Unicorn*, which for him is merely a collector's item belonging to a complete set. In his hands the ship is reduced in significance to a purely aesthetic object.

The second character to obtain the parchments is Aristide Silk, a tidy, elderly little man in old-fashioned clothes who wouldn't merit any attention apart from the fact that he steals wallets. Mr. Silk's first and last names suggest a connection with Hergé's professors, but he is more a failed artist than a scientist. Instead of creating an original work of art, he creates his "unique and rare" collection of wallets "hand-picked" from his "clients." When Thomson comes to arrest him, Silk at first vehemently denies having stolen the wallets, but then the collector's pride takes over and he proudly displays his "work": "When I tell you it took me only three months to assemble my collection, you'll agree that it's a remarkable achievement!" (*SU*, 59, III, 2). This gentle kleptomaniac has in his possession two "items" catalogued under Mr. Bird. But like Sakharine, he does not look beyond appearances. He is fixated, in the psychoanalytic sense of the word, on his collection: the object of desire is the wallet as such, the "external envelope" whose meaning he can manipulate at will. Sakharine and Silk each preserve only one aspect of the ancestral message, that of the foundling. But the manic nature of their collecting is perversely introverted. Rather than exert any real influence on the social world, their collecting is a kind of "nonrelation" to the world, a will to impose order fixated on objects that are merely fetishes.[3]

In the end, only three characters are worthy of receiving the inheritance: Tintin, Haddock, and Calculus, the latter making his appearance in the second part of *The Unicorn* adventure. Their participation in the common quest reveals their sense of brotherhood and transforms them into spiritual sons of the ancestor. Before actually recovering the inheritance, however, they have to undergo a series of initiation trials to prove they have understood the message. Rather than reunite the two opposing tendencies of the bastard and the foundling into one and the same person, Tintin and Haddock integrate these tendencies within the family unit. These tendencies are no longer involved in a "civil war" but complement each other within the family community. Thus, the enigma of the legacy will be unraveled. The new family will inherit the two aspects of the ancestor at the same time that it constitutes itself as "the three brothers reunited."

Each of the putative heirs bears a piece of the puzzle of the legacy. Tintin accomplishes the first step by buying the scale model at the flea market. By withdrawing the vessel from commercial circulation, he restores the ship to its original purpose: to be a gift, not a piece of goods to be bought and sold. Once he decides to give it to the captain, Tintin absolutely refuses to resell it to Sakharine or Barnaby, even when they offer him ten times the price. For Tintin, objects have meaning; they are not soulless, commercial goods, mere commodities. Haddock agrees. Although Haddock might have acted like the Bird brothers in transforming his inheritance into commercially valued antiques, he manages to conserve its true value.

Unlike Tintin's living quarters, which bear no trace of his previous adventures, Haddock's apartment in town is full of souvenirs. The captain keeps in his attic a chest containing several relics of his ancestor: his hat, the saber he probably used to kill Red Rackham, and the three volumes of *Memoirs*. A portrait of the lord decked out in his handsome finery hangs in his living room. Once Tintin obtains the model ship, Haddock decides to open the *Memoirs*, which he feverishly reads all in one night. The *Memoirs* are a revelation, provoking Haddock to set out very soon on an expedition to the Antilles to retrieve the treasure from the wreck of the *Unicorn*. To this end, he hires his friend Captain Chester's trawler, the *Sirius*. Calculus also joins them and brings along his own boat, a submarine to facilitate deep-sea diving. Later, the professor reconstructs the manuscripts discovered at the bottom of the sea, which allows Haddock to trace the ancestral castle. Finally, Calculus offers the captain the necessary funds to purchase Marlinspike Hall and at the same time to recover the pirate treasure.

The three characters do not approach the ancestor empty-handed. Each of them bears the temperament of the foundling or the bastard and offers something in addition that allows the soul of the ancestor to be resuscitated. The gift of a symbolic boat—Tintin's scale model, Haddock's trawler the *Sirius*, and Calculus's submarine—brings the three of them together. They realize that instead of discovering the ancestral hero, they come to found their own family, which is worth much more, for its spirit permeates the entire group.

## THE RETURN OF THE FATHER

Reading the *Memoirs* provokes an identity crisis in the captain. Even more than the others, he feels he has to prove himself worthy of the lord whom he needs as an excuse to justify his life. When he tells Tintin about the ancestor's feats, he enters into a trance, akin to the madness recorded among certain initiates at the moment of climbing the next rung on the ladder to holiness. He embodies the spirit of the story, making the past events come alive in the present. He *becomes* the lord; he takes on his voice, his body. He feeds on his fury, reliving all his actions, especially the murder of Red Rackham, the bloody act founding the family dynasty. When François fights against the pirates, Archibald Haddock wears the same plumed hat while dueling with their shadows. When François is taken prisoner, Archibald relives all his pains, not least of which is thirst. He imitates the life of the ancestor not merely as an actor taking on a role but taking on his very soul, his *mana*, and is transformed in the process. A mysterious alchemy takes place, not changing metal into gold but transforming a weak, drunken sailor into a noble hero. Haddock needs this ancestor to rewrite his own history, to substitute the more famous one for his own. This transference permits the captain to completely forget, even to unconsciously misread, the extreme misery and folly of his former life, which he henceforth never mentions. In the future, the image of François de Hadoque remains his inspiration. Before a crowd of opportunists who claim to be descendants of Red Rackham, Haddock affirms his own high lineage: "You're all descendants of Red Rackham, are you? Good! Well, I'm descended from Sir Francis Hadoque, who killed Red Rackham in hand-to-hand combat and blew up his ship. And there are times when my ancestor's fighting blood begins to boil!" (*RRT*, 4, I, 2; III, 1). When Tintin informs him about the castle, Haddock unceasingly praises the taste of his ancestor, finding everything totally wonderful. When he takes over the castle, he becomes interested in preserving the souvenirs of the past and transforms the reception hall into a museum honoring the founder. The maritime gallery, open only on special occasions, exhibits the relics of François and his *Unicorn*: the three models of the ship now reunited forever, the famous parchments, the *Memoirs*, and numerous other articles brought back from the wreck of the *Unicorn*. In this way, the ancestor continues to live, as if Archibald were only a recent addition to the long line of Hadoques. The family invented by the bastard is modeled on the royal dynasties at just that time in Europe when there were no longer any strong monarchs.

One might think that inventing these glorious family roots would put an end to the captain's psychological instability, but that would be too simple. To be sure, the family myth lends a certain solidity to his personality. He does abandon his great adventures on the sea to stay home to lovingly tend his garden. He who was master of Water now returns to Earth, reigning at Marlinspike Hall like a good-natured king. But his identification with his ancestor crushes him as well. The days of heroism are over, the fight is no longer permitted, and the rascals have a house of their own. How can one be a great man when all one has to deal with each day are crowds of social climbers, journalists, professional loan sharks, interviewers, and theft-insurance salesmen? Archibald's secret fear is to become merely a parrot, to repeat the life of a forefather too great for himself.

Between the lord and the sea captain, there is a greater break than indicated simply in the different spelling of their names. The first one is of noble birth, having his place secured in the hereditary hierarchy. The second has merely invented his nobility, but he continues to live in a debased world where traditional values no longer matter. Haddock glimpses what Tintin has always refused to take into account. But his own constant fear of being only a phony is the price he has to pay for his delusions of grandeur. When Haddock arrives on the ancestor's island, he is struck by his own fate: the parrots only repeat his own repertoire of insults, reducing him to nothing but an echo of another. His history is already written, and he can relive it only in a diminished form, in his own solitude and madness. Everywhere he goes, the ancestor has preceded him. The ancestor has laid down the Law. Archibald speaks through him, as if the lord had taken over his own unconscious. But the lord can never respond to him directly, as if the Father is deaf to the words of the son.[4]

At the same time he is inventing his admirable ancestor, distant and imaginary, Haddock encounters another Father, close-up and real: Professor

Cuthbert Calculus. The two Fathers complement each other. Hergé splits the father figure into two distinct characters: one idealized, inaccessible, and famous; the other real, obnoxious, and ridiculous. The bastard seems to think it is easier to contend with a father whom he implicitly regards as a brother in the family structure he is building around himself. At first the captain does not stop ridiculing the professor and thus does not immediately see him as a father figure. Like the other professors and scientists who have preceded him, this character initially seems ridiculous. With a Greek first name and a last name of an ordinary plant,[5] a silly pointy beard on his chin, clothes that are too big and old-fashioned, chronically hard of hearing—Calculus is a laughable figure indeed. Nevertheless, there are some significant differences between him and the other professors. Unlike the others, he approaches Tintin, not the other way around. He not only approaches him but stubbornly imposes himself on Tintin's group. When Cuthbert shows the group his studio, he has to put up with Tintin's sarcasm, Haddock's rage, and the Thom(p)sons' open ridicule: "Your machine won't do." They mock his silly inventions and scorn his creative genius, so difficult to detect in the odd paraphernalia cluttering his apartment. But beneath the surface, Calculus nurses a secret wound that reappears only occasionally in one of his memorable fits of anger. Most of the time he is too absorbed in his interior world to register any displeasure. He is in effect deaf to the outside world, and therein lies his strength. When the group refuse to allow him to participate in their expedition, he sneaks onto the trawler. On the eve of the departure, he removes the captain's whiskey from the packing cases and replaces it with detachable metal plates for his submarine. Then he hides away in the lifeboat and passes the first two days of the voyage like a phantom, frightening everyone.

Tintin understands more quickly than the others the importance of this good man for their group. He realizes it especially when they see Calculus in his shark-shaped submarine cruising around among the sharks off the island. The young hero sees that the machine will not only help them explore the shipwreck but also lend a new dimension to the adventure. The invention allows them to cross a boundary previously restricting human beings and to penetrate into another universe, the one beneath the seas that holds secrets hitherto unknown. To venture into this unknown realm, Tintin immediately wants to try out the professor's machine. Cuthbert's submarine, a miniature reproduction of Captain Nemo's, serves as an instrument of initiation for the hero into the mysteries of life. Tintin risks dying from suffocation, but he resurfaces in time, transformed. He is saved by Haddock, who once again throws him the magic rope that binds them together forever.

Haddock may conceal from himself the crushing weight of his exemplary ancestor, but in contrast, from the very beginning he displays a strong ambivalence toward Calculus. From their first to their last expedition, he reacts in a similar way: "That chap will drive me crazy!" (*RRT*, 49, I, 3; cf. *F714*, 2, I, 3). One has to admit, of course, that the professor's attitude toward the captain is often discouraging and punitive. From the beginning, Calculus keeps Haddock from his whiskey, in contrast to Tintin, who simply shuts his eyes to his companion's backsliding, and the ancestor, who even seems to encourage his vice. After all, the group carries many bottles of rum from the wreck of the *Unicorn* that the captain enjoys with abandon. Even when Archibald is happy and tries to share his good feelings, Calculus rebukes him. Not harshly, mind you, but the professor's deafness serves to communicate the reprimand of Father to son. Archibald can never seem to respond adequately to the Father's demands, even when he shouts himself hoarse. From Calculus's point of view, Haddock's loud voice is simply a sign of impotence. Sadly, the captain seems condemned to live as the echo of the Father, only his repetition. Frequently the captain says something that Calculus doesn't understand. Five seconds later, the professor makes the same remark, thus undermining the sailor's originality and personality. Haddock's verbal invention is reduced to nothing; he is forever the parrot of the other. To defend himself against this sort of repetition, Haddock mocks Calculus's proposals. He pushes the echoing effect to excess to lessen its danger:

> Calculus: You see? It's just what I said. Weeds.
> Haddock: Really? I thought they were weeds. (*RRT*, 38, II, 3)

The captain's frequent displays of irritation do not really hide his true feelings for Calculus: he loves him deeply, to the point of falling into a depression when in the adventure of *The Seven Crystal Balls* the Indians kidnap the professor. At the end of *The Unicorn* albums, the family structure is in place. The ancestor claims to be the progenitor, all the more prestigious the more distant he is. But the ancient lord becomes more irrelevant to the daily lives of the group, to the point that they abandon the infantile myths and take up their adult responsibilities. But it is the ancestor, after all, who helps them plant their family roots in Marlinspike Hall, and who in this way contributes to resolving the conflict between worldly values and religious ones, an opposition once considered intractable. That Calculus is the one to pay for the family castle, however, indicates that he takes over the place of the Father, thus relieving the bastard from needing the ancestor for an excuse.

By force of circumstances, Tintin is ousted from his central role. He survives only in relation to others, by integrating himself into a group that teaches him the meaning of symbolic relations. These symbolic relations are founded on the mode of gift-countergift. As a consequence, a merely abstract, monetary exchange is inconceivable between them. Granted, the ancestor's treasure consisted of jewels. If they had been merely converted into cash, no one would have known it. In Hergé's world, the origin of social success is unthinkable because it is always ignoble. If the captain is rich, it is not the result of his own social success but thanks to the discovery of a treasure that belongs to him by right. The family does not enter into concrete social relations with the surrounding world because it lacks a crucial figure—the Mother. Awaiting her coming, the three men share their roles as best they can, remaining silent about the lack of emotional, affective meanings in that apparently asexual world. Domestic work is assigned to Nestor, a character as devoted as he is discreet. He does not receive a salary, for his work is unthinkable in terms of monetary compensation and exists only as a form of social exchange. The aristocratic point of view tacitly endorsed by the bastard takes idleness for a virtue. Hergé gives the captain an ancestor who constantly serves as a justification for his success and allows him to benefit from the inheritance.

As the lord of Marlinspike Hall, Archibald tries to live like a king, but his power is immediately limited by several domestic restrictions. Furthermore, taking on a younger brother still in thrall to his passion for the absolute, and a Father whose status constantly increases, Haddock finds himself uneasy. He is always doubting himself, his real status, his success, and his legitimacy. Only in the final episode does he get the better of his misgivings, when he asks his companion the question that has been plaguing him since the *Karaboudjan*: "Who's the captain here, you or me?" To reassure him of his role, Tintin is quick to respond: "You, of course!" (*TP*, 31, I, 2).

## CHAPTER TEN

# THE TEMPLE OF THE SUN

## PERSPECTIVE

Beginning with *The Seven Crystal Balls*, Hergé changes his technique. Previously, the cartoon panels resembled frescoes. The characters stood out against a plain, colored background to keep attention focused on the foreground. Perspective was introduced only occasionally to emphasize the opposition between the character and the immediate environment. If Tintin was not explicitly clashing with the environment, or was not representing it in some way, the exterior world remained merely in the background. The undifferentiated background reinforced the importance of the characters' actions and contributed to the comic strip's epic quality. For the most part, Hergé continued to use this drafting technique even after he gave up the narrative technique used in the first albums of simply juxtaposing images and frames without explaining their connections (*parataxe*). Hergé followed this narrative practice even after *The Blue Lotus*, when he began to focus more on the intrigues themselves.

In *The Seven Crystal Balls*, however, he introduces perspective into the story itself. By that I mean he focuses on the relations between all the elements of the story: the characters, places, objects, and events within the general narrative structure. Moreover, when perspective is introduced into the picture, the individual elements are in relation to the context pictorially represented. But with the introduction of perspective, Hergé's drawing nevertheless always remains as clear as an etching. Each frame—and one page typically has between twelve and fifteen—is laid out like a painting, with different levels of the action interacting with one another. While the characters act in the foreground, there is often something else happening in the background that sooner or later affects the overall story. Beginning with *The Seven Crystal Balls*, the author and his staff take great pains to make every object—airplanes, automobiles, boats, uniforms—as realistic as possible. They also pay attention to the details of the settings in different countries. This bent toward realism gives the fictitious and unreal world of the comic strip the initial appearance of being "true."

It is interesting to note that perspective became introduced into Western art just when a religious vision of the world was disintegrating and the major "secular" approaches to reality, such as science, politics, and art, were becoming more important or were redefining themselves in opposition to religion. Whereas a scene in a medieval fresco may have a gold background signifying God and unifying the painting, in Renaissance paintings the visual order relies on its own apparently autonomous laws. The divine world that had organized the elements of the fresco is no longer invoked. Now the rules of art—namely, perspective—allow for the representation of the celestial world as well as the social universe. Neither heaven nor earth is immediately perceived but only represented. God is not needed to combine the elements of the representation; rather, consciousness itself does this work of objectifying the world according to mathematical laws governing the relations between the different pictorial elements.

Hergé's own work more or less follows the pattern of this aesthetic revolution. When the foundling's quasi-religious omnipotence dominates his character in the story, his adventures are more like epics, and the author's drafting typically ignores perspective and appears more like fresco. But when this earlier Manichean universe falls apart—leaving Tintin no longer incarnating the Good, and God no longer directly intervening to save his champion—Hergé more systematically resorts to perspective in both the story line and the drawings. The exterior world features more prominently precisely when Tintin has to contend with it more directly. The exterior world is also very important to the bastard Haddock, who feels compelled to leave his mark on the social universe. From a psychological point of view, this period corresponds to the transformation from the infantile world of imaginary relations to the adult world of symbolic relations.

In *The Seven Crystal Balls*, the author also introduces a great variety of framing techniques. Some of these he borrows from film, whereas others

later influence filmmaking itself. These novelties, foreshadowed in the preceding albums, no doubt emerge more from a change in viewpoint than
from his increasing mastery of drawing. The use of perspective, in theater
and in comic strips, allows for many actions to be coordinated at the same
time. Furthermore, grammatical syntax—the element of perspective in the
domain of language—allows for the relation of different actions within one
sentence, thus coordinating them into a whole while simultaneously creating visual and psychological depth. The adventures lose their epic character
and become more like novels. The hero no longer invokes the continual
presence of God on his side to carry out his deeds. Now, the reader's interest
is focused on the characters' actual motivations, actions, and their consequences. Each character becomes more complex, and implicit innuendoes
become as important as explicit deeds. The relationships among Hergé's
three main characters also become more complex and frame the remainder
of the adventures.

If the fresco is the visual equivalent of epic, perspective is that of the
novel. The success of a novel rests not only on the story but also on technique. Once Tintin stops thinking of himself as the incarnation of Western
values, his adventures lose their historical dimension and become totally
fictitious. Instead of political engagement, we find adventure, narrative,
and family history. Instead of relating a "memoir" of the Christian world,
Hergé's albums develop their own memoirs. Just as Archibald preserves his
ancestor's relics at Marlinspike, so too each album preserves the traces of the
preceding ones. In *The Seven Crystal Balls*, we meet the members of Haddock's family and many of the minor characters that Tintin had previously
met along his way, especially General Alcazar and Bianca Castafiore. Tintin's
past now reappears, as if it had been temporarily repressed, and contributes
to changing his present. This "return of the repressed" makes the fictitious
world more coherent and allows for the possibility of its own temporality.
Thus, a double chronology structures each adventure: first, the chronology
of each particular adventure; and second, that particular adventure's place
within the broader chronology of the episodes as a whole. It is this second
chronology that Hergé keeps in mind when he goes back to revise and
refine his first albums.

Hergé attempts to round out Haddock's family by introducing a feminine element. In this album, two women appear, both in the theater: the
clairvoyant Yamilah and opera star Bianca Castafiore. The first one is con-

trolled by a man, the fakir Ragdalam, who utilizes her feminine powers to distract his audience. But Madame Yamilah is too strong and too mysterious a character to become part of the family. She can read everyone's thoughts, and she knows the past as well as the future. Thus, she is too dangerous for our heroes, who would begin to doubt themselves. Which of them, after all, would be able to hypnotize *her*? In the first version, one sees her onstage in the Music Hall Palace revealing to the audience that Haddock has a flask of whiskey in his pocket. She acts like a disagreeable, suspicious wife rifling through her husband's pockets.

The second female figure to show up in this album is Castafiore, whom Tintin has already met in Syldavia. But the family is still too fragile to welcome her into its midst. Her overpowering voice drowns out any other sound. At Marlinspike Hall she does not hesitate to tell everyone else what to do. Like Tintin, Haddock—who compares Castafiore to a hurricane—tries to escape while she is singing her favorite "Jewel Song" from *Faust*. At this point, Haddock does not know that she will one day be heard all the way to the hall dedicated to his ancestor's memorabilia.

## TINTIN AND CALCULUS

If Captain Haddock was preceded by Snowy, Professor Calculus is clearly "engendered" by Tintin. As an older version of Tintin, the professor inherits some of the hero's roles in the primordial universe: he is the technician and the witch doctor, at home with both science and magic. When he rings Tintin's doorbell the first time, he addresses himself to "Mr. Tintin" and to no one else. Both of them are eager to discover the secrets of nature, life, and society, but they themselves are very secretive. Tintin refuses to divulge his "schemes" ahead of time, and Calculus shuts himself up in his laboratory and hates to have anyone poking around in his projects (*CA*, 14, I, 3). The professor is certainly proud to unveil his inventions, but he refuses to reveal his blueprints and ends up throwing them in the wastebasket by mistake (*DM*, 15, I, 3). He is as distracted as Tintin, who frequently bumps into things when he is lost in thought and confuses objects for people (*BE*, 3, III, 1). Tintin and Calculus have a similar sense of humor and temperament; they are both secretive, somewhat distant, and given to fits of pent-up anger—Calculus more so than Tintin. Stubborn and introverted, they do not like anyone to get in their way, and once they decide on a project, they pursue it at all costs. If the professor is deaf in the ordinary sense of the word, his young friend is deaf in the sense that he listens more attentively to his own inner world than to the real exterior one. Ultimately, however, their strength and their willpower allow them to accomplish many extraordinary tasks.

Even the names of these two characters point to a secret affinity: the initials of the Professor are T. T. [in French: Tryphon Tournesol], sounding a lot like "Tintin." Moreover, if one compares the professor to the sun that illuminates the adventures bearing his name (he sheds light on mysteries and dazzles those who approach him), *Tournesol*, the French word for "sunflower," practices a remarkable "heliotropism."[1] From beginning to end he "turns" toward Tintin—as the sunflower to the sun—discreetly, but continually. Although Haddock does not hide his irritation with Calculus's exaggerated introversion, Tintin seems not to even notice it. Tintin manages to get the professor to understand him without raising his voice. Even more so than Snowy and the captain, they seem to understand each other without the need to speak. Calculus inherits his young friend's famous way of swearing ("Crumbs!" or "Great snakes!"). Like Tintin, the professor never makes any allusion to his biological family, except one time, in order to deny its existence: "My sister . . . Let's see . . . My sister? But first of all I have to tell you that I never had a sister!" (*TP*, 42, IV, 2, 3). Although Calculus relies to some extent on the myth of the foundling, he is more successful than Tintin in integrating within himself certain characteristics of the bastard. His dream of the absolute holds only for science, and he does not try to impose his ideal on the world. He is affected by social success, and women do not scare him as much as they scare Tintin.

The two characters also share certain physical similarities. Calculus's brown goatee replaces Tintin's blond tuft, the two men are fairly small, and they have round heads and tiny noses. Their bodies are as supple as those of cats. Cuthbert attributes his agility to playing sports: "Tennis, swimming, soccer, rugby, fencing, skating . . . I did them all in my youth. Let's not forget the ring, too: wrestling, boxing, and even kick-boxing!" (*F714*, 7, I, 2). They do not smoke or drink, and they both seem utterly chaste. Their resemblance is so striking that when Tintin disguises himself to go look for the professor held prisoner in Borduria, he easily makes himself look exactly like Calculus, minus the beard (*CA*, 55, I, 3). The profound similarity between the two characters also shows up in two dreams—one Tintin's and the other Haddock's.

Calculus succeeds where the professors and scientists before him had failed because he becomes a permanent father figure, distinguishing him from the others in many respects. He is unique, avoids any risk of madness, and accomplishes a great deal without stifling Tintin. Anytime his power seems detrimental, he caps it and steps back. Calculus is at once too close and too distant for the hero to risk anything by their association. He is too close in the sense that they are so much alike; too distant, because they do not operate within the same domains, thus avoiding the risk of competition.

Calculus is also a father figure for Haddock. With Haddock, he enjoys a constant rivalry, either with respect to fame and fortune or the one woman they both encounter. Thus, Archibald and Tintin both become rather quickly attached to "the absent-minded professor." Archibald keeps a portrait of him in his gallery at Marlinspike, and Tintin carries a snapshot of him in his wallet (*CA*, 26, III, 2).

Although Calculus might have been humiliated on his first contact with the little clan, one can read this as a "trial," or a rite of passage permitting him to find his place in the family. At first he is a brother, a member of the trio, and a lord of the *Unicorn*. But since he shares the features of both the foundling and the bastard, he soon elevates himself to take the place of the ancestor. Nevertheless, this intrusion into the family is accomplished by a ruse that allows the other two "brothers" to accept him as the new incarnation of the Father. In *The Seven Crystal Balls*, Calculus is kidnapped by the Indians and condemned to death for committing a sacrilege. Walking in the garden belonging to his friend Professor Tarragon, he finds the sacred bracelet of the Inca Rascar Capac and slips it on his wrist. The bracelet is clasped on him like a pair of handcuffs and inadvertently leads him to the summit of the Andes. There he is put on a pyre to expiate his sin. If, on a conscious level, Calculus is innocent, certainly not intending to commit any sacrilege, on an unconscious level, his act has great import. He commits the supreme crime, taking the place of the king and setting himself up as the Father. His fault is as grave in the eyes of the others as that of the young Baron Staszrvich reclaiming the scepter. But Hergé excuses Calculus for doing the deed "in spite of himself," which explains why in the middle of the Peruvian adventure Calculus falls into complete unconsciousness. He has to be unconscious of what he has done so that his companions may also ignore it. The three of them participate in a kind of collective "bad faith." Even on the pyre, Calculus believes he is taking part in some kind of cinematic production. He sees his act of seizing power as only a fantasy, as an act having no meaning. Had he been conscious, his action would have disqualified him from his place within the family. As someone feared as much as awaited, he could have become the Father only by breaking the Law.

## THE SACRED AND THE SCIENTIFIC

The Peruvian adventure is greatly inspired by Gaston Leroux's novel *L'Épouse du Soleil* (*The Bride of the Sun*). From this novel Hergé borrows details of local color, descriptions of places, names of certain characters, and many elements of the plot itself.[2] The heroine of the story, Marie-Theresa of Torre, a descendant of one of the first disciples of Pizarro, is chosen by the Indians to become the wife of the Inca—that is, to be sacrificed to the dead souls of Atahualpa. Without recognizing the significance of her action, she slips on the golden bracelet that designates her the wife of the Sun, and she then finds herself implicated in a whirlwind of adventures leading to the Temple of Death on the island Titicaca, where she will be buried alive. Meanwhile, thanks to the devotion of the high priest Huascar, who is in love with her, she escapes death and rejoins her fiancé, Raymond, who follows her every move across the Andes. In his own version, Hergé eliminates the character of Marie-Theresa and replaces her with Calculus, a move that allows him to adapt the plot to Tintin's world while retaining its principal twists and turns. Despite the heavy borrowing from Leroux, one can read this double album as Hergé's own because he reworks enough of the external elements to give them a meaning in his own universe.

The Peruvian adventure constitutes the first of the author's "summations," where he takes stock of his created world. He structures that world in terms of the opposition between the absolute values of the foundling and the relative values of the bastard. But in this album he keeps this opposition outside the family. These incompatible values are now attributed to two different societies: one is founded on the sacred and closes itself off from the modern world; the other is secular, open to the modern world and engaging with worldly values. In this case, we do not have two individuals struggling against each other but two kinds of civilizations confronting each other, armed in their own particular way. Hergé's main characters travel from one world to the other to choose their final affiliation.

The first society, based on the foundling's search for the absolute, is a theocracy. This is the society of the Quechua Indians of Peru. Following Leroux,

Hergé shows us this world that has been refusing for 450 years to collaborate with the Spanish conquerors and to accept any compromise with Western values. The Incan descendants from Atahualpa, the main dignitaries and the elite from the entire country, retreat to their Temple of the Sun, an impregnable fortress in the heart of the Andes. Hergé's depiction of the temple is drawn from the archaeological site of Machu Picchu close to Cuzco, the former Incan capital, a site rediscovered by Hiram A. Bingham in 1911. Wanting to maintain their ancient traditions, the Incas are fixed in a mythical time frame oblivious to historical events. They collect gold not to exchange it for goods from the outside world but only to honor their gods. They repeat the rituals of the past and venerate the mummies of their deceased rulers as divinities. Their day-to-day life is demanding, setting an example for other societies of resistance. The Incas are hostile to the whites, rarely calling them anything but "foreign dogs." The Incas submit to their own priests, who rigidly uphold their traditional values and show no mercy toward the disobedient. Without this strict discipline, the Incas would be quickly assimilated into the foreign culture. The foothills of the mountains are the limits of the Spanish power. Beyond that, the Incas are in command. The Incan emperor, following Manco Capac, proclaims himself the "Prince of the Sun" and is treated like a god. Respecting tradition is the fundamental dogma of this society. Neither the costumes nor the customs have changed since the fifteenth century. The Incas have not borrowed any Western customs except superficially, only to disguise their real way of life. Because they live within their separate space at the heart of the sacred mountain, viewed as the all-powerful protective Mother, they can remain faithful to their traditional religious practices.

Hergé systematically effaces the real Incas' scientific knowledge, particularly their knowledge of astronomy, in order to make his contrast more compelling. He starkly opposes two systems of values that, historically, always end up combining with one another. In this album, on the contrary, science belongs exclusively to the West, religion to the Incas. The emperor is a god, and the high officials, related to him by blood, have priestly functions. The high priest is named Huaco; according to General Alcazar, who knows him under the name Chiquito, Huaco is "one of the last descendants of the Incas" (7CB, 57, II, 1). In the temple Huaco is in charge of the sacrifices. We see him making the ritualistic invocations to the Sun to ignite Tintin's pyre. Another Incan priest named Huascar (named after the high priest in Leroux's story), who occupies a lesser position in the Incan hierarchy, also intervenes in Tintin's adventure. At first Huascar pursues the hero out of hatred, but eventually comes to his aid.

Hergé reconstructs the Incan society by borrowing historical elements. The Quechuan society resembles a totalitarian theocracy, a form of government that Tintin would no doubt have approved at the time of his first two adventures to the Soviet Union and the Congo. The Incas have to serve their priests. They are bound by their word, not by a written contract, as in the West.[3] After trying to cause Tintin's death, the priest Huascar gives Tintin his word in the form of a *conopa*, a talisman intended to protect whoever wears it. In this way the hero is reconnected to the religious world. But Tintin then gives the talisman to the young Indian Zorrino, thus saving Zorrino's life. The Incan emperor promises Tintin to give him everything he desires (*TS*, 59, II, 1), and near the end of the adventure the emperor reminds Tintin that he had given Tintin his word. But the hero refuses to take advantage of the offer. All Tintin wants is forgiveness for his mistakes, his own and those of the West. To show that he has not entirely abandoned the values of the foundling, he himself gives his word never to reveal to the outside world the secret of the temple tied to the secret of his own past.

This secret society, constantly on the defensive, feels attacked when seven European scientists on an archaeological mission violate the tomb of an emperor and steal the mummy. Professor Hercules Tarragon, a former colleague of Calculus, exhibits in his gallery the mummy of Rascar Capac, adorned with all his royal ornaments, as if this emperor-god were nothing but an object of representation. Indeed, the great emperor Rascar Capac had a premonition that someday his funeral chambers would be violated by infidels, and he announced at that time that a terrible punishment would await the ungodly ones. After the departure of the European archaeologists, the Incas feel vulnerable. Although they retain their current emperor, he nevertheless loses a great deal of his former prestige by allowing the mummy, wearing the *borla*—the royal diamond and the sacred bracelet—to be abducted. In this adventure, the jewels play a role similar to that of Ottokar's scepter in the Syldavian affair. The Incan emperor finds himself in a position similar to that of Muskar XII on the eve of Saint Vladimir's Day. Although the threat to Incan society does not come from within (and there is no Müsstler to imperil their religious unity), the society's potential collapse comes from contact with the exterior world. With the seven archaeologists as its representatives, the entire Western world seems to play the role of traitor.

To avenge the sacrilege, and especially to honor the prediction of the ancestor, the Incan emperor appoints a group of the faithful, under the direction of the high priest Huaco, to recover the jewels and to carry out the prophecy. In the name of Rascar Capac, each of the scientists in turn is cast into a deep sleep, thanks to a solution of coca encapsulated in the crystal ball Huaco throws near the victims. Upon his return to Peru, the high priest bewitches the archaeologists and continuously tortures them by means of seven small waxen statues that he pierces with needles several times a day. But while carrying out his mission in Europe, Huaco loses Rascar Capac's sacred bracelet. Calculus by chance finds it and slips it on his wrist, thus becoming an accomplice to his colleagues' crime. When the Indian sees him do this, he knocks out the professor, drugs him, and takes him to the Temple of the Sun, where he will be executed for sacrilege. Thus far in the drama of the seven scientists, Haddock and Tintin have been merely spectators, but now they actively step in when their dear friend Calculus is directly implicated in the affair.

In contrast to this traditional religious society, in which similar individuals have a definite assigned place within the whole, Hergé constructs another society different point by point from the first. The tradition of the one contrasts with the novel inventions of the other; the sacred opposes the profane. The harmony of the Incan world contrasts with the constant changes of the European one. What has positive value in the one world has a negative value in the other. The Incas accumulate gold for the honor of their gods; the Westerners accumulate gold for business deals among themselves. Whereas the former develop a cult of the dead, the latter violate the Incan tombs and transform the sacred into mere historical curiosities.

Science demands that for an object to be known, it must first be destroyed in order to dissect it and classify its various components. Scientists are the priests of the West, and science takes the place of faith: the notion of truth replaces that of revelation. The seven archaeologists who represent the entire scientific "caste" are highly celebrated: journalists talk about their discoveries, the police protect them, and the state finances their research. The archaeologists bring back the mummy to analyze it. They dissect the elements of the cult to which it belongs in order to give a secular meaning to a religious mystery. But the sacred message of Rascar Capac does not make any sense to them. Professor Tarragon, who deciphers the inscriptions on the tomb, is deeply skeptical: "I've drafted a paper on the occult practices of ancient Peru. It seems to have some bearing, but I doubt if it will solve our problem" (*7CB*, 30, I, 2–3).

The West is out of touch with the sacred. Western hierarchies are not based on the essences of beings but on their wealth or their knowledge— that is, on what they *possess*. Western society lacks rituals and is out of kilter because it has lost an archetypal image, that of King as respected as God to provide the fundamental organizing principle. Modern society experiences a spiritual eclipse and loses the light of its political "sun." By unleashing the lightning, by hurling the balls of fire into the darkness of the West, Rascar Capac illuminates this dark wasteland and for a few seconds lends it a holy light. Like the king's ghost in *Hamlet*, the phantom of the Incan emperor abducted from Peru disturbs the Western world and eats away at it like re- morse. He digs into it like a mole, penetrating the Western conscience. In contact with the sacred lightning, Hercules Tarragon gradually loses his self- assurance and ends up vanquished by a mystery that his science is impotent to explain. The end of *The Seven Crystal Balls* seems to mark the triumph of the primal, magical world of the foundling.

Rascar Capac represents the quality of uniqueness we saw earlier in the Syldavian monarch. Rascar Capac's presence, beneficial in Peru, becomes harmful in Europe, where he reintroduces the sacred but only in a prohibi- tive mode, as a collective punishment. Tintin, Haddock, and Calculus each have the same dream simultaneously that the mummy is sneaking into their rooms to throw the dreaded crystal ball. This communal nightmare signifies that they are sacrificial individuals, separated from the rest, and that they must return to the world of the absolute to confront it directly. Everything religious that they—especially Tintin—have tried to shrug off returns here in the form of the repressed, along with the classic symptoms of repression: the inadequate defense mechanisms of delirium, compensatory actions, and disoriented behavior. If the scientists transform the emperor-god into a sci- entific object, the Incas transform these same scientists, as well as Tintin's clan, into religious subjects. They become sacrificial offerings because they embody the opposite of the Indian culture. The sacrifice of the archaeolo- gists, repeated each day as in the Mass, fuels the religious life and confirms the beliefs of the Quechuas. Thus, the Incas remain closely tied by their dog- mas and are not tempted to leave the sacred realm where they are confined. By magic, the priests show themselves to be superior to the scientists and preserve their prestige. On their side, the scientists find themselves weakened precisely because they display their knowledge and enter into a rivalry with religion. In this conflict, the sacred and the scientific make use of all the weapons at their disposal.

## THE DISGUISE

The opening of *The Seven Crystal Balls* displays the triumph of the bastard. Haddock has left the city and his old apartment to take up residence in Marlinspike Hall, where he lives with Calculus. His success comes like a windfall, and he lives like a nouveau riche. He is finished with his sailor suit and his navy pullover with the rolled collar. He now dresses like a true gentleman, in a tweed jacket, well-cut trousers, a felt hat, and a silk scarf fastened with a stickpin. In the evening he wears a bowler and tuxedo. He becomes as obsessed with his appearance as Snowy once was with his. Tintin, on the other hand, continues to wear the same old golfing pants that never seem to wear out. The captain now has an automobile and even a horse to better imitate the aristocracy of yesteryear. He hides his old pipes at the back of a cabinet and now smokes only Havana cigars. Even more astonishing, he has stopped drinking whiskey, but only because it seems too vulgar. He now takes cocktails that his servant Nestor ceremoniously prepares for him in a silver shaker. Following his master's example, the servant also ditches his yellow-and-black striped jacket for the more elegant morning coat. Haddock plays the role of a little king and cultivates the life of a prince. He wears a monocle, calls everyone "dear chap," and frequents the chic spots where one goes to be seen.

But the transformation of the old seadog into a gentleman is too sudden to be entirely credible. This role does not suit him well. Although his horse is a purebred, Haddock cannot stay in the saddle. He is constantly losing or breaking his monocle, and Nestor always has to have an extra on hand. Many years after Haddock has gotten over this temporary role of "snob," one of his monocles is found in the nest of the thieving magpie (*CE*, 60, II, 2). Haddock is too rich, lives in a house too large, and climbs the social ladder too quickly. As a result, he confuses real life with spectacle. He changes his life as quickly as one changes decor. He tries to regain the power he had on his ships, before his "retirement," but one cannot become lord of the manor in a few months, even if one can boast of having a prestigious ancestor. Mr. Cutts and Mr. Bolt, the butcher and handyman for the castle, gossip behind his back. Just at the time the captain needs him the most, Tintin becomes most estranged from him. The foundling has always fled from grand palaces, for he was hesitant to take up residence at a place where he had first been held prisoner. Tintin lets himself be won over to the grand life only gradually, like his friend the cat. His distrust is actually more justifiable than the captain's sudden success. The distance between them shows up when the captain addresses his friend with social formulas devoid of feeling: "Delighted to see you, my dear chap!" (*7CB*, 3, II, 1).

The bastard views the exterior world like a theater that he can modify at will. If he needs spectators to be fully convinced of his own success, and thus is always dependent on the judgment of others, he is also haunted by the idea of being nothing but a fake. Haddock swims in this world where the most stable things begin to float; they lose their stability precisely because they are regarded as mere props. When Nestor imitates Snowy's antics and contorts himself ridiculously so as not to drop his tray, the captain's first reaction is to applaud his performance, as if the servant were an actor in the Music Hall. When the castle's windows begin shattering, the captain leaves, disappointed like a spectator awaiting an act that never happens. The foundling's sacred values, when not transformed into the absolute of science, are degraded for the bastard to mere spectacle. From the captain's point of view, spectacle is the only form in which religion can survive. Upon his entrance into public life at Cana, Jesus changed water into wine. Similarly, Haddock wants to accomplish a miracle to prove to Tintin that religion is nothing more than white magic and that nothing can limit the powers of the bastard.

The captain's error soon shows up in his fascination with a little man resembling Tintin named Bruno, the king of conjurers, whom the captain takes on as a rival. For fifteen days following Bruno's first performance at the Music Hall Palace, Archibald attends every session, hoping to discover his conjuring secret. Not being able to overpower Calculus directly, Haddock tries to find a substitute father figure whom he can conquer more easily. Copying Bruno's every move, Haddock buys the same equipment, goes through the same actions with the same formulas, and expects identical results. If he could manage to change water into wine, Haddock would have the power to satisfy his daily desire for drink. Indeed, he would be able to erase the difference between his fantasies and the capacity to realize them. He would be the incontestable ruler. But his dream of omnipotence obviously fails. The capacity for metamorphosis—whether to transform creatures or things—is the privilege of the foundling.

Having decided to beat Bruno at his own game and at whatever cost, Haddock elicits Tintin's help, and together they head for the Music Hall Palace. Before the magician's act, they watch the acts of the fakir Ragdalam, Ramon Zarate the dagger thrower, and then Bianca Castafiore. What is billed in the theater as a single show actually has very different origins. The clairvoyant Yamilah belongs to the religious world, similar to that of the Incas. Possessed by spirits, she can actually see into the future and even understands the vengeance of the sun-god. Ramon Zarate is the stage name of General Alcazar, who was chased out of his country by his rival Tapioca and joins up with Chiquito to perform his act. True to the theatricality of his name, Alcazar goes from politics to show business. During his performance, his true identity is revealed, but he is able nevertheless to hide that of his partner, Chiquito, for the high priest Huaco is there only to avenge the Incas. Castafiore's journey is the opposite of Alcazar's, though still in his company. She goes from the stage of the Music Hall to the arena of politics, demonstrating on the way the profound identity between theater and government. The famous, or infamous, Bruno does not have the gifts of Madame Yamilah. He is more like the bastard than the foundling, for he is adept at fooling people and takes advantage of his technique to make them believe he can accomplish miracles.

Under the stage lights, the various activities of these characters become equivalent. They transform everything into mere show in the eyes of the Westerners, who like to compare everything but cannot distinguish the difference between genuine mysticism and mere trickery. The music-hall stage forms the microcosm of the *theatrum mundi*, the world theater, where everything appears the same because everything can be exchanged with everything else: real qualitative differences are reduced to mere measurable quantities. Furthermore, each of the actors hides his or her origin. Their acts come together to form the unity of the show, spreading the general illusion that envelops the spectators in a haze of meaningless signs. The Western world's capacity for constant transformation renders all human actions not only equivalent but also meaningless. Politics, religion, art—everything dissolves into mere images and ends up being a single performance during which the opposed values of the foundling and the bastard are both merged and conflicted. A real action is indistinguishable from an illusion; the boundaries between reality and fiction are wiped out. Genuine and disingenuous feelings play an equal role. Mrs. Clarkson, a member of the audience whose husband has just been targeted by the Incas for revenge, is falsely believed to be in cahoots with Ragdalam, who himself is likened to another Bruno. Chiquito, who is on a sacred mission, is mistaken for a fairgrounds barker. During the performance, all the dramatic signs in play are presented both on the stage and in the audience. But neither Tintin nor Haddock can distinguish them because they themselves are caught up in the whirlwind of the performance.

Viewed from the audience, the *theatrum mundi* keeps its secret. But we can spell it out here in the following way. In the performance, all the elements of the real are equivalent. They are no more than empty shapes combining into a whole. They constitute a general signifier that has no relation to any signified. In order to get to the bottom of the mystery, Haddock and Tintin sneak back and wander through a labyrinth of stage sets. Under the effects of the alcohol offered by Alcazar, the captain loses his footing. He suddenly finds himself in an incoherent world, both joyous and agonizing, where everything seems possible. The usual laws no longer apply. Gravity no longer holds: everything is floating, weightless. A wall collapses when Haddock closes a door. A marble column falls over when he leans against it, as if he were suddenly endowed with superhuman strength. Faced with his dream of power, Haddock loses his grip and becomes part of the general performance. A giant mask of a cow's head lands on his own head, transforming him into the Minotaur. He wanders onto the stage, where he interrupts the magician's act. Without a guide, he regresses to the animal level, to that primordial chaos where man and beast are one. Here we find one of Hergé's most constant themes: the union of human and animal.

Since the Music Hall reveals only deceptions, Haddock and Tintin do not return there. The key to the mystery is not to be found backstage in the theater but in the more hidden "backstage" of the West—in this case, in South America. They have to go back to the origins of the history of our society and of their own; they have to return to the world of religion in order to fathom the secret of life and death. As in the adventure of *The Unicorn*, the treasure is elsewhere, no longer in the material universe but in a spiritual one, symbolized by the globe at the feet of Saint John the Evangelist at Marlinspike Hall.

Marlinspike Hall itself provides a nice analogy for the evolution of Tintin's world. The part of the castle where Archibald lives is only the "worldly," visible part, but beneath that level Tintin explores its crypt. The former chapel is the perfect place for the foundling obsessed with absolute values. There in the crypt he finds the vestiges of history (the Bird brothers use the crypt to store their antiques) and the ancestor's treasure. In the current adventure, the characters again have to explore the subterranean region, now not merely of a Louis XIII castle but of an entire civilization. After Calculus disappears, Tintin and Haddock embark on this voyage of initiation to find the Father. At that moment, Haddock sheds his well-cut clothes and his monocle. Rather than wait for the reports of some incompetent detectives incapable of finding the professor, he prefers to follow the foundling on this new journey of discovery. Haddock pulls on his navy blue sweater, his old coarse uniform, picks up his sack, and heads for the sea. Before finding Calculus, he returns to his original element: "Just think: the port, the docks, the jetties, the ocean, the sea breeze whipping the spray in your face" (7CB, 54, I, 3).

## HUACO AND TINTIN

Each of the opposing two societies sends one of its heroes to the other world to learn about its dominant set of values, the sacred or the scientific. For Peru, their champion is Huaco-Chiquito. The whites have left his country, making off with the mummy and the jewels, thus in effect emptying the place of the Father. Genuine authority is vested not so much in the reigning emperor but in the founding Father, more distant and more powerful, for the actual ruler is only a temporary incarnation of that original one. Thus, the archaeologists disturb the theocratic order and cause an eclipse of the royal image. Huaco is sent to Europe to bring back the royal insignia and to reinforce the demands of the sacred by punishing the guilty. But the mission of the high priest is multifaceted. As Huaco, he prepares the sacrifices, but as Chiquito, he himself is sacrificed. In Peru, he is at the summit of the social hierarchy because he belongs to the bloodline of the Incas. In Europe, he plummets to the lowest level. Harassed by the police who confiscate his papers, he conceals his identity by pretending to be a performer in the Music Hall. In his free time, he takes up his mission in the name of Rascar Capac by throwing the crystal balls at the European archaeologists.[4] How he himself is being sacrificed is more apparent during the performance in the theater. Huaco stands against an executioner's pillar, as if Alcazar condemns him to death (the same situation Tintin faces in The Broken Ear). However, Huaco is not tied up there, for his sacrifice is voluntary, even while he plays the role of victim. The risks he takes are palpable, especially at the finale of the act when his partner is blindfolded and throws a dagger at a target held at the level of Chiquito's heart. As Haddock whispers to Tintin, just a few days earlier the act nearly turned into a tragedy: "The dagger landed just on the edge of the target. Half an inch further and that Indian would have been skewered!" (7CB, 10, IV, 1).

What the audience sees as just a theatrical performance more deeply resembles a religious ceremony. It is a matter of a sacrifice, renewed each evening, of a relation of the Inca, of a sacred individual becoming the substitute victim of the emperor. The other aspect of Huaco's activity, his sacrificing of others, makes him a criminal according to European law. He becomes liable to imprisonment, if not death. Thus, accomplishing a role most noble in the eyes of his own society renders him most ignoble in the eyes of the West. But in carrying out the vengeance of Rascar Capac, he liberates the ancestor from his carnal imprisonment. By allowing the mummy to revert to its original nothingness through purification by fire, Huaco lets the emperor-god cross over into another stage of the cycle of life.[5] Thus, Huaco restores the divine significance to the founding emperor who returns to the Sun, now at one with the god. Finally, Huaco returns to Peru and takes with him a person of equal importance to the world of science and to Tintin's family, Cuthbert Calculus, who will himself be sacrificed in the Temple of the Sun for making off with the bracelet of the king.

Tintin takes the reverse path. After the Incas kidnap the family member representing the ancestor, the young man leaves the realm of mere performance to bring Calculus home. Tintin also plays the dual roles of the sacrificer and the sacrificed. For a long time he has acted as a righter of wrongs, helping the weak recover their rights, disarming bandits, and dispensing justice wherever possible. Although he mainly persists in his role as the foundling, he becomes a kind of younger Chiquito, a universal avenger, the champion of absolute values. He is also frequently sacrificed. This particular adventure comes to a climax with Tintin bound to an executioner's pillar similar to Chiquito's. Having entered the Temple of the Sun, Tintin is charged with sacrilege. From the religious point of view, he is the most despicable, the abject, and cursed. But thanks to his knowing the exact time of a solar eclipse, he escapes death. What the Incas at his execution see as a religious mystery turns out to be a theatrical trick, resting on the ingenious use of a purely natural phenomenon. But the Incas do not understand what has happened under their very eyes. They are blind to everything but their own conception of reality, and hence prisoners of a holy fear. By carrying out his feat, Tintin manages at the same time to free Calculus, to return the Father to his rightful place after confirming his innocence.

Tintin and Huaco are in some ways perfect opposites. The Inca is old; Tintin is young. The former has a double name; the other, only one. True, they also have several things in common. The cat's presence around Chiquito certainly connects him with Tintin, but they share a number of more important characteristics. They are courageous, inscrutable, and strong willed. They both have the gift of metamorphosis. Despite the constant surveillance of the police, Huaco is able to throw the crystal balls without getting caught. At the home of Professor Tarragon, where all the shutters are closed, he slips down a chimney. Wounded by a bullet, he manages to climb a tree, overpowers Calculus, who puts up a fight, and finally leads him to the getaway car driven by his accomplices.

Tintin and Huaco are pitted against each other several times. Their first encounter takes place in the dressing room Huaco-Chiquito shares with Alcazar. He observes Tintin without saying anything. Tintin first fights with Huaco, without knowing who he is up against, in Tarragon's garden, and then aboard the ship *Pachacamac*. Their last encounter takes place in the temple, where Huaco the high priest invokes the sun-god to ignite the pyre. The two men no longer fight with weapons but with signs. Like two witch doctors in competition, each one pronounces incantations to see which ones will be most effective. Just as Ottokar IV used trickery to vanquish the young rebel, so too Tintin only appears to fight with the priest. Instead, he cheats. He seems to speak in religious terms but in fact relies strictly on his scientific information. Faith is vanquished by science. If faith knows only the holy rule, science can predict the exception and explain its meaning. Knowing the exact time of the solar eclipse, Tintin seems able to command the Sun not to ignite the pyre. His mystification proves stronger than the mysticism of his rival. This momentous duel, where each stakes everything—a duel between two individuals who seem to invoke the same order of meaning—is in fact a conflict between two very different ways to understand the world. The conflict also represents two periods of Tintin's world confronting each other. Chiquito fully incarnates the foundling, while Tintin does so only in appearance. In reality, his capacity for metamorphosis has dissipated. Tintin's power now relies on ruse. Science alone is true, and religion has only moral value. The hero successfully completes the double exploit by maintaining the illusion of the sacred while relying solely on science. Rather than Chiquito, Calculus is actually Tintin's chief rival, for both Calculus and Tintin give up magic and take advantage of rational knowledge. Tintin's feat is of the bastard type that Haddock tries so hard to develop in himself. But Tintin's skills are not as great as the Incas believe. If the captain had been the one to read in the newspaper about the date of the eclipse, and if he had dared to take on the trappings of an imaginary world of salvation, he would have done just as well as Tintin in pulling off this exploit.

## THE INITIATION

Hergé's work is in many ways similar to Jules Verne's. Just as has been argued for Verne's novels,[6] each of Tintin's adventures can be read as a novel of initiation. Through a series of trials, Tintin leaves behind the world of the child to acquire knowledge, a land, or a treasure reserved exclusively for the initiated. Surely this formula can be applied to many of the albums, but to apply it too broadly would lead to finding the same pattern repeatedly and thus would occlude the internal dynamic of Tintin's universe that interests us in this study.

Nevertheless, the adventure of the Temple of the Sun lends itself more than any other to an interpretation centering on initiation. This adventure is a voyage during which Tintin tries less to acquire a superior form of wisdom than to regain the power of the foundling that he previously possessed. He is accompanied by Haddock, who undergoes similar trials but only in a degraded way appropriate to the bastard. Furthermore, Haddock is especially preoccupied with restoring the Father to his rightful place in order to have someone to pit himself against and, if possible, come out the winner. Each step of the journey is marked by a rite of passage. At each stage, the heroes have to abandon things more or less important to them in the material world to attain a deeper purity and to confront what they do not recognize in themselves.

The first step of their journey of initiation begins at the doors of the Music Hall Palace. Tintin and Haddock have to go beyond appearances and cross forbidden boundaries: the doors backstage are marked "do not enter," and this interdiction is noted not once but twice in this context. Haddock tries to be Tintin's guide, but without success. He tumbles into a primordial chaos, an undifferentiated universe where humans are not separated from beasts. Tintin also finds himself in a confusing, circuslike world, similar to the old flea market where he purchased the scale model of *The Unicorn*. Tintin has to distinguish the important from the incidental, and the scientific from the sacred. He renews his acquaintance with Alcazar, who later reveals to him Chiquito's true identity and allows him to discover the first serious lead for finding Calculus.

The second trial concerns the balls of fire at Professor Tarragon's estate. Before vaporizing the mummy of Rascar Capac, the lightning bolt flashes around them, branding the three members of Tintin's family as the devil used to brand his victims. They find themselves isolated from the broader community and designated for sacrifice. This second trial ends with two departures: Haddock from his manor house, and Tintin from his apartment on Labrador Street.

Their investigation takes them to Callao, the port city of Lima, where the *Pachacamac* steams into the harbor. The story should end here, but instead it takes a new turn. The investigation ends, and the true quest begins. Tintin and Haddock have to decipher hidden meanings in what is said. Thus, they do not believe the doctors who claim there is yellow fever on the ship. Despite the official quarantine our heroes decide to sneak aboard the *Pachacamac*. This episode constitutes the third trial, rendered even riskier when the young hero has to swim to the boat through what Haddock notes are shark-infested waters. Once on the *Pachacamac*, Tintin dodges Chiquito's bullets, but only after Chiquito reveals the sacred character of the adventure by claiming that Calculus has committed a "sacrilege." The hero comes through this third trial fully resolved to follow Calculus despite lack of help from the police.

The last city they see with a Christian name and where Western values hold sway is Santa Clara. From there on begin the mountains and the Incan kingdom, separated geographically as well as culturally from the West. In Santa Clara, Tintin and Haddock buy train tickets for Jauga to follow the kidnappers' trail. On the train, under Huascar's orders, they are isolated from the native people, as if their sacrilegious character would contaminate them. This fourth trial is formidable, for it brings them to the brink of death. Huascar orders the engineer of the train to detach the last car containing our two heroes just when it begins plunging down the highest mountain. Once more, they come through. Tintin jumps off the train exactly at the border of the two worlds.[7]

A Spanish administration runs Jauga, and several whites live there. But the whites are unfriendly and aggressive because they feel constantly threatened by the Indian majority. In Jauga, the typical power relations are inverted, and

Western values are not dominant. When the mixed-race police commissioner learns that the Incas are involved in the case, he refuses to help Tintin. Having only the appearance of power, he is forced to obey the natives and to reveal no secrets. Like all the people in the town, the only thing he says is, "I don't know." Jauga is a small mountain village, very poor by standard economic criteria, but it is the frontier to the Incan territory. In this sense, it is a religious outpost. Tintin and the captain attract a lot of attention, since they seem to be the usual tourists, ignorant of traditional rituals and hierarchies, carelessly profaning religious grounds. One more time, our young hero finds a way to escape, thanks to his meeting with Zorrino, a young Indian harassed by two Spaniards. Tintin is shocked by the Spaniards' brutality and intervenes to teach them a lesson. Since young Zorrino is powerless in the face of their violence, the hero takes on the adults and, with Snowy's assistance, beats them up. This is the fifth trial, which benefits Tintin twofold: he converts two important people to his cause. The first is Huascar, who gives him the magic amulet. The second is Zorrino, who guides them all the way to the temple. These two characters are at the juncture of the two worlds. More easily than others, they understand the dual systems of values and agree to deal with Tintin. In the eyes of their religious compatriots, these two are traitors to their faith. In the eyes of the heroes, Huascar and Zorrino display a generosity equal to their own.

Haddock and Tintin, led by Zorrino, set out for the forest. He is only a child, the most vulnerable of all creation but also closest to the origin of sacred values. In traditional societies, the child sometimes takes on the role of priest. He holds the place next to Tintin formerly occupied by Coco and Chang. He takes the big brother for his model, even though he himself is participating in Tintin's initiation. Imitating the hero, Zorrino becomes Tintin, and this identification leads him to replay an episode of the foundling.

Jauga marks a new stage of the quest. Haddock and Tintin have to leave civilization, divesting themselves of its trappings, to return to a primordial state of being where humans are equal, or equally vulnerable, in the face of a hostile and all-powerful nature. For Hergé, nature—especially in the form of mountains and forests—generally connotes the primal Mother, both ambivalent and monstrous. When the heroes later enter the Incan labyrinth, hierarchies of wealth or poverty no longer hold. One must try to recover the ways of being forgotten by "the civilized" and return to the very source of human history. Zorrino prepares them for all this by asking them to provide the essentials—guns. Meanwhile, he obtains ponchos, food, and llamas, the animals that pose some difficulties for the captain. When they leave Jauga, they cross another gateway, the Bridge of the Incas. From here on, they give up the last vestiges of comfort, including regular meals and beds.

The first trial in this new stage of the quest consists in passing the night in the *chulpa*, the former Incan tomb. They have to come to face up to death in order to emerge from the tomb more mature. During the night, Tintin has nightmares. The physical trial is duplicated in a psychological one, for he has to confront his former demons (*PS*, 23, I, 1–3).

In the first part of the nightmare Tintin sees Calculus with his hat, umbrella, and pendulum. The professor discovers a glass bowl containing a fish and three skulls growing on stalks, called the Inca flowers. Is this a premonition of future punishment, or is it simply reminiscent of the three little monsters from Gaston Leroux's novel that left such an impression on Hergé?[8] Totally caught up in his study of the "plants," Calculus does not notice the death threat weighing on any individual seeking to discover the secrets of life. Behind the professor, an Inca decked out in oversized earrings, a plumed headdress, and a colorful shield is ready to pierce him with his lance. A fantasy or latent homosexual desire seems closely tied to death. The scene takes place on a beach at the seashore. This setting allows the dream to stand out more clearly than the one in *The Crab with the Golden Claws*, where Haddock had threatened to devour Tintin-as-bottle after having pierced him with the corkscrew. The fantasy confounding desire and

Panel 1: "Amazing! An Inca plant in bloom!"
Panel 2: "Excuse me, Señor Inca, but have you a license for that gun?"
Panel 3: "A license? Sacrilege! Sacrilege! The fire of heaven will strike you down!"
*PS*, 23, I, 1–3. © Hergé/Moulinsart 2007.

death is pre-Oedipal and belongs to Tintin's phase as the foundling. In this current episode, Calculus plays the same role Tintin played in the earlier adventures: he is searching for absolute knowledge and believes he is safe from all danger because he thinks he is omnipotent. Meanwhile, wearing the bracelet of Rascar Capac, the Incan parental figure—undifferentiated between Father and Mother—threatens him with death: Calculus-the-son discovers the scene—in this case, the flowers of the Inca—which he is not supposed to see.

Panel 2 continues the preceding scene but also changes it. The two characters are now replaced by Tintin and Haddock. Also, through a change in the elements of costume—the headdress, the earrings, and the shield—a device that Roman Jakobson identifies as metonymy,[9] Haddock now becomes the Incan chief. The lance becomes a rifle, and with a menacing air and his pipe in his mouth, the captain confronts Tintin. The setting now shifts to a theater stage with grass and sky in the background; the theater setting is appropriate to Tintin's bastard side. The parental figure incarnated by Haddock is clearly paternal. He no longer wears the religious bracelet but instead carries a rifle, smokes a pipe, and wears trousers. From now on the son has to face up to the Father and measure up to his demands. Tintin frowns just like the captain, an expression that Snowy and the llama also repeat. As the primal figure of the son as foundling, Calculus shrinks to tiny proportions and finally disappears from the scene. Tintin wears the outfit of a game warden who is asking Haddock if he has a license to hunt, that is, if he has the right to kill the all-powerful and sexually undifferentiated parental figure. The religious murder in panel 1 is contested in panel 2 and is prevented by the game warden. Whereas the foundling accepts the absolute values, the bastard challenges them in the name of a Law that ought to be respected by both Father and son (the right to hunt). From one scene to the next, the son grows up. He moves from the imaginary relation to the Father (the power to kill without having to realize any consequences) to a symbolic relation. Actions follow a system of codified relations. Right takes the place of might: to satisfy certain drives (sexual desire or aggressive impulse), one has to accept the Law governing that sphere (the taboo against incest and murder). Tintin and Haddock are both subject to the same Law; they both carry a rifle. Even if the Father has a more imposing stature than the son, they are both armed. Not everything is allowed.

In panel 3 the theater scene disappears. Now there is a plain background, the kind Hergé uses during Tintin's religious phase; in this instance, the background is the same color as the blue sea in the first image of the nightmare. This third stage of the dream marks a regression in relation to the second. The son once more becomes the foundling, punished by the all-powerful Father. Haddock is transformed into Huascar, the Inca who orders the train car to be detached to kill Tintin. Although the plumed headdress shrinks to a decoration on a helmet, the man still wears the oversized earrings and carries the colorful shield. He again wears the mummy's bracelet on his right wrist. The parental figure is once again sexually undifferentiated, both maternal and paternal, and condemns the son in the name of absolute values ("wretched sacrilege"). The son's crime is to have challenged the Father, to have set himself against the Father in the name of the Law that limits the parental authority ("Do you have a license for that gun?"). Tintin is struck by a flame coming from the heavens that is ignited by the miracle of the Father's raising his hand. The flame strikes Tintin on the head, the same place the Fathers (Ottokar IV and Philippulus) hit their rebellious sons. This punishment connects the recent balls of fire with the fire that will eventually ignite the ordained pyres of execution. Tintin, who has betrayed the religious world since his meeting up with the bastard, now sees himself as the victim of a religious punishment. This is a clear indication of the hero's unconscious guilt and his desire to be punished for having chosen worldly values over absolute ones.

After this episode in the tomb, several other trials await the travelers. They have to deal with the forces of Mother Nature (the snow) as well as many terrifying animals: a condor, a bear, flying monkeys, a gigantic serpent, a tapir, and crocodiles. The three companions outdo each other in generosity and ceaselessly come to one another's aid. Each time they leave behind some of their baggage. Haddock takes his last swig of alcohol, and the llamas run off with the provisions. All they have left are two boxes of cartridges wrapped in newspaper. They reenact all the discoveries of the first human beings: they make fire, fashion crude utensils (a walking stick, some rope out of twisted vines), and explore the natural caves. The captain grumbles but holds up; Zorrino and Tintin get to know each other better.

One can classify their trials according to the four elements. After the trial by fire come trials by water, air (falling into the abyss), and earth (the subterranean). When they finally arrive at the Temple of the Sun after many days of arduous hiking, they cannot find an entrance. The temple is surrounded by a gorge filled with rushing waters, like the moats of medieval castles. To enter, they have to ford the waters and pass through a series of caves and tombs, another journey to the realm of the dead. At last, having penetrated into the interior of the sacred place, they are thrown into prison, where they await their judgment from the Incan priest. Zorrino is judged first and is condemned to death in the name of religious values. The Incan high priest orders that his throat be cut on the altar of the Sun.

Tintin treats Zorrino as he always treats his doubles: he separates from them just at the opportune moment so as not to share in their faults. When the hero acts as the foundling, he returns Didi Wang, the typical bastard, to his family. Now that he himself is influenced by the bastard's values, he can no longer rely on any religious guarantee to endure his trials. Moreover, he gives away the sacred talisman that Huascar gave him. But again he sends Zorrino back into the world of the sacred. The little native boy is a perfect example of the foundling. Without any family, unselfish, and enamored with justice, Zorrino very much resembles Chang. Nevertheless, he betrays the secret of the Incas to help Tintin, whom he sees as a brother. In this sense, then, Zorrino is as guilty as Tintin.

Instead of continuing his worldly adventures with this companion, who is very similar to his earlier self, Tintin chooses to distance himself from Zorrino by giving him the protective amulet. In this way he saves Zorrino's life but also eliminates him from being an annoying witness. As a good foundling, Zorrino returns to the shadow of the Father, agreeing to spend the rest of his life serving the religious values of the Temple of the Sun. Having been threatened by the all-powerful Father, as Tintin had been, Zorrino finds himself protected by this self-same Father, who accepts him as soon as the young child agrees not to struggle with him any longer (PS, 61, I, 1). Thus, partially expiating his guilt by sending his double back into the world of the absolute, Tintin confronts the Inca.

At first he finds a kind of advocate in the person of Huascar, who translates Tintin's intentions in terms of the religious worldview and thus establishes a connection between the two opposing worlds. According to Huascar, Tintin and Haddock represent the Western judicial system, which rests on the notion of intention—specifically, good intentions. But they are being judged according to a religious code that rests on the notion of contamination. When the captain shouts at the Incan high priest that he does not have "the right" to put them to death (49, II, 1), he is relying on the law that limits the Father's power (the license to hunt). But for their Incan judge, the gravity of their misdeed is not reducible to their intentions. The judicial system founded on the absolute does not recognize any middle ground between Good and Evil: these are absolutes strictly excluding any relativism. For the Incan judge, Tintin and Haddock can either be pardoned or put to death. The confrontation between the two accused and the Incan high priest thus reproduces the combative structure of Tintin's dream. Nevertheless, Huascar insinuates some elements of the modern world into the conscience of the judge and thus manages to soften the strictures of the law. At least Tintin and Haddock are allowed to choose the hour of their death—a factor that eventually leads to their escape.

Faced with the judge who sentences them, the two friends react quite differently. Archibald is beside himself with rage, but his yelling and shouting do nothing to move the judge. Tintin, on the contrary, as if he were still the perfect foundling, totally accepts the pronouncement of the Father-Judge. He seems to accept the sentence but is still looking for a way to get around it. As a one-time journalist he finds the solution in the newspaper where he reads the announcement about the eclipse. This scrap of paper, the only thing they have left in the prison, this piece of paper with so little value from the Western perspective, becomes their most precious possession. It stands for all secular knowledge and proves to be more efficacious than all the sacred parchments where Rascar Capac had inscribed his absolute will.

## THE PYRE

Claiming his choice has something to do with the captain's birthday, Tintin chooses the day of their execution. But the choice reveals to what extent he makes the bastard the key character of their trio. From then on, Tintin is treated as if he belongs to the Incas. The "sacrificer" and the "sacrificed" are united in one religious act. In the magnificent apartment that then serves as their prison, Tintin continues to deceive those around him. He does not reveal his secret even to the captain, allowing him to wallow in the depths of despair (55, II, 1), thus showing how much power Tintin still exerts over him. While Archibald becomes more and more miserable, Tintin remains calm. As he faces death, Tintin's stoicism contrasts sharply with his companion's impotent rage. Haddock surely believes that Tintin's noble attitude reveals the superhuman heroism of the foundling, as serene before insult as before honor. But of course, this is pure show on Tintin's part. In the end, he is a tricky bastard who keeps a cool head so that his ruse will work, not an all-powerful hero who can pull off miracles.

The final trial rejoins the trio of "the lords of *The Unicorn*." The young Zorrino gives up his place in the trio to the older Calculus, and the young native returns to the primordial world that the three men will leave behind together. The three of them have opted long before for a life steeped in worldly values. When the three men are led to the pyres, Calculus emerges from his deep sleep and regains consciousness, although he remains ignorant of all the events that brought him there since his kidnapping. He connects what he sees going on around him with the time when Haddock spent every evening at the Music Hall. This is the first reason for Calculus's believing he is on a movie set. But there is another, deeper reason. Since he is so immersed in Western values, he cannot imagine that he could be the central character involved in a religious ceremony. He thinks of the world only in two categories: science and theater, the two opposing factors in the modern world. This is the reason he believes that he is witnessing a cinematic presentation extremely faithful to the original: "Ah, the cinema! Those people there are dressed like the Aztecs, I think. Or rather, I should say, the Incas. Yes, their makeup is perfect. And look at those dancers: so natural; who'd believe they are acting?" (57, III, 2–3). At that moment, Calculus caricatures the Western mind that cannot conceive of the Other except in the form of a pure representation that it conjures up to better control the potentially threatening Other. The Incas exist for him only on two "screens"—those of the cinema or exact historical science. Calculus himself as the spectator is thus "alienated" from the performance.

At this point the Thom(p)sons are finally linked to the Calvary-like experience of the little clan. They literally relive the sufferings of the condemned, thus creating a ridiculous counterpoint to the actual dramatic events. When Tintin reaches the temple, the summit of a spiritual as well as physical ascent, the detectives look for him in a "high place"—the top level of the Eiffel Tower, the highest place they themselves can attain (apart from the height of foolishness). When the captain falls into the abyss, the detectives look for the missing clan in a dark and deep pit, the bottom of a coal mine. When the sun is about to burn the condemned, the Thom(p)sons go to Egypt, to the Pyramids, "where there is a lot of sunshine." When their friends escape death and Haddock crashes into the wood pyre, the twin detectives check out the bumper cars at an amusement park: "No one! Yet the pendulum shows they are someplace getting bumped about!" (59, IV, 4). Although the detectives use the pendulum, the instrument of the Father (Calculus) that indicates the right direction ("a little to the west"), they cannot make it work except in a parodic manner, since they themselves are unable to avoid the attraction of the theatrical pole.

Because of his former familiarity with things divine, Tintin is the character best equipped to vanquish the Incas on sacred ground. But he is able to do so only because he relies on rational knowledge. He treats the Incas the way he treats Haddock: he does not reveal his secrets. He lets them believe he is still the all-powerful foundling, when he is really nothing more than a bastard a bit more gifted than his companion. Earlier in the adventure, we see the young hero fighting with the condor and taking on the figure of the Spirit-Bird (*Démon-Oiseau*). On the pyre, he communicates with another god from the Incan pantheon, Pachacamac (confused here with Uiracocha), the divinity who creates and commands the Sun. One last time Tintin defies Huaco the high priest. Pretending to command the Sun, he takes on the figure of the god Uiracocha. He restores to the Incas their own myths by reliving them, as one might do with a once-successful play: run it again to revive interest in it. When the Moon covers the Sun, the Indians are terrified, fearing that Tintin has plunged them into eternal darkness. This eclipse is more frightening than the one for the Syldavian monarchy, for it is not merely a matter of the downfall of a political order but of the very end of the world. In effect, concerning the analogy with the Sun, the Incas think of the physical, political, and religious realms as one; if it is extinguished, everything else disappears along with it. The Indians are in a situation similar to that of the Westerners confronting the mysterious shooting star heralding the apocalypse. Just as Chiquito fulfills the prediction of Rascar Capac, so too does Tintin seem to fulfill the great Incan myths. Having plunged the world into chaos, he brings it back to life in response to the emperor's pleas.[10] Thus, the hero is reintegrated into a religious world, returning to his former status if only for a moment. In the eyes of the Indians, he becomes Uiracocha himself, the white god who departs after his second creation and who promises to return. When Tintin returns the Sun to them, the Incas believe themselves utterly indebted to him. The power relation between Tintin and the emperor is reversed. The Incan emperor becomes the "sacrificed" and Tintin the "sacrificer." With this role reversal, the two become more intimate, as is appropriate for those in close relation with the gods. While the emperor continues to call himself the Prince of the Sun, Tintin, who has the power to control this most luminous star, can now be considered the Father.

Tintin's return to the religious world takes place only in the form of spectacle, of performance, a ruse of the bastard. His "return" lasts only as long as it takes to free his friends. After that, since he would not be able to maintain his divine reputation any longer, he flees from the temple, leaving the boy Zorrino behind as a kind of hostage. By stunning the Indians with the eclipse, the hero performs an act more appropriate to the Music Hall. Haddock, the great lover of theater, knows full well that this is only a performance and contributes to the theatrical atmosphere by breaking into a song by Charles Trenet.

Learning from his previous adventure, *The Shooting Star*, Tintin knows how to interpret the apocalyptic myths, and he uses this knowledge to convey yet another important message. He fulfills the promise of Uiracocha; he satisfies the messianic hopes of the Incas. In this way, he performs the same role as Pizarro, who was the first to take advantage of the myth of the return of the white god. Tintin apparently agrees to be sacrificed in expiation for the murder of Atahualpa.[11] But in reality he extends the power of the Spanish conqueror by substituting reason for violent warfare. He shows the Incas that their time of isolation from the exterior world is over. The magical universe is no longer justified and has been replaced by science. Tintin puts an end to the Incas' primitive period by introducing them to world history. He explains to the Incan emperor the foundational beliefs of the West by revealing to him the true motives of the archaeologists. He teaches him to distinguish noble motives (science) from base ones (Pizarro's lust for gold). The emperor tacitly accepts Tintin's defense, for he ends the torture of the seven scientists by ordering Huascar to destroy the seven statues used to bewitch them. Although the memory of Atahualpa's murder is not entirely obliterated, at least the relations between the Incan and European civilizations can be reestablished on friendlier terms, where blood no longer has the same role.

Tintin relies on his personal experience to help the religious society integrate into the modern world. Although he still carries traces of the foundling's rigid moralism, he no longer accepts the alienation from worldly values. After all, the moral individual has to belong to the moral community, for he no longer has at his disposal the resources and tricks of the bastard. Under the pressure of external circumstances and, of course, after meeting up with Haddock, Tintin changes his original attitude without totally assuaging his guilt. Because he changes, he believes the world has to change also so that he can think of himself as innocent. This is what he accomplishes in the adventure of *The Sun*: he uses the remaining resources of the hero to convert the Incas to his new set of values. When the absolute abandons him on the threshold of the Oedipal complex, such an absolute can no longer exist anywhere. Just as at the beginning he tried so hard to convert to the Good all those societies ensnared by consumerism, so too he now tries, a bit less single-mindedly, to transform the theocratic world, where he now feels too constrained.

The benefits Tintin draws from his Music Hall performance are many, both for the world of religion as well as of science. For the latter, there are advantages in both the private and public spheres. For the family, he restores the innocent Father to take his place between the two sons. Haddock is no longer alone in his rivalry with Calculus. Now Tintin shares that position insofar as he has used scientific knowledge to save the Father's life. Most important, the hero now feels secure within the family, for the Incan emperor offers him a treasure. Just as Lord Hadoque leaves to Archibald the treasure chest of Red Rackham, so too does the Incan emperor leave to Tintin a portion of Rascar Capac's fortune. Now Tintin can feel like an heir, an individual tied to the sacred. Tintin uses this gold to pay for his right to participate in the family structure that he had struggled against for so long. At the conclusion of this adventure, he discreetly moves out of his apartment on Labrador Street to move in with the other two in Marlinspike Hall.[12] He becomes a full-fledged member of the family, without having to worry about the threat of castration that the Father had always held over the son for wanting to take his place.

With respect to the broader society, Tintin now feels more in tune with its dominant values. Far from feeling drowned by the masses, he lives as an exemplary individual. In effect, his adventure in Peru allows him to acquire a quasi-religious dimension within the secular world. Mounting the sacrificial pyre, accompanied by the two thieves, Tintin recalls the sacrifice of Christ on the cross. Surviving the trial by fire, he also evokes the figure of the Phoenix, the bird-king, the bird-Christ, the unique bird who consumes itself only to be reborn from its ashes. But his death is no more real than his sacrifice. Deprived of his capacity for metamorphosis, he may well replay his former role, but he will never be more than an actor like the others. He is now condemned to the world of the theater, even though he saves himself by science. Tintin may be able to accumulate for himself all the sacred images of the world (that is, his capital), but he will only sink further into the world of representation.

The Incas constitute the last religious society. Not only does the hero flee from them but he also contributes to contaminating their purity by introducing them to the notions of relativity, intention, exchange, tolerance, and the search for truth—the bases of modernity. If a society with absolute values still exists, Tintin would never know it. It would be a society beyond human beings, a society of extraterrestials. The hero now has the choice between being a Pelican or a Phoenix, acting on the great stage of the public world, or playing the role of a cat, his other emblematic animal, in the domain of private life.

## CHAPTER ELEVEN

# DANCING ON THE MOON

## MAMMOTH AND WHALE

Now the family is together again. Despite the absence of the mother, the family invents its own rituals and hierarchies. While Tintin and the captain pursue an adventure in Khemed, where they lock heads with Dr. Müller, Calculus deepens his transformation at Marlinspike Hall. From the small-time, ridiculous "Rube Goldberg" inventor, he becomes a scientist with an international reputation. In the adventure *Land of Black Gold*, he alone is able to analyze the composition of element N14, which increases the combustion power of gasoline, and he invents the cure for the Thom(p)sons' curious hair-growing affliction. Although in the course of his research he blows up the castle, by the time Tintin and Haddock return to Europe, the damages are repaired (*DM*, 1, I, 3). In the following adventure, he sets off for the moon.

What is striking about the double album dedicated to the lunar conquest is its meticulous attention to scientific facts. At the beginning of the 1950s, Hergé wanted to offer some elementary scientific explanations to a public unfamiliar with atomic physics. This explains the rather pedagogical tone of these volumes, although they are also tempered by Hergé's refusal to take himself too seriously. To make Calculus's conquest of the moon more credible, it had to be set in the not-too-distant future when a voyage of this magnitude was imaginable a good fifteen years before its actual realization.

This new escapade is undertaken in the name of science. Its criteria are no longer Good and Evil, but Truth and Error. On several occasions Calculus worries about the precision of his calculations, for even a minor error would be fatal for the members of the expedition (*DM*, p. 59; *EM*, p. 14). Phenomena that used to be explained morally now become matters for physical explanation. For example, in the analysis of *The Blue Lotus*, we emphasized that Good and Evil were conceived as dual magnetic attractions: every creature is attracted to either one pole or the other. To help maintain their pull toward the Good, people create support systems, such as secret societies, religious institutions, and so on. We see these same phenomena in the lunar adventures. Haddock has a difficult time shaking his origins (from the time of the *Karaboudjan*) and suffers a relapse. He is not in his element with either air or fire, and he cannot stand the oxygen tank or the weightlessness he experiences in the spaceship. After gulping down quite a lot of alcohol, he decides to eject himself from the spaceship in full flight and to return to Marlinspike Hall (*EM*, pp. 7–11). Once outside, he is sucked into the orbit of Adonis, an asteroid formed from a former planet. Now he is no longer attracted to the world of crime but to a lifeless planet that changes him into its satellite and thus impedes his freedom.

Calculus is the star of this adventure. This is a story of how the creation of the Father can be diverted from its goals and become an instrument of Evil in the hands of the unscrupulous. Here we meet several traitors. Boris, the former chief counselor to the king of Syldavia, now is operating under the assumed name Colonel Jorgen as a spy for a powerful totalitarian regime. Out to steal the secrets of Western technology, the members of this spy ring probably belong to the former Syldavian aristocracy disavowed by Muskar XII. As in former times, they still address each other as "Baron." They hide out as undercover agents and set up a secret laboratory in Sprodj that doubles as a factory. Through their agent Frank Wolff, who is also Calculus's assistant engineer, they keep up to date on the stages of the lunar exploration, which they christen "Operation Ulysses." Each of the "factory workers" has a code name or number. Haddock becomes "Whale," and Calculus is "Mammoth." The spies give Calculus this name not because of his physical appearance but undoubtedly because of his intellectual weight. He holds the place of the kings Tintin had met earlier in his life, and as happened to these kings, the professor's power is weakened by a villainous adviser whose very name suggests his secret flaw. Although the first name of Frank Wolff may suggest honesty, his family name testifies to his cruel and duplicitous character.

Meanwhile, Calculus seems to be a reliable monarch, competent, respected, but sometimes difficult to take, especially for the captain! Dominated by Calculus as the overbearing Father, the captain regresses to an infantile stage. With the launching of the spaceship, Archibald experiences its incredible acceleration as overwhelmingly crushing. As he puts it, "It's like having an elephant on my back!" (*DM*, p. 60). The captain and the professor have now established their places in the family hierarchy. They cannot change them without risk. On the evening of the arrival of their hosts, Mammoth inadvertently switches his ear trumpet with Whale's pipe. This reversal of masculine symbols provokes the outbreak of a fire that threatens the security of the factory.

In a sense Calculus returns to his submarine project by substituting for water the elements corresponding to his nature: air and fire. The submarine and the spaceship have roughly the same shape, except that the machine lying horizontally to explore the bottom of the sea now stands vertically to conquer the heavens. It becomes enormous. In this respect, Hergé enjoys playing with extra-large plates to reinforce the majestic appearance of the spaceship. Earth is seen from a strange, interplanetary perspective that makes it seem minuscule. The spaceship, in contrast, is shown the first time on take-off, magnifying its power. On page 42 of *Destination Moon*, a tiny Calculus exhibits his most formidable creation to a dumbfounded Haddock: "Look what I created, me, Cuthbert Calculus! And that, I suppose, is what you call 'acting the goat'?"

The lunar adventure is presented in homage to the Father's creative power, whether artistic or scientific. Even the skeptics—and they include those close to Calculus, especially Haddock—cannot hide their admiration. When he climbs into the spaceship for the first time, Archibald is as dumbstruck as on his first visit to Marlinspike Hall: "Amazing! Astonishing!" (*DM*, 44, II, 3). One of the first words spoken on the moon is Haddock's testimony to the scientist, the kind of praise the captain usually reserves only for Tintin: "The Moon! Just imagine, walking calmly along on the Moon! Old Calculus is an incredible fellow!" (*EM*, 26, IV, 2). When the spaceship is safely back on earth, Tintin speaks for all of them by welcoming Calculus in these grand terms: "Here comes the conqueror of the moon!" (*EM*, 62, I, 2).

The lunar adventure clearly marks a change in point of view. Creatures and things are no longer perceived on an earthly scale but in terms of the entire universe. On the one hand, human beings become minuscule, and the planet they inhabit floats like a big balloon in the sky. On the other hand, these dwarfs are capable of gigantic creations such as the spaceship itself. Calculus encapsulates in his own person this dual viewpoint. Without ceasing to be the fussy and somewhat ridiculous character we know from earlier adventures, he becomes at the same time a creative genius, capable of producing a work greater, more lasting, and more impressive than himself. His creation, realized under his direction but with the help of numerous collaborators, transcends the individual personality of the scientist and endows him with the stature of a giant. That explains the rage that overwhelms him when Haddock treats him like an "old goat." The professor makes the captain follow him from one laboratory to the next to teach him about the precise conditions and measurements of his scientific creation. He ends the visit with an exclamation that contrasts the smallness of the man with the grandeur of his accomplishment: "Well, what do you think of that? Look what the old goat created!" (*DM*, 41, IV, 3).

Identifying completely with the spaceship, Calculus grows in size until he reaches the proportions of the founding ancestor. In the lunar adventure, neither Tintin nor Haddock can easily communicate with Cuthbert, who is always preoccupied with resolving some problem or other. But they also lose the opportunity to compete with him. So that the Father does not revert to the all-powerful being he was in the first albums, Hergé resorts once again to the principle of twinness, or duplication. While Calculus takes the place of Lord Hadoque, the ancestral Father, Baxter, the director of the factory, plays the role of the ordinary, everyday father. Baxter views the captain as simply a large, rather backward child whose childish antics get in the way of the collective operation. The director is forever scolding the captain, usually with good reason. One such incident occurs when he surprises Archibald in the act of imitating the opera star Castafiore in front of the control panel of the trial spaceship.[1] After snubbing the captain ten times, Baxter finally proposes to Haddock that he start acting like an adult and asks him to uncork the champagne. This scene takes place before the launching of the spaceship, and the men have a good time together on the eve of the greatest trial of their lives. Archibald, however, cannot manage to control his actions. The champagne cork pops into his mouth, the champagne spills on the ground, and Snowy is the first to lap it up. In contrast to Haddock, Tintin never has to be reprimanded: he observes all the rules, asks permission to do things, and never directly challenges Baxter's authority.

Calculus is reduced to being the ordinary father only when he has a fall and loses his memory and his ability to continue the project. This accident is as dramatic for the science laboratory as the fall of the king for the nation. This is really the second image of the death of the Father Tintin and Haddock experience. The first occurred upon their arrival at the factory in Sprodj. They saw one of the workers apparently bludgeoning the professor on the head (*DM*, 7, IV, 3). But what the sons interpreted as an attempted murder was actually a scientific experiment to test the strength of the Plexiglas space helmet.

But now Calculus's amnesia benefits only Haddock, who secretly is relieved that the Father has lost something of his "mammoth" importance. Under the pretext of trying to cure him, Whale expresses his unconscious ambivalence toward the Father, whom he wants to eliminate by taking his place. First, Haddock disguises himself as a policeman on horseback threatening to charge at the professor. The latter's total indifference to this ploy incites Haddock to brandish an immense phallic object shaped like a serpent that springs out of a trick camera. Calculus does not react at all, even when Archibald threatens him with a gun: "Calculus! Prepare to die!" (48, I, 3). Then Haddock places a firecracker under the professor's chair, singeing only himself while Calculus remains immovable. Later that evening Haddock returns disguised as a ghost, haunting the conscience of the scientist. "Beware, Cuthbert! I am a gho-o-ost! Shake in your sho-o-oes! I have come for your soul!" (49, I, 2, 3). Nothing happens. Each threat backfires on the impious son. Haddock cannot satisfy his desire, even in the form of playacting. In the end, instead of killing the Father, he ends up curing him and restoring his power—a fact he later regrets: "And to think I gave that gherkin Calculus his memory back!" (59, II, 3).

Tintin adopts quite a different attitude. Toward Calculus as well as Baxter, Tintin is always submissive and agreeable. Only through his contact with the professor is Tintin able to come up with certain scientific ideas of his own. It is Tintin, for example, who suggests to Calculus a device that will blow up the trial spaceship in flight (33, I, 4). Each time Tintin has the opportunity, he imitates the Father, learns how to manipulate the controls, and thus manages to replace him at the opportune moment. In fact, Calculus's temporary amnesia reappears during the return of the spaceship. When Cuthbert loses consciousness and is obviously incapable of taking command of the landing on Earth, Tintin takes his place and becomes the scientist's rival. Always full

of tricks, the hero nevertheless lives in the shadow of the Father, and he lets
Calculus take all the credit for the expedition. Calculus has the final word,
even if it is thanks to Tintin that the astronauts return safe and sound.

## THE VOYAGE

Although the lunar expedition theoretically takes place in the name of pure
science, technology, and contemporary rationality, it quickly changes its course
and becomes a mystical quest to the extent that Calculus takes on the role of
the sacred ancestor. As in the Incan adventure, we witness an initiation process,
except that now the heroes operate within the sacred realm instead of outside
it. The religion is, of course, science itself, now the only religion recognized
in the West. Even if the author struggles to explain its operations, science still
remains a mystery to most. When Calculus lapses into amnesia, Baxter insists
on the fact that Calculus "*must* be cured! He alone, he alone knows the secret
of the nuclear engine!" (*DM*, 46, IV, 3). Although mastering the atom is conceived here less allegorically than in *The Shooting Star*, the atomic project still
remains within the alchemist tradition: controlling the atom replaces making
gold. The atomic project is the Great Work of contemporary society and offers formidable power to whoever masters its secrets. Thus, it is imperative that
the forces of Evil do not gain access to this knowledge. While Baxter plays the
role of the Incan leader—and even has the same profile—Calculus takes over
the more powerful role of high priest of the scientific faith. Just as in the case
of the Incas in *The Prisoners of the Sun*, all the workers in the Sprodj factory
wear uniforms and strictly obey orders. Each one has a number indicating his
place in the hierarchy and allowing him to prioritize the collective over the
personal. Tintin and Haddock are no longer religious so much as scientific
initiates. They arrive at the factory only after a voyage filled with several trials,
but these are less harrowing than the ones they experienced in Peru. After all,
the real voyage takes them to the deserted "planet"—the Moon! On a light
note, the captain is squirted a few times with mineral water, as in the episodes
with the squirting llamas in Peru. But on a more serious note, the two brothers once more have to rejoin the Father, who calls them to participate in a
new quest. Calculus remains within the interior of the holy tomb, this time
not as a victim but as the high priest. He no longer plays the role of the sacrificed but of the sacrificer, as a way to connect with the absolute.

Landing at the airport in Klow, Tintin and Haddock have to negotiate a
certain number of passageways, customs, barriers, helicopter controls, and so

forth. A road sign tells them they are in a restricted zone, but since the Father is summoning them, their difficulties are ironed out. Their guide is no longer the child Zorrino but a mysterious chauffeur, as mute as a harem guard, whose only response to all their questions is "Sprodj." Like the Temple of the Sun, the atomic factory is built on an elevation, atop the Zstopnohle, the summit of the Zmyhlpathian Mountains. To get there, one has to cross various uninhabited and inhospitable areas. The entrance to the Temple of Science is not a tomb but an underground parking garage under strict surveillance by armed guards. Once in the factory, the two aspiring scientists are subject to special training, marking a rupture with their former lives. Frank Wolff and Calculus himself serve as their mentors. After some months of interminable waiting, they are finally "pure" enough, worthy scientists ready to undertake the grand voyage—an experience they will come to regard as a provisional death sentence. Haddock prudently draws up his will, and Tintin wonders "if this adventure isn't going to be the very last" (*DM*, 59, II, 1). As for Calculus, he knows there is only one alternative to success: "Will the rocket take off as planned when I press this button, or will everything blow up?" (59, III, 3).

Whereas the adventure of *The Sun* highlighted the contrast between the sacred and the scientific, the adventure of *The Moon* tries to reconcile them in the name of the Father. In the preceding quest, Tintin managed to unite the two worlds only by a compromise based on a lie, which in fact rested on his technological prowess. Hergé thus surrounded his hero with a sacred aura by underscoring the continuity between the archaic and the modern. In this respect, Hergé opposes an entire line of contemporary thinking that insists on the idea of rupture, or discontinuity, in the epistemological field.[2] The objective, scientific knowledge Hergé introduces into those albums initially served to reinforce the religious image of his three adventurers. After having shown in the previous albums by what stretch of the imagination the sacred could still exist today, Hergé now attempts an about-face. He does not dare to push his claim regarding the relation of science and religion to its logical conclusion. Rather, it seems that his heroes can survive in the contemporary world only if they are supported by an ancestral narrative preventing them from becoming rootless and alienated like the rest of modern humanity. Arguably, the traditional notion of heroism running through *The Adventures of Tintin* is incompatible with modern life, and modern fiction can present only lesser human beings.[3] Hergé's work opposes this modern tendency by regilding the iconic image of his three protagonists.

After successfully completing a series of preparatory trials, Tintin, Haddock, and Calculus are symbolically sacrificed in the name of all humanity. The day and the hour of this sacrificial ritual are fixed as precisely as those of their execution on the Incan pyre. They are separated from the rest of humanity and led into a sacred space (on the launching pad), then locked within the spaceship that they come to see as their tomb. In the Incan adventure, Tintin is likened to the figure of the Demon-Bird; in this adventure, he becomes the figure of Icarus, and Calculus takes over the role of Daedalus. But the modern Icarus does not disobey the Father and does not fly too near the Sun. Haddock, on the contrary, in jumping out of the spaceship to fly home on his own ("I have become a finch!") barely escapes becoming a permanent satellite of Adonis.

Before the actual moon-landing, the space voyage itself is the heroes' ultimate test. Like Jonah in the belly of the whale, they have to live in the spaceship, a technological monster both male and female, red and white. On the one hand, Calculus's invention is an immense phallic object, pointed toward the Moon, a "forbidden" virgin territory, unsullied by any living creature. On the other hand, the spaceship is a maternal belly, a womb where the heroes go to sleep, even at the risk of being suffocated. They pass out after the launching, experiencing a kind of temporary death that cuts them off from Earth's atmosphere. Each of them regresses more or less to earlier phases. Haddock falls back into alcoholism. The Thom(p)sons go through the same experiences as the heroes but in a comic mode. To add to the levity, for example, they have a relapse of their hair-growing affliction. Human laws become unstable and unpredictable; the physical universe moves in ways never before experienced. Whiskey forms itself into little balls, and the men float upside down. Earthly time and space no longer apply on the moon, where one day equals fourteen ordinary ones. Although they walk on the Moon dressed in space suits like medieval armor, the three knights of *The Unicorn* realize that this adventure is the beginning of a brand-new relation between humanity and the cosmos.

In some ways, this initiation voyage marks Tintin's return to the imaginary world of the foundling. The Moon plays the same role as the meteorite in *The Shooting Star* episode. The heroes discover a maternal universe, unknown and stifling. While their apocalyptic adventure subjects them to this irrational world, they are also protected from it by the Law of the Father. Star, sun, and moon represent three stages in their allegorical quest. Using these cosmological forms, Hergé explores the fantasies of childhood. From one episode to the next, Tintin discovers that these "worlds" are less frightening and less unpredictable than he had thought, and thus more manageable by reason. On the Moon, the hero once more has to negotiate deep subterranean caverns. He falls into a cave and discovers ice at its bottom. These extreme conditions threaten to kill Tintin, but the captain manages to save him by throwing a rope down to bind them together once again. But on this occasion Tintin does not regress to his primal fears and fantasies. A different experience with ice and snow later in Tibet will stir up those primordial anxieties.

Despite its traps and dangers, the Moon is the Good Mother because it is subordinated to the Father who lays down the Law. Calculus keeps the daily log and thus controls the discourse, incessantly explaining, analyzing, and predicting various events to keep his sons informed and forewarned. Protected as much by their space suits as by the professor's scientific information, the sons give themselves over to the poetry of childhood. Frolicking on the moon, they revert to a boyish world of fun and games, where the adult laws are turned topsy-turvy and allow for the frivolity of youth.

When the Thom(p)sons confuse Hipparchus's crater (*le cirque Hipparque*), where the spaceship is supposed to touch down, with an amusement park (*un cirque forain*), the twins once again introduce the clown theme. This initial blunder leads to many others that pave the royal road to the collective unconscious of the little family. Haddock echoes the detectives' mistake when he announces a bit later: "We're on the Moon [*la Lune*], you know, not at some amusement park called 'Luna Park'" (*EM*, 33, II, 1). Because gravity is six times less than on Earth, they all become weightless and "lose their gravity." Their slightest jump becomes a giant step. The detectives soon get used to it, and their ridiculous behavior reaches poetic heights in the surprising scene where the two of them hold hands and dance a ballet on the surface of the moon.[4] Following their example, Snowy flies "like a dragonfly," Haddock skips like a puppet on his strings, the lunar ship transforms into a set of bumper cars, and Tintin slides on the ice as if on a toboggan and crashes into Snowy. They lose all their disciplined, adult behavior and regain the free and easy movement of childhood. Tintin introduces his companions to a world close to the primordial world of the Congo, where they regress to the primitive state of half human, half animal. Perhaps they even regain the gift of metamorphosis.

No matter how severe, the Law of the Father that protects them is now nevertheless contested. If Calculus thinks that the expedition is entirely directed toward the Good, he becomes progressively disenchanted—the first time when he realizes they have set off with the Thom(p)sons on board, and then again when he learns of Wolff's betrayal. The high priest of science has certainly preached solidarity ("My friends! Calm down, please! Are the first men to land on the Moon going to begin by quarreling?" [*EM*, 19, II, 4]). But he cannot prevent rivalry or the infiltration of Evil. On several occasions, Boris and Wolff try to commit a crime. During the voyage home, the first of them is killed, and the second commits suicide, trying to make amends to those who had trusted him.

The heroes' return to childhood signifies neither a confrontation with the primal maternal image nor a return to innocence. The sons remain at the Oedipal stage, which means that they are potential rivals to the Father. Tintin exhibits no desire to take over the place of the Father, but Haddock manifests his latent aggression several times. The third "son," Frank Wolff—neither wholly good nor wholly bad—does not directly pose a threat as a rival to the Father, but he does allow the Law to be put on hold by the forces of Evil. Just as Alcazar had done earlier, Wolff introduces into the former Manichean universe a certain complexity and ambiguity prefiguring the values of the final segment of Hergé's work. At the end of the lunar adventure the Father has to choose. On the one hand, he may grow in stature and run the risk of turning into the undifferentiated parental figure; he would become the all-powerful being of the opening adventures and tip the universe in favor of the absolute values of the foundling. On the other hand, he can remain the Father with whom the sons have to compete and accept the risk of being overcome. He would thus collapse the world of Tintin-the-foundling in favor of relativity, complexity, and ambiguity—that is, he would assure the triumph of the values of the bastard. The fact that the author gives the last word to the captain suggests the direction of his preferences.

# PART THREE
# WAGG

What is this world, Mr. Holmes? A vast composite subject to revolutions
that all indicate a continual tendency toward destruction; a rapid
succession of beings that follow one another, push to the forefront, and
then disappear; a fleeting symmetry; a momentary order.

—Diderot, *Letter on the Blind*

## CHAPTER TWELVE

# THE DEGRADED WORLD

## THE SACRIFICE OF THE FATHER

*The Calculus Affair* marks the beginning of the final period of *The Adventures of Tintin*. This third phase can be distinguished from the others even by the albums' titles. In the first phase, the titles indicated the geographical nature of the adventures: *Tintin in the Land of the Soviets, in the Congo, in America, in the Land of Black Gold, in the Orient, in the Far East,* and *in Syldavia*. (The last three were the original titles of *The Cigars of the Pharaoh, The Blue Lotus,* and *King Ottokar's Scepter*.) Instead of attaining some psychological depth or becoming more mature, the hero simply travels to the four corners of the globe. What he is unable to accomplish in a temporal sense, his career as reporter allows him to accomplish in a spatial dimension.[1]

The second phase of the adventures, which includes the three albums *Star, Sun,* and *Moon*, begins with his meeting Haddock. This phase tries to work out a balance between transcendent and worldly values, between the worlds of the foundling and of the bastard. The other titles from this period—*The Secret, The Treasure,* and *The Crystal Balls*—highlight the mystical dimension of the world that can be revealed only in an esoteric knowledge acquired through an initiation process involving a journey to outer space or to a distant, sacred past.

The third phase of the adventures brings us back to earth, but to a world that Hergé henceforth presents as run by the logic of "wheeling and dealing." *The Calculus Affair, The Red Sea Sharks, Flight 714, Tintin and the Picaros,* and even *The Castafiore Emerald* show us a world of unsavory trafficking,

**191**

where violence imposes its own laws and eliminates every trace of mystery.[2] The initiation process is completed. Detective work takes precedence over any mystical quest. The qualitative dimension gives way to the quantitative. Only one album escapes this sort of universe: *Tintin in Tibet* has the hero return to his past and openly confront the myths he represented at the beginning of his journey. Thus, this title is similar to those from the first phase.

As we noted, the second phase of Hergé's work revolved around the conflict between the foundling and the bastard. Although Tintin is transformed as much by his dealings with Haddock as Haddock is by his contact with the hero, neither one of them achieves a decisive victory over the other. The final phase of the adventures shows us an unstable but enduring equilibrium between absolute and worldly values. These final adventures attempt to synthesize the opposing values in new ways that at least satisfy the two parties involved. Since the Father participates in both systems of values, one side or the other could win if he were to take sides. But the Father refuses to interfere with the sons, both of whom resemble him to some extent. To maintain this dynamic balance between the opposing values as well as to solidify the father figure, Hergé has Calculus revert to his former self. The only album that bears his name marks both his triumph and his defeat. The title page of *The Calculus Affair* shows us the back of the diminutive scientist, with a suitcase in one hand and his umbrella in the other, walking along a road toward the Marlinspike station. The picture itself forms a circle, as if it were taken through the sights of a rifle. We soon learn that Cuthbert is indeed being targeted.

Upon his return from Syldavia, Calculus retires to his laboratory at the far end of Marlinspike Park to finish his latest invention. Although he is deaf—or at least deaf to whatever he does not want to hear—he invents an ultrasound device whose potentially destructive powers "will soon make H bombs and ballistic missiles as obsolete as pikes and muskets" (*CA*, 51, III, 2). On the trip to the moon he seemed to be an impartial father figure, but now, thanks to his powerful invention, he could become the Bad Mother by further distancing himself from the sons and destroying whoever does not conform to his wishes.

To begin with, Calculus endangers the tranquility of Marlinspike by shattering all the windows and mirrors. In other words, he destroys the fragile barriers that protect the little clan from the outside world (the windows) and the objects that provide them with satisfying reflections (the mirrors). Since many nations are interested in procuring this powerful invention, Calculus also threatens the political world order. Spies are continually watching his work, and eventually they kidnap him on his trip to Switzerland, take him to Borduria, and keep him prisoner in the fortress of Bakhine. Although Tintin and Haddock desire only peace and quiet at home, they once again set out to bring Calculus back to Marlinspike. At the end of a hair-raising adventure, the Father decides to put an end to his power: "We mustn't dilly-dally: the sacrifice must be made" (*CA*, 62, II, 1). The sacrifice definitively designating him as Father and not the Bad Mother consists in burning the blueprints for his ultrasonic device. In putting an end to his power, Cuthbert enacts a symbolic castration. His action signifies that he accepts the Law that he is responsible for establishing for his group, but that the Law is greater than himself. He acknowledges that he is merely a temporary representative of the Father as such. Refusing to transform himself into the all-powerful Mother, he opts once and for all to be the Oedipal Father with whom the sons can compete. Thus, Cuthbert completes his journey, becoming once more the small-time inventor he was before his involvement in Tintin's clan. Moreover, his sacrifice allows him to avoid the excessive pride and foolishness that beset his main predecessors, such as Decimus Phostle and Philippulus. In the future Cuthbert will spend his time on such innocent inventions as motorized roller skates, color TV, and even a cure for alcoholism.

The castration of the Father has many consequences. One is that it stabilizes the family hierarchy. Since the Father no longer runs the risk of being identified as the Bad Mother, the place of the Bad Mother remains forever vacant. A more adequate feminine presence can henceforth be introduced into Tintin's world. In fact, the last six albums tell a story about how the family members more or less successfully accept a female presence in their midst. Another consequence of the Father's sacrifice is that the family members can again struggle against the external world but now more realistically than in the first phase of the adventures. Since Tintin can now deal with the external world through symbolic relations and not merely through imaginary fantasies, the final phase of the adventures can allow the hero to return to his origins.

In *The Calculus Affair*, Tintin returns to a country that resembles "the land of the Soviets." He travels to Borduria, ruled by the dictator Marshal Kûrvi-Tasch, a slimy, Stalin-like figure whose picture hangs everywhere.[3] The temptation to cling to absolute values, which until then had characterized Tintin's clan, is now rejected out of hand and even viewed negatively. In place of the Incan emperor, we find Colonel Sponsz. The mystique of the hero is transformed into the cult of the tyrant. Traditional balance and harmony give way to a bureaucracy where people become merely interchangeable pieces within an inhuman matrix, a system where people blindly obey and even inform on one another. In the face of this bureaucratic dictatorship, the temptation toward totalitarianism presented in the first albums gives way to a form of liberalism whose values are grounded in the private realm.

The final album, *Tintin and the Picaros*, also marks a return to San Theodoros. This time, however, Tintin tries not to get involved with a political regime slanted toward a totalitarian ideology. The two extremes of the public realm are reflected back to back, as two figures in a mirror. The last phase of Hergé's work displays both a mistrust of and an openness to the real world. What Hergé represents in this phase are the complex relations between the family and the exterior world, between private and public values, that cannot be fully captured by the opposition of the foundling and the bastard.

Even in avoiding extremist tendencies, however, the liberal public realm is scarcely more appealing than the totalitarian regimes. Dominated by quantity, without any other motivation than profit, the public world is judged from the perspective of Marlinspike, that is, from the viewpoint of Tintin, who still constitutes the "sun" of the familial universe. Even when he is not directly confronting it, Tintin judges the public realm negatively. Relative to traditional, religious values, the modern world has fallen into decadence, where the excesses of market relations cloud any hope for authentic communication.[4] This noisy, decadent world full of "junk" seems incapable of moral improvement. The residents of Marlinspike thus try to avoid it, but the commercial world infiltrates their private sphere through the smallest gadgets of daily life. How this degraded world constantly intrudes upon the life of Marlinspike constitutes the framework for the final *Adventures of Tintin*.

## THE WORLD OF WAGG

The final phase of Hergé's work highlights this degraded world itself, artfully represented by the colorful figure of Jolyon Wagg, insurance salesman. The genesis of Wagg's world goes back to the first period when Tintin, in contact with Alcazar, becomes a hero of "junk" in a cardboard world. The second album featuring this theme is *Land of Black Gold*, especially in its second and third versions.[5] Hergé situates his characters in the Arabian Desert, a land of

oil and mirages created either by the sun's rays or by the powerful lust to
control the oil wells. *Land of Black Gold* develops a theme already elaborated
in *The Cigars*.

The sheik of Khemed, Mohammed Ben Kalish Ezab, is threatened by his
rival Bab El Ehr. Under the pretext of tribal conflicts, their rivalry is really a
matter of continuing the cold war and dividing the zones of power between
East and West. Two oil companies are trying to control Khemed's wealth: the
Arabex Company and the Skoil Petroleum Company. The representative of
the latter is none other than Dr. Müller, whom Tintin had met in Scotland.
Müller was formerly assistant to the villain Wronzoff, the Slav. Now we meet
him again working for a Middle Eastern political power, but he has not really changed camps. Müller, like Rastapopoulos earlier, kidnaps the crown
prince of Khemed, the young Abdallah, in the hope of deposing the sheik.
Tintin intervenes, sneaks into the villains' fortress, rescues the young prince,
and returns him to his father.

Meanwhile, at Marlinspike Calculus's experiments threaten the lives of
the residents of the estate; but in Khemed, Tintin and Haddock are enjoying
rather peaceful days as guests of the sheik. In a manner similar to the beginning of *The Cigars of the Pharaoh*, Hergé displays the world of Wagg caught
in the grip of carnivalesque decadence. In this album, Tintin manages to
preserve something of his heroic image, but the Thom(p)sons are totally submerged in the ridiculous. We see them continually lost in the desert, tricked
by mirages, spinning hopelessly round and round, and ending their odys-
sey in the Wadesdah prison. Shortly after their release, they are once again
subject to an uncontrollable, comic metamorphosis: as in previous episodes,
their multicolored hair keeps growing and growing, transforming them into
two outlandish clowns.

In the *Land of Black Gold*, the sheik holds the traditional place of the
king, but his personality has little resemblance to that of the Maharajah of
Gaipajama. Whereas the latter always maintains his dignity and faces his trials
with admirable composure, the sheik conducts himself like a king in some
operetta whose misadventures are laughable. According to the judgment of
Señor Oliveira da Figueira, Sheik Ben Kalish Ezab is "a cream of a man."
But above all he is a weak ruler, incapable of ending the tribal conflicts and
dominated by a feudal aristocracy as warlike as it is incompetent. His military adviser, Youssouf Ben Moulfrid, is the perfect model of the bellicose
elite. The sheik is so weak willed that he cannot control his own desires.

He moves from laughter to tears, and from anger to despair, without ever making any real decisions. In his private life, he is a father without authority, dominated by the whims of his seven-year-old son.

One of the remarkable characters in *Black Gold* is indeed young Prince Abdallah. Focusing on him allows us to appreciate the continual transformation of Hergé's world. Just as the forces of Good revolve around the adolescent figure of Tintin, the decadent world of Wagg is personified by Prince Abdallah. Whereas the earlier characters Coco, Chang, and Zorrino belonged to the lineage of the foundling, Abdallah revives the lineage of the bastard. The angelic behavior of the former stands in stark contrast with the devilish behavior of the latter. Unfeeling, self-centered, spoiled by his weak father, the young prince dissolves the tension between the poles of Good and Evil by rendering them equivalent. Wherever he goes, he reduces everything to farce, as if he wants to leave his devilish mark on the world as his way of gaining revenge. Contrary to Tintin, Abdallah has a family, above all, a father, whom he secretly detests. Every time the sheik offers some object, especially those that civility demands from him, such as cigarettes, cigars, and matches, his ability to dispense the goods and to conduct himself like a real king backfires: the object explodes between his very fingers. The mischievous son thus prevents his father from acting like a king. Meanwhile, Abdallah himself as a good bastard looks for a substitute father figure more suitable to his tastes. He finds such a person in the captain, whom he calls familiarly "my good Milsabor," someone he sees as an ancestral "practical joker" worthy of himself. Abdallah interprets the captain's every blunder as a good joke, the attitude adopted later on even more annoyingly by Jolyon Wagg. But Abdallah's mischief is not exclusively directed toward the forces of Good. If the young prince tries to prevent Tintin from rescuing him because he wants more time to "play train" in Müller's bunker, Abdallah also foils the plans of the bandits, who are equally unable to control the little brat. Because of the young prince, the struggle between Good and Evil changes its rhythm.

In the earlier album *The Black Island*, a fight between Tintin and the villain Dr. Müller took place in the doctor's waiting room and ended with the hero's temporarily being knocked out. In this new adventure the second round also takes place in the villain's office. Although some of the same things happen the second time, such as the picture falling off the wall, Abdallah's mighty sneezing powder changes the rhythm of the fight. The sounds coming from the office are not gunshots or heavy punches but the incessant sneezes of the adversaries.[6] Whenever Abdallah gets mixed up in something—which happens constantly—the tragedy turns into farce. For example, when Dr. Müller is captured, he is so terrified of the end awaiting him that he prefers to commit suicide. Since he doesn't have any more bullets in his own revolver, he uses the gun Abdallah had given him. Instead of blowing his brains out, however, the revolver sprays him with black ink. Neither the hero nor his enemies can continue to fight according to the Manichean rules of the game. Abdallah's actions reduce both Good and Evil to nothing but appearances that he himself can manipulate.[7]

Wagg, who makes his entry in *The Calculus Affair*, is the veritable symbol of the degraded world. If Abdallah is the "bastard" brother of Chang, Wagg is the despicable twin of Archibald.[8] Like the son of the sheik, the insurance salesman attaches himself to the captain with an extraordinary perseverance that can be explained only by their secret affinity. Wagg also belongs to the "bastard" side of things.[9] Just as Haddock had immediately remembered his mother, so too does Wagg. He is very close to his mother, both figuratively and literally, for she lives under his roof as a silent witness to her offspring's exploits.[10] Just as with our captain, the biological father of our insurance agent is never mentioned. Again, similar to Archibald's relation to his ancestral Lord Francis, Wagg extols his heredity in the person of his uncle Anatole. But the treasure that he inherits from Uncle Anatole is a gold mine of dirty jokes that Wagg repeats wherever he goes. His "motormouth" is his passport for opening doors everywhere: "You know me; I don't stand on ceremony. A bit of the clown, that's me. Never a dull moment with me around, you bet! I take after my uncle Anatole; he was a barber" (*CA*, 5, IV, 1–2). In Wagg's mouth, the captain's verbal proclivities are reduced to the level of locker-room jokes. Jolyon's propensity for partying combines with his bent for scheming. Wagg not only insures people's property but also reassures them by his own self-satisfied mediocrity, his shallow inventiveness, and his cheerful freeloading. When he travels, he does not look for anything different but only what is familiar. He never goes anywhere without his group with whom he forms a "club." The only question he ever poses to himself is where to go on the next vacation—a place that is exotic, yet comfortably the same. As in the case of Abdallah, Wagg is impervious to tragedy: the drama and misfortunes of others are for him only fodder for more jokes. With such a personality, the insurance agent "gets around." He is president of several charities, organizes a club, and is chummy with the local elites, calling them "my dear chaps" and giving them a friendly poke in the belly. We find him at all crossroads of communication. Wherever the residents of Marlinspike travel, they inevitably bump into him, as if the "Wagg species" had taken over the planet. Far from facilitating genuine exchange, Jolyon constantly disrupts it with his "counterfeit" puns and banalities. For example, in *The Calculus Affair*, he picks up Haddock's SOS but interprets it as nothing but a good joke, and thus does nothing to prevent the spies from kidnapping the professor.

Whereas Tintin chooses his family members for their unique qualities, Wagg is stuck with his biological family, whose members all resemble one another. Besides his mother, his family consists of a wife, who puts up with her husband's wordplay, and seven children, including a pair of twins, very badly behaved. The Wagg "tribe" in all its dreary normality embodies everything Tintin has been avidly avoiding his entire career. Such a family stands in the way of adventure and tarnishes everything beautiful. As soon as the Waggs set up camp inside Marlinspike Hall, they transform the grand interior into their own ugly and conventional image. The kids damage the walls, tear up the bound volumes, and strew their toys everywhere. The mother hangs her laundry in the living room, and the father uses the grounds for his automobile rallies.[11] The rightful residents of Marlinspike do their best to avoid the Waggs' bad manners, but the unrelenting insurance agent pursues them all the way to the heart of the Amazon jungle.

Wagg does not show up by himself. He brings with him a host of parasites, people interested in information and spectacle, who lie in wait for the least tidbit of gossip to spread and magnify. For example, in *The Castafiore Emerald*, the article written by Jean-Loup de la Batellerie about the pseudo-marriage of Archibald and the opera diva draws a crowd of curiosity seekers to Marlinspike. The crowds take over the estate, transforming it from a private to a public space. What the heroes have taken years to build—a place where they can adhere to their own values—is threatened in just a few hours by the formidable powers of the media. On the basis of a pseudoevent, the media generates something "real" that ends up being "true" simply by being reproduced to infinity.

We come to understand that totalitarian governments control an instrument that has the capacity to engender reality simply by representing it. Hergé shows how this happens in *The Picaros*, where something eventually turns against what instigated it. The tyrant Tapioca, manipulated by Colonel Sponsz, concocts a plot that ends up working against himself. By simply broadcasting the news, what had originally been a lie turns out to be true. Tintin, Haddock, and Calculus gradually begin to conspire against Tapioca. Thanks to their plot, General Alcazar is able to oust Tapioca from his position as leader of San Theodoros.

Contemporary communications use a complex, unified technology whose various apparatuses are linked to one another to form a self-enclosed system. The complexity of the instruments is such that they can introduce at every step a multitude of discrepancies created by the "parasites" that reduce reality to nothing but what can be displayed. The criteria of truth no longer reside in an ethics but in mere representation: whatever can be staged and performed is true.[12] Alienation through appearances becomes the contemporary outcome of ideology. The walls of the ancestral estate are not thick enough to protect the small clan from this aspect of modernity. During the adventure in Borduria, Haddock establishes that the least little object of daily life becomes identical to everything else. He thinks he has gotten rid of a small Band-Aid stuck to his fingers, but it eventually circulates like money among other people, creating a kind of identity relation among them (*CA*, pp. 45–49). In a world unified by communications, no one can escape the sticky Band-Aid or the banalities of a Jolyon Wagg. These are the things that replace the Arumbayan fetish from former times. Even an emerald becomes a mere sign without real value.

## GLOBAL EXCHANGE

On his first trip to Syldavia, Tintin opted to save the Good monarchy against the Evil revolutionaries. In *The Calculus Affair*, he is no longer concerned with figuring out which country harbors the Good but instead focuses on extracting Calculus from the public world in order to restore him to the private sphere. From now on the Father belongs within the family. The broader society no longer offers a vantage point for making clear choices. Modern society revolves around a vast emptiness, the place left vacant by the kings of old. This place cannot be filled because it was founded on an absolute no longer available for a society geared to global consumerism. From now on anyone who makes himself out to be the father figure on the state level is defined as a dictator.

During their escapade at the Bordurian Embassy in Switzerland, when spies from various countries are vying to kidnap Calculus, Haddock asks Tintin "how to distinguish friends from enemies" (*CA*, 30, I, 2). The one who claims to be the moral conscience of the captain responds: "Go for the ugliest!" (ibid.). Although this might sound like practical advice, it turns out to be totally unworkable. The secret agents, whether Syldavian or Bordurian, wear the same hats and the same trench coats and even have the same brutish faces. Unable to distinguish the "good guys" from the "bad guys," Haddock resolves the problem by simply knocking their heads together.

At this point in his career, Hergé seems to see his work as a whole. The theme of the general equivalence of everything, only suggested in *The Broken Ear*, is now amplified in *The Red Sea Sharks*. Like *The Seven Crystal Balls*, this album is a kind of retrospective, where the author reintroduces characters from the first and second phases of his work. In this one story he integrates several witnesses to Tintin's past, meanwhile creating new relationships between characters or their worlds formerly considered separately. Tintin, however, is no longer at the center of the universe. The villain Rastapopoulos now occupies that position. The hero, often excluded, finds himself torn between one group or another and has to make an effort to break into social circles where he may be only marginally accepted. Rastapopoulos, meanwhile, has extended his network over the entire planet. He has become the embodiment of the global market. As the international entrepreneur, he manages to hire Dawson and Dr. Müller, become intimate with Castafiore, aid Alcazar in his struggle against Tapioca, and support Bab El Ehr's rebellion against Sheik Ben Kalish Ezab.

Total confusion puts an end to the Manicheanism of the opening adventures. The former opposition between Good and Evil now becomes the opposition between the private and the public. Unable to judge such a complex world, Tintin prefers to withdraw from it. He reluctantly takes on this adventure as a traveler without baggage and spends little time with people whom he formerly would have gotten to know quite well. The only individual he identifies with is the pilot Piotr Skut, someone who like Tintin himself seems without a country. Actually, Skut is from Estonia, a country occupied first by Germany and then by the Soviet Union, but he flees his homeland in order to hire himself out to the highest bidder. Tintin avoids the other characters in this album, for he doesn't really know how to cultivate genuine personal relationships in the public realm.

The hero makes a third trip to Khemed and is tricked by several mirages—not the sort created in the desert, the land of the foundling, but those created by society, the realm of the bastard. In the Arabian Desert, everything turns out to be phony, starting with General Alcazar's speech and ending with Abdallah's final letter to his "dear Milsabor." Even some of the leading characters are false: the names Dubreuil, Mull Pacha, and the Marquis di Gorgonzola are mere smoke screens for the real villains Dawson, Dr. Müller, and Rastapopoulos. On a list of equally fraudulent "factors" in the story appear the cuckoo clock offered to the captain, the socialites aboard the *Scheherazade*, Rastapopoulos's dinghy, Tintin's pass to Khemed, and Alcazar's friendly advances. We also find out that Allan Thompson's bright smile is a flash of false teeth. Everything becomes a mere sign, even classical culture flaunted by the imposter Prince Gorgonzola. What appear to be volumes of Molière's works are really empty bindings that conceal the secret code Rastapopoulos uses to communicate with his accomplices. To fight against all these counterfeits, the heroes sometimes adopt their strategy of deceit. For example, Tintin lies to the Thom(p)sons to procure the general's address. Later on, to escape the police in Wadesdah, Tintin and Haddock disguise themselves as Arab women.

The degradation of traditional values to mere signs circulating at an ever-increasing velocity has its origin in the global exchange, that is, in the transformation of every object into a commodity. Commerce is the sole tangible, historical reality; everything else is merely the play of appearances. Rastapopoulos sells anything, anywhere, to anyone, provided the sale is lucrative for himself. He traffics in arms as well as drugs; he sells films or package tours, oil or slaves. He deals in life or death with the same degree of indifference. After selling a dozen "Mosquito" aircraft to Alcazar, Dawson expresses this total absence of feelings and morals very well: "It's in the bag! Twelve Mosquitoes there, too. To help him chuck out his rival General Tapioca. Suits us. Let them fight. So long as we can unload our junk on them, why worry?" (*RSS*, 12, IV, 1).

Since everything can be quantified, people too become mere things to be measured quantitatively. One is judged no longer in terms of quality but merely in terms of quantifiable productivity, or labor power. It is not just because of skin color that the traffickers in human flesh call the Africans "coke"; like coal, the African slaves are a source of quantifiable energy. "Is the coke of best quality this time? H'mm, yes, strong muscles. You'll do. And teeth? Come on, open your mouth, you. H'mm, not too bad. Teeth quite sound" (*RSS*, p. 48). In this mass circulation of people and things, there are no innocents, for the communication technologies generate connections among everyone. Victims as well as perpetrators are incapable of exiting from the global commercial network. To try to protect themselves against it, the heroes return home as quickly as possible. Unfortunately, the return to Marlinspike Hall brings a new trial. Although Abdallah's tribe has decamped, Wagg's has taken over. Jolyon fittingly warns the captain: "The final test will take place in your own home!"

## CHAPTER THIRTEEN

# THE WHITE GODDESS

Blood? No, it's the blood I don't want to see.

—Federico García Lorca

## THE THREESOME

With the public realm so noisy and full of hustle and bustle, the heroes withdraw into their domestic world, whose dimensions they will explore in more depth. An adventure dedicated to the private life of the foundling, *Tintin in Tibet* marks a return to the first phase. With his name on the album cover and his picture on every single page, Tintin is once again the star of this adventure. He is the leader for the others to follow wherever he wants. This return to the past, however, cannot take place without considering the preceding developments. Those developments explain why Tintin cannot identify with the all-powerful, religious hero he once was. That former life now seems like a dream. Noticing the change, Haddock makes this remark: "*I* don't behave like a sleepwalker" (*TT*, 10, IV, 2). The observation is astute; Tintin goes through this adventure like a dreamer. He is obsessed with one idea that he cannot shake off. In no other story does he appear so worried, tense, and withdrawn. His return to the past is a therapeutic opportunity for the hero to take stock of his life and sort out his issues.[1]

The story begins with a dream. Tintin sees his friend Chang "lying there hurt, half buried by snow" (*TT*, 3, II, 1). Chang is calling out desperately, holding out his hands: "Help, Tintin! Help!" Like a true foundling, the hero does not interpret this nightmare as the product of his own subconscious but as an external reality that he can access because of his preternatural capacity to live in harmony with the cosmos.[2] Tintin believes his dream is a premonition. Contrary to the reports in the newspaper, he is convinced

Chang has not been killed in the plane crash where seventeen people were found dead. Thus, Tintin wants to set out to look for his friend. But every reasonable person, especially Haddock in this case, tries his best to dissuade him: "This is crazy!" Tintin will have none of it, replying each time: "Chang isn't dead!" He embarks on a journey that eventually leads him back to himself. However, even if he regains some of his former characteristics, Tintin now recognizes his limitations, which Archibald is quick to point out: "Why should you be able to find him, when Sherpas and experienced mountaineers have failed?" (6, III, 2).

The hero tacitly admits he has lost his almighty powers, and this loss has several consequences in this story. The return to the origin is not experienced directly by the young man but through the mediation of several doubles whom he meets along the way. The first of these doubles is Chang, who is practically Tintin's twin. Each of the other characters who have strongly influenced his life—the figure of the king, Captain Haddock, Professor Calculus—also split in two. This process better allows Tintin to grasp the nature of his past while giving him the opportunity to free himself from its grip by reliving it like a dream. The Tibetan adventure thus marks for Tintin a kind of mourning that uses Chang for its excuse but whose real object is the foundling himself.

In this adventure, Tintin's relation to the captain recalls their first encounter in *The Crab with the Golden Claws*. To be sure, Tintin no longer believes that Haddock's affections will take on cannibalistic dimensions. Nevertheless, Tintin mistrusts him. On the journey, the captain cannot stop shouting at everyone and provoking people against himself. On several occasions he even wants to abandon the journey because he feels like returning to Marlinspike.

Although Tintin no longer harbors any fantasies of being devoured by the captain, the fantasies now are projected onto the games the captain plays with other children. In Katmandu, Archibald is constantly yelling at the porters he bumps into, causing a stir in the streets, and frightening the children (p. 11). Later, in Charahbang he terrifies another child by making horrible faces at him, baring his teeth as if he wants to gobble him up (p. 54). The boy runs off, believing he has just seen an ogre.[3] No doubt the children of Katmandu are not really worried that Archibald is going to eat them up, but they play along with him. When the captain approaches them with his mouth wide open, they trick him in their own way. They get him to taste the red peppers that are so hot that the captain has to throw himself into the nearest well to cool down.

To offset any real danger, the children resort to the trickery of Little Poucet. To escape being devoured by the ogre, Little Poucet switches his brothers' nightcaps with the ogre's daughters' golden crowns, with the result that in the middle of the night the ogre devours his own daughters. This, of course, is taboo, even for an ogre. The boys of Katmandu get Archibald to eat the red peppers, a "forbidden fruit" that cannot be eaten raw but needs to be prepared according to strict culinary methods. The children feed the red pepper, as a substitute for raw human flesh, to Haddock the ogre. What was formerly for Tintin a horrifying fantasy (the red wine in the earlier nightmare standing for blood) is now played out as a kind of parodic or derivative game.

Calculus also appears in this adventure but with some uncharacteristic traits. He is extremely strict with Tintin, as if Calculus-the-Father had interiorized the punitive role of the Thom(p)sons, who themselves do not appear in this volume. For the first time, Calculus does not understand his young friend. Before reading the news about the airplane crash, Tintin receives a letter from Chang and is overjoyed at the prospect of seeing his friend again. But the professor misinterprets Tintin's high spirits and scolds him for having drunk champagne. According to the symbolic equivalences we have already established, that amounts to accusing Tintin of having sex with the young Chinese boy. A moment later, when Tintin becomes totally distraught at the news of the plane crash, Cuthbert comments ironically: "Look what happens when you drink too much champagne!"—as if the plane crash were divine retribution exacted on the two young sinners. Finally, when the young man leaves the table infuriated, the professor calls after him drily: "That's right! You go and sober up!" (*TT*, pp. 4, 5).[4]

The Father-Judge also splits into two. Because the professor is too much involved with modern technology and, furthermore, would not be a likely leader on a Himalayan expedition, Hergé substitutes the character Tharkey for Calculus. Tharkey is the "professor" of mountaineering, "the best Sherpa in the whole region, and the bravest" (13, III, 1). He will initiate Haddock and Tintin into the mysteries of the mountain and save them from death on more than one occasion. Appearing in only this one adventure, Tharkey becomes a well-balanced father figure, exhibiting aspects of both the bastard and the foundling.

At first, Tharkey seems reasonable and prudent, refusing to get involved in such a crazy adventure. But then he agrees to lead the expedition—but no further than to the wreckage of the airplane. Haddock causes Tharkey to change his mind by promising him and the porters a considerable salary. At the first crisis, when the other mountaineers want to turn back, Tharkey reminds the porters of the "sahib's" generous promise (25, II, 1). When the Sherpa fulfills his end of the bargain, we see Tintin for the very first time dealing with money with an equal. Tintin does not give the Sherpa merely baksheesh, as he did formerly with the Indian Caraco (*BE*, 46, II, 1), but a real salary to which he adds, on Haddock's prompting, family allowances and paid holidays (37, III, 1). But their financial arrangement is followed by a genuine friendship. After exhibiting some bastard-type characteristics, Tharkey follows the example of the foundling and acknowledges absolute moral values: "You, young white sahib risking your life to save Chinese friend. Me yellow man, like him, but I not want to help. I tell myself I am coward, I turn back, and follow you" (41, III, 1). With Tharkey's confession, Tintin has to see in the Sherpa the same brand of idealism he had previously attributed to the captain: "You are a really good man!" (ibid.). Of course, Tharkey's place in the threesome is only temporary. Once he shares his knowledge and expertise with Tintin and the totally exhausted Haddock, Tharkey cuts himself loose from their rope, leaving the third place in the trio open for Chang.

Being a threesome constitutes a preferable alternative to twinness. From now on, the twin relation is rejected because of its inherent dangers: the mirror situation, narcissism, even homosexuality. Thus, Chang does not encounter Tintin again except in the presence of the captain. In fact, even Tintin and Haddock are only rarely together face-to-face. More often, they participate in some triangular situation that allows them to preserve their uniqueness. During the rare moments when the heroes are together on their own, they are not fearful of becoming too close but, rather, of dying. For example, after Tharkey's first departure, Tintin and Haddock attach themselves to each other with a rope, the younger one leading the older. Haddock again has a fall—not a spiritual one this time but a purely physical one with tragic consequences. Although the captain reaffirms their strong tie, in this case the strong rope attaching them together is literally cutting into their flesh. Even when the captain resolves to sacrifice himself and to "cast off moorings," neither of them can really save himself or the other. In this situation they both would have died had Tharkey not returned to save them, thus reconstituting the threesome (pp. 40–41).

Whereas the more fainthearted Calculus is replaced by Tharkey, Tintin himself will be replaced by the monk Blessed Lightning in order to salvage the quest. The monk obviously embodies Tintin's former religious aspect. But far from being all powerful, the simple-minded monk is un-controllably subject to mystical visions, levitation, and clairvoyance. Just as Tintin sees Chang by telepathy, so too Blessed Lightning sees Tintin, then Chang, when they are in mortal danger. The three of them—Tintin, Chang, and Blessed Lightning—form a new, decidedly spiritual trio. Although they speak to one another very little, they can communicate in ways inacces-sible to other people. The monk's name evokes the Incan emperor Rascar Capac, "he-who-unleashes-the-fire-of-heaven" (7 CB, 28, I, 2). In the case of the Tibetan monk, however, his "lightning" is beneficial. However, Blessed Lightning does not have the powers of the religious leaders of the first phase; he has access to the beyond only for brief moments. The rest of the time he acts like a simple, somewhat obtuse monk, ridiculed by the others. He is also amnesiac, for he quickly forgets what he has seen in his visions. It is really in spite of himself that he has access to the supernatural. Furthermore, he does not take advantage of his access to the divine for the purposes of imposing his law on the monastery. Even though he has some of the foundling's traits, those are effectively cut off from his everyday personality and keep him subordinated to the group.

Blessed Lightning plays another important role in this adventure: he gives each of the heroes a new name. He duplicates the characters' human dimen-sion by rebaptizing them, and thus reintroducing them to a religious world they had lost sight of by becoming too wrapped up in the world of Wagg. Milou/Snowy becomes "Powder Snow";[5] Tintin is called "Great Heart"; and the captain, "Rumbling Thunder." Whereas in the earlier adventure the names given by the Syldavian spies drew attention to the characters' animal side (Mammoth and Whale), those given by Blessed Lightning elevate them to the high heavens.

Although Calculus gives up his privileged place in this adventure, he is not entirely absent from it: his memory haunts the captain by appearing in his nightmare. Haddock's nightmare, however, is different from Tintin's fore-boding dream about Chang. Whereas Tintin's dream had a religious content and role, Haddock's can be interpreted in strictly psychological terms. After Haddock gulps down an entire bottle of whiskey, he falls asleep while walk-ing (16, II, 2, 3; III, 1, 2).

Panel 1 shows the captain walking on a path that symbolizes not the Way of Bernard of Clairvaux but the royal road leading to the unconscious.

Panel 1: "Hello, Professor. What are you doing here?" "I've lost my umbrella."
Panel 2: "Your umbrella? Why, I've got a shipload of them here. Heaven knows where they've come from." "Rubbish! This is a red pepper!"    Panel 3: "Checkmate!"
*TT*, 16, II, 2, 3; III, 1, 2. © Hergé/Moulinsart 2007.

The setting suggests both Middle Eastern architecture and the interior of the observatory from *The Shooting Star*, the secret chamber of the Father. As in the dreams of the foundling, we find an image showing a forbidden entry. The bastard shows up in a place he does not have the right to be, for he crosses the Father's path. In the dream, Haddock doesn't sport his usual rucksack and pullover but wears a red formal dress suit and carries a silk rope with a fringe. His hard-soled shoes make clicking sounds on the pavement, and he carries an eight-stringed guitar. His getup evokes the world of show business. Indeed, the bastard views the world as a theater where all he has to do is change the scenery in order to become the star. Since his early days on the *Karaboudjan*, when he took himself to be an actor with multiple roles, Archibald is familiar with such changes. This flexibility, however, has a negative effect: the bastard feels he never actually finishes his act. He lacks a sense of belonging anywhere. Here in the dream Haddock acts the clown, with Calculus as his straight man.

On the ground in the middle of the road are three green objects shaped like pyramids or cones, symbolizing perhaps the triangularity of the relationship. Just before the dream, Haddock had wandered off from the rest of the expedition while merrily singing "The Grand Old Duke of York." He thinks he is doing just fine (although he is drunk and asleep!) and is totally surprised to see Calculus: "Hello, Professor, what are you doing here?" He asks the Father to justify his presence in his life. In the course of this adventure, Haddock believes he has gotten rid of Calculus and considers himself worthy of guiding Tintin, constantly nagging him and calling him "brat," "sonny," "rascal," and even "young whippersnapper."

Fittingly, Calculus himself shows up in the dream dressed like a "young whippersnapper" whose youthful costume is complemented by the adult accoutrements of spectacles and goatee. Calculus is whining like a spoiled brat about "losing his umbrella." Remember that for the professor, this item is the symbol par excellence of virility, from which he never wants to be separated. Calculus even carried his umbrella onto the lunar spaceship, where he used it to shield the Thom(p)sons from the captain's drool. In *The Calculus Affair*, Cuthbert hid his blueprints for the ultrasonic device in his trusty umbrella. The last part of that adventure was punctuated by his anxious cries: "My umbrella! You haven't lost it, have you?" The umbrella was finally found, minus the important documents, and the very end of the story presented the Father's sacrifice, his symbolic castration. In the dream, Haddock revisits the traumatic event: the Father seems to be accusing the son of castrating him, the deed that Didi Wang actually tried to enact in an earlier album.

Panel 2 from the dream shows us the same characters but in closer view. Haddock is again on the left, the typical position of the dreamer in Hergé's dream sequences. The captain secretly believes he is guilty because he shows up with an armful of umbrellas and claims not to know their owners. At this overt claim of being innocent, Cuthbert rightly replies: "You're lying!" Not only does the professor accuse the captain but also Calculus shows him a child-sized yellow umbrella that he brandishes about and says: "This is a red pepper!" This exclamation, previously spoken by Tintin, leads us back to the theme of the ogre. On the one hand, Haddock tries to take the place of the Father by seizing the phallic umbrellas; on the other hand, the Father tries to wheedle the son by offering him the child's umbrella, a child-sized phallic symbol. Moreover, following the instigation of the youngsters of Katmandu, Calculus takes advantage of his childish appearance to palm off on Haddock a "red pepper" shaped like an umbrella. Although the captain wants to compete with the Father—that is, to live in the Oedipal situation—Cuthbert returns him to the earlier oral stage, trying to fixate him there, in the psychoanalytic sense of the term. Indeed, following a bout with the whiskey bottle, the captain often regresses to that stage. Alcohol has a double effect on Archibald: alcohol, after all, is the synthesis of the symbols of fire and water.[6] If it sometimes gives him greater courage, at other times it causes him to regress, dissolving him in a whirl of childish fantasies. In the second panel from the dream sequence, the whiskey has the latter effect. The guitar is transformed into a giant empty bottle, and the captain's suit begins to shrink, reducing him little by little to the size of a child. To gain his victory, the Father resorts to a trick that easily dupes the son. In the guise of a simple offer (of the equivocal umbrella/red pepper) Calculus confines his rival to the world of the child. Calculus shows he is as quick as Ottokar IV in the earlier adventure, who also defeated the young baron seeking the scepter of power by saying, "Here, take it!"

In Panel 3, we go from theatrical games to board games—chess. We find Haddock and Calculus at the "endgame," as in Samuel Beckett's play, when the players are totally identified with their chess pieces. Chess is highly symbolic because the game consists in checkmating the opposing king—in other words, annihilating the father figure. Near the beginning of this album, Tintin plays chess with the captain, who hopes to win by sacrificing his bishop.[7] In the dream, Haddock does not sacrifice his "bishop" but instead gives him free rein, as when he was previously dressed as the showman. Haddock definitively loses the game, and Calculus playing the white king regains the place of the Father. Now Calculus is giant sized. He gathers up the bundle of umbrellas and gives Archibald a tremendous blow on the head. This blow recalls the incidents of Philippulus striking Tintin (SS, 9, II, 2), King Ottokar hitting young Baron Staszrvich on the head with his scepter (KOS, p. 21), and the balls of fire hurled at the scientists in The Prisoners of the Sun (PS, 23, I, 3).

The castration of the son is one of Hergé's recurrent metaphors. Despite his worldly success, the bastard feels guilty in competing with the Father.

With the blow from Calculus's umbrella, Haddock is put in his place. He becomes nothing more than the "young whippersnapper" and remains so to the end. "Eih Bennek, eih blavek." The endgame is observed through the ironic eye of a cow, an animal always troublesome for Snowy and the captain.

In Panel 4, Hergé offers a realistic explanation for Haddock's blow: he simply bumped into a tree. This explanation allows Haddock not to question the meaning of the dream any more than the author does himself.[8] In a few seconds the captain relived the entire history of his relationship with Calculus, whom he at first dismissed as a pint-sized fool but then came to admire as a great genius. But the captain does not draw any positive conclusions from the dream. Its explicit content, presented in a surrealistic mode, completely covers up its latent psychoanalytic meaning.

## THE LOST CHILD

In the early adventure *The Blue Lotus*, Tintin and Chang met for the very first time. Tintin's railway journey from Shanghai to Hong Kong was disrupted by flooding, and he was continuing his journey on foot when he heard a cry for help. He jumped into the river and saved a young boy, Chang Chong-jen, from drowning (*BL*, pp. 42–43). During their first encounter, the two adolescents shared their fantasies with each other, which led to ridding themselves of these beliefs. Chang saw all Europeans as "white devils," as narrow-minded, brutish colonizers. Tintin imagined the Chinese as sophisticated, sadistic executioners, who feast on little dogs, rotten eggs, and swallows' nests. He was especially struck by the torturous practice of foot binding inflicted on little girls and by the idea that "all the rivers of China are full of Chinese babies thrown into the water at birth" (*BL*, 43, III, 3).[9] Although Tintin pretended to reject these stereotypes, he himself had propounded them only shortly before during his adventures in the Soviet Union and America.

From the beginning Chang appeared as Tintin's twin. Having lost his parents with no idea of their whereabouts, Chang attached himself to the hero and shared his quest for the absolute. One highly significant scene among others showed Tintin, wounded, letting Chang take care of him by wiping away the blood flowing down his arm. Contrary to the recent accusation leveled by Calculus, on that earlier occasion it was not "champagne" at the source of their relationship but real blood. Their mutual attachment was based on feelings more sexually undifferentiated than a nascent homosexual relationship would suggest. But their love for each other was also inextricably bound up with cruelty. That explains why Tintin had to put a quick end to what otherwise seemed their almost perfect twinlike resemblance. Nevertheless, he did not dismiss Chang the way he did Coco or the son of the maharajah—disappearing as if by magic—but integrated Chang into the bosom of a newfound family, that of Mr. Wang Jen-ghie. By curing the son Didi of his madness and by introducing Chang into the family, Tintin reinforced the authority of Mr. Wang, who then became Chang's father. Mr. Wang invited Chang to feel at home as his son and "to become the brother of his own son" (*BL*, 62, I, 2). Thus, with Didi Wang as his new brother and new role model, Chang left the world of the foundling and took on that of the bastard.[10] He was no longer an orphan but now the son of a prestigious man. The family romance was reproduced here in a reverse manner: the child was not "adopted" by his initial family but by another one, more suitable to his own desires for grandeur.

During the period separating *Blue Lotus* from *Tibet*, Tintin never mentioned this episode with Chang. But now, as his memory is jogged by the captain's reading a newspaper article about Nepal, Tintin comes to remember his earlier career and, especially, his long-lost "twin." Tintin receives a letter from Chang whose envelope bears the traces of the past. The letter was initially addressed to Labrador Street, then to Marlinspike Hall, and finally forwarded by Nestor to their hotel on the summit of the Vargese Mountains in Switzerland. The envelope informs us of the date of the opening of the Tibetan adventure—the end of July 1958. The envelope also suggests that Mr. Wang's family, compromised by serving Chang Kai-shek, took asylum in Hong Kong. It is from Hong Kong that Chang sets out on his trip, stopping off in Katmandu before continuing his journey to meet his adoptive family in London. In the course of the journey from Patna to Katmandu, Chang stops off at exactly the same point where the Shanghai–Hong Kong railroad had been flooded years before, as if history were repeating itself. But this time the raging elements cause a plane crash rather than a railway disruption. Although Chang escapes death a second time, the accident leads him back to his earlier relationship with the foundling. This time, it is not a river that threatens to overcome him but the snows of the Himalayas.

For both Chang and Tintin, the Tibetan adventure is a series of abandonments. Chang calls for help, but no one can hear him. He is lost in a kingdom of silence and death, the mountain of the White Goddess. "White

Goddess" is the name the Tibetans give the mighty mountain, recognizing it as a living being whose reactions they try to interpret. Thus, when there is an avalanche, Blessed Lightning, the goddess's interpreter, affirms: "The White Goddess is angry! It is a portent!" (44, I, 3). Even if the monks refuse to believe in the mystical visions that transport their peer ("Blessed Lightning and his visions! When you think, he's as blind as a bat from Wei-Pyiong!"), the monks deify that part of the mountain covered with eternal snow. The grand abbot himself considers the mountain a being endowed with special powers. He informs the Western visitors that "the mountain keeps those whom she takes" (49, IV, 2). Thus, Chang is a prisoner of Nature, who, since the flood, is seen as an implacable monster overwhelming her prey.

In this part of the adventure Hergé is drawing on a long tradition attributing symbolic powers to the mountain. Among many possible interpretations, he chooses the one that best accords with his own personal universe. He describes the mountain as the Mother to whom Chang has been sacrificed. Regressing from the Oedipal stage of the bastard to that of the foundling, Chang finds himself confronted with origin fantasies, engulfed by an all-powerful, immaculate Nature, always virginal because no one can master her. Chang's adventure replicates Tintin's on the meteorite in the final section of *The Shooting Star*.

To save his twin, Tintin takes a similar route back to his former self. He leaves the comfort of his town that boasts all the worldly advantages the bastard Haddock has been able to acquire and ends up faced with Chang's situation. Tintin is virtually alone, face-to-face with the White Goddess.

On the expedition to find Chang, contemporary technology is the first thing that lets down the hikers. No technological apparatus can be used in the highest mountains of Gosianthan. With only a guide and experienced porters, they have to hike to the plane wreck on foot. Like the llamas in the Andes, the porters abandon the expedition when they are frightened by the cry of the Abominable Snowman. With the porters gone, Tintin, Haddock, and Tharkey have to leave behind most of their provisions: "Everything that is not strictly essential has to be dumped" (27, IV, 2). But soon they have to get rid of even the essentials: the propane stove the captain blows up, the main tent, and finally the extra tent that is torn. After these accidents, they have nothing left. They can neither eat nor sleep. Even the shortest stop for rest prolongs their trek and becomes equated with death. Like the monarchical eclipse in *King Ottokar's Scepter*, their "calvary" in the snow lasts for three days. In the end, they are saved by the providential intervention of Blessed Lightning.

Those who abandon them like disposable objects show little regard for human solidarity. After the porters leave, even Tharkey deserts them. Later, Haddock himself refuses to go on, even with the enticement of brandy: "Even if you fill me up with jet fuel, I won't budge another inch" (43, II, 3). Snowy, too, the shining example of loyalty, betrays his master. When Tintin explains to Snowy that their "lives depend upon you," Snowy lets their SOS note blow away while he enjoys "a magnificent bone, certainly a five-star model" (45, IV, 1). Tintin himself abandons Chang, the first time at the site of the plane wreckage, and a second time at the end of their stay at the monastery. Nevertheless, all of these abandonments will be reversed. Tharkey, Haddock, Snowy, and Tintin each renew the commitments they had temporarily abandoned.

The ascent to the summit of the White Goddess seems like a mystical quest similar to the hero's first adventures. Appropriately, Hergé varies the narrative structure, at times reverting to the epic style. Thus, the way Haddock recounts their trek in the mountains, with his repetitions of "we did this; then we did that," evokes the epic rather than the novel. When the great abbot honors the heroes, his discourse recalls certain expressions Homer puts in the mouth of Priam when Priam comes to Achilles to recover the dead body of Hector.[11]

The Himalayas are the rooftop of the world. The heroes have to struggle to those great heights to escape the temporality and pervasive values of Wagg's universe.

## THE SECRET LIFE OF THE ABOMINABLE SNOWMAN

The Yeti, also known as the Abominable Snowman, kidnaps Chang. Hergé revisits the theme of "the good monster" elaborated earlier in *The Black Island*, a theme richly developed in nineteenth-century literature. The Abominable Snowman and the gorilla Ranko differ, however, in several respects. Ranko is a gorilla of colossal strength, manipulated by the villain Wronzoff, who uses the monster to prevent curiosity seekers from approaching the Castle of Ben More. If Ranko comes to embody death, inscribed in the very name of the castle,[12] he himself is neither good nor evil. After Ranko trips on the stairs, Tintin takes care of the monster, transforming him into a docile creature who ends his career in the London zoo. Nevertheless, the mytho-

logical dimension of this animal is noticeable from the very first version of
the album. Hergé was inspired by Cooper and Schoedsack's film *King Kong*,
which had been released about three years earlier. Ranko's behavior toward
Snowy can be interpreted as frustrated love. The gorilla becomes impotent
in the presence of the little dog, incapable of carrying out his mission, and
fascinated by the fragile creature he holds at his mercy. Their final separation
is heartbreaking, and Ranko bursts into tears when Tintin leaves him at the
zoo (*BI*, p. 62). Here Snowy plays the role of the young girl with whom King
Kong falls in love, a role later filled by Chang in the Tibetan adventure.

But Ranko also has an ogre side to his personality. The inhabitants of Kiltoch, who never see him, call him "the beast" to emphasize his sexual indeterminacy. They tell Tintin about his legendary exploits, including his feast-
ing on little boys and girls, as if Ranko is Nature's revenge on the region.
The old folks at the hotel pour out a litany of names of those recently
devoured by the ogre (*BI*, 42, I, 1–3). The encounter between Ranko and
Tintin accentuates the animal's bestiality. Sporting a Scottish beret signifying
his ability to mimic humans, the gorilla comes upon the young man, opens
his huge mouth, and bares his teeth, as Captain Haddock does later. When
Ranko grabs Tintin, Snowy cries out: "He's going to eat him!" (*BI*, 53, I, 3).
Fearlessly, the little dog leaps onto Ranko, causing him to drop his prey and
return to his cage.

"Aaahh!" *BI*, 46, II, 2. © Hergé/Moulinsart 2007.

Dans la pénombre d'une grotte, une tête énorme était penchée sur moi et deux yeux brillants me regardaient fixement...

"In the half light of a cave, an enormous head was looming over me, and two gleaming eyes were staring at me." *TT*, 58, IV, 2. © Hergé/Moulinsart 2007.

The Abominable Snowman is a much more complex character than the gorilla of *The Black Island*. Contrary to Ranko, who needed a master to control his instincts, the Yeti is the veritable incarnation of the Mountain and lives in harmony with her. The Yeti internalizes certain human characteristics that Ranko displayed only occasionally. The Yeti, after all, is called "the Man of the Snow." He is a creature with two sides, half wild and half tamed. If Tintin embodies the highest aspects of human nature, the Yeti may be said to embody the lowest. Yet both of them are unique. Coincidentally, their names contain only two syllables: Tin-tin and Ye-ti. Like the Phoenix, the Yeti is the sole survivor of his "species." He emerges from the darkest of times, the last witness to a universe before human beings. As the sole survivor of the natural catastrophes of evolution, he seems immortal. With neither a partner nor offspring, like the original Adam before Eve, his behavior and morphology suggest "he" is androgynous, both male and female, father and mother, human and animal. Just as in his first adventures Tintin incorporates the social roles and values that will later be personified by various characters, so too the Yeti seems to embody within himself all possible familial relationships. He has no Other with whom to engage in any objective, external relationship. He revives the world of childhood not only because this adventure deals primarily with children but also because he manifests the maternal White Goddess and thus replays the infant's earliest fantasies. As a prehuman, he condenses the evolutionary development of the species and the psychological development of the individual all within his own personality.

Whereas the Yeti recalls Tintin in the uniqueness of his situation, he also resembles Haddock in various ways. The captain immediately intuits their secret resemblance and transforms the quest into a settling of scores between them. Like Archibald, the Yeti is a bastard with a double lineage, both noble (human) and base (animal). When Haddock "discovers" the existence of his ancestor Lord Francis, he becomes entranced and performs for Tintin the legendary murder of Red Rackham. To identify completely with his ancestor, Haddock drinks some red wine, signifying the blood spilled by the pirate that the lord soon repays. In a different time frame, Haddock participates in the sacrificial ritual: under the appearance of red wine, the same blood passes from the victims' bodies to the pirate's, then to that of Lord Francis, and finally to the captain's. Thus, Archibald reinforces his ties to nobility in two ways. On the one hand, he claims to issue from the blood of his ancestor, and on the other, he imbibes an equivalent of the blood in the course of a communion where the profane mixes derisively with the sacred. The basic way Haddock apprehends the exterior world is to drink it, and his oral "grasp" of the world lies at the origin of his reputation among the children as an ogre.[13]

The Yeti also exhibits this same oral fixation. Whereas the captain desires to "drink Tintin" (*CGC*, p. 30), the Abominable Snowman is accused of "drinking chang" (*TT*, 23, III, 1). This accusation is ambiguous, for "chang" is the Tibetan name for strong beer as well as the name of the Chinese boy. But the captain understands this accusation in terms of his own phantasmic universe. The scene where the Yeti gets entangled in the tent and is transformed into a ghost-monster recalls the incident when Haddock disguised himself as a ghost to try to frighten Calculus back to consciousness (*DM*, p. 49). This scene also evokes the time the cow's-head mask lands on the captain, transforming him into the Minotaur, the monstrous creature to whom the ancient city of Athens regularly offered a sacrifice of human flesh (*7CB*, pp. 15–16).

Like the captain, the Yeti is fond of tobacco. "His nose is so sensitive!" (*TT*, 54, IV, 2), declares Haddock. The Yeti also loves whiskey and swipes a bottle "barely opened." As one can see from his tracks, he gets miserably drunk, stumbles around in all directions, crashes into the rocks, and finally passes out on the ground (p. 26). His yells also remind us of the captain's, especially when the latter take on a metaphorical sense that gives them more weight (26, II, 3). To emphasize the similarities between Snowy, the captain, and the Yeti, Hergé highlights their respective shrieks against the same red background that stands for both anger ("to see red") and blood. If Haddock tastes human flesh only in the symbolic form of red peppers (which he has to immediately spit out), the Yeti has a long-standing reputation for eating raw human flesh.

Archibald thinks of him as a werewolf (35, II, 2).[14] The theme of the werewolf runs through the entire Tibetan adventure. Considered since the sixteenth century as some kind of mental illness and not a matter of witchcraft,[15] the metamorphosis of a human into a beast is a common theme in medicine, religion, and mythology. In traditional classifications of illnesses (*nosographie*), the werewolf is catalogued as a melancholic, what we would call today a depressive. If the Yeti is thought of as a werewolf, this is another way he resembles the captain, who frequently falls into depression.[16] The Abominable Snowman flees from humans at the same time he is constantly fascinated by them. If he does indeed eat them—and Tharkey testifies that the Yeti eats the eyes and hands of those he kills—it would be to incorporate their strength and to become more like them. When the airplane crashes, the Yeti shows up on the scene immediately. Perhaps he devours the survivors; Hergé does not go into that. Much later, the Yeti discovers Chang in a cave. Rather than leave the scene of the accident with his prey, the Yeti searches the ruins for provisions. When the rescue squad arrives, he watches them constantly. When Tintin comes to the same spot, we see the Yeti still fascinated by the presence of human beings in his territory. The Yeti immediately understands the reason for their coming. While they are sleeping, he approaches their camp, sniffs out everything, and makes off with whatever seems appealing. He spies on them until the very last day, and it is his image, watching the humans leaving his territory, that appears on the last page of the album. It is telling that Tintin confuses him with the captain (p. 31): the Yeti personifies all the traits that the hero has projected onto Haddock since their very first encounter.

Tintin's quest is a *regressus ad uterum*, a return to the origin. Close to the scene of the crash, he enters the first cave where Chang carved his name on a rock. When Tintin's companions join him in the cave, they find no one: "I tell you, Sahib: your friend come here, yes. But afterward, Yeti kill him, and eat him up" (34, IV, 2). Tintin objects: if that had happened, one would surely find "some traces of the tragedy." At that moment, Snowy shows up with a bone in his mouth! But the bone turns out to be an animal bone, probably of a mountain goat, not a human. When it seems their search for Chang has reached a dead end, Tintin discovers the yellow scarf stained with blood. Just like Little Poucet, Chang left behind some signs so that he could be found—not pebbles but bloodstains.

Tintin encounters the Yeti not in the region of the eternal snows but on a mountain called "Horn of the Yak." There he waits for three days, on the constant lookout for the Yeti and his friend Chang. A cave called the "Eye of the Mountain" seems to be the monster's den: "You remember, Captain. We must keep watching the eye" (54, IV, 1). To rescue his friend, Tintin has to forcibly enter the cave. Throughout his career, he has often had to go underground to emerge on the other side, into another world. This time, he has to enter and leave in the same place. The entrance to the cave represents the mouth of the Mountain, both her eye and her sex. The entrance clearly is shaped like the female sexual orifice. Armed with his pickax and camera, Tintin enters the cave. Although the pickax seems the best weapon to ward off the monster, the flash of the camera is what saves the hero by blinding the beast. In one flash, Tintin puts out the "eye" of the Horn of the Yak, re-peating the feat of Ulysses against the Cyclops, another monster that devours human flesh.

At the rear of the cave Tintin discovers Chang, still alive. Rather than being devoured by the ogre, Chang has been nourished and cared for by him. The Yeti offered him little rodents and birds that the boy managed to eat despite his revulsion. Would he have gone even further by sharing human flesh with the Yeti? Neither Hergé nor anyone else dares to envision such a thing, though it appears possible, especially in this album with its theme of cannibalism. Each time the boy might have been able to tell what was really going on between him and the monster, Chang passed out into a state of semiconsciousness and let himself be carried away like an infant. He claims that with the arrival of the first rescue team, the Yeti carried him off on a fantastic journey (59, IV, 1), but several days later he seemed to be still at the same spot. Had he really left the scene of the accident?

Tintin's story of what happens when he first sees the beast in the snow-storm is also unclear. On page 31 the hero leaves the first cave, stumbles along in the blizzard, and sees the Abominable Snowman, who is carrying Chang in his arms. Tintin calls out to him, taking him for the captain, then falls into a crevasse from which he manages to climb out after many hours of struggle. When he recounts this episode to his friends later (33, IV, 1), he claims first to have tumbled into the crevasse and climbed out, and *then* to have met up with the Yeti. One is left to wonder if Tintin sees the Yeti one or two times, and where exactly. One can imagine that his confrontation with the monster causes amnesia. Perhaps something similar occurs within the author himself. Considering his extremely careful attention to the coherence of the story line, the author—like Tintin—may make certain slips without even recognizing them.

In Chang's story Tintin recognizes a monstrous relationship, like the one he had first with Snowy and then with the captain. In the Tintin-Snowy relationship, however, there was a superior and inferior: the superior human controlled the inferior beast. If Snowy at times stuffed himself with raw meat, for example, at least Tintin was unaware of it (*KOS*, 7, I, 1). In the Tintin-Haddock relationship, the hero initially projected onto the captain his fantasies of being devoured. He prevented the sailor from actually eating him by muzzling him like a dog, cutting him off from his beloved whiskey, and forcing him to spit out his vice (*CGC*, 16, III, 2). The initial violence of Tintin and Haddock's relationship was rather quickly sublimated into a brotherly rivalry arbitrated by Calculus.

The relationship between Chang and the Yeti represents everything Tintin has rejected and continues to reject. In this case the beast guides the human, nourishes him—perhaps on human flesh but in any case with raw meat—and smothers him with an abominable love, which turns out for Tintin to be an ominous sign. What is merely suggested between Ranko and Snowy is now explicit. The monster loves Chang with a love as unconditional as Tintin's love for his friend. The hero could read into this love the duplication of his original relationship with Chang, also under the sign of blood. He could acknowledge the strength of the Yeti's tie to his friend only by denying it. Hearing the cry of the Abominable Snowman ringing out on his mountain, Tintin says: "My god! What a heart-rending cry! You'd think he was in distress!" (*TT*, 59, I, 1). The beast is so deeply and sorrowfully shaken because Tintin has deprived him of the only human mirror he ever held and thus thrusts him back into his primordial animality. The beast is once more abandoned to the destructive forces of which he is both the instrument and victim.

By comparing the relationships of Ranko and Snowy with the Yeti and Chang, one can understand their differences. The gorilla expresses his beastly passion by trying to devour the object of his love. The Abominable Snowman, in contrast, manages to sublimate his cannibalistic desire in his purely loving look. Whereas Ranko was identified with a mouth, now we find the Yeti has two organs with separate roles: his mouth and his eyes. At the very same time he is taking Chang away to his lair, initiating him into the inhuman practices of feeding on raw animals, the Yeti himself becomes human by refusing to devour the being he loves. With the same oral drive, he differentiates what is good to eat from what is good to love. He acknowledges the taboo against cannibalism, even after transgressing it for so long. He becomes human, and he is at least capable of thinking in rudimentary terms. Instead of facing an undifferentiated universe, he can imagine a world divided into Good and Evil, a Manichean world similar to the one in the first *Adventures of Tintin*.

While the Yeti advances from the prehuman to the human, the hero himself returns to his origins and imagines himself, instead of Chang, in the arms of the monster. In the look of the Other he realizes his past. His imaginary omnipotence was born of a union with Mother Nature, and his rigid moralism stemmed from his overly simple division of the universe into Good and Evil. He recognizes that uniqueness is an illusion, but that twinness is also a trap. He comes to see that if a relationship of two is based on unconditional desire, it ends up being monstrous. Only a relationship of three allows for symbolic, meaningful interaction.

Tintin went to look for his twin in the mountains in order to allow himself to retrace his steps so that he could overcome the dual relationship and become integrated into a threesome. The two friends look at each other face-to-face only for a short time. There is between them a smell of blood that Tintin cannot accept and that all of the snows of the Himalayas will not sweeten. Once out of the ogre's den, Chang takes the place Tharkey left vacant for him between Haddock and Tintin. Beneath the successive masks of Snowy, Ranko, and Haddock, and finally in the monstrous face of the Yeti, Tintin discovers his own face. In the face of the Yeti, he recognizes himself for a minute before the monster disappears again in the snows of the White Goddess and Tintin could forget what he had seen. Thus, the adventure to Tibet, the favorite of its author, seems to end with a question that once again casts into the shadows the incomprehensibility that lies at the bottom of Tintin's universe: "Who knows?"

# CHAPTER FOURTEEN

# THE LADY IN WHITE

Take care! Take care!
The White Lady is there
Watching you, listening . . . !"

—F.-A. Boieldieu—E. Scribe, *The Lady in White*

## OF ANIMALS AND MEN

With the collapse of both the Manichean worldview and Tintin's reign over primeval Nature, the animal kingdom was relegated to the background. Supplanted by Haddock, even Snowy became a secondary character of only occasional interest: "You know, Tintin, you ought to take me more seriously" (*RSS*, 20, III, 1). Snowy still talks to his master but usually only barks. Most of the time he hangs out with the animals with whom he shares some affinities, especially the Siamese cat at Marlinspike. But the adventure of *The Castafiore Emerald* again showcases the world of animals. In this album animals appear from the first to last page. The opening scene pictures a magpie perched on a tree branch while Snowy follows the scent of a rabbit down into its hole. The captain is delighted by "the twittering of birds" in the underbrush. Two panels further along show some horses in a field, with Snowy chasing another bird. Finally, on the same page, a squirrel is observing the humans passing below. Later, Hergé puts other animals into the foreground: a dog and cat, a parrot, a multicolored bird with a worried expression, some wasps, a ladybug, a great-horned owl, and again the magpie. Other animals in this story are more worrisome because one senses their presence without actually seeing them: the great-horned owl that scurries around in the attic, the Gypsies' monkey long suspected of thievery, and Mr. Wagner's racehorses that are the object of his obsession.

In this album more than in any other, Snowy is just a dog. He barks a lot and talks only to the cat. He runs, follows a scent, chases animals and birds, mistrusts human beings, dashes after cars, and becomes frightened when other animals take him by surprise (*CE*, 40, IV, 4). On only one occasion does he regain his former intimacy with Tintin—when the two of them are hiding like children in the trunk in the attic (54, I, 1–3).

On the whole the animal kingdom, both hidden and familiar, rarely intrudes on people's daily lives. Most of the animals go along, minding their own business, too insignificant to be noticed by the humans (the ladybug, the squirrel). Others, however—like the blackbird, the parrot, and the owl—are constantly interfering and stirring up trouble.

Another way the animals make their presence felt in this adventure is through the behavior of the residents of Marlinspike. In various situations, Tintin and his friends display their secret affinities with emblematic animals. In Castafiore's presence, for example, Haddock typically reacts like Snowy—he flees. When Tintin is embroiled in a situation he cannot control, he characteristically maintains the coolness of a cat. The great-horned owl, otherwise known as the brown owl [*chat-huant*, literally, the "booing cat"], becomes the emblematic animal of Tintin's older self—Professor Calculus. Both the owl and the professor have much in common. They have the same round heads and the same absent looks. The eyes of the nocturnal animal, "sparkling like diamonds," are reflected in Cuthbert's round glasses. Whereas Castafiore mistakes the owl for a ghost haunting Marlinspike, Tintin and Haddock had earlier associated the scientist with the phantom of the estate (*RRT*, 63, IV, 2). The footsteps frightening Castafiore were heard the first time in the crypt, the scene already associated with a story about jewels and the discovery of pirate treasure. The "brown owl" and Calculus also share behavioral similarities. Both nocturnal, Cuthbert and the owl are the soul of the estate although they live at some remove from it. The owl resides in the attic, whereas Calculus sets up his laboratory at the far corner of the estate grounds. By taking up residence among the humans, the owl distances itself from the animals it hunts. Similarly, by setting up his workplace close to the animals in the park, Calculus distances himself from the other humans under his tutelage. The owl and the professor are both uncommunicative, even secretive, and share the reputation of being "the bird of bad omen"—the owl literally according to popular tradition and the scientist figuratively because his inventions often threaten the security of his friends. The Thom(p)sons, who show up in this adventure only peripherally, revive their former ties with the monkey featured on Lord Francis's deserted island (*RRT*, pp. 30–31). This time, too, the detectives are obsessed with a monkey's presence. Attributing to "their" animal the penchant for stealing that secretly fascinates them, they accuse the Gypsies' monkey of taking the emerald. After Tintin discovers the emerald's nesting place, and the detectives finally get their hands on the "stolen goods," they immediately lose it again, as if the jewel were too hot to handle.

In this album other animals also acquire a symbolic value: the wasps, for example, are associated with the journalists. The journalists buzz around Castafiore like wasps around a flower. After sucking her dry, they sting her with their venomous news article. But the diva will have her revenge, for the real wasps sting the paparazzi before they are able to get to her again (21, I, 2).

To reinforce the parallelism between humans and animals, Hergé gives the animals human attributes. Like Snowy, the parrot talks, of course, although more mindlessly. Defending animals, Castafiore asserts that "animals immediately attach themselves to those they love" (10, I, 3) and later praises the "intelligence of the beasts" and "their artistic instincts" (34, III, 2). If she takes the great-horned owl for "a man, no doubt about it," the only real thief in the story turns out to be the magpie. The racehorses that are virtually Igor Wagner's "wife" have female names that the musician lovingly whispers into the telephone like a secret code: "Sarah, Oriana, Semiramis" (23, IV, 3).

While many of the animals take on human characteristics, many of the humans become identified with animals. The young Gypsy Miarka is called "the little tigress," and the woman on the telephone takes offense at being addressed as "you old cackling cockatoo" (19, II, 5). When Haddock sees Castafiore hanging out with the journalists, he "smells a rat." To the captain the journalists are like "zebras" who "bolt like rabbits" when they are surprised by the wasps. Later, when the *Paris-Flash* runs a full-page article announcing "Milanese Nightingale Will Marry Old Sea Lion" (27, II, 1), Wagg advises Archibald to stop "playing the goat."

In contrast to the animals, the humans do not form a homogeneous group but, rather, three "clans" that constantly intersect but do not share the same values or interests. The first group, with the most members, populates Wagg's world, personified in this album by the journalists and the media people interested in spectacle and performance. The second group includes the residents of Marlinspike who try to prevent the "wasps" of the outside world from overrunning them. If most animals generally respect the territory of other animals, humans do not share this trait. They take advantage of the smallest breach in a boundary to invade another's territory. Haddock, Calculus, Gypsy Mike, and Castafiore, respectively, are ready to pounce on such an aggressor. Whereas the first two express an impotent rage in the face of the invaders, Castafiore is strong enough to show the door, literally, to insurance salesmen (42, IV, 1–3).

The third group is the Gypsies, who were originally to have a more prominent place in the adventure.[1] The Romany Gypsies play a role similar to the Yeti in the previous adventure or the Incas in *Prisoners of the Sun*. They are the Other, the unassimilable stranger, who both fascinates and repulses. They are "damned" not because they are in touch with the beyond but because they move around in the lower realm, in the margins. They are the excluded ones, the abject who live among filth and garbage. The Marlinspike police allow them to camp only on the rubbish heap "where the filth from every garbage can in the neighborhood is chucked" (*CA*, 4, II, 2). Whereas the Marlinspike clan wants to put down roots, the Gypsies are by definition wanderers. The two clans are as opposed as Abel the settler and Cain the wanderer, the older of the two children of the original couple.[2] Occupying the cursed position of abjection, the Romany people are associated with the mystical. They know the future as well as the past. When the old Gypsy woman meets the captain, she predicts exactly what unfolds in this adventure. But Archibald does not give any credence to her words (4, I, 2, 3). Tintin, in contrast, listens more attentively. Although he has chosen the camp of Abel the settler, he is endlessly fascinated by the itinerant Romany people, as if they belonged to his former but now inaccessible world, as if they knew the secret of his birth. When Tintin hears the Gypsy guitars, he nostalgically regrets his choice: "What haunting music this is!" (40, III, 3). For the foundling, after all, the Gypsies play a very important role. They are the ones accused of kidnapping the infant from his original family to sell him to another, typically less famous. But in this adventure the myth is reversed: the foundling belongs to the Gypsy clan. It is the little girl Miarka, lost in the forest, whom Tintin brings back to her family, as he has always done in similar cases. But for the first time, the hero does not find himself confronted by a male twin but by a little girl who adopts him with the same trust that he himself had shown to the boys in previous stories.

Having returned Miarka to her family, Tintin is very happy that the captain offers to have the Gypsies camp nearby on his estate. Instead of Nestor, who is definitely prejudiced, Tintin offers to show them the camping place himself. During their entire stay in the Marlinspike meadow, Tintin tries to get to know how the Gypsies live. He snoops around their horses' watering hole on the pretext of trying to figure out the owner of some footprints he had discovered near the main house (*CE*, p. 16). Some days later, he again hangs around in their vicinity but does not dare make himself visible in order to avoid setting off Mike's aggressive temper. Given the choice, he much prefers to listen to Mike's singing than Castafiore's (*CE*, 40, II–III). Mike intuits that Tintin is drawn to his people, so he tries to scare him off by throwing stones at him: "The little brat! I don't like the way he's always snooping around" (16, III, 6). But Tintin does not show any resentment toward Mike. On the contrary, he tries to defend the Gypsies by solving the mystery of the missing emerald so that the police will stop harassing them: "What pleases me the most is the relief for the Gypsies. They'll be completely cleared of suspicion now" (60, IV, 2). The hero who has scaled the steepest mountains, reached the most inaccessible summits, and discovered the best-kept secrets is powerless in this case to break down the barrier separating him from these strangers. They reject him, knowing that he belongs to a different class, another world, and that he has opted for the worldly values of the bastard.

The parallel worlds of animals and humans come together through the secret affinities of several of the characters for particular animals. Of course, each animal does not always represent or symbolize a human being. Trying to draw a strict correlation risks becoming tedious. Nevertheless, against a general background of living creatures, one can pick out certain characters that have their doubles, their echoes, in the opposing world. This is true not only for the humans but also for the animals.

Mike-the-gypsy and Haddock-the-sailor are two men with striking similarities. Both of them are always hurling insults at others but move from insults to songs according to their moods. The old Gypsy man who tries to make peace very much resembles Professor Calculus; the old fortune-teller who rambles on like the parrot is reminiscent of Castafiore because of their similar noses as well as their moralizing tone. Miarka, as beautiful as Esmeralda in *Notre Dame de Paris*, has an aura of infantile sexuality previously attributed to Tintin when the captain desired "to drink him." They call Miarka "the little tigress," and she definitely resembles a cat, especially when she bites the captain and "draws blood" in response to the captain's attempts to tame her. Archibald quickly realizes his ambivalence: first he calls her "the little devil" and then soon after, "the little angel."

The symbolic structure of the three main groups can be summarized in Table 1.

Table 1. The symbolic structure of the three worlds in *Tintin*

| Role | Place | | |
|---|---|---|---|
| | *Animal world* | *Gypsy world* | *Marlinspike Hall* |
| Father | Owl | Old Gypsy man | Calculus |
| Mother | Parrot | Old Gypsy woman | Castafiore |
| Bastard | Snowy | Mike | Haddock |
| Foundling | Cat | Miarka | Tintin |

## THE JEWEL SONG

Tintin is the first character to meet Castafiore. In *King Ottokar's Scepter*, when he stops at the Hotel Crown, he meets the diva on her way to Klow with Mr. Wagner, her accompanist. Tintin asks if he can share their car, and they agree. En route, Bianca Castafiore tells him that she is an opera singer and makes him an apparently generous offer: "Would you like to hear me now?" (*KOS*, 28, I, 2). She treats him not as an adult, however, but as an adolescent whom she can easily please by giving him a sample of her performance rather than by inviting him to the opera itself, which is reserved for mature adults. Recognizing his place, Tintin accepts her offer and for the first time hears her rendition of the "Jewel Song" from the second act of Gounod's *Faust*.

The scene from the opera takes place in Marguerite's garden. Siebel, her young suitor who is trying to seduce her, brings her flowers. But just as Mephistopheles had predicted, the flowers immediately fade and die. Beside the faded bouquet Mephistopheles places a jewel box engraved with Faust's name. The beautiful young woman has to choose between the flowers and the jewels, a choice that will dictate her entire life. As Calculus slipped the Incan bracelet on his wrist, Marguerite fatefully fastens the jeweled bracelet on her arm. The jewels wed her not to the Sun but to the Devil. At the bottom of the jewel box, Marguerite discovers a mirror, and now she can contemplate how the diamonds have transformed her. Her laugh of surprise is not innocent; it echoes Mephistopheles' diabolical laugh running throughout the entire piece:

Ah! I laugh to see how lovely
I look in this mirror!
Is it really you, Marguerite?

Answer me, answer me quickly!
No, no, it is you no longer,
It is the daughter of the king,
To whom everyone bows as she passes.[3]

Castafiore's performance in the car makes the forest animals scurry off, and they are quickly followed by Tintin, who slips out as soon as possible. Granted, this meeting with the opera star saves his life, insofar as Müsstler's villains—hot on his trail—ambush the hay wagon where he had previously been hiding. But he is not saved from having to hear her voice again. On a cell mate's radio in prison, he hears her concert broadcast from the opera house in Klow. Another time he inadvertently hears her again when he breaks into the reception hall at the royal palace where she is performing (*KOS*, p. 38).

The "Jewel Song," the only thing we ever hear the diva sing, perfectly reflects her narcissism. Evoking themes of the family romance, the song also connects the singer to other characters. When Marguerite is transformed by putting on the jewels, she goes from being middle class to "the daughter of the king to whom one bows as she passes." She breaks with her own family, transgresses the prohibitions laid down by her brother (since her father is dead), and thinks only of living with Faust, whom she takes for a young lord whose lifestyle conforms more closely to her social aspirations. When Castafiore intones this song like a personal hymn, she totally identifies with Marguerite's story, a role where she claims to be "utterly divine." She sees the Faustian adventure as an original scenario laying out her future, and her everyday life as merely a temporary, degraded form of the stage drama. Thus, she incessantly tries to transform her daily routine into a grand opera where she will always be the star.

We do not know anything about her actual origins, but Hergé presents some incidents that allow us to know her better. After her concert at Klow, for example, she telephones the palace to say she would be delighted to sing before the king. The king's secretary takes the call and indulgently replies: "His Majesty will be delighted" (*KOS*, 35, IV, 2). Once she is introduced at the court of Syldavia, she keeps elbowing her way into high society until it is rumored that she has a liaison with Baron Halmaszout, the Lord Chamberlain (*CE*, 28, II, 1). This baron does not appear in person, but his last name allows us to connect him with another: Baron Almazout who in 1277 was proclaimed king with the name Ottokar I. The current Lord Chamberlain of Muskar XII, according to Hergé himself, was "obviously the descendant of the one who defeated the Bordurians six centuries before."[4] Nevertheless, one is led to believe that the line between the founding monarch and the contemporary baron is as fictitious as that between Lord Francis and Captain Haddock, for in both cases the spelling of the names is different.

In this story, then, Castafiore is attracted to two males with opposing characteristics: Tintin, whom she tries to seduce by singing to him, and the bastard baron, with whom she has an adult sexual relationship. Her situation duplicates Marguerite's. Marguerite is attracted to Siebel, who is too young for her taste but whom she loves like a brother. But she is also attracted to the lord who gives her the jewels. But like Halmaszout and Haddock, Faust is a bastard whose royal position is due only to the powers of Mephistopheles.

In the earlier adventure, when Tintin tried to escape from his pursuers by breaking into the palace hall, Castafiore fainted into the arms of Mr. Wagner—a scene duplicated, in the same way, at Marlinspike Hall after the false alarm of the jewel theft (CE, 35, IV, 3). The first fainting spell is perhaps due to a similar cause. In the star's automobile, Tintin catches a glimpse of her jewels; later on, when she is performing her twin role of Marguerite, she takes Tintin for a thief. Real life interrupts the theater and changes the scenario. In the opera, Siebel continues to respect Marguerite even after she gives herself to Faust. To Castafiore, it seems that Tintin-Siebel is taking advantage of the situation to steal her jewels. This eruption of violence that Castafiore interprets as a theft provokes her swoon. The hero, however, does not see anything that is happening on stage because he is too absorbed in looking for the father figure of the Syldavian adventure. Indeed, in *The Adventures of Tintin*, the father figure takes a long time to establish itself, thus delaying the emergence of the Mother.

In *The Seven Crystal Balls*, also an adventure dominated by the search for the Father, Haddock has his turn to meet the Milanese Nightingale. For two weeks he attends the shows at the Music Hall Palace to try to figure out the magician Bruno's secret, which would also allow him to oust Calculus from his place of privilege. But before the magician's act, Haddock has to suffer through the diva's singing. After he and Tintin escape through the stage doors, he tells Tintin: "And she's in good voice tonight!" (7CB, 12, I, 1). The captain associates her singing not with the mythical Sirens but with a natural disaster: "Whenever I hear her, it reminds me of a hurricane that hit my ship when I was sailing in the West Indies some years ago" (7CB, 11, III, 2).[5] When Castafiore launches into her "Answer me, answer me quickly," it is Snowy who responds with a howl drowning out the diva's song. The captain has only himself to blame, for he has listened to the same song fifteen times in as many days. On future occasions he even sings it himself: in *Destination Moon*, at the moment of the trial launching, and again at the beginning of *The Emerald* (5, III, 4).

The first more direct meeting between the Nightingale and the Sea Lion takes place at the Hotel Sznorr in Szohod. Haddock tries to avoid "Bianca Catastrophe" by hiding with Tintin behind a pillar (*CA*, 48, I, 1). His negative attitude toward her seems even more extreme before the singer actually meets him. Unintentionally, he encounters her again shortly afterward. Pursued by Colonel Sponsz's police, Tintin and the captain hide in the Opera House in Szohod, where *Faust* is being performed. At the end of the show, the two friends try to escape through the stage door, but they bump into the diva, who assumes they have come backstage to congratulate her on her performance. Bianca asks, "Who is this . . . this fisherman?" At that point Haddock makes his first slip of the tongue loaded with implications. Completely befuddled, he introduces himself as "Hoddack," and then "Haddad," errors the singer later multiplies indefinitely. The first seduction scene in Syldavia is also duplicated here. Bianca invites Tintin-Siebel and Haddock-Faust into her dressing room, where she puts on "Marguerite's prettiest gown" for her backstage admirers (*CA*, 53, III, 4). The only one missing from the scene is Mephistopheles, who shows up shortly afterward in the person of Colonel Sponsz. Once more, real life embroiders a variation into the original operatic scene. Since Haddock and Tintin are desperate to avoid the colonel, the diva hides them among the clothes in her wardrobe. The two "heroes" are reduced to the level of children hiding in their mother's skirts, waiting to discover the parental secrets. But this doesn't immediately happen. As soon as the colonel enters the dressing room, he sits on the captain's cap before beginning to turn on the charm.[6] Rather than rely on his human intermediary, Faust, as in the original scenario, Sponsz-Mephistopheles himself seduces Marguerite. Sponsz begins by making her "blush," a tactic used later on by Calculus (*CE*, 9, I, 3). Castafiore offers to take his coat and asks him to uncork some champagne—always a symbol of sexuality in Hergé's work. Just as the colonel is about to carry out her wishes ("Madam, your wish is my command"), he is interrupted by two of his guards who are searching the theater. Annoyed by the presence of "these brutes," Sponsz experiences a kind of premature ejaculation: as he pops the cork, the champagne runs through his fingers before he can pour it for his partner (*CE*, 55, I, 2). Not to lose face, he brags about his diabolical plans to kidnap Calculus and gradually reveals to the singer all the details of the plot. Still hiding in the wardrobe, Tintin and Haddock do not miss a word. After thus "exposing" himself, Sponsz suggests to his partner that she come home with him "to meet his wife." He takes Castafiore to his home, and the next day he cannot get the "Jewel Song" out of his head (*CA*, 56, II, 1). Following that evening, the local Bordurian journalists spread rumors about the engagement of the colonel and Castafiore. The scene that Tintin and Archibald witness not only teaches them how to make babies (but does Tintin really understand, since he does not drink champagne with the ladies?) but also saves their lives and allows them, later on, to exonerate the Father and bring him back to Marlinspike Hall.

In *The Red Sea Sharks*, a very similar episode unfolds when Castafiore finds herself among Rastapopoulos's guests aboard the *Scheherazade*. This time, the seduction scene is carried out in costume. At a masquerade ball, Bianca disguises herself as Marguerite and the phony Marquis di Gorgonzola as Mephistopheles.[7] In this case the masks do not conceal but actually reveal the true nature of those in disguise. One more time, tongues wag about the diva's engagement to her new host. When Tintin and Haddock are rescued from their raft and climb aboard the yacht, it is as "the mistress of the house" that Castafiore welcomes them "in the name of the Marquis di Gorgonzola" (*RSS*, 40, II, 2). Here again, to the advantage of Faust, Marguerite-Castafiore betrays Mephistopheles-Rastapopoulos even after accepting his presents. When she reveals to the captain the true identity of the owner of the yacht, she prevents the latter from killing Tintin's shipwrecked clan. As in *The Little Poucet*, the wife of the ogre betrays her husband by revealing to the children the true nature of the Father and his secret powers. This is the third time Hergé repeats this theme. Since each of the members of Tintin's group owes her something, Castafiore can now find a place within the family. Afterward, however, the family members try to liberate themselves from "the jewel song" by paying their debt to her the moment it comes due.

## THE LADY WITH THE PARROT

Castafiore is internally conflicted between her desire to end up with a respectable man and her attraction to the "devilish" Maharajah of Gopal, Colonel Sponsz, and Rastapopoulos. The "devils" are notorious givers of jewels, but their gifts smack of foul play. Indeed, the fortunes of these men are based

on blood and the crazed exploitation of others. But there is nothing villainous about Haddock. Although the jewels he possesses may have a checkered
history, at least the success of his ancestor has restored their original honor.
Shedding the blood of Red Rackham expiated that of his victims. Thanks
to Lord Francis's slaughter of this villain, the captain can enjoy his immense
fortune with a clear conscience.

Ignorant of the part the evil Rackham has played in his affairs, Bianca-
Marguerite sets her cap for Archibald-Faust. She offers herself to the captain
under the guise of a symbolic bird—not the nightingale this time but the
parrot whose multicolored plumage evokes the shimmering of jewels. Everything is prepared for her plan to succeed.

In the middle of May, a season ripe for love, she sets out for Marlinspike, persuaded that Haddock will welcome her with open arms. That very
morning, the captain feels nature "bubbling up" inside him and toasts "the
fresh air"—the allusion to champagne again suggestive of sexuality: "Breathe
deeply, Tintin! Fill your lungs with fresh air . . . air so pure and sparkling
you could drink it!" (*CE*, 1, I, 3). Nevertheless, the beauties of spring are
disrupted the first time when "the little tigress" Miarka bites the captain.
Shortly thereafter, he trips on the broken step of the Marlinspike staircase
and ends up with a badly sprained ankle: "A cast and absolute rest for two
weeks." At this moment Castafiore makes her grand entrance and surprises
the captain with his leg stretched out, barefoot, on a cushion. From a psychoanalytic perspective, the bare foot is a phallic symbol. The beauty asks
right off: "What has happened to you?" Reassured that his future "capaci-
ties" are not endangered (the accident will not prevent him from being
captain in other senses), she does not immediately take his foot but at least
initiates a seduction.[8] Right away she presents the parrot in terms suggesting sexuality. It is "a little something" Irma the maid carries in a cage tied
up with a pink ribbon—pink like Bianca's personal writing paper. Bianca's
"hello" sounds like a "cuckoo," and she lists the virtues of her rare bird. His
name is Iago,[9] "a compliment to dear Signor Verdi" (10, I, 1), and the parrot
will be the captain's "constant companion." She attributes to the parrot "an
unfailing instinct," implying that Iago will be an intermediary for her own
affections for the captain: "We love Captain Hopscotch already, don't we?"
(ibid.). When Iago is as wild as little Miarka (who was dressed in the parrot's colors, red and green), Bianca suggests the captain should make the first
move: "Stroke him, Captain, don't be afraid." The morning's incident in the

forest is repeated: the captain's finger is bitten, setting off a spate of curses. Castafiore immediately puts a stop to the captain's bad language. Like herself, her parrot has such modest ears: "Please, Captain! Such language! Poor pollikins might learn it." Beginning with the toe, her project of seduction passes to the finger, another sexual equivalent. Bianca wants to bandage the injured member herself, using the occasion to further her advances: "A pretty little butterfly bandage to comfort the poor sailorman" (p. 10).

Indeed, the captain is going to need some comfort, for unbeknownst to Castafiore, the parrot plays an important role in the captain's history. Without enumerating all the particular incidents in *The Adventures of Tintin*, one can note that the bird introduces the two maladies of psittacism and psittacosis into Marlinspike Hall. Psittacism is the mechanical, even stammering repetition of words and phrases typical of parrots. Psittacosis is an illness transmitted by parrots to humans. The repetitious stammerings start with the parrot ("Hello-o-o-! I can hear you"), pass on to Castafiore ("Mercy! My jewels!"), and spread to the rest of the characters. Haddock is the first to catch it: "How . . . how did you get in?" he repeats two times.[10] Calculus catches it next and passes it on to the doctor: "What happened? What happened?" Calculus asks, and the doctor also repeats it two times (55, II, 2). Irma is no less spared ("yes, Madame; yes, Madame") than is Mr. Wagner. Not only does Wagner repeat his beloved racehorses' names several times but he is also fated to rehearse the scales on the piano all day long. Castafiore treats him like a mechanical toy, even a eunuch, and he winds up installing a recording to simulate his own repetitive playing. The stammering repetitions continue to show up in the characters' speech as well as in their thinking and behavior.

The presence of Bianca-the-parrot provokes some degree of castration anxiety among all the usual characters at Marlinspike, but the anxiety crystallizes in Captain Haddock.[11] After being bitten by the little girl and dropping his walking stick, he suffers a sprained ankle. Once the diva shows up, the symbolic castrations proliferate. First Bianca knocks his pipe out of his hands; then the parrot bites his finger, causing the finger to become red and engorged like an erect penis. After the finger comes the nose, as if Hergé had to multiply the substitutions to emphasize the one unnamable organ. Archibald's nose is targeted first when the parrot bites it (19, III, 4) and then when the wasps sting it. His nose becomes bright red and puffs up in an obscene way. Bianca takes this opportunity to redouble her efforts. She applies a symbolic "wrap" to the organ that is supposed to relieve the stinging and bring the nose back to its normal shape. This time she applies not a little "butterfly" bandage, as for the finger, but crushed rose petals for the aching member. As if his castration anxiety were not sufficiently obvious, it reappears again during the night in the form of a dream (*CE*, 14, IV, 3, 4).

The second panel has to be analyzed before the first since it suggestively replays the day's events. Haddock is unable to move and lies in his bed with his sprained ankle, his finger bitten by Miarka, and the parrot's nick on his nose. He hears a cry in his sleep: "E-e-eek!"—a cry he had heard that afternoon. That time it was the cry of the wild little girl when he tried to grab her to comfort her. In the dream he does not identify the cry as Miarka's but Castafiore's, who does indeed let out a real scream. But Haddock does not know this, since he sleeps in a separate room where ordinarily he would not hear any voices. Only his unconscious is able to equate the two females.

In Panel 1 the captain imagines himself in a theater, where he first saw the diva. He is seated in the first row, completely naked. His face is red, signifying two complementary experiences. He is red with shame for being naked among those who are dressed. The red, which we have just seen on his finger and nose, also suggests an erection. Just as in the look he gave

1                              2

Panel 1: That night: "Ah! My beauty."    Panel 2: "E-e-eek!"
*CE*, 14, IV, 3, 4. © Hergé/Moulinsart 2007.

Tintin in the nightmare from *The Crab*, desire is written all over his face, especially in his eyes. Archibald, in his nakedness, is in sharp contrast with the other spectators, who are dressed for a formal evening or for a wedding. There are two more telling features of the spectators: they are all parrots dressed up like people, and they are judging the captain's indecency very harshly. One can see in these birds a strong connection to the parrots on the ancestor's island. When the inhabitants of the island regressed to barbarism upon Lord Francis's departure, only the parrots were able to preserve the traditional laws of the Father in a derogatory form by repeating his reper-toire of curses and insults. One of those birds provoked Archibald by calling him a "sissy," an insult that really wounds him. If indeed there is one quality he believes he shares with his ancestor, it is courage. It is unacceptable, then, that mere parrots disparage his lineage (*RRT*, 29, II, III). But here, the birds' judgments remind him of the basic law: sexual desire ought to be repressed. If one's sexual desire becomes too visible, the parrot-judges will punish the guilty one by castrating him.

In the current dream sequence, Bianca Castafiore is dressed in a violet nightgown, the same color as her dress from earlier in the evening. She is wearing a pearl necklace and a parrot head. If in the current adventure the parrot represents the female sex, then indeed Bianca is wearing her sexual desire on her face. But this head also represents the parrots in the ancestor's gallery, making her the woman designated for the Father and thus forbid-den to the captain. She is singing the "Jewel Song" to seduce her audience, but her act is undoubtedly more complex. In the circus or the music hall, it is frequently the case that someone has to go onto the stage, an extra or a spectator, to be part of the show or bear witness to its success. The magician Bruno, for example, asks for a volunteer from the audience just at the mo-ment Haddock bursts onto the stage wearing the head of the cow. The act is repeated here: the captain, completely naked, has to go onstage in response to the diva. The bed can be interpreted either as separate from the dream (although Hergé intentionally includes it, as in the dream sequence in *Pris-oners of the Sun*), or as representing the dreamer as a significant element in the dream sequence. The bed is on the stage, after all, and appears an integral part of the act. Haddock probably has to put himself in bed (to see himself onstage) to be an adequate partner for the star. The scene is a wedding night that is at the same time the castration of the male. The song "Ah, I Laugh" is in fact a kind of war cry (E-e-eek!), screeched by Castafiore and Miarka, and with them the entire female-parrot species at the moment when they triumph over the male sex. As the forbidden woman, the woman belonging to the Father but desired by the son, the opera star (*cantatrice*) becomes the castrator (*castratrice*). Thus, Archibald's dream allows us to better appreciate the complexity of his relationship with the diva. If he honestly wants to get away from her, we can nevertheless see in his behavior that he is also secretly attracted to her. Castafiore's overbearing nature is only his pretext to justify his flight and blocks his examining any other aspects of his feelings. Because the son risks transgressing the incest taboo, the singer constantly threatens him with castration in the name of the Father. The only way for the son to remain safe is to reject all advances of the Mother.

## THE SECRET OF THE UNICORN

To be complete, the analysis of *The Castafiore Emerald* has to include the two previous albums featuring *The Unicorn*, for these two albums bear numerous similarities to the later one.[12] In fact, they form a single story—the establishment of the family—where the first part of the episode introduces the Father and the second, the Mother. The two albums appeared in the same season (the first from April 15 to the beginning of August, and the second from May 16 to the beginning of July), revolve around Marlinspike Hall, and feature a story about jewels. In *The Unicorn*, the jewels travel from the past to the present, and the problem remains of keeping them within the family. In *The Emerald*, the jewels move from one place to another, but the problem is the same: how to limit their movement to within the family circle. In each story, the parrot is a nagging presence. As a symbolic animal, its sexuality depends on the main characters of the episode. When it is Lord Francis, the parrot is decidedly masculine. When Castafiore comes on the scene, it becomes feminine. But when she finally leaves Marlinspike, the bird—instantly transformed into the mirror of the captain—reverts to his blustering masculine conduct: "Billions of blistering barnacles! Shut up when I'm speaking!" (*CE*, 57, II, 2).

     The same pattern of switching from masculinity to femininity characterizes the two adventures. When Tintin and Haddock set out to search for the lost treasure of Red Rackham, the old antique dealer predicts that a dark future awaits them: "Remember what I said, my lad! You won't find any treasure!" (*RRT*, 10, III, 1). The same scene replays with the old Gypsy woman who physically resembles the dour antique dealer: "Just a little silver, please! Otherwise you will suffer great misfortune! The jewels will disappear!" (*CE*, 4,

II, 1). In the two stories a doctor intervenes to prevent Haddock from setting off on the adventure. Uninvited guests constantly threaten the tranquility of the little clan: in the one case, the fraudulent descendants of Red Rackham; in the other, the media people and journalists. Without claiming to be exhaustive, we can mention several other incidents that are duplicated. The verbal quid pro quo between Calculus and the journalist Ken Rogers (*RRT*, p. 56) is replayed between the professor and the journalist Christopher Willoughby-Drupe (*CE*, p. 23). The misunderstandings between Haddock and Calculus are common to both adventures. In the first, one understands "whiskey" when the other says "underwater." In the second, the one says "roses" and the other hears "marriage." In the two instances, the rivalry between the professor and the captain ends with a hearty handshake that only prolongs their antagonism (*RRT,* 21, I, 1; *CE*, 28, IV, 1). Whereas in the earlier adventure Haddock "offers a bottle of champagne to the first one to sight land" (*RRT*, 21, III, 1), in the later one he declines to offer the champagne to the first ones—the Marlinspike Marching Band—to congratulate him on his forthcoming marriage (*CE*, 30, I, 3). In the two albums, the Thom(p)sons—now in charge of security on the estate—end up by quarreling with each other after accusing those closest to Tintin of committing the crimes. Other details that may appear insignificant nevertheless contribute to reinforcing the parallels. The mirror Haddock drops in the antique dealer's shop (*RRT*, 10, I, 4) is the very one Bianca later uses to look at herself (*CE*, 27, II, 2). By leaving an antique crossbow on the step of the Marlinspike staircase, Tintin causes Nestor and the Bird brothers to trip. In the later episode, that very same step, now broken, causes the whole family (except Bianca) to come crashing down.

With the help of his more glorious ancestor, Archibald has an opportunity in the adventure of *The Unicorn* to wipe out his "original sin" by rewriting the less savory aspects of his life aboard the *Karaboudjan.* The *Memoirs* of Lord Hadoque are for the captain what Gounod's *Faust* is for Castafiore: an alluring scenario in terms of which they reinvent their existence. The two of them want to be the descendants of more prestigious families, and thus both participate in the myth of the bastard. Furthermore, they are both attracted to the world of the theater, and both are incredibly gullible. Haddock attempts to conduct himself like an aristocrat of former times, while Bianca believes she is living out the role of Marguerite in real life. Meanwhile, the gulf between their aspirations and their actual conduct makes their ordinary lives seem quite dull.

When Archibald compares his life to his ancestor's, the comparison does not speak in his favor. Although commissioned by Louis XIV to undertake a commercial venture, Lord Hadoque is first and foremost a soldier, proud of his brave conduct, and not afraid of mortal danger, as evident in the incident with Red Rackham. Archibald belongs to the Merchant Marines; his activities bear the "disreputable" trademark of commerce. But he cannot even defeat the pirates that attack his own boat, and he jumps ship rather than suffer defeat. Reading about the skills of his ancestor induces such a level of exaltation in him that he falls into a psychotic trance—what sometimes happens to those returning from war.[13] To compensate for his impotence in warfare, he acts out for Tintin the legendary murder of the pirate, reliving the incident through his own hallucinations, confusing past and present, blood and red wine. His imaginary bravado is subsequently negated by the fact that all it takes to get the captain to engage in activities he initially repudiates is to call him a "sissy."[14] The only way to erase his original shame is to imitate the behavior of the ancestor, at first in a totally external and mechanical way and later by internalizing his model and adapting it to new circumstances.

Haddock does follow his role model, especially in the pivotal moments of his existence. Thus, when he associates with the Inca, he gives his solemn oath in the same style as his ancestor: "Me too, old salt, I swear too! May my rum be rationed and my beard barbecued if I breathe so much as a word" (*PS*, 61, I, 3). He feels he has roots only when living in the Father's house (Marlinspike Hall), surrounded by the Father's heritage: the portrait, the fetish, the old armaments, and the relics of the ancestor fill the main reception hall of Marlinspike. By inheriting the jewels, Haddock receives from his ancestor a social confirmation equivalent to Tintin's decoration of the "Golden Pelican" by Muskar XII. The captain arrives at the pinnacle of social success more gloriously than by hard work. The glory of Lord Francis simply reflects on him. Thus, he can enjoy all the advantages of a bourgeois life while maintaining the fiction of belonging to the idle aristocracy.

The fact that the captain's lifestyle is based on such a rudimentary lie partly explains his emotional instability. Never really convinced of being a hero, Haddock constantly looks for compensations in a world of performance designed to grant him the changes he desires. Manic phases follow depressions, the latter typically leading to alcohol or melancholy. We have already emphasized his oral fixations. These do not correlate with the Freudian oral stage because Haddock remains an Oedipal bastard. His behavior seems, rather, to exhibit a tendency toward hysteria. Studies have indeed highlighted the phenomenon of "hysterical conversion" in a type of psycho-infantile personality characterized by passive dependence, oral fixations, and a tendency toward hypochondria—traits one can find at least intermittently in the captain.[15] His identification with the ancestor becomes all the more unbending when the sailor feels unsure of himself. His insecurity translates, furthermore, into his many slips of the tongue. Haddock thus expresses a constant fear of being castrated by the Father, or in other words, as being seen as a "sissy" or a "girl." Sometimes he tries to avert the danger by impos-ing the same threat on the stand-in for the Father, namely, Calculus. In *The Treasure*, several times he snatches and throws away Calculus's pendulum, one of the most frequent phallic symbols along with the umbrella associated with the Father. Each time, Snowy retrieves it, thinking it is only a game the Captain is playing (*RRT*, pp. 52–53).

In contrast to his usual hypermasculinized behavior, the captain some-times acts in a more "feminine" way, suggesting a certain ambivalent iden-tification with the mother figure. Thus, on several occasions we see him imitating Castafiore. In *The Red Sea Sharks*, for example, he dresses up in women's clothing—a disguise Tintin himself adopted earlier, when he still had the gift of metamorphosis (*CP*, 48, I, 2). But the captain's experience as a transvestite deserves a closer look. To escape their pursuers, he and Tintin dress as Arab women carrying jugs on their heads. Despite diligently prac-ticing this task, Haddock trips in front of the guard patrol—the "guardians of masculinity" on the lookout for them. Since he appears not to be their target, Archibald transforms the patrols' search into a sexual one by attempt-ing to seduce the guards with his newly acquired "skills." With a few quick steps, he manages to rebalance the jug atop his head. The guards whistle and cheer, as if he were a showgirl performing in a cabaret. Noting his success, Haddock looks back, leans seductively on one hip, and says to himself: "Well! What about that, eh?" (*RSS*, 25, II, 2). Shortly thereafter, he encounters a real Arab woman who addresses him in Arabic; of course, he cannot reply. The woman pulls off his veil and runs away screaming, terrified at coming face-to-face with "a woman with a beard." In the nick of time the guide arrives on the scene with the horses Tintin and Haddock need for their es-cape. Haddock is relieved and looks forward to getting away on horseback. After all, he had taken up that sport earlier to imitate the aristocrats. The only problem is that his "feminine side" is still in play. He can't get his feet into the stirrups, has a hard time staying on the horse, and ends up riding backward in the saddle. In short, he is mounting his horse in anything but a genuinely manly position.[16]

We see, then, that the captain harbors both a tendency to imitate a masculine ideal, valorized by society and his own superego, and a fear of being treated like a "girl." This fear is all the more repressed insofar as it is the other side of a desire, but the fear is also augmented by the fact that he sees Woman as a phallic and castrating figure, a danger to the Male.

The adventure of *The Unicorn* deals with not only the foundation of the family but also the myth of the triumph of the Father over the Mother. This triumph is signaled by the temporary barring of the Mother from the family circle. The characters abandon strictly dual relationships and arrive at the level of triangularity, the threesome, the only pattern of relationships that allows the connection between generations. But triangularity has also become mythical to the extent that it has been constituted without the female dimension, as if reproduction were exclusively an affair for men. The "secret of the unicorn" may be the secret of bisexuality. However, this secret is not divulged here but remains buried in the carcass of the shipwreck at the bottom of the sea.

Although the Mother is not presented in any realistic way that might assuage the terrors she otherwise inspires, in this adventure the feminine dimension is nevertheless not completely foreclosed (*scotomisée*). As all things repressed, the feminine resurfaces but remains elusive, reappearing just as it seemed to have been symbolically put to rest somewhere else, and temporarily becomes crystallized in images susceptible to various interpretations.

The feminine is instantiated in at least four figures, or "places," in our text. The more powerful she is, of course, the more frightening she appears. The first figure is the sea itself. Without playing merely on words sounding alike,[17] we know that the ocean is traditionally associated with the maternal image.[18] The ocean represents the vital force of the universe, and it both nourishes and engulfs. Thanks to his maritime experience, Haddock's ancestor can sail the sea without succumbing to her traps.

The second feminine figure is the island, a constant theme in the mythology of the foundling. As we have seen, the heroic lord is able to impose his law on the island, but when he departs, the taboo against cannibalism is transgressed. The natives devour each other, and the island reverts to its primeval "virginity."

The third figural incarnation of the primal Mother is the character of Red Rackham, an outlaw yet master of oceans, whose practices are steeped in savagery and blood. Elegant and seductive in his grand red cape, the pirate stands before the captured Lord Francis with his coffer of diamonds under his arm: "Look at these jewels!" The villain condemns his prisoner to a slow and painful death, but the prisoner escapes. Striking a blow to the pirate's vanities ("I'll pluck those feathers, you squawking popinjay!"), the ancestor imposes his own code of honor on the pirate, forces him to fight, and manages to kill him (*SU*, 24, III, 1). The lord also recovers the coffer of jewels, the "feminine finery" that changes its meaning in the symbolic hierarchy. From being objects of scorn and malice, steeped in blood, the diamonds become a sacred legacy handed down from father to son.

Finally, a fourth feminine figure, quite different from the preceding ones, runs through the entire adventure and lends it its name: the unicorn. Just as the whiteness of the Tibetan snow contrasted with the bloodstains left by the Yeti, the whiteness of the mythical unicorn contrasts with the red of the pirate. Traditionally, the unicorn is associated with a nonsexual, sublime love and purity—factors that explain its presence in the iconography of Courtly Love.[19] This animal has the magical ability to detect any impurity, even the slightest imperfection in the brilliance of a diamond. In Hergé's symbolism, the unicorn becomes the "other face" of the primal Mother. The unicorn represents inaccessibility, virginity, unblemished purity, and the all-consuming quest—the sort of quest Tintin takes up for the last time on his Tibetan adventure.[20] Although the unicorn is a positive figure, the ancestor rids himself of it by sending his ship *Unicorn* to the bottom of the sea so that "the red" would not triumph over "the white." Returning to Europe, Lord Francis reintegrates the symbolic animal into his legacy in the form of the three model ships he leaves to his sons. Thanks to Calculus's underwater apparatus, Tintin locates the shipwreck. Along with his team on the *Sirius* he recovers the unicorn figure on the prow and takes it back to Marlinspike with the lord's other relics. When Haddock purchases Marlinspike, he exhibits the inherited treasures to the public, but he subsequently hides the figure from the prow to preserve it as a fetish.

Afraid of being overwhelmed by the Mother, Archibald eliminates every representation of her primal form. The foundling of the family first has to get his issues straightened out with the Father before the Mother can be integrated into their home. In *The Castafiore Emerald*, the sons finally decipher the secret of the unicorn: they figure out its symbolism, or in other words, they come to accept sexual existence. They can do that only by interiorizing the Law that permitted the ancestor to vanquish the primal mother figure and to put her in her place each time he confronted her. When the Mother finally makes her triumphal entry into the ancestral home, the domain reserved for the Father, she does not appear as the all-powerful White Goddess but as the less fearsome "lady in white," Bianca Castafiore.

## PORTRAIT OF BIANCA

Hergé's portrait of Bianca is like a diamond, brilliant and multifaceted, reflecting differently within the various albums. These different reflections nevertheless offer us a faithful likeness because Bianca herself does not exist apart from representation and performance. As Calculus puts it, not even realizing how appropriate his words really are: "Your portraits always display an amazing likeness" (*CE*, 9, II, 1). The most unflattering picture appears in the *Tempo di Roma* news bulletin. In the tradition of the medieval tapestries, it shows us "The Lady with the Parrot." Castafiore is looking at her emblematic bird as if seeing herself in a mirror.[21] If Calculus finds it an "astonishing likeness," Haddock on his part thinks it "not bad at all." But this image of the singer does not make her laugh. Bianca-Marguerite refuses to see herself in this "beastly" reflection. She much prefers the one in *Paris-Flash* announcing the engagement of the "Milanese Nightingale" to the "Old Sea Lion," nicely mixing children's fairy tales with bourgeois aspirations. But if one looks too closely at even this picture, the Nightingale still looks more like an "old squawking parrot." The Sea Lion appears more like a defeated dog, confirming the prediction he made earlier: "Just a bark or two, and you can change my name to Snowy" (*TT*, 18, III, 1).

A different depiction of Castafiore recalls Freud's patient Dora.[22] We noted that Haddock shows occasional signs of hysteria. But with her unending stream of erotically charged behavior and language, his female counterpart does so even more. Systematically mispronouncing men's names is not only a way of cutting the men off from their manly heritage and castrating them but is also a way of sending a message. What is she really saying when she *mis*-names the captain?

The first mis-naming occurs in the opera house in Szohod when Haddock calls himself "Haddada," which can be read as "to dada." This infantile way of asking "to play horsey" (*faire tagada*) can also be interpreted as a disguised sexual invitation. To show him she has understood the unconscious message, Castafiore then calls him "Mr. Paddock," a term meaning an enclosure in a field for mares in heat and slang for a bed. To the invitation to make "a dada" with the captain, the singer offers her bed, while saving appearances by playing on the equestrian double meaning. On several occasions she uses her astonishing ability to lose concentration ("Where is my head today?") to excuse making an off-color remark. Here are some examples. When she sees the captain's naked foot, she calls him "Kapok,"[23] a very light, waterproof fiber made from vegetables; but this word could also be heard as "capote," slang for condom. A little later she asks Iago the parrot if he loves "nice Captain 'Mastock.'"[24] In French slang, *mastoc* means "big, thick, or hefty." One can read here an allusion to the captain's physique but also perhaps to the size of his penis; after all, the captain is still lying there with his bare foot up in the air. The latter interpretation gains more support if one recalls that the parrot symbolizes sex. When Archibald swears at the parrot, the diva admonishes him to be quiet and calls him "Captain Cossack."[25] The Cossack is a member of the Russian cavalry under the czar, and the name itself used to suggest gross and obscene behavior ("he acts just like a Cossack"). The Cossack is also the hero of many sexual adventures and bawdy melodies. When Bianca meets the captain later in the garden and insists on his putting on his coat, she calls him "Captain Kolback" and literally grabs him by the back of the collar, or gets him in her "snare."[26] Finally, when she brings him a copy of the *Paris-Flash* announcing their upcoming marriage, he becomes "dear Captain Kornack," a derogatory term with at least two meanings. A *cornac* is someone who introduces or leads something else, especially an elephant. But *cornac* also comes close to the term *cornard*, which means "a cuckold." In suggesting her future infidelities, Bianca sheds light on what kind of marriage they would have, should it actually come off! At that point she tallies up in front of her "future" man the names of her many ex-fiancés the press attributed to her in the past.[27]

During her first night at Marlinspike Hall, Castafiore experiences a "crisis" that defines her relationships with the other residents. Although in a deep sleep, she believes she is the victim of a threatened sexual assault. At the window, she sees a monster, "a ghost or something," that lets out a "long, mournful cry." The "monster" has eyes "shining like diamonds" that cast on their prey the same look of desire the Yeti showed for Chang. Bianca does not know how such a monster could appear at the second-floor window, but a little earlier she also heard footsteps overhead: "It was a man. I'm certain" (15, III, 4). She awakens the entire household to tell them about the incident. Although Tintin immediately sees the whole thing as a figment of her imagination, he nevertheless tries to find some basis in fact by looking the next day for footprints beneath her window. And he finds them! "Was she telling the truth?" (16, I, 1). The footprints prompt him to continue the game, at least for the sake of the others at Marlinspike.

When the singer believes she is being attacked, she lets out a scream ("E-e-eek!") that sets off the captain's dream. She repeats this same scream on different occasions, but in particular when Calculus (the symbolic equivalent of the great-horned owl) enters the room, like a thief in the night, where the cameramen are videoing her interview (32, IV, 2). Each time she sees a man approach in some sort of aggressive way—especially in a setting where she feels she belongs—she interprets his action as an attempted theft or violation of her person: "Mercy! My jewels!"

Her diamonds not only represent an enormous fortune but serve as her special way of personally communicating with the outside world. The jewels form a kind of discourse that the singer, blocked by her subconscious censor, cannot formulate in socially acceptable language. In Bianca's case the jewels are like the clinical symptoms (in somatic transformations or phobias) of a "classic hysteric." In short, they are a language. To be understood by others, the language still has to be rooted in communal meanings. For this reason Castafiore makes use of things that already "speak" to convey her own personal message.[28] The word *jewel* (*bijou*) is very like the word *gem* (*joyau*) in French, and comes from the Breton word *bizou*, which means "a small finger ring." Gilles Ménage, cited by *Littré*, suggests a different etymology: *bis-jocare*, *bi-jouer*, or "play together," "expresses something that plays with light and sparkles from many angles." Slang has taken over this word with its many sexual connotations. In their literary works, Denis Diderot, Éveriste Parny, and numerous other authors reinforce the erotic overtones of the word *jewel*. This leads to our modern usage of the term "the family jewels" to refer to the penis as well as the female sex organs. The word *joyau*, on the other hand, may come from the pseudo-Latin term *gaudiale*, from *gaudium*, or "joy." Nevertheless, the etymology most accepted derives *joyau* from *jocari* and, in turn, from *jocalis*, meaning *jeu*, or "game." According to *Robert: The Dictionary of the French Language*, *jocalis* is "that which delights or pleases." *Jewel* and *gem* have root connections associated with *joy* (*joie*), *game* (*jeu*), and *enjoy* (*jouir*).

What Castafiore expresses with her "jewels" is the sexuality she cannot otherwise show—that she cannot even verbalize except in the form of slips of the tongue, phonetic twists, and reversals. She reworks the language, playing with its sounds, to bypass the censor and express desires that apparently have no other outlet. She also reworks the gems, playing with their meaning, so that they lose their clarity, allowing her to communicate in a way otherwise impossible. But this exchange of meanings is itself lived out in the mode of the forbidden. The origin of the jewels is unmentionable: they are always the gifts of Mephistopheles or one of his subordinates, who typically ends up exchanging them for someone's soul. Under the tender embrace of Faust, Marguerite detects the claws of the devil that mark the jewels with his indelible signature.

Once the beautiful woman has the jewels, they can no longer circulate except "outside the law," in the form of theft. The men who meet the diva can be divided into two groups equally villainous: the devils who offer her jewels and whose "eyes glitter like diamonds" and the thieves who penetrate into forbidden places with the hopes of stealing (dérober) the jewels themselves.[29] Although these groups may appear different, they are probably the same men who offer with the one hand what they intend to grab with the other. The violence she attributes to men in general allows the opera star herself—whether seduced or robbed—to remain "white," pure, only the victim. Even while taking part in the forbidden relationship, she remains innocent by projecting onto the male Other all responsibility for desire. This explains why she refuses to insure the "whole kit and caboodle," her collection of jewels. An insurance policy would put an end to the game, eliminate the risk, and transform the language of the diva into a monologue with herself. She would then be obliged to invent another "symptom," another external sign perhaps more anxiety provoking, and in any case less meaningful than the language of jewels, and hence less socially recognizable.

To appease the various conflicts that beset her, Castafiore delegates the security of her treasure to her maid Irma. If Mr. Wagner, the accompanist, is the eunuch who bars intruders from her inner circle, Irma's role is to be both confidante and scapegoat for the sultana. The maid who cannot help misplacing her own household items (scissors, thread) will never be vigilant enough to prevent a theft, even if she herself would never steal. On the one hand, Bianca's many precautions undermine any genuine protection: "I'll lock my jewels in this drawer, Irma, and I'll hide the key to the drawer in this vase, over here. Try to remember, girl" (14, III, 1–2). On the other hand, as soon as the jewel box is safely locked up, Castafiore rushes to get it out to contemplate her treasure or to show it to future lovers. As soon as she takes out the jewels, she forgets where she puts them. When Bianca herself needs to remain innocent, Irma serves as an excuse for the mistress's foolishness. In case Bianca loses the jewels, she can always accuse her confidante, as Phaedra accuses Oenone: "It is you who named him."

The sexuality Castafiore tries to repress keeps reappearing, diffracted in various ways by the jewels, the parrot, the step on the staircase, the slips of the tongue that multiply in her presence, and the play of language itself. Her chastity exists in name only. Michel Serres has taught us to read "Bianca Castafiore" as "Blanche Chaste Fleur"—the Holy White Flower. Unconsciously she calls herself Marguerite, and the circulation of her jewels (acquired, then lost) stands in for the forbidden libidinal exchange.

Just as Haddock's relations with his entourage exist in the mode of swallowing and spitting out, Bianca's exist in the mode of giving and taking. These actions imply violence, transgression of taboos, and the disruption of good manners. They are acted out, moreover, by two characters who claim to be fussy about good manners—at least when they manage to control their own impulses. Archibald sees this woman as a typical mother figure, both hateful and desirable: hateful because she is inaccessible, and desirable because she belongs to the Father. Bianca sees the male as having the paternal characteristics. Both the one and the other have difficulty in verbal communication; they scream or they sing to make others listen to them. Because their ability to communicate in symbolic forms has been impeded, their imaginations run wild, thus feeding Bianca's inattention and Archibald's clumsiness.

If they achieve a relationship of three—something the foundling was formerly incapable of doing—they nevertheless cannot escape reliving the Oedipal situation with every new encounter. According to Castafiore, Haddock acts "like a big child." In terms of the symbolic dualism of prostitution and violation (giving and taking), Castafiore herself plays the role of the "sweet young thing," mincing about and trading her "gems" with whatever prestigious man she meets.

Even with Tintin-Siebel, she cannot help herself from trying to seduce. After her first attempt at seduction by giving him the recording of *Faust*—an audio seduction—she loses her necklace, a piece of costume jewelry. Tintin rushes in to retrieve the beads, mistaking for real what is only a fake, a "Tristan Bior" (25, I , II). Inviting the hero to "thread her pearls"—"an activity of an idle gentleman"[30]—Castafiore once more acts the flirt. Here again, the hysteric resorts to a metaphor rather than speak more plainly.

Haddock and Calculus compete with each other to win over the beautiful damsel who quickly becomes the figurehead on the metaphoric ship of Marlinspike. Haddock resumes his habits from his early days at Marlinspike—dressing elegantly, learning to do his hair—thus submitting to each new caprice of his tyrannical beloved. As the captain, and despite his repeated cries of alarm ("Every man for himself!" and "Take cover!), he does not abandon the ship and bravely faces Hurricane Bianca.

Calculus, with his innocent airs, takes a subtler route to conquer the diva.[31] Besides being the authentic father figure—something Castafiore discovers the night of her arrival—his pseudo-deafness also allows him to take advantage of many situations. When the lady gushes, "Professor, you make me blush," he quickly responds, "I sincerely hope so, Madame!" (9, II, 1). Cultivating his garden, he is not really candid and soon proves to know all about the language of flowers, pure and impure. He is constantly offering the diva red and white roses, both appropriate colors for her. He even creates a new variety: "Such a white! Pearly, sparkling, immaculate!" (20, IV, 2). Predictably, he baptizes his new variety with "the beautiful name Bianca." In short, he attributes to her a symbolic virginity that pleases Bianca-Marguerite, who this time chooses the flowers over the jewels. Near the end of this adventure, the opera star kisses the "dear professor," a sign of warmer feelings to come. When the lady departs from Marlinspike, Cuthbert takes the first opportunity to go to Milan, where he will be sure "to call upon our charming friend" (58, I, 3). What happens between him and Bianca is not mentioned in the story. But whatever it may be must surely take place "within the rules," for Calculus has never been a thief: "Fraud? Certainly not. I never do it. I make it a point of honor to declare everything at customs" (61, III, 1).

The different images of this woman come together in a special portrait broadcast on television. The televised scenario appears at the center of the album (pp. 30–40) and takes place in the Maritime Gallery at the heart of the estate. From there the broadcast can spread everywhere in concentric waves. Castafiore arranges the stage set the way she wants, removing the ancestor's antiques to make room for her piano. If the unicorn of yesteryear does not return, the Lady in White takes its place. Even her beaked nose recalls that mythical animal's horn. From this central position, having vanquished the captain, she performs her grand act. All the crisscrossed themes come together in the same person: the ambitious bastard, the seductress, and the sexually violated woman. On this evening, with the television as her mirror, Marguerite performs an updated version of *Faust*. Her portrait is more complete, however, than even she had hoped. Presenting the official broadcast as well as the scenes backstage, Hergé demystifies the show. Letting us see the diva playing to her audience, he allows us to understand the language of the jewels. He also reveals the unconscious structure of the relationships within Tintin's family, just at the moment when the feminine presence is about to overturn them.

## THE ROLE OF THE FABLE

The adventures of *The Unicorn* and *The Emerald* appear as a mystery about the heroes' past whose solution will establish the family. The secret will be deciphered once the Father's code is understood. But the actual sons of Lord Hadoque were not able to decipher it. Tintin's clan is more successful once they learn another language. The original language of *The Adventures of Tintin* is straightforward and unequivocal, allowing one to distinguish clearly between Good and Evil. In this language of absolutes, words symbolize things. But *The Unicorn* makes the hero learn a new worldly, ambiguous language coming from the ancestor, the language of the Father. If this new language remains the model, it is based now on wordplay ("Light will come from light") and requires interpretation. It is no longer a language of symbols but of signs, "liberated symbols," referring to different objects of reality. This new language—no longer absolute but relative—adapts to historical circumstances, thus dissolving the original Manichean dichotomy.

The story of *The Unicorn* is an apprenticeship in several distinct stages for learning the new language. The first takes place when the wounded Barnaby points to the birds and says: "Take care! They will kill you too" (*SU*, 31, III, 3). Tintin figures out only later that Barnaby meant the Bird brothers. The second stage comes with deciphering the three manuscripts that must be superimposed for their meaning to appear. The third takes place when the heroes are near the island but do not find it. Tintin realizes that the meridian used by the French ancestor was Paris, not Greenwich, so they were initially thrown off track (*RRT*, 23, IV, 2). The final stage leads them to the treasure.

They finally realize that everything they have understood literally must be read metaphorically. The eagle's cross stands for the statue of Saint John, the Eagle of Patmos. The coordinates on the ancient parchment indicate a point on the earthly globe and not Earth itself. In other words, the adventure obliges them to rethink more abstractly what they had previously thought of in more concrete terms. This operation is carried out by the same methods—assimilation and accommodation—that Piaget advances in his theory of childhood development.[32] The treasure was right in their hands all along. They could have saved themselves a lot of trouble if they had understood from the start that everything plays out at the level of representation.

In *The Emerald*, Hergé takes up the same pattern of language apprenticeship but at an even higher level of abstraction by getting his readers to play along with him. The album presents not three parchments with one message but one story with three different readings that can be superimposed on it. What we find here is the triple structure we saw previously. Each place is structurally identical to the others, the only difference being the level of abstraction that calls for the interpretation of the mystery. The first place, the Gypsy camp, represents the world of the foundling. Tintin tries to come close to it, not so much to discover the solution to the theft (after all, he believes the Gypsies are innocent) as to come to understand the myth of origins. However, the Gypsies abandon the grounds of Marlinspike without warning, leaving Tintin in the lurch about discovering his origin. At the ancestral hall, an equally dramatic story is developing around the bastard, introduced by the sudden entrance of the Mother and the rivalry with the Father. As in the Freudian account of "the family romance," the Mother is both desired and denigrated by the son. For Archibald, she is both mother and whore. Bianca fits perfectly into the fantasies of the bastard: she scolds him like a schoolboy and openly rattles off the names of her previous lovers, or at least reputed fiancés. Read at this level, it is not the mystery of who stole the emerald that needs to be solved but the meaning of the jewels and, especially, their role in the language of substitutions. The mystery lies there. It can be solved only in the language of the Father, in which words and emeralds refer to an underlying multiple reality.

Finally, the world of the threesome is also the animal world, the only one presented in a tangible, concrete way. It is the world of fable, in every sense of the word: the world of the fabulous, of origins, and of the primordial era, *in illo tempore*. But it is also the world of "fabulation," of storytelling, of the *favola* and the *fola*, which in Italian mean the "fable" and the "joke." Tintin travels from one world to the other, but because he does not fully possess the elements of either one, his investigations put him on the wrong track. The Gypsies are as innocent as Mr. Wagner's passion for the track. Tintin lives within the mystery of the Oedipal relations among the characters, but he does not know how to understand it. The drama plays out between the main characters, the "grown-ups"—Calculus, Haddock, and Castafiore. The hero has access only to the stand-ins, the substitutes, the "Tristan Biors." Like the child to whom one explains the mysteries of birth by introducing the stork, he finds a solution to the mystery that satisfies his spirit only in the animal kingdom. The guilty are no longer the Bird brothers but an actual bird, the thieving magpie who steals the emerald and hides it in its nest. While the hero sees a puzzle where others simply do not—because for them it must be "the Gypsies who did it"—he shows that the adult world has a giant blind spot. Curiously, *The Emerald* puts that lacuna aside. Rejected by the children, we see the hero looking for the solution in the animal kingdom, while right in front of him the adults exchange remarks more or less obscene. Tintin's understanding is limited in a way he just cannot get around. If in the adventure of *The Unicorn* he shows that he can decipher the language of the Father, in *The Emerald* he cannot perfectly master that language. If he could manage it, he would understand the secrets of the adult world, of sexual difference, and the logic of desire—but then he would cease being the childhood hero. By presenting the animal tale as the only truth that allows for "the solution to the mystery," Hergé saves appearances, even after having multiplied the signs of complicity among the adults. The unity of "all the young from seven to seventy-seven years old" can be realized only at the level of the signifier. With the very same images, the author invites us to explore many different readings of his works.

## CHAPTER FIFTEEN

# THE TEMPLE OF SLEEP

## THE VOID

With the adventure of *The Broken Ear*, the original Manichean structure of the foundling's world, patterned on the notion of the double, begins to crumble. In that adventure the characters chase after a fetish that supposedly, but not actually, contains a precious diamond. In other words, the fetish is empty. In *The Seven Crystal Balls*, the empty interior takes on the dimensions of a theatrical stage that sucks Haddock in, as if he were nothing but a wooden puppet. The captain opens doors that lead nowhere, flings himself at flimsy stage props, and finally regresses to the level of pure animality, with a cow's mask on his head. The emptiness not only engenders a perpetual restlessness but also introduces some unexpected, diabolical transformations very different from Tintin's earlier metamorphoses that result from his dedication to and familiarity with the divine. Thus, one can link the scene in the music hall to the desert sands, the "void" on planet Earth.

When Tintin or the Thom(p)sons get lost in the desert, they are taken in by mirages, the play of illusions—as if the ego and the world melted together to produce a fanciful but anxiety-ridden reality operating according to unpredictable laws. When the victims leave the desert, they temporarily lose their essential capacity to distinguish the true from the false, and thus to deal with the external world. In *The Cigars of the Pharaoh*, Tintin's ordeal is all the more disturbing when Rastapopoulos builds a "cardboard city," a film set, in the desert, uniting in one scene two different sorts of "voids" generally separated: the desert and the stage.

A sense of vertigo appears in constructions even more solid than card-board—Calculus's spaceship, for example. The hatches that allow one to move from one level to another are a constant danger. Cuthbert himself ends up falling into one, and his fall causes amnesia. He regresses to an unstable, infantile stage where he needs to be coddled. *The Calculus Affair* is not about gangsters chasing after a fetish but about international spies wanting to get their hands on a powerful weapon. While Calculus is held prisoner, we are led to believe that his famous plans are hidden in his umbrella that inadvertently is sent on a trip far from its owner and ends up in a junk heap for "lost property." But all the fuss over the umbrella is in vain: Cuthbert forgets he left his plans in his night-table drawer. The handle of his umbrella is as empty as the Arumbayan fetish.

*The Castafiore Emerald* is built around a more fundamental emptiness generating all the movement, a symbol of the characters' basic lack. The broken fourth step, symbolizing their emptiness, is both a symptom of general repression and "the image of this gap introduced into the series by the opera singer, the only character who does not trip."[1] The staircase at Marlinspike Hall changes into the staircase at the Paris Casino, where the aspiring stars go up and down—singing, muttering, or crying, according to their moods. Marlinspike gradually becomes "the play of the whole world" (Massillon), a huge stage surrounded by spectators who are stirred up by the media and gathered there to applaud or to boo.[2]

In *Flight 714* the void shows up on many levels. First, the many scenes depicted from a high angle produce a feeling of vertigo. In no other album, even on the adventure to the moon, does Hergé show us the Earth from on high, transforming the human participants into dwarfs. The impression of living in a film set (*décor*) begins on the second page, when the characters land at the Djakarta Airport, which could just as well be in Sydney or Chandernagor. The scenery is functional, international, impersonal, utterly divorced from nature. When Haddock surreptitiously waters the potted plant with his glass of Sani-Cola ("a healthy drink, overflowing with chlorophyll"), the plant immediately shrivels up and dies.

For Archibald the experience of the airport is as stressful as that of the music hall. With so many anonymous, indistinguishable people crammed together, people feel unable to connect with one another on any genuine level, and therefore each traveler conceals his or her personal life. The captain finds it all terribly disagreeable. But then he has an epiphany. He heads toward someone sitting alone on a bench and projects onto this lonely traveler an image of what might have become of him, had he not been saved by Tintin: "Where does that poor chap come from? How long since he had a square meal? Alone in the world, no one to care for him. Human flotsam, one of life's failures" (*F714*, 2, II, 1, 2). Touched by such misery, Haddock discreetly slips a five-dollar bill into the poor fellow's hat, only to find out a little later that he is the millionaire Laszlo Carreidas!

Reminiscent of those in *The Seven Crystal Balls*, the captain's experiences reinforce the impression that the world is only a flimsy make-believe. The conjuror reappears, for example, but this time Calculus, not Bruno, plays the magician. This time the conjuror does not change water into wine but pulls a five-dollar bill out of a spectator's hat. Carreidas is ecstatic: "That's priceless!" Since the millionaire will not have to pay—and will be further entertained—he invites Tintin's clan to continue their trip on his personal aircraft. Haddock is picked to play "battleship" with the master. Like Lord Hadoque of old, the new Haddock hopes to win even if it is only a childish game. But the fight is fixed! Archibald is as bewildered as he was during the magic act of the fakir Ragdalam: "You're psychic! Anyone would think he could see my board." But magical, superhuman powers are now revealed as simple trickery based on advanced technology. A camera placed above the captain's head allows his opponent to see the positions of his battleships. Carreidas fools Archibald the way Tintin had tricked the Incas.

The impression of the world's flimsiness continues elsewhere. On the island of Pulau-Pulau Bompa, the natives collaborate with Rastapopoulos because he tricks them into believing that he will support their national liberation movement. But in fact, the revolutionary rhetoric of Rastapopoulos and his lieutenant Allan Thompson is nothing but hot air. The villain's confederates are acting in vain. Their leader admits as much under the effect of Dr. Krollspell's truth serum; Rastapopoulos has no intention of keeping his promises to the revolutionaries. To repay their help in rounding up Carreidas, the villain intends to bury them in a hole, where they will be left to die. Nevertheless, Rastapopoulos sings his victory song too soon. Who knows if the millionaire's famous bank account, the centerpiece of the intrigue, is not completely empty?[3] The sensation of free fall continues when the gangsters' careful plans backfire.

But even the heroes experience the void. They have to explore the island's underground: first, the bunkers left by the Japanese at the end of

World War II; then, the abandoned underground temples. It is there in the underground hole that, just like Calculus aboard his spaceship, they discover the truth, as well as fall victim to amnesia.

*Flight 714* links up with themes from two previous adventures: *The Prisoners of the Sun* and, to a lesser degree, the adventures to the moon. In *Flight 714* the relation between the sacred and the scientific is taken up again but from a different point of view. Once again the characters set out on a voyage, not to a deserted planet this time but to a supposed island. Although the first part of the trip is voluntary, the rest is not. Just like the Thom(p)sons on the rocket to the moon, Calculus, Haddock, and Tintin are unaware of their own risk as they set out for the island. They toast their departure not with a bottle of champagne, as on previous occasions, but with a bottle of "Sani-Cola," far from the real thing.

Carreidas is a type of Baxter but craftier, more childish and inhumane, less interested in research itself than in technological applications. In contrast to the Syldavian scientists who work for the good of humanity, the extravagantly wealthy engineer works for his own profit. Science, technology, and art are for him nothing but signs of power that he manipulates with pleasure, even while taking risks. For him, life is a poker game where all moves are allowed, and he counts on having the "the four aces" in his hand.[4]

Where once Good and Evil could easily be distinguished, now we find only a meaningless void. Haddock would love to send Wagg "to the devil," but how is this possible when even the devil has been reduced to such a weak specimen of human being? In *The Cigars of the Pharaoh*, Rastapopoulos made his first demonic appearance; his second, in *The Red Sea Sharks*. Apparently unchanged, his activities are still focused on Evil. But now the Grand Master of former days has become a mere hoodlum, living in luxury, and putting himself above others by ostentatiously flaunting his wealth. His disguise as Mephistopheles is no mere illusion, but it reveals not so much the depths of his character as his cunning plan to dazzle Castafiore. What was once considered divine, even as its devilish opposite, has become mere spectacle.

The devil's fall does not stop there. In *Flight 714* Rastapopoulos sinks to the level of mere farce. Master of the island of Pulau-Pulau Bompa in the Celebes Sea, he plays his final trick to try to regain his former position. Rather than rebuild his fortune from ground zero, he kidnaps Carreidas to swipe the millionaire's hoard. He has the devil on his side, after all: "The devil could not have done any better!" But following Tintin's lead, he also relies on science. For his team he recruits a former Nazi, Dr. Krollspell, inventor of an effective truth serum. Unfortunately for the villains, nothing goes as planned. When science lets them down, Rastapopoulos resorts to worn-out religious formulas: "I'll get you, if I have to demolish this temple stone by stone!" (48, IV, 3). He also invokes the devil as his ally: "What have I done to Lucifer to deserve all this?" (50, III, 1). But his invocations are in vain; his bad angel has abandoned him. Rastapopoulos's Hollywood-style cowboy outfit is now in shreds, his face covered with wounds, and his head, with bumps. His colleagues betray him or cannot rise to the occasion. Allan Thompson, his loyal lieutenant, shares his defeat. Having lost his false teeth in the scuffle, he shows up with a swollen face (*F714*, 51, II–IV).

The carnivalesque atmosphere erases the differences between Tintin's clan and Wagg's counterfeit world. By all rights, Carreidas belongs to Wagg's camp. If Tintin and Haddock save him from the grip of Rastapopoulos, it is only because they accidentally are mixed up in his affairs. Like his fellow travelers, the millionaire is strongly attracted to farce. As hard-nosed as Abdallah, he uses Spalding, his secretary, as his whipping boy. When he meets Calculus for the first time, his reaction is worthy of Jolyon Wagg: the professor is "a scream . . . the life of the party!" Since he sees other people only in caricature, he judges them all as clowns or comedians. Even in the course of a drama where he risks losing everything, he refuses to consider the consequences, confident that something will turn up to get him out of the mess. For him, all human beings are equivalent, thus interchangeable. He sees uniqueness only in trivial objects, like his classic hat, which he fetishizes: "A prewar Bross and Clackwell, and that's absolutely irreplaceable" (60, II, 2).

One of the best scenes in this album is the meeting between Carreidas and Rastapopoulos. In principle, these two men belong to opposing camps, but their opposition is merely superficial, like that between Alcazar and Tapioca. Under the effect of the truth serum, Carreidas willingly lists his former misdeeds: "There are lessons to be learned from a dishonest man" (25, III, 2). He never spends time in prison, as his alter ego does, only because he is luckier. Under the truth serum he admits to cheating at cards and to the childhood origins of his obsession to become a millionaire. When Rastapopoulos turns to beat up the doctor whose truth serum has worked only too well to reveal Carreidas's secrets, if not his bank-account number, the villain himself accidentally receives a shot of the serum and displays a similar need to air his dirty laundry. His likeness to Carreidas is stunning. The "twins" strenuously

compete to establish which of them is more wicked. Each proves worthy
of the title "the devil incarnate," but their rivalry for being the worst devil
would have ended violently in bloodshed if Tintin had not shown up in time
to stop the fracas. The hero separates them and in a perfectly arbitrary way
condemns Rastapopoulos to the camp of Evil and takes Carreidas with him
to that of the Good. This was not a moral judgment but merely a conjuring
trick where no one is really fooled, neither the author nor his readers.

## EDUCATING TO FORGET

In contrast to the distant times invoked in the background, the action in
this adventure takes place within twenty-four hours. Like the island of Lord
Hadoque, the island of Pulau-Pulau Bompa contains traces from different
time periods. First, we see signs from the Second World War: shipwrecks
floating near the shore and Japanese bunkers used by the villains for hide-
outs. However, guided by Mik Kanrokitoff's telepathic powers, the heroes
soon discover the remains of a more ancient period that first shows up in the
form of a prehistoric lizard: "What's it doing here, pestilential pachyderm?
Looks as if it escaped from the Ice Age!" (35, IV, 1). When they descend into
the subterranean caves, Tintin and his band come face to face with the prehistoric, their own prehistory, and that of all humanity. They enter a temple
built millennia ago, then abandoned and forgotten by human beings. The
native islanders do not know anything about it, other than that they may not
descend into its darkness. Naturally, this place reminds Tintin of the Temple
of the Sun (43, I, 1), because of the phosphorescent coating on the walls and
the giant statues he discovers there (*F714*, 43, I, 1). To emphasize the parallels,
Hergé offers us numerous other reminders. On the island, Haddock slips on
a flagstone (*F714*, 29, I, 3), recalling the incident when they had to remove
the same kind of stone to get into the Temple of the Sun (*PS*, 46, IV). Weird
animals appear in both episodes. In one there is an eclipse; in the other, a vol-
canic eruption. The statue that hides the secret entrance to the island temple
(*F714*, 43, I, 2) conjures up the statue sealing the Incas' treasure room (*PS*, 61,
IV, 1). In both cases, the initiates have to press on the left eye and poke it in
to enter the heart of the sacred compound.

In the earlier adventure of *The Sun*, the Indians incarnated the religious
pole; Calculus and Tintin, the scientific. Hergé stripped the Incas of their
genuine knowledge of astronomy in order to make his contrast between
religion and science starker and to present the West as the ground for the

new truth, more certain than that of religion. That was a time of optimism for science, when the hero discovered a Father as congenial as himself, who soon guided his sons on a trip to the moon. But *Flight 714* takes place in a different context. Science has revealed its limitations, especially its negative consequences. Science has become subservient to technology and, thus, to a commercial venture. Whereas Professor Calculus embodied the first and higher type of scientist, he has been eliminated and replaced by Laszlo Carreidas, the millionaire engineer.

Hergé invents another world, inaccessible to human beings but nevertheless a model for them, in contrast to this contemporary world of only relative values. Without access to the absolute, the author reintroduces a kind of absolute in the form of extraterrestrials. Whereas the Temple of the Sun was populated by natives who continued their ancestral rites, the temple of the forgotten island seems to be abandoned. The heroes encounter a guide who seems more like a child than an adult. The guide, Mik Kanrokitoff of *Comet* magazine,[5] immediately establishes telepathic communication with Tintin, although Tintin seems no more ready than any of the others to be introduced to the mysteries of this new faith. Mik tells them about the history of the place they have discovered.

For millennia, mysterious creatures regularly visited Earth to check its progress. In former times, these creatures would show themselves to humans, who consecrated temples, such as this one, to these aliens, who were revered as gods. The frescoes of the "chariots of fire" represent the space travelers; and the grand statue, "an astronaut with a helmet, microphone, and earphones" (47, IV, 2). For unknown reasons, the humans were not faithful to these gods, so the astronauts no longer appeared. But the aliens still haunt the places of old, even though they are empty and people have lost their faith. Only a few initiates have kept the faith, and they maintain the connection between Earth and the wider universe by playing the role of double agents.

To be sure, as Hergé does himself, one can believe in the existence of extraterrestrials who are tracking the development of our planet. But it is preferable to read this adventure that was so disconcerting to Tintin's followers as merely a follow-up to the preceding albums. I personally see it as a projection of the hero's individual history onto the community. In attributing to everyone the same sort of abandonment of religion as Tintin goes through himself, Hergé absolves the latter and allows him to appear, if not as an outright conformist, at least as similar to others. At the same time Tintin's status as hero is preserved.

Like Tintin, the first inhabitants of the island start out as believers. Those whom they take for gods are only superior creatures, but the natives interpret their actions as miracles. Then, like the foundling himself who ends up opting for the bastard's values, these people forget about their gods. The absolute formerly projected into the distant past is now cast into the future, when human beings will become mature enough to reconnect with these superior creatures. Just as Hergé idealizes history, when in *King Ottokar's Scepter* he depicts a sovereign straight out of a fairy tale, so too he idealizes the future in projecting the dream of a perfectly controlled and unproblematic technology.

As an individual, Tintin is torn between two conflicting tendencies. On the one hand, he ought to remain faithful to what he was; on the other, he ought to leave behind his imaginary grandeur to become an adult. To reconcile these two leanings, Hergé resorts to amnesia. Throughout the adventures, we find many cases of amnesia or some kind of madness resulting in forgetfulness. That "forgetting" allows an individual in difficult straits to choose evil "innocently," or even to erase a preceding period of his life. Professor Sarcophagus, Didi, the spy Kaviarovich, Philippulus, the sailor on the *Speedol Star*—all of these become amnesiacs. In the Incan adventure, the seven scientists, who were guilty from the standpoint of faith and innocent from that of science, sleep through the adventure in which they star by becoming bewitched by the magic crystal balls. Once Tintin secures their pardon from the Incas, the scientists do not have any recollection of their experience. The same thing happens to Calculus, who lives through the drama totally unconscious. In *Destination Moon*, the professor is again the victim of amnesia when he falls through the hatch on the spaceship. Haddock is also subject to a kind of "hysterical" amnesia, especially when he is drunk. He seems totally oblivious to the evil he is about to commit. In *The Picaros*, he receives a blow to the head and experiences amnesia similar to Cuthbert's on the lunar voyage.

In *King Ottokar's Scepter*, when the Thom(p)sons are leading Kaviarovich to the hospital, they make a slip of the tongue that confuses amnesia with amnesty and then armistice. The collective amnesia of the seven scientists in *Prisoners of the Sun* and of Tintin's group in *Flight 714*—the latter case the result of Kanrokitoff's hypnotic spell—is a kind of armistice and amnesty. This last case of amnesia puts an end to the war between the foundling and the bastard, whose values have been in conflict since the beginning. It also marks the voluntary erasure of the past, with its errors, disavowals, and betrayals. The entire album appears as a sort of education in forgetfulness that allows Tintin to reach maturity, to become a man among others. In *Prisoners of the Sun*, even though he opts for science, he still tries to maintain the appearances of faith. He also promises the Incas not to reveal the secrets they have shown him. In this adventure, Mik Kanrokitoff asks him only to forget. By plunging them into a deep sleep, he liberates them from their past and returns them to a primal innocence. "Now, my friends, I wish you pleasant dreams!" Thus, Kanrokitoff exonerates Tintin. Similar to humans' abandoning their gods, Tintin's little "forgettings" or acts of neglect committed in the past are now absolved by being submerged into a far greater forgetfulness. Freed from his past as a foundling, Tintin loses his imaginary grandeur and status as redeemer. He trades the image of the Phoenix for that of the cat. At the same time, he appeals to his first parental figures, his primitive superego, to grant him the "armistice-amnesty" that his (bad) conscience demands.

In this light, the cover of this album seems highly relevant. For the first time in a long while, Tintin is carrying a gun, but for the legitimate reason of defending his group against the evil designs of the wicked. Beside him is Haddock, his brother who has changed his life. Behind is Dr. Krollspell, the former Nazi doctor who ends up on the side of justice. Finally, in the rear, is Carreidas, an ambivalent father figure whose mouth is taped shut so that he can no longer openly espouse Wagg's corrupt values. Snowy is in front of them. From now on Snowy is the only one who really knows Tintin's story, but Snowy is now regarded as nothing but a simple dog to whom no one listens: "I could tell them a thing or two! But no one would believe me!" (62, III, 1). In front of the group stand two immense statues of the ancient gods. They represent not so much the extraterrestrials as the hero's archaic parental figures.[6] They are twins facing each other, like the two Thom(p)sons deified and frozen into a stony sleep. Their huge, closed eyes suggest they have seen everything but now remain shut. Like Augustus at the end of the play by Pierre Corneille, they know everything but have decided on general amnesia-amnesty:

> Let your conspirators hear it publicly decreed
> That Augustus has learned everything, and wishes to forget everything.[7]

## CHAPTER SIXTEEN

# THE SCEPTER OF ALCAZAR

## THE STRUCTURE OF THE WORLD

*Flight 714* may seem like a totally pointless adventure because the characters do not remember anything that happens and their stay on the island does not change them in any way. While showing us something of their daily lives and desire for roots, this adventure otherwise alienates the characters from their readers and encloses them in a fictional universe. At Marlinspike, the family does manage to become close-knit. Castafiore insures her jewels, which no longer circulate in the outside world, and the Thom(p)sons are in charge of safeguarding them (*TP*, 2, IV, 2, 3). Keeping to themselves, the little clan even more strongly opposes the world of Wagg. Each of the family members, however, has a "twin" in the opposing universe who seems to share the same values but who enacts them in some degenerate form. All these pairs meet up in *Tintin and the Picaros*, the last album Hergé finished. This adventure, like *The Red Sea Sharks*, is a kind of retrospective in that many of the characters from previous adventures once again make their appearance. Table 2 summarizes the similar structure of the two worlds.

The pattern of pairing established at the beginning of the adventures seems to continue to the end, but it changes its function and significance. In the adventure of *The Congo*, the relationship of doubling provided balance and order, whereas now it generates disorder. Initially, the Other appeared identical to oneself, but now the Other is simply a caricature. Tintin's formerly exclusive status is now shared by the other family members. Being "the One" in an impossible superhuman dimension is no longer the goal;

rather, being recognized as a unique individual is now the hallmark of a humanism whose values constitute life at Marlinspike.

In this final album, however, a carnivalesque atmosphere highlights the distance between the two "places" and prevents them from becoming totally identical or assimilated. Each pair of individuals embodies a special value, except that each of the "twins" enacts it in different and complementary ways. Thus, Calculus and Alcazar are both masters of power and control, the former in science and the latter in politics. Cuthbert tries not to have to compromise with world powers. Alcazar, on the contrary, solicits the help of the International Banana Company to wrest power from Tapioca. When Calculus comes to understand the possible applications of his discoveries, he prefers to be "castrated," "to cut them off." Alcazar, in contrast, does not even consider the sources of the armaments that he receives. Although in *The Picaros*, Tintin does make the general promise to stage his revolution "without bloodshed" (43, IV, 2), Alcazar wants to make exceptions of Tapioca, his ministers, and his staff officers.

The second pair embodies love, both maternal and romantic. Castafiore lives her personal life in terms of the Faustian myth. Her "twin," Alcazar's wife, is named Peggy, the diminutive of Marguerite. With men, Bianca goes back and forth between the roles of "sweet young thing" and the Mother. Peggy, in contrast, has definitely made her choice; she is the nagging wife, the domestic tyrant who doesn't take "no" for an answer. She follows Alcazar in the name of love—but really because he has promised to fulfill her dreams: "The General promised me a palace in Tapiocapolis! But all the General provides is a beat-up straw hut crawling with bugs and roaches" (41, II, 1). "Peggy-my-dove" incarnates the will to dominate men that expresses itself only periodically in "Bianca-the-parrot." Calculus finds it easy to show the general's wife

Table 2. The symbolic structure of the private
and public spheres in *Tintin*

| Role | Place | |
| --- | --- | --- |
| | *Marlinspike Hall* | *Wagg's World* |
| Father | Calculus | Alcazar |
| Mother | Castafiore | Peggy |
| Bastard | Haddock | Jolyon Wagg |
| Foundling | Tintin | Ridgewell |

the same warm admiration he devotes to the opera star. He does not seem to notice the difference between the elegance of the one and the vulgarity of the other. For him they are both women, so they deserve the same treatment.

Haddock the bastard is duplicated in Wagg, his deformed twin. Both of them are driven to succeed, but the former is happy with playing out his success in private life, whereas the latter tries to aggrandize himself everywhere. Jolyon, the ring leader of the troupe "The Jolly Follies," is invited to the carnival in Tapiocapolis. Less savvy about political power than Haddock, he is delighted by the recognition he gets from Alcazar, who "appoints him and his Jolly Follies to the order of San Fernando" and invites him to next year's carnival (62, II, 2). For Wagg, this public recognition is equivalent to Haddock's legacy of jewels, the signs of success.

Once again, Tintin encounters the English explorer and naturalist Ridgewell. Ridgewell has not lost his "Robinson Crusoe" spirit of adventure, but the results have not lived up to his expectations. In *The Broken Ear* Tintin seemed like a son to the anthropologist, but in *The Picaros* they are now equals. Although he has not really grown older, the hero has matured, whereas Ridgewell has seen his powers decline. The white Arumbayan witch doctor has lost his prestige, with the result that the tribal people now live as they please. Like Tintin, Ridgewell looks on powerlessly while his ideals collapse. The Arumbayas have not improved their golf game, but they have "made great strides in drunkenness" (32, II, 1). Their excessive drinking is resulting in the loss of their culture and their sense of the sacred traditions. They are becoming merely the "flotsam" of a wealthy consumer society. Ridgewell views his Robinson Crusoe lifestyle no longer as the fulfillment of the foundling's dream but simply as retirement. His withdrawal from society has turned out to be much less glamorous than Tintin's move to Marlinspike Hall, for the explorer now lives in just a "beat-up straw hut crawling with bugs and roaches," without any hope of bettering his condition. But he is wise enough not to feel bitter and is resigned to his lot, even if history disposes of him among the downtrodden.

The members of Tintin's clan are distinguished from those of Wagg's world by their different interpretations of the same words. The first group, with no material or financial problems, interpret things morally. Their demands are generated primarily from within themselves. According to David Riesman's categories, they are "inner directed."[1] The second group, in contrast, interpret everything in immediate, materialistic terms. They are the "other directed" and look for apparent success based on money and possessions. In the eyes of the first group, Wagg's values are "fake" because they rely strictly on materialistic gains. The two groups completely misunderstand each other. They may go through the same sorts of experiences but in different ways: the one in a "noble" manner, the other as farce. Like the difference between the master and the valet in classical theater, the power struggle does not play out well for the "nobles." They feel threatened in their very existence and have to shut themselves away to escape the decadence of Wagg's "values."

## THE PUBLIC AND THE PRIVATE

At the beginning of his adventures, Tintin experienced the external world as so threatening that he organized his life around the king, who could guarantee a certain stability and continuity to his existence. At this period his personal life was nonexistent. He tried to establish himself wholly in the public world where he was hailed as the "redeemer," and he put his own imaginary omnipotence at the service of those with legitimate power. The distribution of powers between the public and the private, however, was gradually transformed. The hero discovered that good kings are hard to come by and that their invariably limited power was constantly threatened. To counterbalance this loss of security, Tintin began to establish personal ties, both familial and psychological. This personal development occurred through his contact with ambivalent father figures, in dreams, and through the mediation of monstrous creatures (sharks, Ranko) on whom he projected the fantasies that he initially did not even recognize as his own.

In Tintin's final adventure, the original pattern is totally reversed, and this reversal teaches Tintin to rely on history rather than myth. Nevertheless, he turns away from the unreliable public sphere to take refuge in private life, which seems to him more dependable, if somewhat unstable. Even if Calculus and Haddock are constantly competing, their lots are bound together forever. And even though Castafiore can sing her jewel song on every stage throughout the world, she remains the Mother, at least on an unconscious level. The equilibrium between the bastard and the foundling is duly established, and these two sons can interact without destroying each other. After sharing so many adventures, they have exchanged their respective positions without, however, losing their distinctive characters.

That the interactions among the family members are reciprocal shows up in the fact that the traits originally associated with one of the characters are now transferred onto another. Thus, the Thom(p)sons no longer have the monopoly on spoonerisms and other farcical slips of the tongue. Calculus and Haddock are also afflicted with this mania, and we find the latter even repeating the Thom(p)sons' famous "to be precise" (58, I, 2). Whereas Tintin formerly always had to prod the captain into action, this time it is the hero who refuses to budge, opting for security over risk. Archibald takes this opportunity to reproach him: "All right, stay here, tucked up, safe and warm in your bedroom slippers! Cuthbert and I are going out to defend our honor, and yours too, against that thundering herd of Zapotecs!" (11, II, 1).

If Bianca communicates with the public world through her jewels, Haddock does so through whiskey. Since their first meeting, Tintin has tried to moderate the captain's alcoholic tendencies and to socialize him into better behavior. After all this effort, Haddock now experiences only the positive effects of drinking, as an increase of energy, while the negative effects of dissolving into a hazy oblivion subside.

Although more subtle, Calculus's attitude toward Haddock's habit is actually more radical. Since their first meeting, Calculus has tried to get Haddock to quit drinking. His first attempt involved replacing the captain's cargo of whiskey with the parts of his underwater machine (*RRT*, p. 20). In *The Seven Crystal Balls*, Haddock sees Cuthbert's portrait on the wall scolding him for his alcoholism, so he throws the whiskey bottle in the trash (*7CB*, 53, II, 1). In *Destination Moon*, the professor invites Tintin and the captain to stop off in the land of mineral water. Although Archibald swears he will "never touch a single drop of that nauseating liquid," he proceeds to get squirted in the face with it and inadvertently swallows quite a bit (*DM*, 5, III, 1). During the actual voyage to the moon, Frank Wolff forbids him to drink any alcohol. Archibald disobeys, gets drunk, and climbs out of the spaceship "to return to Marlinspike," endangering the lives of his companions (*EM*, pp. 7–11).

In *The Picaros*, Calculus discovers a definitive cure for the captain's "malady," a nontoxic product of medicinal herbs, without taste or smell: "A single one of these tablets dissolved in either food or drink imparts a disgusting taste to any alcohol taken thereafter" (*TP*, 42, II, 1). He tries his remedy on the captain, who subsequently gets through the entire adventure without one drop of whiskey. Typically, Archibald experiences his relation to the world in the oral mode of swallowing and spitting out, but this intervention of the Father forbids him to swallow any more alcohol and thereby limits his contact with Wagg's universe. Calculus thus reinforces the cohesiveness of the group by cutting off the family from the outside world, whose values are nauseating and need to be spit out once and for all.

The Captain's "excessive" abstinence leads to an identity crisis with multiple consequences. After being hit on the head by a bottle of whiskey, he again develops amnesia. He thinks he is Lord Hadoque, confusing his own adventure with the ancestor's and acting out exactly the same gestures.

*SU*, 15, III, 2. © Hergé/Moulinsart 2007.

"Hard a' starboard!" "That crack on the head must have done it!"
*TP*, 31, I, 1. © Hergé/Moulinsart 2007.

In fact, this hysterical amnesia is more complex than the earlier case in *The Unicorn*. Just as he mouths the words of the ancestor ("Prepare to come about! Iceberg ahead!"), he denies his paternal lineage ("Haddock? That's a ridiculous name"). Furthermore, in his delirium he confuses Hadoque's ship with Calculus's spaceship, thus implying the fundamental equivalence between his two father figures. He relives the original trauma he has in common with them both, namely, the hijacking and subsequent loss of their vessels at the hands of the villains: "To crown it all, I've lost my ship. It's probably flown away" (*TP*, 31, II, 1). Tintin does not see the significance of his ravings and tries to reason with him: "Look, Captain, a ship does not fly!" But Haddock is not dissuaded and responds: "Oh no? That's what you think. Mine does! It's a bateau-mouche" (*TP*, 31, II, 1, 2).[2] As a result of his abstinence and his amnesia, the captain finds himself doubly shut up in a private world of subjective fantasies. At this level his fantasies seem like an excrescence of the psychological universe of the hero. In the end, Tintin agrees to join the fight solely to protect Haddock. Tintin knows he himself is powerless to change the world, not because the world always remains the same but because the laws of transformation do not rely on a single individual, no matter how powerful he may be.

The social and political sphere was formerly considered stable only because the hero thought of it as immutable. His own tendency toward the absolute was based on a twofold original sacrifice: the sacrifice of the son and the castration of the Father. Hergé analyzed this theme mainly in *King Ottokar's Scepter*, but it also reverberates in many other albums as well. In *The Broken Ear*, Tintin discovered the breakdown of the values he had been defending, the corruption of the political world, and the necessity for its regeneration. However, he did not commit to paying the price for that revolution. He refused to cause any bloodshed, whether among the Arumbayas or the San Theodorians. Later, with the Incas he maintained the same attitude and managed to pull off a conjuring trick to stave off a bloody sacrifice. His trick worked to get himself and his friends out of the difficulty. But in fact, he realized he was as incapable of halting the movement of the sun as he was of arresting the deterioration of the world. That revelation was one of the reasons he turned toward the private sphere, where he would henceforth invest all his efforts.

In *The Picaros*, Tintin goes so far as to refuse to get involved in the public realm where Tapioca had treated him and the members of his family as scapegoats. After fifty years of heroism, he has had enough of being the victim and chooses instead to remain in the peace and quiet of Marlinspike, even if it means breaking with the rest of the family. He ultimately gives in, of course, when he realizes that Haddock will not be able to avoid the traps set for him by Colonel Sponsz. The latter has indeed arranged to have Haddock and Alcazar executed next to an ancient pyramid, the former site of human sacrifices. The cover of the album shows the scene where the heroes are fleeing from the sacrificial site, refusing to be the victims of an unjust trial.

Wandering through the Amazon jungle under the leadership of Alcazar, they get as far as the Arumbayan territory, where Chief Avakuki offers to take them in. Tintin then discovers that the aboriginal tribes, in contact with so-called civilized societies, have suffered the same sort of decline. The once reliable structure of the public sphere is in the process of destabilization everywhere. This social decline is due not only to the absence of sacrifice but especially to the excessive consumption of whiskey.

Consider how whiskey relates to the other two alcoholic beverages considered previously: champagne and red wine. We noted that the latter two are symbols: champagne for sperm and red wine for blood. They generally are poured in private gatherings to celebrate special occasions. One drinks champagne, for example, to celebrate the launching of a spaceship to the moon or to announce an engagement of marriage. Red wine shows up in the adventures according to a stricter code: it invokes the primal murder at the origin of the family or the state. In contrast, whiskey is not a symbol but a sign and should be analyzed in the same way as Castafiore's jewels. It is tied analogously to money. In *The Black Island*, for example, the counterfeiting ring set up by Wronzoff intersects on several occasions with bootleggers. The themes of counterfeiting and bootlegging run throughout the adventure. People trade in whiskey, and this liquid gold, a devalued gold, serves as a universal currency. In *The Picaros*, whiskey disappears from the private sphere, where it is merely spit out, to circulate at high speed in the public world. From beginning to end, whiskey is everywhere. To emphasize its universal currency, Hergé presents it under only one label, "Loch Lomond." This one label effectively speaks to the different areas of public life in order to homogenize them. Thanks to the whiskey market, private places are opened up and become submerged into the totality of mass consumerism. When there is no whiskey available at a particular moment, its label reminds us of it and stirs our desires—the point of the commercials on television.

When Haddock offers the journalists whiskey, it is because the journalists
are among those who break down the barriers between the private and public. They invade Marlinspike Hall to reveal its secrets to the public and render
private life increasingly impossible to live out by transforming it into mere
representation. Even Nestor, who shares the captain's taste for alcohol, drinks
in the kitchen to be in step with the others. Loch Lomond shows up everywhere, from the luxurious mansion, where Tapioca is confining Tintin and
Haddock, to the virgin forest. Alcazar explains to Tintin: "Tapioca is trying to
neutralize the Arumbayas and my Picaros at the same time by dropping cases
of whiskey by parachute. You've seen the result: even the monkeys have taken
to the bottle!" (*TP*, 30, IV, 2). The revolutionaries backing Alcazar secretively
get drunk on the slightest excuse. But their leader himself sets the example:
whiskey shows up in his home as well as in the Arumbayan chief's.

The mass circulation of Loch Lomond results in homogenized behavior.
Despite their apparent differences, the Arumbayas and the San Theodorians
display the same artificial joviality that masks their real passivity. Whiskey
unites what formerly had been divided. Social classes and ethnicities melt
into the same amorphous "soup." But instead of being a source of real joy,
the consumption of alcohol produces only a false sense of camaraderie. The
drunkard is as solitary in the crowd as in the desert: he engages in monologue, not dialogue.

## THE FINAL ACT

In *The Broken Ear*, the first album situated in South America, Hergé contrasted the "savages" (the Arumbayas and the Bibaros) with the "civilized"
(San Theodorians and Nuevo Ricans). In *The Picaros*, the original pair-
ings have disappeared. We no longer hear anything about the Bibaros or
the Nuevo Ricans. Furthermore, the basic opposition between "savage" and
"civilized" is dissolving under the influence of whiskey: "Dipsomaniacs!
That's what 'civilization' has done for those 'savages'" (*TP*, 32, III, 3). Tintin's
return to the Arumbayas only temporarily slows their decline. On his first
trip, the dethroned witch doctor had tried to sacrifice Snowy, the animal
equivalent of "the One," but the intervention by Ridgewell saved him. Now
there are no more attempts at sacrifice but only parody. The natives seize
Calculus, undress him, and divide up his clothes. In *Prisoners of the Sun*, the
professor had to put on the garb of the Incas; now the Indians want to dress
in *his* clothes to look more like the Europeans. There is no longer an attempt

at forcible assimilation of the Other through sacrifice, but only a superficial imitation dressed up as theater and lacking any mediating rituals.

When the Arumbayan Chief Avakuki invites Tintin's group to a feast, Calculus uses his "remedy" to reestablish a lost ritual. Despite "the exotic foods," the Arumbayan feast looks like any sort of civilized banquet: it is an occasion to drink alcohol. Following Ridgewell's advice, Tintin agrees to make a toast to the chief's health and to drink the whiskey "straight down in one gulp." But he has to spit it out. Under the influence of Calculus's drug, even the English explorer and the chief himself have to spit out the whiskey. During this feast, the sacred reappears not out of extravagant excess but through "prohibition." Whereas the greater society lives from a frenzied consumption, the mark of distinction comes through abstinence. For one night, the Arumbayas rediscover their opposition to the San Theodorians, and they temporarily regain their ethnic identity by "doing a Tintin." Nevertheless, one guesses that a return to their origins does not follow. The Arumbayan future is not to be found in the jungle but, rather, in mixing with the other Indians in the shantytowns crowding the port areas of Tapiocapolis. They will live amid the waste of the consumer society, among the discarded cigarette packs and empty bottles of Loch Lomond, products they themselves will probably not be able to afford. Their fate seems worse than that of the Gypsies arrested in Marlinspike.

From the standpoint of "the civilized," *The Broken Ear* had highlighted the connection between revolution and carnival. Revolution is tragic, not farcical, precisely because of the bloodshed following in its wake. Continuing to explore this theme in *The Picaros*, Hergé juxtaposes several characters, sometimes literally face-to-face. First, we have Haddock and Tapioca (8, IV, 2): the former representing the private sphere; the latter, the public. From the start, their communication is only one way. Archibald cannot bear to see or listen to Tapioca, who is in effect protected from the captain's rage by being "behind" the television screen. In response to the dictator, the captain has to resort to the newspapers, that is, he has to expose to the general public an affair belonging properly to the private sphere, namely, the kidnapping of the Mother. Later, it is Alcazar who faces Tapioca on the occasion of transferring power from the one to the other (p. 57). Accompanied by Tintin and the Picaros, Alcazar enters the palace he knows so well and brandishes a gun in Tapioca's face. Tapioca, taken completely by surprise, loses his cigar and power at the same moment. To emphasize his victory, the new leader lights up a cigar right under Tapioca's nose. This second face-to-face highlights the two generals as "twins," both in manners and methods (57, III, 2).

Before the coup d'état, two ceremonies were in the making. For those in power, there was the carnival. Thanks to the sponsorship of the Loch Lomond Company, and certain of his position of authority—for didn't he just foil a plot?—Tapioca proclaims a three-day holiday for the San Theodorians. To the extent that his dignified position allows, he himself participates in the public revelries. He appears on his balcony and requests to review up close the "comical" Jolly Follies. However, to solidify his personal position with regard to tradition, he has also ordered the execution of the Thom(p)sons, whom he holds responsible for the plot against him.

From the standpoint of Tapioca's opponents, however, the carnival is in fact a revolution. It will succeed only on the condition that the Picaros distance themselves from the Jolly Follies, stop acting like simple revelers, and agree, like the Arumbayas, to "do a Tintin"—stop drinking. The young hero agrees to help Alcazar regain his power on the promise that he stage the revolution "without bloodshed," a promise the general finally makes, despite many misgivings: "A revolution without executions? Without reprisals? It's unthinkable! You must be joking!" (44, I, 1). For Alcazar as for Tapioca, the "sacred traditions" have to be respected under pain of having the revolution degenerate into a ludicrous public holiday. The danger of this degeneration is all the stronger because the takeover by Alcazar is to happen during the carnival. The Picaros borrow the costumes of Wagg's Jolly Follies, and in this disguise they are able to get to Tapioca. Despite being masked as revelers, they manage to retain the spirit of Tintin by not drinking for two days.

Even if the hero temporarily forbids the Arumbayas and Picaros from becoming soused, he cannot ignore the alternatives: blood or whiskey, sacrifice or conspicuous consumption—the contemporary form of sacrifice for a society based on a consumerist economy. In this last adventure, Tintin definitively refuses the first alternative in favor of the second. Just as the magician Bruno changed water into wine, the hero performs his final conjuring act by changing blood into alcohol and the revolution into carnival. Tintin does not put himself at the service of political power—at least, so he believes—but works only to stage the celebration. Disguised as one of the Follies, he climbs onto the float of the King of the Carnival and parades in the streets of Tapiocapolis as he had formerly done to celebrate the solemn entrance of

King Ottokar, whose reign he had rescued. But the current king in question, the King of the Carnival, resembles Alcazar. He reminds us of the caricature of the general that the Nuevo Ricans brandished at the beginning of the war in their country (*BE*, 42, III, 4). Tintin enters the mouth of this cardboard "monster" without being devoured, and he drives the float toward the prison to prevent the execution of the Thom(p)sons. Accomplishing this feat, he realizes the only difference between revolution and carnival has to do with the amount of alcohol consumed!

Realizing the identity of revolution and carnival leads to another equivalence. Alcazar and Tapioca are not only figurative twins but also mirror the figure of the King of the Carnival. Their scepter is his scepter, a huge cigar that he brandishes to affirm his power. Whereas Ottokar's scepter was made of gold, Alcazar's is made of tobacco leaves that go up in smoke as rapidly as the power he represents. When the scepter does go up in smoke, the structure of the old world dissolves into alcohol.

Cigars and whiskey are the basic emblems of Wagg's fraudulent world. Whereas the emblems of the Syldavian monarchy were unique, those of the subsequent leaders are mass-produced crowd pleasers. The Syldavian emblems were founded on qualitative values, but the latter are based only on the quantitative. They allow for a constant transformation of the world at the same time that they signify its inevitable decline. If the political and social world incessantly changes from one day to the next, Tintin's private world, in contrast, tries to preserve its stability and solidify its heroic image.

The success of the clan's latest exploit is as much to Haddock's credit as to Tintin's. Haddock is really the instigator. He manages to free himself from his haunting ancestral fantasies. He can accomplish this because in this new adventure he manages to reform himself. As a prisoner of the pirates, Lord Hadoque was in a situation similar to Archibald's. Archibald feels he is in fact the prisoner of Wagg's values, which are dragging him down. According to the captain, Francis of Hadoque was also a lover of rum, the equivalent in the days of Louis XIV of modern-day whiskey. Perhaps that is true, but one never sees the ancestor with a bottle in his hands. Furthermore, when he manages to free himself from his chains, Lord Francis agrees, according to Tintin, to remain sober: "This is no time for drinking, he says; I need all my wits about me" (*SU*, 23, IV, 1). Thus, refusing the rum while the pirates get "abominably" drunk, he defeats Red Rackham and escapes from the ship.

The adventures of Tintin's clan unfold in similar circumstances. On the one side is a small group of the righteous, and on the other, the mass of "the lawless" who forget themselves in an artificial joviality. Three hundred years later, the result is the same, but the means are different. Lord Hadoque managed to establish his family by trading the rum for the pirates' blood. Tintin's clan re-creates the situation, but it accepts the demands of sobriety while refusing to spill any blood. The ancestor exploded the former equivalent of Wagg's world, but the captain lets this world self-destruct. The presence or absence of blood makes all the difference between these two foundations. Whereas the ancestor's family repressed the image of Woman, Tintin's family is now consolidated around the Mother. As Castafiore exclaims: "Ah, what joy to be all together again! I simply must sing!" (*TP*, 61, IV, 3).

Between the two episodes of *The Emerald* and *The Picaros*, the feminine figure has been integrated into the family because she has lost her former threatening character. What allows the devouring White Goddess to become the Lady in White—a mother who may be a bit overbearing but who no longer appears utterly monstrous—is the refusal of bloodshed. Blood has been eliminated from all social levels; it has been replaced by whiskey in the public sphere and affection in the private one. The taboo against blood is the price to be paid for establishing an ordinary family, one where the father is no longer viewed as the castrator, the mother as all-consuming, and the son as all-powerful.

## THE WORK AND ITS MIRROR

In both the public and private realms, forgetfulness not only is necessary for survival but is the sole condition allowing for the rejuvenation of the decadent world. In Tintin's clan, forgetfulness was imposed from on high in the form of collective amnesia. In Wagg's world, forgetfulness is produced by whiskey, the language common to everyone, and thus dwells at the heart of social life. The general forgetfulness of traditional values nevertheless goes along with a kind of hyperreminiscence at the level of the structure of the narrative—as if the story itself were the sole witness to what individual consciousness has refused to see.

We have already noted that the later albums should be read as responses to the earlier ones. *The Red Sea Sharks* returned to and reassessed the previous adventures to give them a new meaning. *Tintin in Tibet* put the finishing touches on *The Blue Lotus*. *The Castafiore Emerald* could not be understood without seeing its connections with *The Secret of the Unicorn*. *Flight 714* completed *Prisoners of the Sun*, and *The Picaros* responded to *The Broken Ear*.

In this final episode Hergé multiplies the cross-references, especially in the carnival scenes in Tapiocapolis. The costumes of the San Theodorian revelers evoke the figures from previous albums: Scots, Africans, Chinese, Indians, cowboys, bullfighters, and, of course, the inevitable parrot. Here we have a genuine "inventory," in Jacques Prévert's sense of the term. Furthermore, to avoid presenting a world that seems merely self-enclosed, Hergé offers us glimpses from other works contemporary to his own. Many Walt Disney characters parade beside Astérix and Snoopy. Groucho Marx encounters Zorro, and the Three Musketeers meet Donald Duck. In *The Secret of the Unicorn*, Hergé staged a flea market where objects from different eras meet in one place. Here, in *The Picaros*, the carnival is a market where creatures of all different backgrounds and origins are represented, objectified, and rendered equivalent. The structure of the celebration duplicates that of the social organization of labor: in the first case, exchange takes place through the mediation of whiskey, and in the second, through money. The people lose their ethnic or social identities, even their humanity. Literary fictions or cartoon strips mark their place in history. They are reduced to images, taken out of their original context, that become merely different elements of a code signifying nothing outside itself. Under the influence of whiskey and to the incessant rhythm of the salsa, the "being-signs" (*les êtres-signes*) dance through the streets, intermingling and transforming themselves into the latest figures.[3]

There is yet another sense in which the final albums are linked to memory. With *Tintin in Tibet*, and especially in the final two albums, the former adventures are reflected in one way or another in the newer ones, thus lending a certain autonomy or coherence to Hergé's work as a whole. Particularly in *The Picaros*, there is almost no image or sentence that does not cross-reference, recall, or respond to something else from a previous episode. In this way the work extends itself in many directions that are nevertheless interconnected. The work develops backward, so to speak, because the play of intertextual cross-referencing sheds new light on the previous episodes. We will cite only one example, but the "Tintin idolators" have long been busy uncovering them all. In *The Picaros*, Castafiore's rescue duplicates, even to the point of the position of the characters, that of Aunt Save Hatt in the very early *Adventures of Totor*.

Une seconde après, Totor se jetait
dans les bras de sa tante délivrée qui
pleurait d'émotion de se voir sauvée
par son cher petit Scout.

"A moment later, Totor threw himself into the arms of his rescued aunt, who broke down in
tears at realizing she had been saved by her little Boy Scout."
*AH*, I, p. 37. © Hergé/Moulinsart 2007.

Je savais bien que vous viendriez
me tirer de là !...

"I knew you'd come to rescue me from this dreadful place!"
*TP*, 61, III, 3. © Hergé/Moulinsart 2007.

Thus, the work loops back on itself. After fifty years, the same Oedipal desire motivates the heroism of the masculine character. In *The Picaros*, however, it is the bastard Haddock who accomplishes the deed enacted long ago by Tintin's ancestor Totor. Each adventure has one or more echoes in the final one. Whereas the characters are rendered innocent by their memory loss, for the rest of us the past does not disappear. It takes refuge in the narrative structure that takes the place of the unconscious in individuals. As in the previous example, each sentence uttered, each gesture made becomes a kind of Freudian slip that both reveals and conceals its origin. The story should not be taken merely literally, for it articulates another history, individual and collective, that the reader has to decipher beneath the official story line.[4] As in the art world of Western society, the little world of Tintin feeds on its own history in a way that both limits and enables its capacity to reinvent itself. Because it cannot fully erase the successive layers of its past, it tries to reinvent itself precisely on the basis of what it has been. It coils back on itself in ways that are both humorous and pessimistic, often simplistic and yet complex.

This world of childhood, addressed as well to adults, is born out of the friendship between an imaginative, obsessive adolescent and a clever dog. The characters that follow are descendants of either Tintin or Snowy. The original couple engenders a universe that functions like a myth. The final episode is the reflection of the entire work that, like Castafiore, can contemplate itself and laugh to see itself reflected so beautifully in this mirror.

# CONCLUSION

*The Adventures of Tintin* tells a story in mythical form about political and psychological development. At the beginning of the tale, the main character lives in a world of absolutes, or at least loses himself in the absolute he projects onto parental figures or systems of government. At the beginning of the 1930s Tintin's behavior supports Kurt Lewin's research on theories of personality dating from that same time period. According to Lewin, the weaker the ego, the more it tends to build itself up by adhesion to an authoritarian political system.[1] This explains the hero's sympathy for the right-wing ideas spreading in Europe between the world wars.

Hergé's reworking of the first episodes consists not only in distancing himself from their initial political engagement but also in changing the temporality of the adventures by situating them within an imaginary universe. Whereas the beginning albums evoke a cyclical, noncumulative time, the later ones take place in a linear, irreversible time sequence. Tintin abandons political engagement to take up a psychological venture, the quest for the Father. When he is finally able to deal with his parental figures, he chooses the private realm over the public. Haddock's ever-increasing importance in the adventures bears witness to this change in point of view. Nevertheless, Tintin never totally liberates himself from his initial choices. He manages to rise above one sort of conformism only to take up another. After the war, he ratifies the dominant worldview that "freely" condemns the values of the public realm—in which the individual is powerless—in favor of private values, which are now considered the only important ones.[2]

But the metamorphoses of *The Adventures of Tintin* are not merely psychological in origin. Hergé's success is also due to the social transformations coming after 1945, during the period when the hero was confronting
a new system of values. Edgar Morin argues that the history of publishing
for children reveals a change from an ideology of pedagogy to an ideology
of mass media.[3] Tintin was transformed into an international hero just at
the moment when the Western nations became ever more homogenized by
transmitting commodities and their values on a global scale. The success of
the little Belgian Boy Scout was amplified by the blurring of the distinc-
tions between children and adolescents, and especially between adolescents
and adults, for the sake of promoting a model of "youth" common to all age
brackets. As both adult and child, Tintin could seduce an international public
by incarnating its triumphant vitality.

Although the text of his adventures is allegedly straightforward, many
different readings are possible. In his rivalry with Haddock, Tintin is defeated in the sense that the relative, private, and worldly values of the bastard
have the last word: "Well, I won't be sorry to be back home in Marlinspike,"
says the captain (*TP*, 62, IV, 1). At this point, the hero appears singularly subdued in relation to his companion, but it is not at all clear whose traits will
win out in the long run. Currently we see a change in sensibility similar to
that of the triumph of absolute monarchy under Henry IV or Louis XIII.
Haddock's affectionate, exuberant, blundering behavior, as endearing as it
may be, is nowadays considered rather unacceptable. Constant control of
aggressive or sexual impulses, with its resultant lack of affect, plus the split
between a totally "liberated" imaginary life and a hyperconditioned social-
ization, are no longer negatively classified as "schizoid." Rather, this model
of controlled behavior has become an ideal for a technological world that
demands that human reactions be as reliable and predictable as those of ma-
chines. Tintin's coolness, his quick reactions, his lack of personal life, and his
repressed sexuality have often passed for sure signs of his immaturity. Even
for his creator, he remains "only a sketch of a man." There is something
that seems "unfinished" about him that is expressed even in the simplified
graphics of his face.[4]

But now, on the contrary, we can see that his rather abstracted behavior
and bearing fit very well with the total ease of manipulation demanded
by contemporary technologies. Thus, an advanced technological society
would seem to favor Tintin as the hero of the future. Because Haddock

has such a well-defined psyche, he runs the risk of being less open to new interpretations. Partly because Tintin is rooted in heroic mythology, he is more open, more susceptible to being interpreted in numerous ways. If generations to come are at all interested in his adventures, they will make of Tintin something quite different. The metamorphoses of Tintin may be only beginning.

# NOTES

## PREFACE

1. See J.-M. Apostolidès, "On Paul de Man's War," *Critical Inquiry* 15, no. 4 (Summer 1989). This entire issue is dedicated to articles published by Paul de Man during the war.

2. See Jan Baetens, *Hergé écrivain* [Hergé the Writer] (1989; repr., Paris: Flammarion, 2006).

3. Flammarion published the most recent edition of *Les Métamorphoses de Tintin* in France in 2006 as a boxed set with two other books. The set is titled *La Petite bibliothèque du tintinologue* [The Little Library of Tintinology]. The two other volumes in this set include the biography written by Benoît Peeters, *Hergé, fils de Tintin* [Hergé, Son of Tintin], and the book by Jan Baetens cited in note 2.

4. Pol Vandromme, *Le Monde de Tintin* [Tintin's World] (Paris: Gallimard, 1959; repr., Paris: La Table ronde, 1994).

5. See *L'Archipel Tintin*, papers from a conference at Lyon, edited by Benoît Peeters, introduction by Cyrille Mozgovine (Paris: Les Impressions nouvelles, 2004).

## INTRODUCTION

1. *Libération* 558, March 5–6, 1983, p. 25.

2. Patrick Thévenon, "Tintin et le Temple du Soleil," *L'Actualité* 12, January 8–14, 1970, p. 41.

3. See Nouma Sadoul, *Entretiens avec Hergé* (Casterman, 1983; repr., Paris: Champs-Flammarion, 2003), p. 50.

4. In this regard, see his interview in the magazine *Minuit* 25, September 1977.

5. For the *Archives Hergé* [The Archives of Hergé], citations will be indicated as follows: title of work (*AH*), followed by I, II, II, or IV for the volume, then the page number.

For citations from the Tintin albums, citations will be indicated as follows: first, abbreviated title in italics; second, page number in the album; third, Roman numerals for the "strip" on the page; and fourth, the specific panel of that strip. [In many cases, incidents or images take up an entire page, or incidents run over several pages. In those cases, citations will be as follows: abbreviated title in italics, followed by page numbers indicated as *p.* or *pp.* with no line or panel numbers given.—Trans.]

## CHAPTER ONE

1. "I was seven or eight years old at the elementary school. And I remember drawing in my notebooks. . . . What was I drawing? Well, quite frankly, the adventures of a young boy who flew a thousand missions against the German army. . . . It wasn't very long before I made the connection between these doodlings and the stories of Tintin that were created fifteen years later." Sadoul, *Entretiens avec Hergé*, p. 11.

2. *Scènes de la vie future* (Paris: Mercure de France, 1930), p. 19.

3. Robert Pfeiffer and Jean Ladrière, *L'Aventure rexiste* (Brussels: Pierre de Meyere, 1966), pp. 23–25.

4. Pierre Louis de Cours Saint-Gervais, "Tintin au pays des fascistes?" in *Le Message politique et social de la bande dessinée*, edited by Charles-Olivier Carbonell (Toulouse: Privat, 1975).

5. Paul Radin, *The Trickster, with Comments by Karl Kerényi* (London: Routledge and Paul, 1955).

6. Muganga reveals to his accomplice the existence of the Aniotas and the goals of this brotherhood: "I am telling you there is a secret society, called 'Aniota.' They organized to stop civilization by White men! Aniota kill Black chiefs who support White men. Aniota wear special costume, looking like leopard skin. On they fingers they wear steel claws, like those of the leopard. What is more, they carry stick, with end carved like leopard's paw. To kill they victim, Aniota creep up on sleeping native, tear out him throat, and are running away. But first, by means of stick, they are covering ground with leopard footprints. I have Aniota dress" (*AH*, I, p. 236).

7. Pfeiffer and Ladrière, *L'Aventure rexiste*, pp. 21–22.

8. Joseph Douillet, *Moscou sans voiles* (Paris: Spes, 1928). On the fourth page, the editor suggests other works in a similar vein: *La Tyrannie soviétique, La Menace du communisme*, etc.

9. In February 1941 an anti-Mason exhibit was shown in Brussels. On the first page of *Le Soir*, J. Schieffer gives a complete account of it. After describing the "blue lodge" in the Assyrian-Egyptian style, the journalist turns to the Grand Temple, reproduced on the first floor of the exhibition. "In this immense hall, everything is entirely in Egyptian style. The panels, as high as the lateral gallery, depict the story of Hiram, architect of Solomon's Temple, the temple that the Masons dreamed of building, thus confirming how closely their thinking is to that of the Jews." *Le Soir*, February 2, 1941, p. 1.

10. "L'Amérique et les Américains," *Le Crapouillot*, October 1930, p. 31.

11. In the later versions, the "150 gallons of Javel champagne" is replaced by "one hundred gallons of bootlegged whiskey" (*TA*, 38, II, 3).—Trans.

12. Blanchard, "L'Amérique et les Américains," p. 66.

## CHAPTER TWO

1. *AH*, I, p. 411. The fantasy of being devoured runs through Tintin's adventure in America; Tintin fears being "ground up" in the gears of modernity. Just as Claude Blanchard imagines himself in the Chicago slaughterhouses, becoming meat for the butcher, bloodied like a steer, so too Tintin falls into the assembly line in the slaughterhouse and risks being turned into corned beef (pp. 399–401). In *King Ottokar's Scepter*, Hergé re-creates this fantasy. In a restaurant, the owner explains to Tintin that the "szlaszeck" he has just eaten came from "the leg of young dog prepared in the Syldavian style." Tintin immediately imagines he has just devoured his canine companion (*AH*, IV, p. 153).

2. *BL*, 8, IV, 2. I want to thank Li Jian-jun for translating the inscriptions in this album. The *Hergé Archives*, vol. III, pp. 4 and 5, do indeed translate some of these inscriptions, but they do not translate those with decidedly direct ties to the politics of Chiang Kai-shek, for example, those on p. 157.

3. See *AH*, IV, p. 3.

4. The pilot is the hero in fashion on the eve of World War II. Recall Jean Mermoz, the works of Antoine de Saint-Exupéry (*Courier sud*; *Vol de nuit*), and the Jean Renoir film *The Rules of the Game*, whose main character is a pilot.

5. Sadoul, *Entretiens avec Hergé*, p. 106.

6. He was arrested early in September 1944 but was released soon after. In the course of the trial of the *Soir* collaborators, the military prosecutor responded to the lawyers who questioned the absence of Hergé on the bench of the accused: "I would feel ridiculous if I had him brought here along with Snowy." Cited by Pol Vandromme, *Le Monde de Tintin* (Paris: Gallimard, 1959), p. 52.

7. Henri Vanherpe, "Les Idées politiques de Tintin," *Revue politique et parlementaire* 811 (June 1970), p. 49.

8. Régis Debray, a French author and philosopher, was captured in Bolivia in 1967. He was convicted of having been part of Che Guevara's group. On November 17, 1967, he was sentenced to thirty years in prison. He was released in 1970, following an international campaign for his release. Those campaigning in his favor included Jean-Paul Sartre, André Malraux, General de Gaulle, and Pope Paul VI.

9. An edition of five hundred copies, reserved for the author, was printed in 1969, with the stamp "Studios Hergé."

10. Sadoul, *Entretiens avec Hergé*, p. 78.

11. Hergé learned only later that this name was also an Israeli surname. Sadoul, *Entretiens avec Hergé*, p. 50.

12. Pascal Bruckner, *Le Sanglot de l'homme blanc* (Paris: Seuil, 1983; repr., Paris: Points, 2002).

13. After the capitulation of the Belgian army, "the war seemed over for us. Thus, I didn't have any qualms about collaborating on a newspaper like *Le Soir*. I worked for it; that point is clear. But my work was rather insignificant, like that of a miner, or a tram ticket taker or a baker! Although people find it quite normal that a driver allows the train to go, they claim that journalists are 'traitors.'" Sadoul, *Entretiens avec Hergé*, p. 87.

14. In the issue of *Les Nouvelles littéraires* that came out after Hergé's death, Bob de Moor, his chief assistant and partner, recalls for the journalist interviewing him "those interminable afternoons, when Hergé would tell us all about the lives of his characters. To breathe life and depth into Captain Haddock, the Thom(p)sons, or Professor Calculus, he imagined their whole lives, from birth to death. He knew, for example, who had been divorced, who beat his wife, or who spent his evenings with the bottle." *Les Nouvelles littéraires* 2877 (March 10–16, 1983), p. 23.

## CHAPTER THREE

1. *TC*, 1, I, 2. Snowy shares many traits with Tartarin. To "diminish the reputation of Bombonnel," Tartarin sees a panther as only a big cat; so too Snowy asserts: "A leopard isn't all that scary. After all, it's nothing but a big cat" (*TC*, 31, I, 2).

2. The dog's name in French is Milou. The English translators chose the name Snowy for him, though it is true that the Tibetan monks refer to him as Powder Snow.—Trans.

3. *TC*, 57, I, 3. The relations between Snowy and the cows quickly become more strained. For example, consider the meeting of Snowy with the Indians' cow (*CP*, 48, II, 3, 4).

4. Robert Javalet, *Image et ressemblance au XIIème siècle* (Paris: Letouzey and Ane, 1967).

5. For good measure, one meets a horse named Beatrice and a Pekinese dog named Chang.

6. Roger Caillois, *La Pieuvre: essai sur la logique de l'imaginaire* (Paris: La Table ronde, 1967).

7. To accentuate the parallel between the sharks and the humans, the English translators translated *Coke en Stock*, which would be more obviously translated as *Coke on Board*, as *The Red Sea Sharks*.—Trans.

8. René Girard, *La Violence et le sacré* (Paris: Grasset, 1972; repr., Paris: Hachette-Pluriel, 1998).

9. Roger Caillois, *La Dissymétrie* (Paris: Gallimard, 1973).

10. Patrice Hamel and Benôit Peeters, "Entretien avec Hergé," *Minuit* 25, September 1977, p. 13. In the course of their conversation, the two interviewers share with Hergé their astonishment at the number of circle motifs in his work, but they do not dare broach the subject of Tintin's face. When they ask him if the circle represents

anything in particular to him, Hergé responds: "No, nothing. Or perhaps one could mention the unity in the famous Chinese drawing of yin and yang, with the male dot within the female, and the female dot within the male. Perhaps I am looking for my own unity."

## CHAPTER FOUR

1. According to Freud, the superego, consisting essentially of representations of words, derives from auditory perceptions. Clinical psychoanalytic research shows that it functions in a realist mode. See *grosse voix*, etc., in J. Laplanche and J.-B. Pontalis, *Vocabulaire de la psychanalyse* (Paris: PUF, 1967).

2. Hergé drew the two detectives at least in part from pictures of his father. In an interview with Numa Sadoul, he claims not to remember how he arrived at the idea of them, but he does reveal the following in a kind of free association: "It is true that my father had a twin brother who died two or three years before him. Until the end, the two dressed exactly alike. If my father had a cane, my uncle would get one too. When my father got himself a gray bowler, my uncle would do likewise. So together they sported moustaches, bowlers—they even had their hair cut at the same time. What is curious is that I didn't think of them at all when I was creating the Thom(p)sons." Sadoul, *Entretiens avec Hergé*, p. 99.

3. "In fact, Captain, this is just guano, right?" (*PS*, 4, III, 1).

4. *EM*, p. 30. It is important to note that the word *cirque* in French means both "crater" and "circus." Calculus announces just a minute before that their spaceship is heading for Hipparchus's crater on the moon. They understand and ask Haddock if he knew that there is a crater on the moon, to which he responds: "Of course. Everybody knows that. I also know that they need two clowns there. You'll do perfectly!" (*SS*, 18, III, 2).

5. He takes this up in a different way in *The Seven Crystal Balls*.

6. Tintin shares a number of affinities with cinema. In the Congo, he uses film to convince the Ba Baoro'm that their witch doctor is deceiving them. In *The Blue Lotus* and *The Red Sea Sharks*, we see him in the darkened movie theater watching films. Hergé was definitely influenced by this "seventh art." His earlier *Adventures of Totor* was presented by "United Rovers" and signed "Hergé Moving Pictures." The cartoon panels for *Tintin* are set up like cinematic sets. Whereas the first albums were more like intimate, small-scale films, the later ones are more like grand-scale productions. The techniques of supplying summaries of the events and interjecting hiatuses ("meanwhile," "some days later," and so on) are more developed in the later adventures.

7. *CP*, 17, II, 3. In the first version of this album, he goes so far as to accept being a spy for the villain, that is, to continue to observe the scenes that are forbidden to him (*AH*, III, p. 43).

8. Didi is the Chinese name given to a younger brother.

### CHAPTER FIVE

1. "What I call a sociological revolution is the intellectual process of pretending to be a foreigner in the society in which one lives, to observe it 'from outside' as if one were seeing it for the first time." Roger Caillois, *Rencontres* (Paris: PUF, 1978), p. 92.

2. Georges Feydeau (1862–1921) was a French playwright known for writing farce. —Trans.

3. "Are you familiar with an author who before the war wrote a very important text on ethnographic anthropology? I have in mind Hergé's *The Broken Ear* from this period. It really is a treatise on fetishism. This type of treatise is found not only among specialists but also among observers of society. Not officially, however. But in *The Broken Ear*, one can find this type of analysis." *Libération*, March 5–6, 1983, p. 25.

4. Hergé further develops this theme in *The Seven Crystal Balls*.

5. Roger Caillois, *L'Homme et le sacré* (Paris: Gallimard, 1950; repr., Paris: Folio, 1988).

### CHAPTER SIX

1. See Hannah Arendt, "Qu'est-ce que l'autorité?" in *La Crise de la culture* (Paris: Gallimard, 1972; repr., Paris: Folio, 1989), pp. 121–185.

2. "Opened to the sacred, the battle is a kind of liturgy. Like the divinely sanctioned 'trial by fire,' or ordeal [*l'ordalie*], the trial by combat requires a field." Georges Duby, *Le Dimanche de Bouvines* (Paris: Gallimard, 1973; repr., Paris: Gallimard, 2005), p. 149.

3. The figure of the circle defines the temporality of myth, whereas the line stands for a conception of time and of history both irreversible and cumulative, but not transcendent. Events happen only once, even if they can "serve as lessons for the future," and they are meaningful only at one time. In contrast, mythic time is incomprehensible if not understood diachronically. For a more detailed analysis of these two conceptions of time, see my article "The Problem of History in Seventeenth-Century France," *Diacritics* 12, no. 4 (Winter 1982), pp. 58–68.

4. Jean Chevalier and Alain Gheerbrant, *Dictionnaire des symboles* (Paris: Robert Laffont/Jupiter, 1982).

5. He also doesn't have any initials, in contrast to his creator, who has given himself a pseudonym on the basis of reversing his initials: R. G., Remi Georges.

6. *Roman des origines et origines du roman* (Paris: Grasset, 1972; repr., Paris: Tel-Gallimard, 1997).

7. "He never had any parents. They would be too much in the way. He would have to ask permission to go out each time. We never would have been done with all that." Interview with Hergé by Pierre Ajame, *Les Nouvelles littéraires* 1869 (June 27, 1963), p. 10.

8. "Is the professor part of his gang? Who will ever know?" (*AH*, III, p. 137).

9. The lack of sexual difference of the Thom(p)sons shows up again later in the

album (*CP*, pp. 27–30), when they disguise themselves as women, without any good reason, to save Tintin.

10. Robert, *Roman des origines*, p. 115.

11. Indeed, Tintin sees the family home as a prison that suffocates him. Although the Thom(p)sons are his first parental figures, they constantly attempt to put him in prison or, in other words, to bring him home. Even Marlinspike Hall, where Tintin finally decides to live, was once a real prison in the time of the Bird brothers (*SU*, p. 36ff).

12. Otto Rank, *The Myth of the Birth of the Hero: A Psychological Exploration of Myth* (Baltimore: Johns Hopkins University Press, 2004).

## CHAPTER SEVEN

1. *Faire tintin*, translated here as "to do a Tintin," shows up in the *Dictionary of Non-conventional French*, edited by Jacques Cellard and Alain Rey (Paris: Hachette, 1980). The editors write that "to do a Tintin" refers to "being deprived of some satisfaction or enjoyment expected or owed; to be frustrated."

2. "I've always been interested in psychoanalysis. Besides, I've read a great deal of the works of Jung." Hamel and Peeters, "Entretien avec Hergé," p. 26.

3. *Tintin in the Land of the Soviets* (*AH*, I, p. 60).

4. Hamel and Peeters even claim, falsely, that red wine never shows up in Tintin. "Entretien avec Hergé," p. 21.

5. The French word *conscience* means both "consciousness" and "conscience." In this incident, the author suggests that because Tintin and Haddock have passed out, or lost "consciousness," their "consciences" are also "relaxed," "asleep," allowing for otherwise forbidden acts.—Trans.

6. G. Carloni and D. Nobili, *La Mauvaise Mère* (Paris: Payot, 1977).

7. *CGC*, 57, II, 3. Should we see in "the woman in white" an allusion to the opera singer Castafiore, who had appeared in *The Scepter* and whose first name is Bianca?

8. *En haine du roman* (Paris: Balland, 1982).

9. See the article by Robert Poulet, "Adieu, Georges," *Rivarol*, March 18, 1983, p. 11.

10. The fact that his ancestor's name has a different spelling from his own emphasizes the imaginary character of the connection with the captain.

## CHAPTER EIGHT

1. Tintin finds this figure on his adventure in Tibet precisely at the moment when Haddock totally loses all monstrous, devouring aspects he had in *The Crab*. The evidence comes when Haddock catches his "dreadful" beard in the zipper of his sleeping bag and Tintin comes to his rescue (*TT*, 24, I).

2. In the English translation, the text reads "guardian angel," but in the original it appeared as "God the Father."

## CHAPTER NINE

1. "Moulinsart" is the name of the castle in French, translated in the English versions as "Marlinspike Hall." I give the French name here in the context of the story of Haddock's ancestor, but from now on will refer to it as Marlinspike Hall, as in earlier chapters.—Trans.

2. When he lands on the island, Tintin, who is more familiar with the legend of Robinson Crusoe, takes charge. Tintin establishes the parallel between Defoe's hero and François de Hadoque when he discovers that the lord had counted the days spent on the island (*RRT*, 51, II, 1).

3. Baudrillard, *Le System des objets* (Paris: Gallimard, 1981), p. 127: "Because the collector tries to reconstitute a discourse that seems transparent to him, he is alienated and volatilized in social discourse whose rules escape him. He holds that the signifying and signified are at bottom the same thing."

4. This theme will be developed later [in Chapter 14] in the subsection titled "The Secret of the Unicorn."

5. Professor Cuthbert Calculus is the name given by the English translators of *The Adventures of Tintin* to Hergé's character Tryphon Tournesol. *Tryphon* is the Greek first name, and *tournesol* is the French word for sunflower. In this book, I have used the familiar Cuthbert Calculus for Tryphon Tournesol despite the obvious differences in connotation between the two.—Trans.

## CHAPTER TEN

1. This section of the text plays on the professor's French name and certain French words connected to "sunflower." The author wants to show that this play on words is itself a "figure" or "trope" for sun, light, and flower. A heliotrope is in fact a kind of flower, but the author's play on words also constitutes a verbal "heliotropism."—Trans.

2. Gaston Leroux, *L'Épouse du Soleil* (Paris: J.-G. Leroux, 1913).

3. Strictly speaking, the Incas did not have a system of writing but used instead a system of mnemonics, *quipu*. But this mnemonic system did not have much importance in the everyday language in traditional society.

4. In the first version, he simultaneously throws at the victims a medal that emphasizes the religious nature of the vengeful act. Hergé later eliminates this detail to keep up the suspense, which also accentuates the novelistic aspect of the adventure.

5. The mummy, whose soul awaits its return to its primary state of fire, is in a squatting position, the position of childbirth in primitive societies. For an interpretation of the life cycles, see Jacques Soustelle, "La religion inca," in *Histoire générale des religions* (Paris: Quillet, 1948), vol. I, pp. 200–202.

6. Simone Vierne, *Jules Verne et le roman initiatique* (Paris: Sirac, 1973).

7. During his adventure in Syldavia, Tintin also had to jump from a rock and catch

the scepter exactly on the border of Syldavia and Borduria (*KOS*, 52, IV, 2). But at that time, it was a matter not of entering into a sacred place but of trying not to leave one.

8. See Sadoul, *Entretiens avec Hergé*, p. 106. In the novel, the monsters are called *Crâne pain de sucre*, *Casquette crâne*, and *Crâne petite valise*.

9. Roman Jakobson, "Deux aspects du langage et deux types d'aphasie," in *Essais de linguistique général* (Paris: Minuit, 1963), vol. I, pp. 65–66.

10. The Incan myths tell us that Uiracocha destroys the universe by a great flood but re-creates it.

11. This is the major theme of Leroux's *L'Épouse du Soleil*.

12. One sees him again in his old place in *Land of Black Gold*. But the beginning of that album, which Hergé decided to keep, dates from 1939, before *The Crab with the Golden Claws*, that is, before Tintin even meets Haddock. See Sadoul, *Entretiens avec Hergé*, p. 106.

### CHAPTER ELEVEN

1. Right after that, he passes himself off as "the virtuoso Haddockoff." Is he dreaming of replacing Wagner, that is, of becoming the accompanist of the celebrated contralto? *The Castafiore Emerald* will allow us to answer this question.

2. For example, see Thomas Kuhn, *The Structure of Scientific Revolutions* (Chicago: University of Chicago Press, 1961; French translation, Paris: Champs-Flammarion, 1983); Louis Althusser, *Pour Marx* (Maspero, 1965; repr., Paris: La Découverte, 2005); and Michel Foucault, *Les Mots and les Choses* (Paris: Gallimard, 1966; repr., Tel-Gallimard, 1990).

3. See Michel Zéraffa, *Roman et Société* (Paris: PUF, 1971), p. 9, quoting Saul Bellow's *Dangling Man* (New York: Vanguard Press, 1944) on this point. For Bellow, the diminished status of characters in modern novels does not have to do with any blunting of the powers of human emotions or actions but with the enormity of the scale of modern societies in relation to the individual.

4. They are willing to act like children because they think no one is watching them. Shortly after, Thompson says to his friend: "Come on; be serious! What if someone saw us!" (30, III, 3). They then begin to feel guilty again, especially when they notice tracks made by "extraterrestials" that are in fact their own footsteps. But having engaged in the freedom of childhood pleasures, they become strangers to themselves, for the function of the superego consists precisely in forbidding childhood pleasures (*EM*, pp. 30–31).

### CHAPTER TWELVE

1. "The interesting thing about this career is that it makes up for an inevitable temporality by a fluid spatiality. Time is fixed in the repetition of identical moments, while space, in the sense of various possible places for action, allows the adventure to unfold." Vicky du Fontbaré and Philippe Sohet, "Codes culturels et logique de classe dans la bande-dessinée," *Communications* 24 (1976), p. 66.

2. The shortened title of *Flight 714* in French is *Vol*. The author calls attention to its double meaning of "flight" and "theft."—Trans.

3. In the French, Marshall Kûrvi-Tasch is named Maréchal Plekszy-Gladz, a name that plays on "Plexiglas," or the "artificial plasticity" of his character.—Trans.

4. See Michel Serres, "Les Bijoux distraits ou la cantatrice sauve," *Critique* 277 (June 1970), pp. 485–497.

5. The third version of *Black Gold* takes up the general theme of *The Cigars*, except this time the main characters are no longer heroic.

6. These are just a variation of the continual explosions that occur in this album. In *Land of Black Gold*, we go from explosions of gasoline to firecrackers, then to the sneezing. At the time this album was composed, when the threat of world war weighed heavily on the world, the drama dissolves into farce.

7. Even Tintin himself is indirectly affected by the infectious masquerading (*la vague carnavalesque*). When Señor Oliveira introduces him to Professor Smith, alias Müller, Tintin presents himself as Oliveira's nephew, just arrived from Portugal. And to retain his servants while Tintin is off looking for Abdallah, Oliveira starts an interminable story that is supposed to be the hero's. The story is in effect a parody of the myth of the foundling: an orphan who finds himself embroiled in a series of wild adventures.

8. Hergé gives us a preliminary sketch of their characters in one person, appearing in *The Broken Ear*: the steward on the freighter *Ville de Lyon*. What this character foreshadows about the captain is his alcoholism and his tendency toward depression. This is accentuated in the first version where the steward accuses himself of being indirectly responsible for Tortilla's death in exactly the same terms that Haddock uses in *The Crab*: "I am a miserable person" (*AH*, III, p. 304). What the steward foreshadows about Wagg is his frenetic character, his taste for puns, and his tendency to sponge off others.

9. His first name, Jolyon (Séraphin in French), highlights the absence of the dimension of the foundling in his own character, a dimension that Tintin had managed to inculcate to some degree in the captain.

10. We can assume that she really is Wagg's biological mother, not his mother-in-law, because of the similarity of their noses.

11. The parallel between Abdallah's and Wagg's families' taking up residence in Marlinspike Hall does not speak well for the Waggs. The Arabs do indeed plant themselves in the grand reception hall (*RSS*, 6, IV, 2), but they do not destroy anything and are simply ignorant of the value of the captain's precious objects. In contrast, the middle-class Belgian—or French—Wagg family reduces the ancestral legacy (*sémiophores*) to utilitarian objects, discardable like any industrial products.

12. Guy Debord, *La Société du spectacle* (Paris: Gallimard, 1967; repr., Paris: Folio, 1992).

## CHAPTER THIRTEEN

1. At the time Hergé was working on this album, he began psychoanalysis, although it was quickly interrupted. See Hamel and Peeters, "Entretien avec Hergé," p. 27.

2. This nightmare serves the same function as the one in *The Seven Crystal Balls*, pp. 32–33.

3. In *The Castafiore Emerald*, there is a similar incident. Haddock meets an unhappy little Gypsy girl in the forest and tries to reassure her: "Thundering typhoons, don't be so timid! We're not going to eat you!" (*CE*, 2, II, 3). The little girl does not believe him. In order not to be eaten herself, this new Red Riding Hood resorts to the best tactic in such circumstances: she bites the wolf first!

4. Later, Chang will again be associated with a fermented beverage, but it will be the Yeti who will be accused of having "drunk chang" (23, III, 1, 2).

5. The official English translation of "Snowy" for Milou is supported by the fact that Milou is indeed rebaptized "Snowy" by the Tibetan monk.—Trans.

6. According to Bachelard, alcohol falls under the masculine sign of fire: it leads to inspiration and enflames the creative imagination. But it also falls under the feminine sign of water, submerging consciousness and thus leading to forgetfulness and death. See *La Psychanalyse du feu* (Paris: Folio, 1985), pp. 174–180.

7. In French, the word for the bishop in chess is *fou*, which also means "fool," "court jester," and "madman."—Trans.

8. In Hergé's own words: "There is indeed the captain's dream when he falls asleep while he is walking and bumps into a tree, but this dream is without any real significance." Sadoul, *Entretiens avec Hergé*, p. 110. In his interview with Patrice Hamel and Benoît Peeters, Hergé sticks to the same line about the dream's having no particular interpretation, explaining that it is only a matter of some surreal images. "Entretien avec Hergé," p. 26.

9. Tintin is fascinated by such a custom closely tied to sexuality that both emphasizes sexual difference and focuses sexual desire on the foot. "This deformation is surely sexual in nature. Without doubt, it dates from the time of the court of the libertine kings. Foot binding is pleasing to men because of the cult of the foot and women's shoes, fetishes of sexual love in their eyes. Furthermore, this mutilating practice also affects how their companions can walk." Lin Yu Tang, *La Chine et les Chinois* (Paris, 1937). Cited by J. Chevalier and A. Gheerbrant, "The Foot," in *Dictionnaires des symboles* (Paris: Laffont, 1982).

10. Didi, who wants to castrate his father, is the first figure of the bastard that Tintin encounters.

11. Compare Homer, *The Iliad*, XXIV, ll. 565–566; and *TT*, 61, III, 1.

12. The French word for death is *mort*, pronounced like "more" in the name Ben More.—Trans.

13. In contrast with the captain's, Tintin's basic attitude toward the world is to live in total harmony with it by perfectly adapting to his surroundings. The practices of

swallowing and spitting out seem horrible to him. His anxieties of being devoured are constantly repressed.

14. The English translators translate *loup-garou* as "grizzly bear," a translation that is not only inaccurate but also does not support our author's following note on the significance of the werewolf for psychology.—Trans.

15. "In France one has named those afflicted with *lycanthropie* [a certain delirium or obsessive belief that one has been transformed into a ferocious animal] 'werewolves.' These unfortunate ones flee from their species, typically living in forests, cemeteries, and ancient ruins, roaming through the countryside at night and making great howling sounds. They let their beards and fingernails grow to enormous lengths, thus confirming their appalling beliefs by seeing themselves covered with long fur and armed with talons. Motivated by need or by some atrocious ferocity, they throw themselves onto children, tearing them apart, killing and devouring them." E. Esquirol, *Des maladies mentales* (Paris: J.-B. Baillières, 1838), vol. I, p. 521.

16. When he is depressed, he poses like the "melancholic" represented in paintings for the last five hundred years. For example, see *CGC*, 15, II, 4, and 41, IV, 3; *SS*, 30, III, 2, and 37, I, 1, 2; *DM*, 47, IV, 2, 3; *CA*, 25, III, 2. See Maxime Préaud, *Mélancolies* (Paris: Herscher, 1982).

## CHAPTER FOURTEEN

1. Sadoul, *Entretiens avec Hergé*, pp. 114–115.

2. Furthermore, the period of Tintin's wanderings precedes his period of putting down roots. The symbolic aspect of the Cain-Abel pairing has been developed by Luc Estang, *Le Jour de Caïn* (Paris: Seuil, 1967), and partly by Michel Tournier, *Le Roi des Aulnes* (Paris: Gallimard, 1970; repr., Paris: Folio, 1996), pp. 56–58.

3. J. Barbier and M. Carré, *Faust*, music by Gounod (Lévy, 1890). In the original version of *The Scepter*, Castafiore sings the refrain to the first four verses (*AH*, IV, pp. 186, 191).

4. Hamel and Peeters, "Entretien avec Hergé," p. 17.

5. Precisely in this sea the captain finds the island of his ancestor, Francis of Hadoque. Later, the captain continues comparing her to a hurricane: "Emergency. . . . Take cover!" (*CE*, 33, IV, 3).

6. To eliminate any suspicions of the colonel, Castafiore says that the cap "belongs to the tenor who sings in *Madame Butterfly*. . . . He forgot it yesterday." (*CA*, 54, III, 1). Once again, she associates the captain with a seducer, and she sees herself in the role of the one being "seduced and abandoned."

7. The costume of Rastapopoulos (*RSS*, 36, I, 2) is almost identical to that of Castafiore's partner in the performance of *Faust* at the opera house in Szohod (*CA*, 53, II, 3).

8. In French, the expression *prendre son pied* means "to take pleasure" or "to have an orgasm." So the sentence could read, "She does not have an orgasm right away but initiates a later seduction."—Trans.

9. "Iago" in the English version; "Coco" in the French.—Trans.

10. The author notes the wordplay involved in the French: "Co-comment êtes-vous entrée?"—the French question asking "How did you get in?"—can be heard as "Coco ment, êtes-vous entrée?" "Coco," the parrot's name in French, "lies," "do you get it?"—Trans.

11. When Snowy is bitten by a parrot, Snowy believes he has caught this illness and sees the malady as a castration (*TC*, pp. 2–4).

12. Hergé himself pays particular attention to this connection since the only album to which *The Emerald* refers is *The Secret of the Unicorn*.

13. S. Lisfranc, "À propos de quelques observations d'hystérie de conversion chez l'homme," doctoral dissertation in medicine, École de Medecine, Paris, 1966.

14. The double album dealing with *The Unicorn* appeared in *Le Soir* between June 11, 1942, and September 23, 1944; in other words, at the time when the German occupation outlawed self-defense. Whereas Louis XIV allowed Lord Francis to fight with the pirates, the politics of collaboration advocated by the king of Belgium put an end to all hostilities—except for those who went against orders and chose to resist the German occupants.

15. L. Ljungberg, *Hysteria* (Copenhagen, 1957). Cited by T. Lempérière, "Hystérie," *Encyclopédia Universalis* (Paris: Encyclopédia Universalis, 1974).

16. If one were to develop the symbolic dimensions of this scene, one could see the horseback riding as a sexual act.

17. For example, the French words for "sea" and "mother" sound alike: *mer* for "sea" and *mère* for "mother."—Trans.

18. See Chevalier and Gheerbrant, *Dictionnaire des symboles*, article on "Mer" and "Mère."

19. Bertrand d'Astorg, *Le Mythe de la dame à la Licorne* (Paris: Seuil, 1963).

20. Invoking the Jungian psychoanalysis that he takes up in the course of putting together *Tintin in Tibet*, Hergé tells his interviewers: "This is really about the struggle between two factors within me and indeed in everyone: Purity, on the one hand, a Purity with an enormous capital *P*, and another tendency. And I understand still what Dr. Ricklin said to me with such a strong Zurich accent: 'You have to kill the demon of purity within you.' Yes, he really did say 'the *demon* of purity'! I was caught up in the problem of Purity in all its forms: whiteness, snow, ice, mountain peaks. That was all he had to say to me on that subject." Cf. Hamel and Peeters, "Entretien avec Hergé," p. 27.

21. Here Hergé takes up, or renews, a theme of the comedian Saki, "La Réforme de Groby Lington," in *L'Omelette byzantine*, French translation, pp. 10–18 (Paris: Christian Bourgois, 1982; repr., 2005, p. 122).

22. S. Freud, "Fragment d'une analyse d'hystérie (Dora)," in *Cinq psychanalyses*, French translation (Paris: PUF, 1954), pp. 1–91.

23. In the English translation Castafiore calls the captain "Fatstock."—Trans.

24. "Captain Hopscotch" in the English translation.—Trans.

25. "Captain Stopcock" in the English translation. "Stopcock" suggests even stronger sexual connotations than "Cossack," but I will continue with the author's interpretations here based on the French word.—Trans.

26. The French word for "collar" is *col*, and the word *collet* means "snare" in English.—Trans.

27. *CE*, 28, II, 1. Surely other associations and connotations are possible for the many names Castafiore gives Haddock. For the names he gives her, the connotations are much more obvious: Catastrophe, Calamity, Cataclysm, among others.

28. Proust uses the symbolism of jewels in a more complex way, managing to suggest in the sparkle of precious stones the diffraction of time itself. See Pauline Newman-Gordon, "Bijoux et pierres précieuses chez Proust," *Stanford French Review* 4, no. 3 (Winter 1980), pp. 347–363.

29. In French *dérober* means "to steal or to rob" but also plays on the sense of "derobing," undressing the woman to get at her jewels.—Trans.

30. Jacques Cellard, *Ça ne mange pas de pain! 400 expressions familières ou voyoutes* (Paris: Hachette, 1982).

31. "Calculus in his behavior with Castafiore represents my father to a tee." Hergé, in Hamel and Peeters, "Entretien avec Hergé," p. 18.

32. Jean Piaget, *La Construction du réel chez l'enfant* (Paris: Delachaux and Niestlé, 1963).

### CHAPTER FIFTEEN

1. Benoît Peeters, "Le Sexe des boy-scouts," *Libération* 558 (March 5–6, 1983), p. 25.

2. In *The Calculus Affair*, the journalists break the story of the shattered windows. Around the estate a huge crowd gathers, hoping to catch the show (*CA*, 13, III).

3. When Carreidas realizes he has been kidnapped for his money, he exclaims: "They won't get a penny! Not a penny! Never!" (*F714*, 15, III, 3).

4. The logo of his aviation company is "The Four Aces" in red and black.

5. Hergé gives this character the head of Jacques Bergier, a noted television personality, writer and founder of *Planet* magazine. See Michael Farr, *Tintin: The Complete Companion* (London: John Murray Publishers, 2001; repr., San Francisco: Last Gasp Books, 2006), p. 183.—Trans.

6. When Snowy or Haddock gets drunk, he generally tends to see those who reprimand Tintin or Calculus in double vision, as twins. Snowy even says one day to his master: "You never told me you had a twin brother" (*BI*, 35, II, 1).

7. *Cinna*, ll. 1779–1780.

## CHAPTER SIXTEEN

1. David Riesman, *The Lonely Crowd* (New Haven, Conn.: Yale University Press, 1950).

2. [In French, the Captain says: "C'est un bateau-mouche." *Bateau-mouche* is a large, passenger touring boat on the Seine in Paris. *Bateau* is the French word for "boat," and *mouche*, for "a fly." So, quite literally, a *bateau-mouche* IS a "fly(ing) boat."—Trans.] The captain's reply is indirectly a response to Calculus when the latter defied the sailor during their stay on the moon: "Just you try coming to the moon by boat!" (*EM*, 27, III, 3).

3. The scene of these metamorphoses is the main street of Tapiocapolis, Calle 22 de Mayo. May 22 is an even number composed of 2 and 2, thus linked with the sign of the Twins. It is also the date of Hergé's birth.

4. On the topic of reasons that can motivate the reader to reassess the meanings of even cartoon strips, see the essay on interpretation by Michael Covin, "L'Image dérobée," *Communications* 24 (1976), pp. 197–242.

## CONCLUSION

1. Kurt Lewin, *A Dynamic Theory of Personality* (New York: McGraw-Hill, 1935).

2. On the historical origin of this division, see Reinhart Koselleck, *Le Règne de la critique* (Paris: Minuit, 1979).

3. Edgar Morin, "Tintin, le héros d'une génération," *La Nef* 13 (January 1958), p. 56.

4. "In terms of graphics, Tintin is always just a sketch. Look at his features: his face is a kind of unchanging 'first draft' in contrast with Haddock's, whose face is extremely active and expressive. Haddock obviously lives a much more intense life." Hergé, in Sadoul, *Entretiens avec Hergé*, p. 135.